NUCLEAR TRANSFORMATION

Initiatives in Strategic Studies: Issues and Policies

James J. Wirtz
General Editor

Jeffrey A. Larsen
T.V. Paul
Brad Roberts
James M. Smith
Series Editors

Initiatives in Strategic Studies provides a bridge between the use of force or diplomacy and the achievement of political objectives. This series focuses on the topical and timeless issues relating to strategy, including the nexus of political, diplomatic, psychological, economic, cultural, historic and military affairs. It provides a link between the scholarly and policy communities by serving as the recognized forum for conceptually sophisticated analyses of timely and important strategic issues.

Nuclear Transformation

The New U.S. Nuclear Doctrine

Edited by

James J. Wirtz

and

Jeffrey A. Larsen

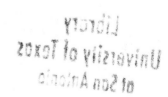

NUCLEAR TRANSFORMATION
© James J. Wirtz and Jeffrey A. Larsen, 2005.

First published in 2005 by
PALGRAVE MACMILLAN™
175 Fifth Avenue, New York, N.Y. 10010 and
Houndmills, Basingstoke, Hampshire, England RG21 6XS
Companies and representatives throughout the world.

PALGRAVE MACMILLAN is the global academic imprint of the Palgrave Macmillan division of St. Martin's Press, LLC and of Palgrave Macmillan Ltd. Macmillan® is a registered trademark in the United States, United Kingdom and other countries. Palgrave is a registered trademark in the European Union and other countries.

ISBN 1–4039–6904–3

Library of Congress Cataloging-in-Publication Data

Nuclear transformation : the new U.S. nuclear doctrine / edited by James J. Wirtz and Jeffrey A. Larsen.
        p. cm.—(Initiatives in strategic studies—issues and policies)
    Includes bibliographical references and index.
    ISBN 1–4039–6904–3
        1. Nuclear weapons—United States. 2. United States—Military policy. I. Wirtz, James J., 1958– II. Larsen, Jeffrey Arthur, 1954– III. Series.
UA23.N7924 2004
355.02'17'0973—dc22   2004061668

A catalogue record for this book is available from the British Library.

Design by Newgen Imaging Systems (P) Ltd., Chennai, India.

First edition: June 2005

10 9 8 7 6 5 4 3 2 1

Printed in the United States of America.

Contents

List of Tables and Figures

Tables

Figures

FOREWORD

There has been a profound change in the strategic security environment since the end of the Cold War. U.S. relations with Russia and China today, while far from perfect, reflect a more constructive and less adversarial approach. The arms control framework that characterized the U.S. relationship with the former Soviet Union has virtually disappeared, replaced by a less intrusive bilateral regime requiring deep reductions in operationally deployed strategic forces. The threat of apocalyptic nuclear war has receded accordingly. Ironically, in spite of these positive changes, we are less secure in many ways than we were before. Over the past 15 years, the confidence we had in our ability to deter potential adversaries has waned and been replaced by a widespread recognition of the uncertainties we now face. Although the likelihood of major nuclear attack has diminished, the likelihood of the use of weapons of mass destruction (WMD) against the United States or its allies has dramatically increased. The proliferation of WMD and their means of delivery to rogue states and the avowed interest of terrorist organizations in acquiring WMD pose the greatest threat to global stability and security and greatest challenge to our national security strategy.

The 2001 Nuclear Posture Review (NPR), which was mandated by Congress prior to the 2000 presidential election, created an opportunity for the new Bush administration to assess how this profoundly changed security environment should transform our national security strategy, strategic policies, and force structure. Prior to completion of the NPR, President Bush had reaffirmed the importance of strategic deterrent forces and of the need to "achieve a credible deterrent with the lowest possible numbers of nuclear weapons consistent with our national security needs."[1] The new Administration had postulated that strategic deterrence, which worked well in the bipolar framework of the Cold War, would not suffice alone in this multipolar environment of more unpredictable and asymmetric threats. In some cases, it is likely to fail. The decision to withdraw from the Anti-Ballistic Missile Treaty and to deploy a limited ballistic missile defense reflected this supposition. The tragic events of September 11 and the ensuing global war on terrorism reaffirmed the conviction that there are some threats we may not be able to deter or dissuade; the use of preemptive force may be necessary.

Thus the NPR was intended by the Bush administration to serve two closely related purposes:

—to create a vision for transformed nuclear forces more effectively aligned with the security challenges facing the nation and more integrated with transformed conventional forces and other instruments of national power;

—to develop a coherent approach to achieve the president's objective: a national security strategy with lower nuclear salience, reduced warhead numbers, and a less adversarial character.

Conducted in parallel but separate from the Quadrennial Defense Review (QDR), the NPR mirrored and reinforced the strategic premises and conclusions of the QDR. In a fluid and unpredictable security environment, the NPR concluded that broader, more comprehensive frameworks for nuclear strategy, policies, and force structure are required to:

—*assure* allies and friends of U.S. commitments,

—*dissuade* adversaries from actions inimical to U.S. interests or those of our allies and friends,

—*deter* threats and coercion against the United States, its military forces, allies, and friends,

—decisively *defeat* any adversary while *defending* against attack if deterrence fails.

These NPR objectives—assure, dissuade, deter, and defend/defeat—were portrayed as a decisive break from America's traditional Cold War doctrine of deterrence. In truth, none of these objectives originated within the NPR or QDR; most had been subsumed in the broad interpretation of "deterrence" and were objectives of our Cold War strategy. But there was a perception that many of these concepts had fallen into disuse since the end of the Cold War. The NPR appropriately forced us to think about the broader objectives U.S. forces are intended to achieve by making them more overt.

To underwrite this new strategic framework, the NPR offered a "New Triad"—a mix of strategic offensive and defensive capabilities that include nuclear and nonnuclear strike forces, active and passive defenses, supported by a robust and responsive research, development and industrial infrastructure—to supplant and expand the existing strategic triad. This New Triad would be further augmented by enhanced command and control, intelligence collection and analysis, and adaptive planning capabilities.

At the same time, the NPR recognized that nuclear weapons will continue to play a unique role in international politics—by shaping the security environment (e.g., assuring allies and dissuading competitors), deterring conflict and the use of WMD and, if necessary, achieving operational and war termination objectives that can be attained no other way. While advanced nonnuclear weapons and defensive systems will assume increasingly important roles as strategic forces, they are not likely to assume the political, psychological, and deterrent role uniquely associated with nuclear weapons—especially in a world defined by increased WMD proliferation and potential adversaries whose intentions and tolerance for risk may not be well understood.

The conclusions of the NPR remain controversial. Its supporters believe that it provides a conceptual roadmap to adapt and transform our national security policies and nuclear force structures to meet the realities of a profoundly changed world. Its critics contend that the approach outlined by the NPR will lead to greater reliance on nuclear weapons, a lower nuclear threshold, and insufficient progress in reducing nuclear stockpiles. Regardless of how one views the Bush administration's policy, nuclear transformation should be viewed as a journey, not a destination, and the approach outlined in the NPR as only a first step forward rather than an exhaustive blueprint.

So there is work to do, and this volume is an important contribution to understanding nuclear transformation. The editors have brought together strategic experts who evaluate the NPR, its strategic meaning, its impact and implications, and its prospects for successful implementation. As commander of U.S. Strategic Command during the period in which the NPR was developed, I can attest to the challenge of rethinking deeply ingrained assumptions and constructs. As you read this book, I ask you to bear in mind several core issues critical to transforming our strategic doctrine and our strategic forces.

First, the NPR has strongly advocated the transformation of U.S. nuclear forces; yet at the time of this writing, three years after the NPR was completed, there is neither a comprehensive plan nor a consensus to implement one. The debate about nuclear force transformation has proven unproductive—too often political and emotional in character and devoid of dispassionate discussion and analysis. A good starting point to shift the debate might be a focus on the strategic effects U.S. leaders will want to achieve in peace, crisis, and war, and the capabilities required to attain those effects. Within such a framework, it is difficult to imagine a world where we would not need some of the unique capabilities of nuclear weapons. Although the new triad holds promise of enhanced conventional capabilities to achieve our strategic objectives, significant deficiencies still exist. Yet much of the discussion on nuclear transformation focuses simply on nuclear weapon numbers rather than on their capabilities. Because the Cold War nuclear arsenal the United States inherited was neither designed nor intended to counter some of the emerging asymmetric threats, officials and planners need to think about how they should adapt and transform our existing strategic capabilities to keep them credible against new threats. They must consider what kind of unique nuclear capabilities (both in warheads and delivery platforms) must be preserved or developed to credibly respond to future challenges, provide a cushion against imperfect intelligence and surprises, and enable a reconstitution capability as a hedge against unwelcome political or strategic developments. To do otherwise runs the risk of being "self-deterred"—of sustaining capabilities irrelevant to the threat at hand or allowing our legacy capabilities to atrophy and lose credibility.

Second, the debate on nuclear transformation must address the nuclear infrastructure as well as the arsenal. Although the NPR recognized that the capability to adapt our deterrent forces to a rapidly changing and unpredictable strategic future is critical, there has been insufficient debate on whether or how to make our nuclear infrastructure more responsive. Policymakers must consider whether the creation of a robust, latent infrastructure to agilely respond to an uncertain future, changing environments, and new threats might be as important as the arsenal itself. Could the existence of such a latent infrastructure not only respond to emerging threats but also discourage future competition such that its full potential never has to be realized?

Finally, we must continue to build and sustain a community of strategic thought that can provide the nation's leaders with innovative ideas, solutions, and tools at the intersection of policy, operations, and technology. In the decades following World War II, such a community of theorists and practitioners played a vital role in helping the nation successfully meet the challenges of Cold War deterrence and containment. Today, facing different but equally daunting challenges, serious and creative strategic thinking remains essential. I commend this book to you in that spirit, and am certain that policy makers, operators, academics, and students will find it helpful in understanding the issues shaping U.S. strategic policy in the years to come.

Richard W. Mies, Admiral, US Navy (ret.)
President and CEO, Hicks and Associates, Inc.

NOTE

1. "Remarks by the President to Students and Faculty a National Defense University," May 1, 2001, Office of the Press Secretary, The White House <http://www.whitehouse.gov/news/releases/2001/05/20010501–10.html#>.

ACKNOWLEDGMENTS

Although this is the third collection of essays we have coedited together, *Nuclear Transformation: The New U.S. Nuclear Doctrine* is a significant milestone in our scholarly agenda. Most of the chapters in this volume are the product of what turned out to be the first of an annual event, the *Monterey Strategy Seminar*, hosted by the Center for Contemporary Conflict, the research arm of the Department of National Security Affairs at the Naval Postgraduate School. The workshop that led to this volume, "Implementing the Nuclear Posture Review," was held in Monterey, California, September 17–19, 2003. It was attended by a small but highly talented and enthusiastic group of scholars, officers, and policy makers: Charles Ball, Nathan Busch, Christopher Craige, Kevin Farrell, Charles Glaser, Dennis Gormley, David Hamon, Kerry Kartchner, Bret Kinman, Feroz Khan, Jeffrey Knopf, Jeffrey Larsen, Peter Lavoy, Scott Levac, Brad Martin, Robert Ord, David Pervin, Joseph Pilat, James Russell, Alexander Saveliev, Thomas Skrobala, James Smith, Marc Trachtenberg, and David Yost. In addition, we appreciate those contributors who were commissioned to write chapters after the kickoff conference, and who did so in a timely fashion: Bill Berry, Stephen Burgess, and Steven Maaranen. We would especially like to thank David Hamon and the Defense Threat Reduction Agency, Thomas Skrobala of the Navy's Strategic Systems Program Office, and James Smith of the Air Force's Institute for National Security Studies for their support of our ongoing efforts to make the Center for Contemporary Conflict a source of policy-relevant research and education.

This volume is also significant to us because it marks the beginning of another venture: Palgrave Macmillan's new series, *Initiatives in Strategic Studies: Issues and Policies*. The series will explore the role played by strategic studies as a bridge between the use of force or diplomacy and the achievement of political objectives. We also hope to provide a link between the scholarly and policy communities by becoming the recognized forum for conceptually sophisticated analyses of timely and important strategic issues. We are especially grateful to David Pervin at Palgrave Macmillan for his support, encouragement, and willingness to publish work on important national security issues at such a critical moment in history.

Two individuals have played a key part in the success of all our scholarly efforts, yet have received far too little credit. We would thus like to thank our wives, Cyndy Larsen and Janet Wirtz, for all they have done to keep our lives grounded and handling the home front as we jet off to another conference or spend too much time in our offices. Both ladies work outside the home and still find time to take care of six children, no small matter when two additional kids they put up with have undeniably entered middle age. We would like to proclaim, as we did so many years ago, our love for you and our thanks for our good fortune in having you beside us.

The opinions and analysis expressed here are the views of the authors, and do not reflect the policies of the United States Navy, SAIC, or any other government agency or corporation.

James J. Wirtz   *Jeffrey A. Larsen*
Monterey, California   Colorado Springs, Colorado

About the Contributors

Charles Ball is Senior Scientist at Lawrence Livermore National Laboratory, Livermore, CA. He holds a Ph.D. from the London School of Economics.

William E. Berry, Jr. is a private consultant in Colorado Springs, CO. He earned his Ph.D. at Cornell University.

Stephen Burgess is Assistant Professor and Deputy Chair, Department of Strategy and International Security, U.S. Air War College, Maxwell Air Force Base, AL. He earned his Ph.D. at Michigan State University.

Nathan Busch is Assistant Professor in the Department of Government and Public Affairs at Christopher Newport University. He holds a Ph.D. from the University of Toronto.

Steve Fetter is Professor in the School of Public Policy at the University of Maryland, College Park. He holds a Ph.D. from the University of California, Berkeley.

Charles L. Glaser is Professor and Deputy Dean at the Irving B. Harris Graduate School of Public Policy Studies at the University of Chicago. He holds a Ph.D. from the Kennedy School, Harvard University.

Dennis M. Gormley is Senior Fellow at the International Institute of Strategic Studies in Washington, D.C. He holds an M.A. from the University of Connecticut.

Kerry M. Kartchner is Senior Advisor for Missile Defense Policy, Bureau of Arms Control, U.S. State Department, detailed as Foreign Affairs Advisor to the Defense Threat Reduction Agency's Advanced Systems and Concepts Office. He earned his Ph.D. from the University of Southern California.

Jeffrey W. Knopf is Visiting Associate Professor of national security affairs at the Naval Postgraduate School, Monterey, CA. He holds a Ph.D. from Stanford University.

Jeffrey A. Larsen is President of Larsen Consulting Group and Senior Policy Analyst with Science Applications International Corporation, both in Colorado Springs, CO, and Adjunct Professor of International Studies at the University of Denver. He holds a Ph.D. from Princeton University.

Steve Maaranen is Senior Scientist at Los Alamos National Laboratory, Los Alamos, NM. He holds a Ph.D. from Claremont Graduate University.

Joseph F. Pilat is Senior Analyst at Los Alamos National Laboratory, Los Alamos, NM. He holds a Ph.D. from Georgetown University.

James A. Russell is Senior Lecturer in the Department of National Security Affairs at the Naval Postgraduate School, Monterey, CA. He holds a Masters degree from the Graduate School for Public and International Affairs, University of Pittsburgh.

Alexander G. Saveliev is Senior Analyst at the Institute of World Economy and International Relations Russian Academy in Moscow.

James M. Smith is Director of the USAF Institute for National Security Studies at the U.S. Air Force Academy, Colorado Springs, CO. He holds a Ph.D. from the University of Alabama.

Marc Trachtenberg is Professor of Political Science at the University of California- Los Angeles. He holds a Ph.D. from the University of California, Berkeley.

James J. Wirtz is Professor and Chairman of the National Security Affairs Department at the Naval Postgraduate School, Monterey, CA. He holds a Ph.D. from Columbia University.

David S. Yost is Professor of National Security Affairs at the Naval Postgraduate School, Monterey, CA. He holds a Ph.D. from the University of Southern California.

The Context

INTRODUCTION

James J. Wirtz

By the time the September 11, 2001, attacks against the Pentagon and the World Trade Center focused global attention on the terrorist threat, the George W. Bush administration was already developing a series of initiatives to transform Cold War nuclear force structure and policy to meet a changing security environment. Responding to a congressional requirement contained in the FY2001 National Defense Authorization Act, the Bush administration issued a comprehensive review of U.S. nuclear forces on January 8, 2002.[1] This Nuclear Posture Review (NPR) remains classified, but officials have described it as calling for a fundamental change in U.S. nuclear weapons policy and a departure from the traditional U.S. approach to deterrence. The NPR calls for the U.S. nuclear deterrent to transform slowly into a more broad-based *strategic* deterrent that now includes nuclear weapons, conventional precision-strike forces, and missile defenses. The NPR is not current doctrine; it is a roadmap for change.

For many outside experts and members of the administration, the traditional approach to nuclear deterrence applied by the Soviet Union and the United States during the Cold War had become obsolete by the turn of the century.[2] They believed that the U.S. nuclear arsenal, which was intended to guarantee destruction of the Soviet Union, or at least neutralize the instruments of Soviet military and police power in the event of a nuclear exchange, no longer posed a credible threat. Administration officials doubted if either friends or foes believed that the United States would detonate one of the large nuclear weapons contained in its Cold War–era arsenal in response to what would likely be a relatively limited provocation on the part of Iran, Iraq, North Korea, or some terrorist syndicate or isolated lunatic. Instead, they believed that a variety of credible deterrent capabilities was required to deter a range of actions while still providing a capability to preempt a looming threat or to terminate a war quickly if deterrence should fail. To transform the old nuclear deterrent into a new strategic deterrent, the administration called for a new triad—a plan to combine the existing nuclear arsenal and the conventional precision-strike capability demonstrated in the skies above Iraq and Kosovo, nascent missile defenses, and a revitalized nuclear research and development infrastructure into one synergistic force. The effort to modernize command and control, intelligence, technology, strategy, and tactics to make this new triad a reality became the central mission of the United States Strategic Command, located at Offutt Air Force Base, Nebraska, in the former headquarters of the now-disbanded Strategic Air Command.

TODAY'S THREAT ENVIRONMENT

Military planners and policy makers will continue for the foreseeable future to face the same political, technological, and strategic trends that shaped the current NPR. In terms of the political setting, the collapse of the Soviet Union created an opportunity to foster a new strategic relationship between Russia and the United States. Bush administration officials believed that massive nuclear arsenals were no longer relevant in Russian–American relations and that the time had arrived for deep cuts in the Cold War nuclear force structure. They also believed that traditional arms control was made obsolete by increasing Russian–American strategic cooperation and that the existing arms control regime actually prevented both sides from adjusting their force structures and doctrine to meet fiscal realities and new threats.[3] Thus, a central tenet of the NPR was that Russia would no longer dominate nuclear war plans; as a result, more cooperative methods to manage strategic relations with Moscow could be undertaken. In the future, a key challenge facing U.S. policy makers will be to continue to transform the U.S. strategic deterrent while undertaking military, political, and especially collaborative efforts to reduce the role deterrence plays in Russian–American relations.

The information revolution also continues to transform U.S. deterrence and warfighting capabilities. This revolution is part of the phenomenon referred to in academic literature as the revolution in military affairs (RMA) and as "transformation" by U.S. Department of Defense officials. The application of the information revolution to the realm of warfare is facilitating the integration of surveillance and reconnaissance sensors, information processing capabilities, tactical and operational communications, and long-range precision-guided munitions. In real time, operational commanders can now use multiple data feeds from a variety of sensors (generically called the global command and control system) to create a coherent operational picture of the battle space that can assist in target identification. This emerging ability to employ precision-guided munitions on very short notice against targets at intercontinental ranges, often referred to as "global strike," barely existed twenty years ago. Although the Bush administration wants to use the advances in command, control, communications, computers, and intelligence (C^4I) to integrate nuclear and conventional forces to make them responsive to short-notice contingencies, future administrations will have to continue to transform military institutions, capabilities, and plans to capitalize on the RMA.

Although a declining Russian threat and an emerging global strike capability bodes well for U.S. national security, concern is rising in Washington about the proliferation of chemical, biological, and nuclear weapons and associated long-range delivery systems to unfriendly states and non-state actors. In its report to Congress on January 30, 2002, the Central Intelligence Agency identified nine countries that are developing or seeking to acquire weapons of mass destruction (WMD).[4] The classified version of the NPR apparently identified several countries that could be involved in "immediate, potential, or unexpected" nuclear contingencies, including North Korea, Iraq, Iran, Syria, and Libya.[5] Various non-state actors and terrorist organizations, such as al Qaeda, which is rumored to be trying to acquire chemical, biological, nuclear, and radiological weapons, also are depicted as posing a serious threat to the United States. Despite recent successes in rolling back Libya's WMD program and forcibly terminating the threat of Iraq's WMD, the fact remains that chemical, nuclear, and biological weapons capabilities continue to proliferate. Today, the threat that non-state actors will somehow acquire these weapons keeps policy makers and their public on edge.

When combined, these emerging trends over the last decade have created a challenging set of circumstances for U.S. officials and defense planners. Unless some sort of cataclysmic break down in Russian politics or society occurs, it is likely that Russian–American strategic relations will continue to improve in the decade ahead. Simultaneously, the failure of nonproliferation efforts during the 1990s confronts U.S. planners with a host of relatively small-scale threats (when compared to the Cold War challenge posed by the Soviet Union) that could quickly become serious civil, political, and military problems. It now appears increasingly likely that the U.S. military might encounter opponents willing to use chemical, biological, or nuclear weapons. To deal with this challenge, planners look to the RMA to provide new ways to use conventional weapons to undertake missions once reserved for U.S. nuclear forces. Yet, the RMA requires planners and strategists to undertake a sustained effort at transformation to capitalize on emerging technologies. In that sense, the NPR is not about current capabilities. Rather, it provides a roadmap for the process of transformation of the U.S. nuclear arsenal over the next several decades.

THE WAY AHEAD

Critics were quick to condemn the NPR as a dangerous escalation of the nuclear arms race. It calls, for instance, for maintaining a substantial reserve force of nuclear warheads to hedge against future threats, dissuade potential opponents from trying to run a nuclear arms race with the United States, and assure allies about the U.S. ability to maintain its extended deterrent commitments indefinitely. Disarmament advocates, however, lamented the Bush administration's failure to make "irreversible" cuts in the U.S. nuclear arsenal following the 2002 Moscow Treaty. They believe that the maintenance of a reserve force is an unnecessary measure that calls into question the sincerity of the administration's effort to reduce further not only the size of the U.S. nuclear arsenal, but also its reliance on nuclear weapons as a strategic deterrent.

In fact, most of the attention generated by the NPR is negative and has been centered on the Bush administration's interest in exploring the military utility of developing a new generation of earth-penetrating, low-yield nuclear weapons that are intended to hold at risk hardened underground targets. Military planners are concerned that these deeply buried underground facilities can serve as command and control centers as well as storage and manufacturing facilities for nuclear, chemical, and biological weapons. States are "going underground," especially as U.S. precision-strike capabilities improve. In a manner that mirrors earlier opposition to the development of missile defense, critics of the so-called mini-nuke concept question both the feasibility and the desirability of developing a new generation of nuclear warheads. Some suggest that it is impossible to contain nuclear weapons' effects by deeply burying incoming warheads because existing designs only allow warheads to penetrate about twelve meters of steel-reinforced concrete. A penetration this shallow probably would not contain the explosive blast produced by even the smallest nuclear warheads currently available, making it likely that radioactive fallout would contaminate areas near the blast. Critics suggest that innovative methods of burying conventional warheads deeply underground, not necessarily a new nuclear warhead, are needed to hold deeply buried targets at risk.

Even if one could develop effective ways to bury incoming nuclear warheads deeply so that their effects could be contained, critics charge that the idea of developing a more useable generation of nuclear weapons is strategically flawed and likely to break a nearly six-decade tradition of nuclear nonuse in battle. They believe that integrating earth penetrating, low-yield nuclear weapons or other types of exotic nuclear devices into deployed forces and operational plans will lower the nuclear threshold. Yet, supporters of the plan suggest that a credible deterrent requires the presence of forces that can be used effectively if deterrence should fail. They want potential opponents to recognize that U.S. military planners and officials have a range of capabilities that can respond to limited provocations with locally devastating results. They believe that the prospect of "self deterrence" on the part of policy makers in Washington—a reluctance to use large nuclear weapons because of the prospect of staggering collateral damage—should not be a factor in the calculations of opponents who seek to challenge U.S. interests.

Although the Bush administration's foreign and defense policies have received ample attention from their critics, the fact remains that the administration has set in motion a complex and demanding initiative to transform U.S. nuclear forces into a strategic deterrent to meet emerging security challenges and opportunities. The NPR seeks to reduce the role of nuclear weapons in Russian–American relations while increasing the credibility and capability of its strategic forces in the minds of several potential adversaries. The administration has adopted a policy that seeks to reduce U.S. reliance on nuclear forces, while exploring new roles for a new generation of nuclear weapons. The NPR also calls for the deliberate integration of conventional and nuclear forces into this new strategic deterrent, a call for action that is reminiscent of the years of work needed to produce the doctrine of flexible response adopted by the North Atlantic Treaty Organization in 1967. Even more challenging is the integration of offensive and defensive forces into the strategic deterrent. A key item of the NPR calls for the creation of new doctrine and command and control to realize synergies produced by an offense–defense strategy intended to bolster deterrence. The NPR also calls for improvements in the U.S. ability to sustain and even improve its nuclear arsenal in the future without ongoing nuclear weapons development or testing. None of these tasks is easy, but each of them is a direct response to the security challenges and opportunities facing today's policy makers and military planners.

About the Book

Given the challenges and paradoxes contained in current U.S. nuclear policy, the purpose of this volume is to identify and explore the impediments and problems that must be overcome to implement the NPR. Although members of the administration sometimes speak about the capabilities outlined in the NPR as if they already existed, the reality of the situation is that it might take decades of sustained effort to produce the strategic deterrent envisioned by the Bush administration. For instance, no new nuclear weapons are under development by the United States, and only rudimentary missile defenses will be deployed by the end of the decade. Thus, the NPR is best thought of as a process intended to transform a Cold War nuclear arsenal and strategy, updating it for the challenges that the United States is likely to face in the coming decades.

Our purpose is not to critique the NPR, but instead to trace the logic of its recommendations and identify what remains to be done to make it a reality. Our underlying assumption is that the NPR offers a reasonable, albeit far from perfect, response to the political, technical, and strategic challenges and opportunities faced by U.S. policy makers and planners and that this threat environment will likely dominate planning for at least the next decade. Our contributors also have been asked to discuss the policy implications the NPR will have on a variety of issue areas and regional settings. We hope to provide a more detached and less polemical view of evolving U.S. deterrence strategy than critics of the administration. Our goal is to assess the strengths and weaknesses of the NPR and to identify the key roadblocks in the path of any effort to transform the U.S. nuclear arsenal into a new type of strategic deterrent that embodies nuclear and conventional weapons and missile defenses.

Our contributors address the NPR in a variety of ways and from a variety of perspectives. Mark Trachtenberg, Charles Glaser, and Steve Fetter place the NPR not only in its historical context, but also assess the logic of its deterrence and warfighting strategies. Joe Pilat, Dennis Gormley, Kerry Kartchner, and Steve Maaranen examine the main doctrinal issues and transformational initiatives embodied by the NPR: global strike, offense–defense integration, developing a responsive nuclear infrastructure, and the concept of a new triad. Support functions related to the NPR—command and control, intelligence, and the role the military services must play in the process of transformation—are addressed by Nathan Bush, Charles Ball, and Jim Smith. Jeff Larsen and Jeff Knopf then debate the impact of the NPR on the arms control and nonproliferation regimes. Allied and Russian reactions to the NPR are described by David Yost and Alexander Saveliev, while Stephen Burgess, Bill Berry, and James Russell survey the impact of the transformation of U.S. deterrence policy on the security situations in South Asia, Northeast Asia, and the Middle East.

We expect that neither supporters nor critics of the current policy will be completely satisfied with our description and analysis of the Bush administration's NPR. Nevertheless, we believe that a debate on the current and potential U.S. response to the emerging strategic environment is crucial to global security.

NOTES

1. Excerpts from the classified version of the report were first reported in the *New York Times* and the *Los Angeles Times*. See William Arkin, "Secret Plan Outlines the Unthinkable: A Secret Policy Review of the Nation's Nuclear Policy Puts Forth Chilling New Contingencies for Nuclear War," *Los Angeles Times*, March 10, 2002, and Michael R. Gordon, "U.S. Nuclear Plan Sees New Targets and New Weapons," *New York Times*, March 10, 2002. Most of the NPR text has been posted on the globalsecurity.org website at <http://globalsecurity.org/wmd/library/policy/dod/npr.htm>. This quote is taken from that text, cited as the NPR's Executive Summary on page 1, which was released by the Department of Defense.
2. Keith B. Payne and C. Dale Walton, "Deterrence in the Post–Cold War World," in John Baylis, James J. Wirtz, Eliot Cohen and Colin Gray, eds., *Strategy in the Contemporary World* (Oxford: Oxford University Press, 2002), 161–182.
3. Robert Joseph, "The Changing Political–Military Environment," in James J. Wirtz and Jeffrey A. Larsen, eds., *Rockets' Red Glare: Missile Defenses and the Future of World Politics* (Boulder, Colo: Westview Press, 2001), 55–78; and Bradley Graham, *Hit to Kill* (New York: Public Affairs, 2001).
4. Central Intelligence Agency, *Unclassified Report to Congress on the Acquisition of Technology Relating to Weapons of Mass Destruction and Advanced Conventional Munitions*, January 1 through June 30, 2000.
5. NPR, 16. By contrast, the NPR does not depict Russia as a country of immediate or even potential concern.

2

The Bush Strategy in Historical Perspective

Marc Trachtenberg

In September 2002, a year after the terror attacks on New York and Washington, the U.S. government published an important document, *The National Security Strategy of the United States of America*. This document laid out what was called a strategy of preemption. The enemies of the United States—countries such as Iraq and North Korea—were intent on acquiring weapons of mass destruction (WMD), and those weapons, it was argued, could be used "offensively to achieve the aggressive designs of these regimes." In such circumstances, a purely "reactive" policy—a strategy of "deterrence based only upon the threat of retaliation"—was no longer sufficient to defend the United States. America would instead exercise its "right of self-defense by acting preemptively," that is, by dealing with "such emerging threats before they were fully formed." And in dealing with these threats, the U.S. government would "not hesitate to act alone." "In the new world we have entered," the *National Security Strategy* document declared, "the only path to peace and security is the path of action."[1]

THE BUSH ADMINISTRATION AND PREEMPTION

The George W. Bush administration was sharply criticized both at home and abroad for embracing a preemptive strategy; however, this was not the first time the media reported this interest in preemption. A half-year earlier, a leak to the press of the Pentagon's Nuclear Posture Review (NPR) had touched off what one observer called a "mini-firestorm."[2] At that time, the administration was charged with moving toward a policy of *nuclear* preemption. "U.S. Nuclear Arms Stance Modified by Policy Study: Preemptive Strike Becomes an Option"—thus did the *Washington Post* headline its main article on the NPR.[3] And according to a *New York Times* editorial titled "America as Nuclear Rogue," the NPR showed that the government was "contemplating preemptive strikes against a list of non-nuclear powers."[4] The critical coverage argued that with the NPR, the administration had broken with tradition. In the past, "non-nuclear states were exempt from U.S. nuclear attack," but now it seemed that this policy had been abandoned.[5] In the past, U.S. nuclear forces had been maintained "for the single purpose of deterring a nuclear attack." But, critics said, the NPR signaled "an unfortunate reversal" of that "longstanding policy, ending the taboo against nuclear weapons by including them in the full range of weapons to be used against countries with which the U.S. has major disagreements."[6]

Administration officials denied that the NPR was to be interpreted in those terms. Secretary of State Colin Powell, for example, happened to be testifying before a Senate Committee the day the *Times* editorial appeared, and he was asked about the press stories on the NPR. He replied: "With respect to reports that we are thinking of preemptively going after somebody or that, in one editorial I read this morning, we have lowered the nuclear threshold, we have done no such thing. There is no way to read that document and come to the conclusion that the United States will be more likely or will more quickly go to the use of nuclear weapons."[7] Secretary of Defense Donald Rumsfeld, in testimony before a Senate committee a couple of months later, said much the same thing: the press reports were inaccurate; the "recently concluded Nuclear Posture Review does not change the threshold for the use of nuclear weapons one bit."[8] And indeed, from the excerpts from the NPR that were posted on the internet—presumably the most revealing parts of the document—it does not seem that the authors were calling for a strategy of nuclear preemption. In fact, the main problem with the NPR, or at least with its excerpts, was perhaps that it failed to give a very clear sense for when or how nuclear weapons actually were to be used.

The Bush strategy was thus not quite as extreme as it was made out to be. Yes, the United States felt free to deal with developing threats before they got totally out of hand. And yes, the U.S. government felt free to use force before an attack had actually been mounted or was even considered imminent. But one gets the sense from the NPR that in acting preemptively, the United States basically would use only nonnuclear force. To be sure, in certain cases the Americans might use nuclear weapons first, even against a nonnuclear state. If the United States were attacked with biological or chemical weapons, the document did not rule out a retaliatory nuclear strike (and, indeed, nuclear retaliation in such circumstances had not been ruled out by previous administrations).[9] And in the event of war, certain specially designed types of nuclear weapons might be used to destroy facilities where an enemy's most dangerous weapons were stored before they could be used.[10] But to the extent that the United States contemplated military action to prevent dangerous regimes from acquiring WMD, those military operations normally would not involve the use of nuclear weapons of any sort.

But even a policy of preemption that relied on conventional forces was considered quite extreme, especially after it became clear during the run-up to the war with Iraq in 2003 that the Bush administration was serious about pursuing a policy of this sort. That war was widely seen as a preemptive operation—that is, designed to prevent an intolerable situation from emerging. Indeed, the administration explicitly justified its Iraq policy in those terms. It stressed the importance of resolving the Iraq problem before that country's weapons programs developed to the point where the threat had become much greater. In one key policy speech, Vice President Dick Cheney quoted Henry Kissinger as saying that the various elements in the Iraq problem had combined to "produce an imperative for preemptive action." Cheney continued: "If the United States could have preempted 9/11, we would have, no question. Should we be able to prevent another, much more devastating attack, we will, no question. This nation will not live at the mercy of terrorists or terror regimes."[11]

This policy was characterized not just by its many critics but also by its defenders as radically different from anything the country had known in the past. Kissinger, for example, thought that a "revolutionary" change in strategy had taken place.[12] The whole idea of the international system as a system of sovereign states—and the idea that force cannot be used simply because one believes that the development of military power by another state is potentially threatening—was going to have to be rethought, he argued. In the new environment, a simple strategy of deterrence might no longer provide an adequate basis for American security.[13] The Bush administration basically felt the same way. Given the nature of the states and terrorist groups the United States now had to deal with, "traditional concepts of deterrence" were no longer valid, and a far more active policy was called for.[14]

But how new *was* the Bush strategy? Was it the case that U.S. policy in the past had been essentially defensive and reactive in nature, and was this the first time that the idea of preemption was taken seriously in high policy-making circles? To what extent was the Bush administration really breaking with traditional American policy or, more generally, with the way international politics had traditionally been conducted?

PREEMPTION IN THE EARLY COLD WAR

This issue must be broken down into two parts. First, there is the question of preemption in the traditional sense of the term: striking first when it becomes clear that an enemy attack is imminent, or, somewhat more loosely, when it is believed that war is unavoidable. The key matter here is whether, during the Cold War, the U.S. government had opted for a strategy of deterrence pure and simple—that is, for a "second strike strategy"—based on the idea that the threat of retaliation could deter an enemy from launching a nuclear attack. Was it true that the U.S. government during that period had ruled out the very idea of using nuclear weapons first? Was it true, as three prestigious critics of the NPR argued, that throughout the Cold War, the United States "maintained an enormous nuclear force for the single purpose of deterring a nuclear attack" and that all American presidents until now had rejected the nuclear option "as too dangerous to the planet and to humanity?"[15]

The second question has to do with preemption not in the traditional sense of the term, but in the sense in which it is currently used, that is, with what used to be called a "preventive war" strategy. Was the whole idea of dealing with developing threats relatively early on—of launching an attack well before a threat became unmanageable—more or less inconceivable until now? Was the United States in particular the sort of country that traditionally would never dream of conducting a preventive war?

On the first question, the basic facts are well known and the story can be reviewed quickly. During the most dangerous phase of the Cold War, the period from 1946 to 1963, the U.S. government did *not* view nuclear weapons as too dangerous to be used under any circumstances, nor did U.S. officials believe that nuclear forces would only be used if America or one of its allies had first sustained a nuclear attack. The United States had a nuclear monopoly until 1949; if Western Europe had been attacked in the late 1940s, America would have gone to war with the Soviet Union, and it certainly would have used nuclear weapons. Of course, those weapons were not used during the Korean War—but not because the use of nuclear weapons was inconceivable as a matter of principle. The U.S. government thought the West was too weak and vulnerable during the early part of that conflict to risk taking measures that might have led to a third world war. During the later part of the conflict, nuclear options were taken quite seriously, and U.S. decision makers might well have used nuclear weapons if no armistice agreement had been reached in 1953—a circumstance that was probably an important reason why an agreement *was* reached at that time.

The U.S. government had a much freer hand in the area of nuclear policy by late 1952 because by that point, the United States had re-armed and the country was in a very strong position vis-à-vis the Soviet Union in terms of the nuclear balance. In that new and vastly different strategic environment, nuclear escalation was by no means out of the question. It is clear that the Dwight Eisenhower administration took for granted that nuclear weapons would be used in a major war with the USSR; they might even have been used in a minor war outside Europe with a large Communist power. In a war with the Soviet Union, the U.S. government intended (if it could) to be the first to use nuclear weapons, and it intended to use them quickly and massively. America, Eisenhower himself said, "must not allow the enemy to strike the first blow."[16] As David Rosenberg, the most serious student of the history of American nuclear weapons policy, pointed out long ago, massive retaliation, the famous Eisenhower policy, really meant "massive preemption."[17] From Eisenhower's point of view, a full nuclear attack would be ordered as soon as it became clear that war was unavoidable—and that meant, ideally, *before* the enemy had launched its own attack. In 1959, the president thought that if the conflict over Berlin came to a head—that is, if the "acute crisis period" were reached—the United States would have to "engage in general war to protect our rights." His "basic philosophy," he said, held that America had to be prepared to push its "whole stack of chips into the pot when that became necessary."[18]

President John F. Kennedy also was willing to use nuclear weapons rather than accept an American defeat in Europe. "I suppose if we get involved in a war in Europe," he said in 1962, "we will have no choice but to use nuclear weapons."[19] If war broke out and the Soviets threatened to overrun Europe, he said the previous year, the United States would have to "strike first with nuclear weapons."[20] And during the Cuban missile crisis, officials in the U.S. government believed they might have to be the first to use military force. As Secretary of State Dean Rusk told the Senate Foreign Relations Committee (in executive session) shortly after the crisis, "it certainly was our clear thinking at the time if we saw these missiles in a readiness position, we would have to strike them. . . . Raised and ready, they would have to be hit."[21] So, under Eisenhower and Kennedy at least, U.S. government officials believed they might have to go first in a crisis; a strategy of preemption, as the term was understood at the time, had by no means been ruled out.

PREEMPTION OF NASCENT NUCLEAR ADVERSARIES

But what about the second question? Was the U.S. government ever willing to consider a strategy of preemption as the Bush policy documents use the term—that is, a strategy of attacking a hostile power, or of destroying its key military programs, before that power could pose a serious threat to the United States? Eisenhower and Kennedy might have been willing to go first in a crisis, or to use nuclear weapons first once fighting had broken out. But was the United States ever willing to begin military operations, even if an enemy was not preparing to attack—in other words, even if the threat was not imminent?

The answer is that American governments have been much more attracted to strategies of this sort than is generally realized. Both Eisenhower and Kennedy seriously considered operations along these lines to prevent first the Soviet Union then China from developing a substantial nuclear capability. The whole idea of taking military action to prevent the Soviets from building a nuclear force was widely discussed in American policy-making circles during the early Eisenhower period—in fact, from 1945 on.[22] In the later years of the Harry S. Truman administration, such key U.S. policy makers as Secretary of State Dean Acheson and his close associate Paul Nitze wanted to pursue a very aggressive policy toward the USSR. One famous policy document from the period, NSC 68 of April 1950, called explicitly for a rollback policy—a "policy of calculated and gradual coercion" designed to "check and to roll back the Kremlin's drive for world domination."[23] This policy could not be implemented in 1950 because the United States did not have the military might to back it then. But by late 1952, the situation had changed dramatically. The massive buildup of U.S. military power that attended the Korean War made it possible for the United States to take a much tougher line. Indeed, the goal of the buildup was to put in hand a policy of forcing the nuclear issue with the Soviet Union before it was too late or, as Nitze put it, "to lay the basis for taking increased risks of general war in achieving a satisfactory solution of our relations with the USSR while her stockpile of atomic weapons was still small."[24]

Under Eisenhower, top officials continued to worry about what would happen once the Soviet Union developed a strong nuclear force and whether some action should be taken to deal with the problem sooner. This issue lay at the heart of military exercises in 1953, and it came up in various key policy documents and in a number of NSC meetings in the early Eisenhower period.[25] Eisenhower himself wondered at one point "whether or not our duty to future generations did not require us to *initiate* war at the most propitious moment that we could designate."[26]

The United States eventually learned to live with a Soviet nuclear force. But a decade later, U.S. leaders had to face the same kind of issue with China. Kennedy thought that the development of a Chinese nuclear capability would pose very serious problems for the United States. In his view, a nuclear China would be intolerable.[27] Military authorities were asked to deal with the issue, and they analyzed America's options. The U.S. government also broached the issue of joint action to destroy China's nascent nuclear capability with the USSR on a number of occasions, but the Soviet government rebuffed these American overtures.[28]

In neither case—the Soviet Union in 1953–1954 or China in 1963–1964—was anything actually done to curtail the development of a nuclear adversary. No preemptive attack, to use the current terminology, was actually launched. But the policy discussions within the U.S. government on both occasions are important and instructive.[29] Responsible leaders were far more open to the notion of preventive war than one might have imagined. It was not as though a policy aimed at destroying the heart of an adversary's military power before it was too late—a policy of "strangling the baby in the cradle," to use a phrase from the title of one of the most important scholarly articles on the subject[30]—was dismissed out of hand. As far as the U.S. government was concerned, a military operation to destroy the Chinese nuclear program might well have been undertaken, if, for example, the Soviets in 1963 had been willing to cooperate in this endeavor—something that was not out of the question, since just a few years later it was the Soviets who were pressing for a preventive strike against China's nuclear infrastructure.

PREEMPTION AND THE CUBAN MISSILE CRISIS

Moreover, there have been times when considerations of preemption do play a key role in shaping actual political behavior. For example, the United States took the world to the brink of thermonuclear war in 1962 to prevent the Soviet Union from deploying a nuclear force in Cuba. The fact that Cuba was a sovereign state—or that an attack on America was not imminent—did not mean that the U.S. government believed it could not take military action to ensure that the deployment did not take place. American policy in the Cuban missile crisis was rooted in concerns about the future, about the way the strategic balance was shifting, and about the importance of taking action sooner rather than later.[31] To be sure, the Kennedy administration did not emphasize this point when defending its policy; a defense that rested on sanctions from the Organization of American States was considered preferable for political reasons. But if the Latin American states had been unwilling to support the United States on this question, the U.S. government still would have threatened to attack Cuba. As it was, the preemptive argument, though muted, was by no means missing from official pronouncements. The president had a passage that invoked this principle in his October 22, 1962, speech to the nation on the crisis. Even the relatively dovish Adlai Stevenson, the U.S. ambassador to the United Nations, spoke in these terms when he famously addressed the UN during the Cuban missile crisis. "Were we to do nothing until the knife was sharpened?" Stevenson asked. "Were we to stand idly by until it was at our throats?"[32]

PREEMPTION BEFORE THE NUCLEAR AGE

It merits mention here that preemption or the pressure to act preemptively is not a product of the nuclear age. The basic tenets of preemption have informed U.S. policy and global affairs well before anyone knew that atoms could be split to such explosive effect. The United States came out of World War II a nuclear power; it went into the war with preemption on policy-makers' minds. In the second half of 1941, the United States was not a country that "asked only to be left alone."[33] Robert Dallek, perhaps the leading student of American foreign policy during the Franklin D. Roosevelt period, notes that the president "wished to take the United States into the war." As Roosevelt told the British prime minister, Winston Churchill, at the Atlantic Conference in August 1941, he would instead "wage war, but not declare it." "He would become more and more provocative." His goal, he said, was to "force an 'incident.' " He "made it clear that he would look for an 'incident' which would justify him in opening hostilities."[34] The story of U.S. policy in late 1941—and especially the role that preemptive thinking played in it—is important because the real story here is so much at variance with the conventional wisdom that says the United States entered World War II for one simple reason: because of the Japanese attack on Pearl Harbor. That story is conceptually important because it is empirically surprising. The key to understanding what happened in 1941 is the realization that America was not a passive victim of attack, but rather that the U.S. government was pursuing a very active policy in the months before Pearl Harbor, and that that policy played a central role in the process that led to American involvement in the war.

The escalation of naval operations in the North Atlantic, especially the adoption of a policy of "shooting first" in September 1941, is to be understood in the light of Roosevelt's remarks. Roosevelt announced the policy in a "fireside chat" broadcast on September 11, 1941—sixty years to the day before the terror attacks on New York and Washington. Over and over, he argued that the country had to take action before it was too late: "One peaceful Nation after another has met disaster because each refused to look the Nazi danger squarely in the eye until it actually had them by the throat. The United States will not make that fatal mistake." He continued: "The time for active defense is now. . . . [T]his is the time for prevention of attack. . . . When you see a rattlesnake poised to strike, you do not wait until he has struck before you crush him."[35]

But why did Roosevelt want to provoke a war with Germany? Why was he unwilling to wait for Germany to attack America before taking the United States into the war? The heart of the policy was laid out in the so-called Victory Program signed by General George C. Marshall, the Army Chief of Staff, and Admiral Harold R. Stark, the Chief of Naval Operations, also dated September 11, 1941. After Germany attacked the Soviet Union in June 1941, U.S. policy makers feared that the USSR would be defeated and that the Germans eventually would be able to mobilize the resources of all of continental Europe up to the Urals, ultimately building their military power up to extraordinary levels. In this event, American security would be imperiled; the United States would therefore be well-advised to act quickly, before the Germans were able "to bring order out of chaos in the occupied areas" and harness the resources of those areas to their war machine. "Time is of the essence," the authors of the Victory Program strategy document argued, and "the longer we delay effective offensive operations against the Axis, the more difficult will become the attainment of victory."[36]

There was nothing anomalous about Roosevelt's behavior in 1941. International relations theorists often argue that states are led to pursue aggressive policies for essentially defensive purposes. Such policies, in other words, need to be seen as natural—that is, as built into the basic structure of the system. In the midst of the Iraq crisis, for example, Secretary of Defense Rumsfeld justified American policy by telling a group of European journalists that preventive war was as "old as history itself."[37] Rumsfeld was on to something: preventive war logic is more powerful than people think, and in many contexts, people have no problem accepting that kind of logic.[38] After 1945, for example, one of the lessons drawn from the story of World War II was that the Western powers had waited too long to take a stand against Germany. Appeasement was more or less universally condemned; the idea was that it would have been better to deal with the German problem early on, while it was still manageable. This point was central to Winston Churchill's history of the origins of the war, *The Gathering Storm*. Churchill took as his theme in this volume: "How the English-speaking peoples through their unwisdom, carelessness, and good nature allowed the wicked to rearm."[39] At the time, no one was shocked by the argument that the Western democracies should have taken more forceful measures to prevent this development.

And this was not simply because everyone took it for granted that Nazi Germany in the 1930s was such an extreme case that the standard rules did not apply. It is important to remember that traditionally even the most moderate statesmen assumed that some dangers had to be dealt with before things got totally out of hand. Lord Castlereagh, the British foreign secretary in the post-Napoleonic period, was one of the most reasonable, thoughtful and distinguished diplomatists in modern history. But even Castlereagh recognized that it might be important to take action even if there was no immediate threat of military attack. In fact, he was prepared to take action even if the balance of power was threatened by developments of a purely internal nature—for example, by a revolution in the Low Countries that would take that area into union with France. According to Castlereagh, it was better for the statesmen of Europe to "meet that danger which they cannot avoid" than to wait for it to be "poured in the full tide of military invasion upon their own states." "The actual existence of such a danger," he recognized, "may indeed be inferred from many circumstances short of the visible preparations for attack." If the threat was serious enough, action would be warranted even if an attack was not imminent.[40] It is not the least bit unusual to find statesmen arguing along such lines. But the fact that this kind of thinking was so common historically suggests that the approach embodied in the Bush strategy documents is more deeply rooted in the basic structure of international politics than one might think.

CONCLUSIONS AND CONTINUITIES

International relations theorists often argue that states are led to pursue aggressive policies for essentially defensive purposes. In other words, such policies must be seen as natural; they are built into the basic structure of the system. The fact that preemptive strategies were so common historically suggests that the approach embodied in the Bush strategy documents is more deeply rooted in the basic structure of international politics than one might think.

This basic point is also reflected in the fact that the U.S. government had been moving toward a preemptive policy for some time. In 1994, the William Clinton administration seriously considered taking preemptive action against North Korean nuclear facilities; in 1996, the U.S. government also threatened to take preemptive military action against Libya if that country moved ahead with its chemical weapons program.[41] The elements of continuity from the Clinton to the Bush period are quite striking. For example, the September 2002 *National Security Strategy* document called for an active "counterproliferation" policy, but the term "counterproliferation" (which in itself implied a need for something more energetic than the old nonproliferation strategy) had been coined during the Clinton period. The original architects of this policy described it in terms that are virtually indistinguishable from those used by the Bush administration in describing its own counterproliferation policy.[42]

If these continuities exist, and if preventive war thinking is so common historically, it is because the incentives to pursue this sort of policy are much stronger than people seem to realize. The Bush strategy is no transitory notion, and the basic idea of preemption is not going to disappear when the Bush administration leaves office.

NOTES

1. *The National Security Strategy of the United States of America*, September 2002 <http://www.whitehouse.gov/nsc/nss.pdf>. The passages quoted are from the introduction signed by President Bush (dated September 17, 2002), 6, 14, 15.
2. Andrew Krepinovich, "The Real Problems With Our Nuclear Posture," *New York Times* March 14, 2002. A copy of the report was given to *Los Angeles Times*

contributor William Arkin. See William Arkin, "Secret Plan Outlines the Unthinkable: A Secret Policy Review of the Nation's Nuclear Policy Puts Forth Chilling New Contingencies for Nuclear War," *Los Angeles Times* March 10, 2002. Another copy was leaked to the *New York Times*. See Michael R. Gordon, "U.S. Nuclear Plan Sees New Targets and New Weapons," *New York Times* March 10, 2002. Key excerpts were soon posted on the internet <http://www.globalsecurity.org/wmd/library/policy/dod/npr.htm>. Unless otherwise noted, references in this chapter to the NPR, including page numbers, refer to these published excerpts.

3. Walter Pincus, "U.S. Nuclear Arms Stance Modified by Policy Study: Preemptive Strike Becomes and Option," *Washington Post* March 23, 2002.

4. "America as Nuclear Rogue," *New York Times* March 12, 2002.

5. Mary McGrory, "Nuts About Nukes," *Washington Post* March 14, 2002.

6. "Three Nobel Laureates Criticize Bush Nuclear Posture Review," press statement of the Council for a Livable World, March 18, 2002 <http://www.clw.org/control/nprnobels.html>.

7. U.S. Senate, Hearings before a Subcommittee of the Committee on Appropriations on S. 2778, 107th Cong., 2nd sess., March 12, 2002, 264 <http://frwebgate.access.gpo.gov/cgi-bin/getdoc.cgi?dbname = 2003_sapp_com_1&docid = f:78462.pdf>. See also the transcript of Powell's appearance on *Face the Nation* March 10, 2002 <http://www.state.gov/secretary/rm/2002/8704.htm>.

8. "Transcript of testimony by Secretary of Defense Donald H. Rumsfeld at Defense Subcommittee of Senate Appropriations Committee," May 21, 2002 <http://www.dod.mil/speeches/2002/s20020521-secdef.html> (response to question from Sen. Feinstein).

9. After the NPR was leaked, the White House took care to point out that there was nothing new to the policy of threatening to use nuclear weapons against nonnuclear states if those states sought to use chemical or biological weapons against the United States or its allies. Two statements to this effect from top Clinton administration officials were quoted by the White House press secretary shortly after the original stories appeared. Press briefing by Ari Fleischer, March 14, 2002 <http://www.whitehouse.gov/news/releases/2002/03/20020314-8.html>. See also Richard Sokolsky, "Demystifying the US Nuclear Posture Review," *Survival* 44, no. 3 (Autumn 2002): 136.

10. As the NPR put it in one widely criticized passage, "Nuclear weapons could be employed against targets able to withstand non-nuclear attack (for example, deep underground bunkers or bio-weapon facilities)." Nuclear Posture Review, 12–13.

11. Vice President's address to VFW 103rd National Convention, August 26, 2002 <http://www.whitehouse.gov/news/releases/2002/08/20020826.html>. For the Kissinger article Cheney was quoting, see Henry A. Kissinger, "The Politics of Intervention: Iraq 'Regime Change' Is a Revolutionary Strategy," *Los Angeles Times Syndicate* August 9, 2002.

12. Kissinger, "The Politics of Intervention."

13. Ibid.; Kissinger testimony in Senate Foreign Relations Committee hearings, September 26, 2002, 59, 61 <http://frwebgate.access.gpo.gov/cgi-bin/getdoc.cgi?dbname = 107_senate_hearings&docid = f:83463.pdf>. See also Henry Kissinger, *Does America Need a Foreign Policy? Toward a Diplomacy for the 21st Century* (New York: Simon and Schuster, 2001), 21, 236.

14. *National Security Strategy of the United States of America*, 15.

15. "Three Nobel Laureates Criticize Bush Nuclear Posture Review."

16. NSC meeting, March 25, 1954, in U.S. Department of State, *National Security Affairs*, vol. II of the 1952–1954 series, Foreign Relations of the United States [FRUS] (Washington, D.C.: GPO, 1984), 640–642.

17. David Rosenberg, "Toward Armageddon: The Foundations of U.S. Nuclear Strategy" (Ph.D. diss., University of Chicago, 1983), 221.

18. Eisenhower meeting with congressional leadership, March 6, 1959, in U.S. Department of State, *The Berlin Crisis, 1958–1959; Foreign Ministers Meeting, 1959*, vol. VIII of the 1958–1960 series, FRUS (Washington, D.C.: GPO, 1993, 433; and meeting with a group of congressmen that same day, *Declassified Documents Reference System* [DDRS], 1996/3493.

19. Quoted in John Ausland, "A Nuclear War to Keep Berlin Open?" *International Herald Tribune* June 19, 1991.

20. Kennedy–de Gaulle meeting, June 1, 1961, DDRS 1994/2586. See more broadly Marc Trachtenberg, A Constructed Peace: The Making of the European Settlement (Princeton: Princeton University Press, 1999), 89 (especially n. 91), 158–165, 286–297, 318.

21. Dean Rusk testimony before Senate Foreign Relations Committee, January 11, 1963, *Executive Sessions of the Senate Foreign Relations Committee (Historical Series)*, vol. 15 (Washington: GPO, 1987), 10. The approach is not distinctly American. Note, for example, a comment made in March 2003 by the Japanese defense minister, Shigeru Ishiba, in connection with the North Korean threat. If North Korea started fueling its missiles, he told a parliamentary committee, "then it is time to strike." Quoted in Howard French, "Japan Faces Burden: Its Own Defense," *New York Times* July 22, 2003.

22. The issue is discussed in some detail in Marc Trachtenberg, "A 'Wasting Asset': American Strategy and the Shifting Nuclear Balance, 1949–1954," in Marc Trachtenberg, *History and Strategy* (Princeton: Princeton University Press, 1991).

23. NSC 68, April 7, 1950, in U.S. Department of State, *National Security Affairs; Foreign Economic Policy*, vol. I of the 1950 series, FRUS (Washington, D.C.: GPO, 1977) 253, 255, 284.

24. Paul Nitze, "A Project for Further Analysis and Study of Certain Factors Affecting our Foreign Policy and our National Defense Policy," September 15, 1954, Project Control Papers, U.S. Air Force Historical Research Center, Maxwell Air Force Base, Alabama.

25. For the details, see Trachtenberg, *History and Strategy*, 132–146.

26. Eisenhower to Dulles, September 8, 1953, *National Security Affairs*, vol. II of the 1952–1954 series, FRUS, 461. Emphasis in original text.

27. Kennedy's views described by his National Security Advisor McGeorge Bundy in a January 10, 1963, meeting with CIA director McCone, quoted in William Burr and Jeffrey Richelson, "Whether to 'Strangle the Baby in the Cradle': The United States and the Chinese Nuclear Program, 1960–64," *International Security* 25, no. 3 (Winter 2000/2001): 67.

28. Burr and Richelson, "Strangle the Baby," especially 67–72 and 75. See also Trachtenberg, *Constructed Peace*, 385–386, and the sources cited there.

29. Burr and Richelson make the point explicitly with reference to the China case in "Strangle the Baby," 54–55.

30. Ibid.

31. See Kennedy's remarks in a meeting with his top advisors on October 16, 1962, in Ernest May and Philip Zelikow, eds., *The Kennedy Tapes: Inside the White House during the Cuban Missile Crisis* (Cambridge: Harvard University Press, 1997), 71, 90; and Trachtenberg, *Constructed Peace*, 350–351.

32. The decision to go to the OAS was made only after Edwin Martin, the assistant secretary of state for Latin American affairs had given his strong assurance that the United States would be able to get the necessary vote in that body. See the record of a top-level meeting, October 19, 1962, *Cuban Missile Crisis and Aftermath* vol. XI of the 1961–1963, FRUS (Washington, D.C.: GPO, 1997), 117–118. See also May and Zelikow, *Kennedy Tapes*, 256–257. Note also the discussion in Abram Chayes, *The Cuban Missile Crisis* (New York: Oxford University Press, 1974), 16, 32–33, and esp. 63 (where it is shown that one draft of the president's speech on the crisis contained a reference to Article 51 of the UN Charter, which, in the opinion of the State Department legal advisor's office, would have amounted "to a full-scale adoption of the doctrine of anticipatory self-defense"). This explicit reference was dropped for mainly political reasons, but the passage in question in its final form did implicitly invoke the principle of preemption. The president declared: "We no longer live in a world where only the actual firing of weapons represents a sufficient challenge to a nation's security to constitute maximum peril. Nuclear weapons are so destructive, and ballistic missiles are so swift, that any substantially increased possibility of their use or any sudden change in their deployment may well be regarded as a definite threat to peace." For the quotation and a brief discussion, see Theodore Sorensen, *Kennedy* (New York: Harper and Row, 1965), 699–700. For Stevenson's remark, see Arthur Schlesinger, *A Thousand Days* (Boston: Houghton Mifflin, 1965), 823–824.

33. A. J. P. Taylor, *The Origins of the Second World War* (New York: Atheneum, 1961), 278.

34. Robert Dallek, *Franklin D. Roosevelt and American Foreign Policy*, 1932–1945 (Oxford: Oxford University Press, 1979; paperback edition, 1981), 285.

35. "Fireside Chat on National Defense, September 11, 1941," *Public Papers and Addresses of Franklin D. Roosevelt*, comp. Samuel Rosenman, vol. 10 (New York: Harper, 1950), 388–390. George Shultz also used the rattlesnake metaphor in his article calling for action against Iraq; "Act Now," *Washington Post*, September 6, 2002.

36. The "Victory Program" of September 11, 1941, officially titled "Joint Board Estimate of United States Over-All Production Requirements," was published in Steven Ross, ed., *American War Plans*, 1919–1941, vol. 5 (New York: Garland, 1992), 160–189 (for the main study), 190–201 (for the appended "Estimate of Army Ground Forces"). For the passages quoted, see 4–5 in the original study (193–194 in the Garland volume) and 4 in the "Estimate of Army Ground Forces" (193 in the Garland volume).

37. Charles Lambroschini and Alexandrine Bouilhet, "Donald Rumsfeld: 'La guerre préventive est aussi vieille que l'Histoire,' " *Le Figaro*, February 10, 2003. Rumsfeld specifically alluded in the U.S. policy in the Cuban missile crisis in this context.

38. By far the most important book on the subject is Dale Copeland's *The Origins of Major War* (Ithaca: Cornell University Press, 2000). This book should be read with some care by everyone interested in this question.

39. Winston Churchill, *The Gathering Storm* (Boston: Houghton Mifflin, 1948). The "Theme of the Volume" appears at the beginning of the book, just before the table of contents. A key passage from the Churchill book, stressing the importance of acting before it is too late—i.e., while the balance of power is still favorable—was quoted in one document that made the case for a preemptive attack on the Chinese nuclear facilities: "Can the Genie Be Put Back in the Bottle?" This document, probably written by Deputy Assistant Secretary of Defense Arthur Barber around June 1963, was declassified in 1997 and can be found in the "Briefing Book on US–Soviet Non-Diffusion Agreement for Discussion at the Moscow Meeting," in box 265, National Security Files, John F. Kennedy Library, Boston.

40. Lord Castlereagh State Paper of May 5, 1820, in Harold Temperley and Lillian Penson, eds., *Foundations of British Foreign Policy from Pitt (1792) to Salisbury (1902)* (Cambridge: Cambridge University Press, 1938), 60, 62.

41. On the question of an attack on North Korea, see Ashton B. Carter and William J. Perry, *Preventive Defense: A New Security Strategy for America* (Washington: Brookings, 1999), 128–131. For the threats to Libya, see Philip Shenon, "Perry, in Egypt, Warns Libya to Halt Chemical Weapons Plant," *New York Times* April 4, 1996.

42. Compare the passage on counterproliferation in *The National Security Strategy of the United States of America*, 14, with the passage on the same subject in Carter and Perry, *Preventive Defense*, 142. Both called explicitly for active and passive defenses and—more important in this context—for counterforce capabilities.

3

CRITIQUING THE NPR'S NEW NUCLEAR MISSIONS

Steve Fetter and Charles L. Glaser

This chapter explores the most controversial aspect of the Nuclear Posture Review (NPR): the identification of possible new roles and missions for U.S. nuclear weapons.[1] The NPR lists three ways in which the United States might use nuclear weapons in future conflicts: (1) to destroy underground facilities that house weapons of mass destruction, leadership, and command and control assets; (2) to defeat chemical and biological agents; and (3) to attack mobile and relocatable targets. Although the United States long considered many or all of these missions vis-à-vis the Soviet Union (and now, presumably, Russia), the NPR states that "new capabilities must be developed to defeat emerging threats," which presumably refers to North Korea, Iran, Iraq, Syria, and Libya, which are apparently mentioned in the document. As a result of the NPR, an "advanced concepts initiative" was established to explore "possible modifications to existing weapons to provide additional yield flexibility in the stockpile; improved earth penetrating weapons (EPWs) to counter the increased use of potential adversaries of hardened and deeply buried facilities; and warheads that reduce collateral damage." According to the NPR, the Department of Defense (DoD) and the National Nuclear Security Agency will "jointly review potential programs to provide nuclear capabilities, and identify opportunities for further study, including assessments of whether nuclear testing would be required to field such warheads."[2]

To analyze these possible new roles and missions, this chapter explores the following questions:

- What new capabilities might nuclear weapons provide, in addition to those provided by conventional weapons?
- What are the costs and benefits of using, threatening to use, and planning to use nuclear weapons in these ways?

Our assessment raises serious doubts about the case for these new nuclear missions. Conventional weapons can be quite effective at destroying or disabling many of the types of targets that the NPR identifies for nuclear missions, and nuclear weapons are not necessarily more effective against some of the targets that conventional weapons cannot defeat. Adversaries are unlikely to attack the United States with weapons of mass destruction, because they will be deterred by existing U.S. retaliatory capabilities, both conventional and nuclear. Overall, we find at most a very limited role for nuclear weapons in the damage-limitation missions identified by the NPR. Further technical and strategic analysis is required to determine whether even these quite circumscribed roles are warranted and should be included in U.S. nuclear doctrine.

NUCLEAR VERSUS CONVENTIONAL WEAPONS

Typical strategic nuclear weapons have yield-to-weight ratios a million times larger than conventional explosives; that is, a nuclear bomb weighing one ton can have an explosive yield equivalent to about one million tons of TNT. This high-energy density produces much higher temperatures and greater thermal effects than can be achieved with conventional weapons. Nuclear weapons also produce an initial burst of radiation and, if the weapon is detonated close to the ground or on the surface, intense fallout, although fallout has not been relied upon by U.S. military planners as a method to disable targets.

Nuclear weapons are uniquely capable of destroying targets that cover a large area, such as cities, industrial complexes, and large military bases. These targets can be destroyed completely by a single nuclear warhead detonated at a relatively high altitude, without requiring high accuracy of delivery. For point or hardened targets, on the other hand, accuracy is far more important than explosive yield. A mobile missile launcher or a shallow-buried bunker can easily be destroyed by existing conventional weapons if they are delivered precisely on target. But because blast and shock effects decrease rapidly with distance, very large increases in yield are needed to compensate for inaccuracy in weapon delivery or uncertainty about target location. For example, compared to a conventional weapon with an explosive yield of one ton of TNT, a one-kiloton nuclear weapon would have a radius of destruction only about five times larger against belowground targets and ten times larger against aboveground targets.[3] Thus, the ability of nuclear weapons to compensate for uncertainties in target location is limited unless one is prepared to use very high-yield weapons, which already exist in large numbers and which would have large collateral effects. These general observations are relevant to each of the three new missions proposed for nuclear weapons.

Defeating Hard and Deeply Buried Targets

According to the NPR, the U.S. Department of Defense has estimated that more than 10,000 underground facilities exist worldwide. Some 1,400 of these facilities are known or suspected strategic sites intended to protect weapons of mass destruction (WMD), leadership, and command and control centers. The majority of these are difficult to defeat because they are hardened and deeply buried, and because their exact location is unknown. The NPR states that "current conventional weapons are not effective for the long-term physical destruction of deep, underground facilities," and that current nuclear weapons, which have limited ground penetration capability, do not "provide a high probability of defeat of these important targets. With a more effective earth penetrator, many buried targets could be attacked using a weapon with a much lower yield. . . . [T]his lower yield would achieve the same damage while producing less fallout (by a factor of ten to twenty) than would the much larger yield surface burst. For defeat of very deep or larger underground facilities, penetrating weapons with large yields would be needed to collapse the facility."[4]

The NPR, however, greatly overstates the number of deeply buried underground facilities that must be held at risk by the United States. Only a handful of these underground facilities are strategically vital, in the sense that they would be used to protect weapons or command and control assets necessary to carry out devastating attacks against the U.S. territory, soldiers, or allies. Any scenario for using nuclear weapons would require knowing which few of these facilities were strategically vital. Thus, good intelligence is far more important in defeating underground facilities than are the types of weapons available to attack them. But recent performance of the intelligence community in this regard is not encouraging. The United States carried out a massive bombing campaign against suspected WMD facilities during the first Gulf War, but inspections undertaken after the war showed that the majority of actual WMD sites had not been attacked. In the opening salvo of the second Gulf War, the United States dropped four one-ton bombs on a site U.S. intelligence believed was a command bunker containing Saddam Hussein. According to news reports, later inspections by U.S. Army revealed that no underground facility existed at the site.[5] Intelligence of the highest accuracy and reliability would be required before using a nuclear weapon against such sites.

Most underground facilities also can be defeated with conventional weapons if good intelligence is available.[6] Existing conventional earth penetrating bombs can collapse facilities located under less than ten meters of concrete or hard rock if the location of the bunker is known precisely. Moreover, underground facilities can be defeated short of physical destruction by attacking surface features such as tunnel entrances, airshafts, power supplies, and communication lines and antennas. Subsequent surveillance by fighter aircraft or armed unmanned aerial vehicles (UAVs) could detect and prevent attempts to remove weapons or to place the facility back into operation.

Most importantly, facilities that are not located precisely or are buried very deeply underground cannot be destroyed even by new, deep-penetrating nuclear warheads. The practical limit to warhead penetration is ten meters in hard rock,[7] and facilities located in hard rock can be confidently destroyed only if they are within the zone of fractured rock formed by the explosion.[8] Thus, facilities deeper than 50 or 250 meters could not be destroyed with high confidence by EPWs with yield less than one kiloton or one megaton, respectively. Even shallow facilities in hard rock could not be reliability destroyed if their location, which could be many hundreds of meters from tunnel entrances and other surface features, could not be determined (nor the weapon delivered) with similar accuracy (i.e., within 50 to 250 meters).

Thus, nuclear weapons would be useful for defeating hard and deeply buried targets only under a fairly narrow range of circumstances. The facility would have to be strategically vital, in the sense that defeating the facility would significantly reduce the probability of enemy WMD attacks against the United States, its allies, or allied troops. U.S. intelligence would have to be confident about the nature of the facility and its location and depth. And the facility would have to be too deep to be vulnerable to conventional attack, but not too deep to be vulnerable to nuclear attack. Such facilities likely exist, but developing new nuclear weapons to destroy them probably would lead determined adversaries to simply dig deeper.

The utility of nuclear EPWs is further diminished by that fact that they would produce substantial fallout, which in most cases would cause serious collateral damage and significantly complicate other U.S. military operations in the area. Because EPWs cannot penetrate more than ten meters in hard rock, most of the radioactivity produced by the explosion would be released into the atmosphere. As noted by the NPR, the area receiving high radiation doses from fallout would be ten to twenty times smaller than would be produced by a surface burst with equal radius of destruction against underground targets. Nevertheless, the area contaminated by even low-yield EPWs would be substantial. Fallout from a one-kiloton EPW would deliver a lethal dose over an area of five to ten square kilometers, which would kill thousands of civilians if used in or near a city.[9] The high-yield EPWs that would be needed to destroy very deeply buried facilities would contaminate vast areas. One group estimated that a 300-kiloton EPW detonated near Pyongyang, North Korea, would cause 500,000 casualties—with the wind blowing *away* from the city.[10] A one-megaton EPW would produce a lethal area of more than 1,000 square miles and would likely cause thousands of civilian deaths unless used in extremely remote areas. Doses in excess of international standards would extend over areas hundreds of times larger than the lethal areas produced by an EPW.

Defeating Chemical and Biological Agents

The NPR mentions the possibility that nuclear weapons might be used to neutralize stocks of chemical and biological weapons (CBW). This point arises from a concern that conventional weapons may not be able to destroy these facilities and prevent the use of these agents, and that conventional attacks might expose civilians and U.S. soldiers in the area to these agents. Extensive analysis, however, has shown that the effectiveness of nuclear weapons for this mission also is limited.[11] To neutralize chemical or biological agents, the nuclear explosion must occur at very close range and within the bunker in which the agents are stored. For example, an EPW with a yield of one to ten kilotons could sterilize all or nearly all biological agents stored within a radius of only five to ten meters of the detonation. Thus, nuclear weapons could only be effective in neutralizing CBW if stocks are in surface or shallow-buried facilities, and if the facilities—and the CBW stocks within the facility—can be located precisely. If the nuclear explosion occurs close enough to rupture but not completely neutralize CBW stockpiles, active agent will be dispersed by the explosion, posing a hazard to surrounding civilians and U.S. soldiers. The lethal area from BW agents dispersed by a nuclear EPW could exceed the lethal area from radioactive fallout.[12]

An alternative approach would be to attack shallow-buried facilities with conventional weapons. Although this also would risk releasing active agents into the environment, the overall risks to nearby civilians and U.S. soldiers, including the risks of fallout, are likely to be smaller than with nuclear attacks. Even a worst-case release of CW from a conventional attack on a storage facility would most likely kill fewer civilians than would the blast and immediate radiation from a low-yield nuclear EPW.[13] Moreover, new non-nuclear weapons are being developed which could disable or destroy CBW storage and production facilities with much lower risk of dispersal. If occupation is the military objective, the best strategy may be to prevent access to CBW facilities by destroying roads and entrances and to monitor the facilities using armed aircraft or UAVs to prevent access to the CBW. The agents can then be neutralized with far greater safety after U.S. troops arrive and secure the site.

Attacking Mobile and Relocatable Targets

The NPR also mentions that "one of the greatest challenges today is accounting for the location uncertainty of mobile and relocatable targets." These targets might include road-, rail-, or ship-mobile missile launchers, command posts, and mobile CBW production facilities. If such targets can be located precisely, they easily can be destroyed with existing conventional weapon systems, such as fighter aircraft or armed UAVs. If the target location is not known precisely, the use of nuclear weapons, which have a much larger radius of destruction, might be considered. Target location uncertainty might result from the time interval between spotting the target (e.g., with photoreconnaissance satellites) and delivering a weapon on the target (e.g., with a ballistic missile).

Large increases in explosive yield, however, would be required to compensate for relatively small increases in distance due either to inaccuracies in target location or weapon delivery. A one-kiloton weapon can severely damage vehicles, rail cars, or ships at distances of up to about 200 meters; a one-megaton weapon can do so at distances up to about two kilometers.[14] These ranges are small compared with potential location uncertainties. Consider, for example, a target moving in one direction along a straight road or rail line at an average speed that is uncertain by plus or minus ten kilometers per hour.

Thirty minutes after locating the target (the flight time of an ICBM), the target could be anywhere along a line ten kilometers in length, requiring twenty-five one-kiloton or three one-megaton bombs to destroy it. If the target (e.g., a ship or mobile missile launcher) could travel in any direction at speeds up to twenty-five kilometers per hour, it could be anywhere within an area of 500 square kilometers after thirty minutes; a single one-megaton bomb would have less than a three percent chance of destroying it.

The effectiveness of nuclear weapons for destroying mobile and relocatable targets could be improved substantially though the development of advanced surveillance, tracking, and guidance systems that would allow ballistic missile warheads to home on their targets. Of course, further improvement in such systems would allow the use of conventional warheads for the same purpose. Thus, nuclear weapons might be useful when target location uncertainties are less than a few hundred meters, but greater than a few tens of meters. Because in this case the lethal range would be maximized by detonating the warheads well above the ground, there would be no local fallout and few civilian casualties would result from the use of kiloton-yield warheads in remote areas (e.g., more than ten kilometers from the nearest village).

BENEFITS OF NEW NUCLEAR ROLES

The benefits of being able to destroy an adversary's ability to attack with weapons of mass destruction are potentially very large. In countering the worst scenario, the United States might prevent an adversary from attacking American cities with nuclear or biological weapons. Other horrible outcomes that might be prevented include nuclear or biological attacks against allies or against deployed American troops. It is the possibility of truly catastrophic damage that most clearly motivates interest in using nuclear weapons for damage limitation and requires a judicious evaluation of the option. In addition, the ability to destroy an adversary's WMD could enhance the U.S. ability to deter aggression and to terminate a war on favorable terms. A country that has a survivable WMD capability might be able to deter the United States from intervening in a regional conflict by threatening to escalate to WMD attacks against U.S. interests. The ability to destroy the adversary's WMD would undermine this threat and thereby help deter an aggressor from initiating or escalating the conflict.

The United States should have a strong preference for being able to perform these missions with conventional weapons—because it has a variety of reasons for not using nuclear weapons and because an adversary might therefore question the credibility of nuclear threats, which would reduce their counter-deterrent value. If, however, conventional weapons are incapable of destroying the adversary's ability to attack with WMD, then there may be valuable roles for nuclear weapons. Of course, this will only be the case if there are scenarios in which using nuclear weapons would significantly increase U.S. prospects for destroying an adversary's capability, which might be true only under a very limited set of conditions. Still, assuming that such cases exist, we need to explore more thoroughly the benefits of using and threatening to use nuclear weapons.

First, the benefits of developing new nuclear capabilities to enhance deterrent threats are limited because the United States can probably deter the adversary's use of WMD. We greatly exaggerate the value of new U.S. nuclear forces, doctrine, or use if we assume that the adversary actually would use WMD against U.S. interests. The U.S. ability to inflict massive nuclear retaliatory damage is likely to deter all states under all but the most extreme conditions.[15] Moreover, the U.S. deterrent is not limited to nuclear threats. The United States also could rely on its conventional superiority to threaten to retaliate against states or overthrow regimes that use WMD. Intimidating conventional threats would enable the United States to avoid relying on threats of first use of nuclear weapons, while adding to U.S. credibility. Furthermore, the one scenario in which an adversary might be likely to use WMD against the United States is largely under U.S. control. If the United States makes clear that it intends to conquer a state, the leader of that state may decide he has little to lose by using WMD, either in a last-ditch effort to deter the United States or simply to exact revenge. Fortunately, the United States can essentially eliminate this rationale for enemy attacks with WMD by choosing not to invade and overthrow the regime.[16] The possibility that a U.S. invasion would lead an adversary to escalate to nuclear attacks, together with the military, political and humanitarian costs to the United States of using nuclear weapons to preemptively destroy the adversary's WMD, would likely be critical considerations in deciding against invasion.

The U.S. ability to deter WMD attacks is less clear-cut if the adversary has a survivable WMD capability, especially a nuclear capability, which it could use to deter U.S. retaliation.[17] In this case, the adversary would be more willing to attack, believing that U.S. retaliation might be deterred by the prospect of additional attacks. Therefore, if nuclear weapons are required to make the adversary's WMD capability vulnerable, then they would increase the U.S. ability to deter WMD attacks, as well as enabling it to reduce the damage if escalation to WMD became likely.

Second, the benefits of using nuclear weapons to destroy WMD depend on the type of WMD involved. Although frequently lumped together within this category, nuclear, chemical, and biological weapons inflict drastically different types and degrees of damage.[18] An attack on a large U.S. city with even the most primitive nuclear weapon is certain to be a true catastrophe, with the dead numbering in the tens of thousands. Passive defenses would be largely ineffective short of complete evacuation. By contrast, the potentially lethal area created by even a large-scale attack with chemical weapons would likely be a hundred times smaller, and it could be much less if the agent was distributed inefficiently or under unfavorable weather conditions. Moreover, casualties could be greatly and reliably reduced by passive defensives (e.g., shelters, masks, atropine injections, evacuation of contaminated areas, etc.). Biological weapons are more difficult to characterize. Inefficient or small-scale attacks or attacks with less deadly agents might kill no one; efficient, large-scale attacks with deadly agents such as anthrax could kill as many people as a primitive nuclear weapon; attacks with contagious agents such as smallpox could trigger an epidemic and kill millions. Thus, the case for using nuclear weapons to destroy nuclear and certain types of biological weapons is much stronger than for chemical weapons.

COSTS OF NEW NUCLEAR ROLES

Critics of the NPR have argued that establishing new missions for nuclear weapons is a bad idea for several reasons: It encourages states to acquire nuclear weapons or improve their nuclear forces, while undermining the U.S. ability to slow proliferation,[19] and it makes adversaries more willing to use nuclear weapons.[20] These ideas are more fully examined in chapter 12 of this book. To explore these criticisms here, we must flesh out the arguments and scrutinize the logic that underpins them.

Acquisition of Nuclear Weapons

How might U.S. adoption of new nuclear missions influence decisions by other countries to acquire nuclear weapons?[21] One line of argument focuses on an adversary's security requirements: The shift in U.S. nuclear policy leads the adversary to believe that nuclear weapons are now necessary to protect its security. A state that has chemical or biological weapons might conclude that it now needs nuclear weapons to deter American attacks against its WMD; a state that already has nuclear weapons might conclude that it needs more weapons—and more survivable weapons—to deter American nuclear attacks.

While the logic of these arguments is sound, the magnitude of the effect is unlikely to be very large. First, a country that sees the United States as a potential threat to its security or regional goals would likely already place substantial value on nuclear weapons, because they are the only means of offsetting U.S. conventional superiority. Second, because U.S. conventional capabilities already pose a serious threat to any target that the United States can find, emerging nuclear states already have an incentive to build more survivable and larger nuclear forces. This incentive is further increased by the potential inherent in existing U.S. nuclear forces. Therefore, although explicit nuclear threats may push states further in this direction, the effect should be small because these threats do not significantly increase states' incentives to acquire nuclear weapons or improve existing nuclear capabilities.

There also are considerations that cut in the opposite direction. U.S. threats to use nuclear weapons against nuclear targets could decrease incentives to acquire nuclear weapons by making explicit that possessing nuclear weapons puts states on the U.S. nuclear target list. Moreover, if nuclear threats increase the adversary's assessment that the United States would use nuclear weapons to destroy the adversary's nuclear capability, then these threats could reduce the value of acquiring nuclear weapons in the first place, by reducing the expectation that they would be available for deterrence.[22] These considerations by themselves are unlikely to convince a state to forego nuclear weapons, but they push in that direction.

Another line of argument suggests that states will become more likely to acquire nuclear weapons if the U.S. advertises the military utility of nuclear weapons against certain new types of targets. But the key reason for acquiring nuclear weapons, especially for a state that suffers conventional inferiority, is for deterrence, which depends primarily on their countervalue potential, not their utility against these sorts of counterforce targets. Moreover, a conventionally inferior adversary might want nuclear weapons because they could be effective against concentrations of conventional military capabilities, including ports and airbases, and could therefore help to undermine American conventional superiority. In contrast, the missions that the NPR does highlight are likely to be of at most secondary interest to potential and emerging nuclear states: they will be unable to acquire a damage-limitation capability against U.S. nuclear forces and may not face regional powers that possess potent WMD capabilities.

There is, however, a second layer of argument that deserves consideration. By emphasizing the possible uses of nuclear weapons, the NPR weakens the taboo against using nuclear weapons. If the taboo is weakened, potential proliferators may find nuclear weapons more attractive because they can be used more easily for coercion and for deterrence of conventional attacks. By this logic, U.S. nuclear doctrine, the nuclear taboo, and the nonproliferation regime are all linked, and to achieve its nonproliferation goals, the United States should downplay all uses of nuclear weapons instead of highlighting new missions.

Evaluating this argument requires understanding the sources of the nuclear taboo.[23] Specifically, we need to consider the link between nuclear doctrine and capabilities on the one hand, and beliefs about the appropriateness of nuclear use on the other. It is hard to see how the relationship could be a strong one. The nuclear taboo developed during decades in which the United States planned for the use of nuclear weapons in increasingly varied ways, including the first use of nuclear weapons to deter conventional attack and to bring about the termination of a conventional war that the United States and its allies were losing. The NATO allies acquired increasingly advanced nuclear forces to perform these missions. The threat of first use to protect America's NATO allies played a central role in driving U.S. nuclear force requirements; in addition to guiding U.S.–European force requirements and command and control, extending nuclear deterrence was the most prominent rationale for the extensive strategic counterforce capabilities that accounted for the majority of U.S. force modernization during the 1970s and 1980s.[24]

This leaves open the possibility that the nuclear taboo would be strengthened by doctrinal changes that reject the use of nuclear weapons. Some proponents of a policy of no-first-use have identified strengthening the norm against using nuclear weapons as a key rationale for changing U.S. nuclear doctrine.[25] Again, however, the strength of this potential effect must be analyzed relative to the sources of the nuclear taboo. The nuclear taboo reflects the widespread recognition of the destructive potential of nuclear weapons, the difficulty of establishing hard lines between different types of nuclear use, and the weight of decades of nonuse. These factors are so powerful that doctrinal shifts alone are unlikely to strengthen or weaken the taboo significantly.[26]

Instead, the NPR is more likely to have a negative effect on nonproliferation by increasing the probability of nuclear use by the United States, which could in turn encourage other states to acquire nuclear weapons. As discussed below, new roles and missions (and corresponding new weapons and targeting plans) increase the likelihood of nuclear use by the United States, which could shatter the nuclear taboo. With this barrier to U.S. nuclear use reduced, other states would be more likely to acquire nuclear weapons for deterring American nuclear attacks. In addition, states that were restrained by the nuclear taboo might then see nuclear weapons as more usable and, therefore, more valuable for coercion.

In addition, the NPR and related weapons development—particularly weapon testing—could hurt U.S. multilateral nonproliferation efforts. By continuing to emphasize the military value of nuclear weapons, the United States may inadvertently strengthen the hand of pronuclear elites in debates within nonnuclear states, while undermining those opposed to acquiring nuclear weapons.[27] It could also undermine the ability of the United States to form and maintain strong international coalitions opposing proliferation (e.g., vis-à-vis North Korea and Iran), or to get broad international agreement to strengthen barriers to proliferation (e.g., export controls and enhanced safeguards and physical protection measures). Although these effects are undoubtedly negative, their magnitude is hard to judge.

Use of Nuclear Weapons by Adversaries

Another concern is that adopting new roles and missions for U.S. nuclear forces might make adversaries more willing to use nuclear weapons. The basic argument is as follows: the NPR increases the probability that the United States will use nuclear weapons by promoting new roles and missions for them; if the United States uses nuclear weapons the taboo would be shattered,[28] and as a result other states would become more willing to use nuclear weapons, either against the United States or regional adversaries. According to this line of argument, if, in the recent war against Iraq, the United States had used nuclear weapons to destroy Iraqi WMD or deeply buried command bunkers (assuming they existed), in a future conflict North Korea would be more likely to use nuclear weapons against the United States, U.S. military forces, or America's allies in the region, or India might be more willing to use nuclear weapons preemptively to destroy Pakistani nuclear weapons.

The first step in this argument is correct: The NPR increases the probability that the United States would use nuclear weapons—both by identifying and legitimizing new roles and by calling for improvements in the U.S. arsenal that would increase the effectiveness and reduce the collateral damage of nuclear use. The Bush administration believes this is warranted in light of the dangers the United States faces. Moreover, the NPR argues that this change in nuclear doctrine will discourage proliferation and will therefore ultimately decrease the number of situations in which nuclear weapons might be used to counter proliferation. We doubt that this will be a dominant effect and judge that, on balance, the probability of U.S. nuclear use will increase as a result of policies promulgated by the NPR.

The second step—American nuclear use would shatter the nuclear taboo—is also basically correct, although the long-term effects are less clear. Nuclear use would end a very long period of nonuse, which is now approaching sixty years. Analyses of the nuclear taboo emphasize that its strength increases as the period of nonuse increases; use of nuclear weapons would weaken this dimension of the taboo. In addition, if American first use against military targets is effective and results in limited collateral damage, the sharp distinction between nuclear and conventional weapons might be reduced and the nuclear taboo would be eroded severely. Nuclear use also would weaken the identity-based prohibition on the use of nuclear weapons because the leader of the Western world and the world's most powerful country would have once again used nuclear weapons. As a result, other states would not be as severely stigmatized or ostracized if they used nuclear weapons, and it would be more difficult to marshal coordinated international action against countries that use nuclear weapons.

At the same time, other factors do not work so sharply against the taboo, and might even reinforce it over the longer term. As explained above, the impact of using nuclear weapons could depend on the scenario and purpose for which they are used. If the United States used nuclear weapons preemptively when its adversary was preparing to launch a nuclear attack against the United States, the rationale for American nuclear use might be sufficiently compelling that most observers and nations would accept its legitimacy, particularly if the collateral effects of the attacks were modest. The result could be a further articulation, but not necessarily a weakening, of the nuclear taboo. The aversion to using nuclear weapons would largely stand, but under very narrow conditions, nuclear use would be recognized as acceptable and perhaps even necessary, although undesirable.[29]

On the other hand, if American use of nuclear weapons resulted in tremendous destruction, or if it resulted in catastrophic retaliation, governments and publics might come to better appreciate the danger posed by nuclear weapons, with their destructive potential made more vivid and horrifying, which in turn might strengthen the taboo against using nuclear weapons. It is not unimaginable that this would lead to serious efforts to prohibit nuclear weapons, just as the use of chemical weapons ultimately led to prohibitions on their use and, ultimately, their possession.

The third step in the argument—that other states will become more willing to use nuclear weapons—is more complicated and less clearly correct. We do not know much about whether the adversaries in question embrace the nuclear taboo. The most extensive work on the nuclear taboo focuses on the United States; for states that do not yet have nuclear weapons there can be no direct evidence of their attitudes toward use. Iraq repeatedly violated the taboo on the use of chemical weapons, which at least raises doubts about whether it would be constrained by a nuclear taboo. If the United States is facing an adversary that does not accept the nuclear taboo, there is little, if any, cost in weakening the convention against use except for the possibility that the adversary would have embraced the taboo eventually but for the American nuclear attack. Moreover, the effect of the nuclear taboo is likely to be less important than other considerations. An opponent that otherwise can be deterred will not be significantly more likely to use nuclear weapons simply because the United States weakened the nuclear taboo by using nuclear weapons in an earlier conflict. On the other hand, an adversary that the United States cannot deter is not likely to be influenced very much by the nuclear taboo—either because the state perceives itself to be in a desperate situation or because a state that is willing to risk high levels of damage to its own people is less likely to be repulsed by inflicting massive damage on others. A weakening of the nuclear taboo would thus appear to have its greatest effect on the remaining cases: states that are difficult but not impossible to deter, and that recognize and are influenced by the nuclear taboo. This seems likely to be a quite small, but possibly nonzero, set of adversaries and scenarios.

CONCLUSIONS AND RECOMMENDATIONS

Overall, we find at most a very limited role for nuclear weapons in the damage-limitation missions identified by the NPR. Adversaries are unlikely to attack the United States or its vital interests with WMD, because the United States possesses highly capable deterrent forces and the will to use them if attacked with WMD. Moreover, if deterrence fails, U.S. conventional forces can be quite effective at destroying or disabling the new types of targets the NPR identifies for nuclear weapons, with much smaller collateral effects. Consequently, there is at best a very limited role for nuclear weapons in these missions.

Nevertheless, no matter how well the United States designs its deterrent policy, there remains some possibility that deterrence could fail and conventional weapons would be ineffective against strategically critical targets. Given the enormous destruction that an adversary could inflict with nuclear and certain types of biological weapons, we can imagine scenarios in which the United States would benefit from using nuclear weapons in a damage-limitation attack. Using nuclear weapons would generate a variety of costs—including possibly increasing the probability that other states would use nuclear weapons, hurting U.S. nonproliferation policy, and damaging the United States' international reputation (as well as its self-image). But we cannot rule out the possibility that the benefits of damage limitation could exceed these costs if the adversary was armed with nuclear or sophisticated biological weapons, if the probability that the United States was going to be attacked with these weapons was high, and if conventional weapons had significantly poorer prospects of defeating targets essential to these enemy attacks.

Although such scenarios are not impossible to imagine, it may be that there are no realistic scenarios in which employing nuclear weapons would be the United States' best option. The NPR does not provide an assessment of whether the types of targets with which it is concerned can be destroyed or disabled with conventional weapons. The first step in assessing the value of nuclear options is to determine whether there exist targets that cannot be destroyed with conventional weapons, but that could be destroyed with nuclear weapons. If such targets exist, the next step is to determine whether any of these targets are in countries that possess nuclear or sophisticated biological weapons and whether the targets would play an essential role in an adversary's ability to launch a devastating attack. Thorough analysis of these questions is required for understanding the implications of the NPR. Because answers to these questions are critically important, we believe technical experts from outside the government, such as the Jason scientists—a group of elite academic scientists who have advised the U.S. government on national security for decades—or a committee of the National Academy of Sciences should be consulted to offer critiques and alternatives to classified DoD studies.

Once this assessment of targets is complete, and assuming that there exist high-value targets that can be defeated with nuclear but not with conventional weapons, further analysis is required to assess the costs and risks of a nuclear attack. The collateral damage from a nuclear attack should be estimated for each target, including blast and thermal effects, fallout, and the possible dispersal of chemical and biological agents. U.S. confidence in its characterization of each target should be evaluated, because U.S. decision makers must consider the true urgency of launching a nuclear attack. The scenario in which a target might need to be attacked should be analyzed to provide guidance on when in a crisis the United States would need to launch a nuclear attack. All of this information would be essential to U.S. leaders faced with the momentous decision about whether and when to order a nuclear attack. U.S. leaders, including the president, should be briefed fully about the effects to ensure that they appreciate the urgency, risks, and complexities before becoming involved in a crisis or war.

In sum, the NPR raises more questions than it answers, and it overstates the extent of new roles for U.S. nuclear weapons. We anticipate that more thorough study of possible targets—and the risks and costs of nuclear attacks on these targets—will lead to a more measured nuclear doctrine in which there are, at most, a few scenarios in which the United States might use nuclear weapons preemptively. There may not be any.

Notes

1. *Nuclear Posture Review* [excerpts], January 8, 2002<http://www.globalsecurity.org/wmd/library/policy/dod/npr.htm>. References in this chapter to the NPR refer to this text, which we assume to be authentic.

2. *Nuclear Posture Review*, 34–35.

3. The range for a given level of air-blast damage (peak overpressure) is proportional to the one-third power of yield; thus, a one-ton explosion produces about the same peak overpressure (about 100 psi) at a distance of ten meters as a one-kiloton explosion produces at a distance of 100 meters (for a fixed scaled height of burst). The radius of destruction for very hard buried targets is given roughly by the apparent crater radius, which is roughly proportional to the 0.22 power of yield for explosions in hard rock at constant depth of burial; the crater radius for a one-kiloton explosion is 4.6 times larger than that produced by a one-ton explosion at the same depth. See Samuel Glasstone and Phillip J. Dolan, *Effects of Nuclear Weapons*, 3rd ed. (Washington, D.C.: U.S. Department of Defense and Department of Energy, 1977).

4. *Nuclear Posture Review*, 47.

5. "U.S. Can't Find Hussein Bunker," *Washington Post* May 30, 2003, A19.

6. For a more detailed analysis, see Michael A. Levi, "Fire in the Hole: Nuclear and Non-Nuclear Options for Counterproliferation," working paper (Washington, D.C.: Carnegie Endowment for International Peace, November 2002) <http://www.ceip.org/files/pdf/wp31.pdf>.

7. Robert W. Nelson, "Low-Yield Earth-Penetrating Nuclear Weapons," *Science and Global Security* 10, no. 1 (2002): 5–10; Michael May and Zachary Haldeman, "Effectiveness of Nuclear Weapons against Buried Biological Agents," report (Stanford, Calif.: Center for International Security and Cooperation, Stanford University, June 2003), 5–6, 25–26 (an updated version is available at <http://iis-db.stanford.edu/pubs/20216/MayHaldeman0104.pdf>); Christopher E. Paine, principal author with Thomas B. Cochran, Matthew G. McKinzie, and Robert S. Norris, "Countering Proliferation, or Compounding It? The Bush Administration's Quest for Earth-Penetrating and Low-Yield Nuclear Weapons," (Washington, D.C.: Natural Resources Defense Council, May 2003), 9–11 <http://iis-db.stanford.edu/pubs/20216/MayHaldeman0104.pdf>.

8. May and Haldeman, "Effectiveness of Nuclear Weapons," 17–18; Glasstone and Dolan, *Effects of Nuclear Weapons*, 265.

9. Nelson, "Low-Yield EPWs"; Paine et al., "Countering Proliferation"; and Frank Serduke, "Standard KDFOC4 Fallout Calculations for Buried Nuclear Detonations," UCRL-ID-146937 (Livermore, Calif.: Lawrence Livermore National Laboratory, September 2001).

10. Paine et al., "Countering Proliferation," 7.

11. May and Haldeman, "Effectiveness of Nuclear Weapons against Buried Biological Agents"; Robert W. Nelson, "Nuclear 'Bunker Busters' Would More Likely Disperse than Destroy Buried Stockpiles of Biological and Chemical Agents," *Science and Global Security* 12, nos. 1–2 (2004): 69–90.

12. May and Haldeman, "Effectiveness of Nuclear Weapons," 21.

13. Author's calculations, comparing a 10-ton release of sarin (assuming 5% of a 200-ton inventory is released by the attack) with the effects of a 1-kiloton nuclear explosion at a depth of 10 meters.

14. Glasstone and Dolan, *Effects of Nuclear Weapons*, 221–224.

15. On uncertainty about the effects of nuclear threats in the Gulf War see Scott D. Sagan, "The Commitment Trap: Why the United States Should Not Use Nuclear Threats to Deter Biological and Chemical Weapons Attacks," *International Security* 24, no. 4 (Spring 2000): 91–96.

16. An important qualification is that U.S. military operations required to retake territory could be confused with the operations required to conquer a country. On this danger and approaches for reducing it, see Barry R. Posen, "U.S. Security Policy in a Nuclear-Armed World (Or: What if Iraq Had Had Nuclear Weapons?" *Security Studies* 6, no. 3 (Spring 1997): 1–31.

17. For a more detailed analysis of this issue see Charles L. Glaser and Steve Fetter, "National Missile Defense and the Future of U.S. Nuclear Weapons Policy," *International Security* 26, no. 1 (Summer 2001): 66–68.

18. Steve Fetter, "Ballistic Missiles and Weapons of Mass Destruction: What Is the Threat? What Should Be Done?" *International Security* 16, no. 1 (1991): 5–42.

19. Michael May, "An Alternative Nuclear Posture," *Physics and Society* (October 2003) <http://epswww.epfl.ch/aps/units/fps/newsletters/2003/oct/oct03.pdf>; available alternately at <http://www.aps.org/units/fps/newsletters/2003/october/articles.cfm#2>; Henry Kelly and Ivan Oelrich, "Will New Nuclear Weapons Make Us More Secure?" <www.fas.org/ssp/docs/030916-newnukes>.

20. May, "An Alternative Nuclear Posture."

21. For analyses of states' nuclear acquisition decisions see Scott D. Sagan, "Why Do States Build Nuclear Weapons: Three Models in Search of a Bomb," *International Security* 21, no. 3 (Winter 1996/1997): 54–86; T. V. Paul, *Power Versus Prudence: Why Nations Forgo Nuclear Weapons* (Montreal: McGill-Queen's University Press, 2000).

22. The NPR argues more generally: "Systems capable of striking a wide range of targets throughout an adversary's territory may dissuade a potential adversary from pursuing threatening capabilities."

23. see Nina Tannewald, "The Nuclear Taboo: The United States and the Normative Basis for Nuclear Non-Use," *International Organization* 53, no. 3 (Summer 1999): 433–468; Elizabeth Kier and Jonathan Mercer, "Setting Precedents in Anarchy: Military Intervention and Weapons of Mass Destruction," *International Security* 20, no. 4 (Spring 1996): 77–106.

24. On U.S. nuclear doctrine see Lawrence Freedman, *The Evolution of Nuclear Strategy* (New York: St. Martin's Press, 1983); on the relationship between extended deterrence and U.S. counterforce requirements see Charles L. Glaser, *Analyzing Strategic Nuclear Policy* (Princeton: Princeton University Press, 1990), chap. 7.

25. See, for example, Committee on International Security and Arms Control, National Academy of Sciences, *The Future of U.S. Nuclear Weapons Policy* (Washington, D.C.: National Academy Press, 1997), which calls for shifting to no-first-use to support U.S. nonproliferation goals (71), and argues that the practice of nuclear deterrence can fuel proliferation by, among other reasons, "lending respectability to reliance on nuclear deterrence."

26. For example, Thomas C. Schelling, "The Role of Nuclear Weapons," in L. Benjamin Ederington and Michael J. Mazarr, eds., *Turning Point: The Gulf War and U.S. Military Strategy* (Boulder: Westview Press, 1994), 113, argues that "the inhibition on any president's authorizing the use of nuclear weapons was already far stronger than any no-first-use declaration [or even treaty] could make it; an official announcement of a no-first-use policy would have the same effect as adding a hemp rope to an anchor chain."

27. Sagan, "Why Do States Build Nuclear Weapons," 72–73, makes this point in a related context.

28. Another possibility is that the NPR weakens the nuclear taboo simply by making clear the U.S. willingness to use nuclear weapons and does not depend on the United States actually using them. This argument has already been discussed above and does not appear very strong, although there is the possibility of missing the opportunity to further strengthening the taboo.

29. Schelling, "The Role of Nuclear Weapons," comments on many of these considerations.

IMPLEMENTING THE NPR

4

THE NEW TRIAD

Joseph F. Pilat

At a time of great change, marked by the decline of the old Soviet threat and rising concerns about terrorism and weapons of mass destruction (WMD) proliferation, the Bush administration has put forward a new strategic vision in the Nuclear Posture Review (NPR), the Quadrennial Defense Review (QDR), and the new national security strategy issued in September 2002. The strategy is being honed in the context of the Afghanistan and Iraq campaigns, which are providing valuable lessons and reinforcing central tenets of strategy.

The new strategy reflects a changed security environment and newly formulated strategic objectives: assure friends and allies, dissuade future military competition, deter threats against U.S. interests and allies, and defeat adversaries if deterrence fails. To meet these objectives, there is a call for a new triad consisting of nuclear and nonnuclear offensive strike forces, including offensive information operations (IO) and special operations forces (SOF); active and passive defenses; and a revitalized defense infrastructure (including the nuclear weapon complex). Command and control, intelligence, and a new planning approach support this triad.

Is the new triad new? Does it portend strategic revolution or evolution? Will it survive the Bush presidency? With these questions in mind, this chapter explores the prospects and issues related to the integration and transformation of the new triad.

OFFENSIVE STRIKE FORCES

The element of the triad that comprises nuclear and non-nuclear strike forces is designed to provide effective and flexible offensive capabilities and to expand the options available to the president if international conditions deteriorate. This approach has the potential to reduce dependence on nuclear weapons in the strategic deterrent. Current nuclear forces, including nuclear-capable strike aircraft and nuclear-armed submarine-launched cruise missiles (SLCMs), will remain core U.S. capabilities for some time, and these forces must be sustained and modernized while other capabilities of the new triad are being developed and fielded.

Nuclear Forces

The U.S. stockpile of today was largely designed during the Cold War to deter a single, large, technologically advanced enemy with a great number of readily deliverable nuclear weapons. Consequently, the current stockpile consists of weapon systems that were not designed for deterrence in the new, primarily regional contingencies the United States is likely to face in the future. In some contingencies, U.S. nuclear weapons in their current state may not be seen by adversaries as a credible deterrent. If nuclear weapons are to play an important deterrent role in regional contingencies, the stockpile must evolve to respond to requirements in an increasingly complex world. It will need to be integrated with conventional strike forces to create mixed nuclear-conventional and wholly nonnuclear options where possible.[1] The NPR offers a road map to address these and other nuclear issues, and it embodies both continuity and change.

The U.S. nuclear deterrent will rely for many years on current forces, albeit reduced in number. These forces are projected to remain until 2020 or longer (as the old triad is embodied in the new). Replacements for current delivery systems are under consideration. The NPR makes no explicit call for new nuclear weapons, although the document also does not foreclose the possibility that the United States might develop new nuclear designs. The NPR does call for improved capabilities to defeat hard, deeply buried, and mobile targets, as well as chemical and biological agents. These capabilities could utilize nuclear or nonnuclear weapons. No new nuclear testing is mandated by the NPR, but it calls for enhanced test readiness. There is a requirement for a responsive force that provides a capability to upload existing weapon systems rapidly if the decision is made to increase the size of the U.S. nuclear arsenal.

All of these changes were underway before the conclusion of the George W. Bush administration's NPR, reflecting a reduced U.S. reliance on nuclear forces after the Cold War ended. In this sense, the NPR's vision of nuclear roles is evolutionary.

New Directions for the NPR

Four new initiatives in the NPR suggest more dramatic changes in U.S. nuclear doctrine and force structure. The NPR removes nuclear weapons from the center of U.S. deterrence and defense strategy, it decouples the U.S. force posture from that of Russia, it acknowledges the need to address new contingencies, and it calls for new ways to conduct nuclear planning.

Some have claimed that the Bush administration's NPR, unlike the one of 1994, did not reduce the role of nuclear weapons. In fact, some have even argued that it expands their role. Such criticism, however, fails to acknowledge that the NPR removes nuclear weapons from the center of deterrence. The NPR envisions lower numbers of nuclear weapons, and substituting conventional weapons for nuclear where possible. Finally, the NPR highlights the role of defenses in deterrence and dissuasion.

The United States will no longer plan, size, or sustain forces based solely on the Russian threat. The United States is working to encourage a cooperative, non-adversarial relationship with Russia that sets aside Cold War hostilities and antagonisms and seeks to eliminate the outdated relationship of mutually assured destruction (MAD) as the basis of Russian-American relations. Of course, Russian (and Chinese) nuclear capabilities remain a long-term concern, and the responsive force is sized in part on the prospect of potential contingencies involving these and other states. Today, however, WMD proliferation and terrorism are of greater concern to U.S. policy makers than Russia's nuclear arsenal.

Nuclear Deterrence

Nuclear deterrence was a focal point of Cold War strategy and set the parameters for nuclear forces and for formal bilateral arms control between the United States and the former Soviet Union. The changes outlined in the NPR do not alter the need for a credible nuclear deterrent but they do make clear that the Cold War approach to nuclear deterrence, with its dominant reliance on massive offensive nuclear forces and its focus on Russian nuclear forces, is no longer appropriate.

The credibility of nuclear deterrence has been estimated, at least in the minds of U.S. policy makers, largely by relying on measures of existing capabilities. If the capability did not exist to undertake the threatened action should deterrence fail, the deterrent threat was not viewed as credible. A misunderstanding of this long-standing relationship between deterrence and capabilities seems to be a major factor behind the charge that the NPR outlines a nuclear-warfighting strategy. In the current climate, there are important questions about the credibility of future deterrence. These questions are made more acute by significant constraints on U.S. nuclear forces and associated capabilities, including a decade-long testing moratorium and the problems with a nuclear-weapon complex that has been in decline since the end of the Cold War. U.S. nonproliferation policy, especially its negative security assurances, is also a complicating factor.

Conventional Capabilities

Advanced conventional strike forces, nuclear strike forces, offensive information operations, and special operations forces constitute one element of the new triad. The many capabilities provided by these new forces and operations will be needed to address the full spectrum of contingencies faced by the United States today. These forces are intended to increase the options open to the president and military commanders. They are expected to provide nonnuclear attack options if deterrence or dissuasion fails. It also is assumed that these capabilities will be needed to make preemptive (or preventive) attacks, if necessary, in pursuit of this newly formulated element of U.S. national security strategy.[2]

The NPR suggests that the United States must have an enhanced global strike capability, that is, rapidly deployable, fully integrated joint land-air-sea-space forces with global reach, capable of striking rapidly and effectively at all ranges and in all weather and terrain conditions. No single weapons system can provide a global strike capability. Global strike options must be integrated with nuclear and other capabilities in military planning.

Achieving a real global strike capability is critical to the new triad and will require new capabilities to create and reinforce U.S. asymmetric advantages against adversaries. Weapons development efforts will focus on identifying, leveraging, and strengthening U.S. technology in the fields of power projection, precision strike, space operations, undersea warfare, and intelligence collection. Future forces will be transformed from manned to unmanned, short-to-long range, and non-stealthy to stealthy systems.

Missions and Objectives for Nonnuclear Strike

For preemption, prevention, and counterforce missions, the United States is exploring the possibility of developing conventional precision-guided munitions, earth-penetrating munitions, and munitions designed to counter biological and chemical weapons. All of these munitions concepts will have to be assessed in terms of their ability to fulfill specific missions and to minimize casualties and collateral damage during strikes on various facilities and sites related to weapons of mass destruction production and storage.[3] Sensors that would help target underground bunkers and mobile missiles must be developed.

The suite of technologies referred to as non-kinetic strike capabilities, including information operations, could in principle meet certain counterforce needs and create new arenas for military action with minimal costs and limited amounts of damage and death. If non-kinetic strike capabilities prove technically feasible, they could reduce collateral damage that has been traditionally associated with strategic attacks.[4]

Conventional Dissuasion/Assurance

The role of advanced conventional forces in dissuasion has not been articulated by the Bush administration. Strong U.S. naval and air forces ideally will dissuade potential adversaries from direct military or political competition with the United States. These same capabilities should assure allies in times of war or crisis of the ability of U.S. policy makers to honor their treaty commitments.

The U.S. conventional superiority evident during the Gulf War in 1991 and the belief that this heralded a technology-driven revolution in military affairs (RMA) has also created the expectation that a viable conventional deterrence posture will become available shortly. Although the NPR does not advocate relying solely on conventional deterrence, it opens up the prospect of a greater role for conventional forces in the deterrence formula. Some analysts believe that conventional deterrence may allow the United States to forego nuclear deterrence, at least in some contingencies. Such beliefs are based on speculation about the likely behavior of so-called rogue states when they are confronted with overwhelming conventional power. In this type of crisis, however, a regional aggressor might decide that the best means to negate the conventional advantages of the United States and the West is to threaten or to use WMD. This lesson was drawn by regional leaders from the first Gulf War. And the continued horizontal and vertical proliferation of nuclear, chemical, and biological weapons can affect U.S. power projection forces in the future, especially if the U.S. military fails to take steps to counter these new threats. Efforts to enhance the survivability of weapons, military bases, troop concentrations, and logistical infrastructure are likely to become increasingly important in the years ahead.

Even if U.S. forces and the United States itself can be made less vulnerable to attack, too great a reliance on conventional capabilities for deterrence may be imprudent in the long term. Doubts exist about the effectiveness of conventional deterrence, and the causes of its failure are well understood theoretically. If advanced conventional capabilities are used decisively in battle, and particularly in preemptive actions, however, they could have a deterrent effect on other adversaries or potential adversaries. The initial reactions of North Korea, Iran, and other states to the rapid coalition victory in Iraq may suggest this effect. To try to ensure that conventional forces sufficient to deter a threat are available in a region of concern in time to prevent aggression, there is a new focus on deterring forward and developing the capabilities to do so.

DEFENSES

How are defenses likely to play in the new triad? Active and passive defenses reduce vulnerabilities. Defenses will never be perfect, however. The U.S. homeland, as well as U.S. and allied nuclear and conventional forces, logistics, and command and control, will always face a threat of chemical, biological, or nuclear attack. The credibility of deterrence and defense will increase to the extent that the U.S. and allied militaries and civilians can be protected from WMD attack. Defenses also can help achieve the goals of dissuasion and assurance. As a consequence, they are seen as an important feature of the new strategic framework.

Active Defenses

The scope, depth, and effectiveness of coverage by missile defenses have yet to be determined. A limited capability against states with modest ballistic missile forces will be deployed over the next several years. The cost–benefit analysis of deploying limited systems will continue to be debated, even as systems are deployed initially. Decades will elapse, however, before anything but a limited system can be deployed. Budgetary competition with counterterrorism, defense transformation, infrastructure renewal and other national military and nonmilitary priorities will influence both the timing and effectiveness of future systems.

The technical challenges of ballistic missile defenses are known. What are the anticipated benefits? The deployment of ballistic or cruise missile defenses might force states to conclude that proliferating missile technology—or considering the use of ballistic and cruise missiles against the United States or its allies—is not in their best interests. Defenses may, to the extent they are seen as effective by U.S. decision makers, increase the attractiveness of preemptive or preventive strikes against an adversary's WMD. They also could be critical for defense in the event deterrence and dissuasion fails or if preemption or prevention is undertaken without complete success, allowing an opponent to launch a retaliatory strike against the United States.

The current missile defense program reflects a broad-based research, development, testing and engineering effort (RDT&E), designed to provide a layered defensive capability against limited ballistic missile attacks on the U.S. homeland, U.S. forces, and the territory of allies. The program explores a variety of technologies and approaches to intercept missiles of different ranges and trajectories, and in different stages of flight. Ground-based kinetic kill interceptors (late-midcourse phase) and airborne lasers (boost phase) are key elements of the current program. Little attention, however, has been given to the development of cruise missile defenses. For political, military, and technological reasons, international participation is an important long-term aspect of the U.S. missile defense program.

Despite the developmental status of the program at present, there is a sense within the Bush administration that an emergency capability is needed. This sense of urgency has led to a decision to deploy as much capability as possible, as soon as possible. On December 17, 2002, the White House announced it was directing the Pentagon to field initial missile defense capabilities in 2004 and 2005. The expectation is that following the initial deployments of ground-based interceptors, development and testing will continue.[5]

Passive Defenses of Military Assets

Passive defenses are designed to reduce or remove vulnerabilities, especially those of U.S. warfighting forces. These capabilities are more advanced than active defenses, but they can and must be improved.

Redundancy is one way to reduce vulnerabilities. Given the costs of transforming the military, of conducting the war on terrorism, and nonmilitary expenditures, redundancy within the U.S. military can be expected to decline. To some extent, vulnerabilities can be reduced through improvements in survivability (dispersal, mobility, hardening), but a lack of redundancy might emerge as an American Achilles heel in the twenty-first century.

The vulnerabilities that cannot be reduced or eliminated through redundancy and survivability must be addressed by other means. For example, standoff radiation, optical, or spectrometric detectors can provide the capability for battlefield early warning, which is currently limited. Development of detection systems that can quickly identify biological or chemical agents is a priority. Chemical and biological warfare protection can be improved further by the development and acquisition of advanced protective clothing and inhalation toxicology. Also, defense mechanisms can, in principle, be built into forces to protect them from radiation, electromagnetic pulses, or chemical and biological threats. Environmental remediation technologies, including the destruction of biological or chemical agents and the cleanup of radiological contamination, are being pursued.

INFRASTRUCTURE

For both conventional and nuclear forces, a robust, modernized, flexible, and responsive infrastructure is critical to overall national security. In many respects, infrastructure supports other capabilities. But its ability to augment U.S. capabilities in a timely manner by developing new systems or accelerating production of existing systems through rapid prototyping or surge production capabilities provides adaptability and defense in depth. This warrants its treatment as one leg of the new triad.

Seen in the context of an ability to sustain (through life-extension programs), modernize, and augment existing forces; to develop replacements for existing systems; and to adapt capabilities to new challenges, infrastructure can help achieve assurance, deterrence, and dissuasion. Perhaps its greatest contribution will be to deterrence and dissuasion, especially if it can be demonstrated that the infrastructure can out-produce potential adversaries.

Defense–Industrial Base

Although the U.S. defense–industrial base remains the largest in the world, it is slowly contracting, due in part to the Pentagon's procurements of smaller numbers of often more expensive weapon systems. Moreover, the industrial base is no longer entirely independent and relies heavily on commercial and foreign suppliers for key weapons components. Because the Pentagon is no longer at the cutting edge of innovation in many critical technologies, this loss of independence is likely to continue to grow over time. This is not necessarily a debilitating situation. In fact, it can even promote technological advancement while reducing costs, but only if supply can be assured against surprise by creating a network of diverse multiple suppliers.

Reforms in Pentagon procurement procedures must be undertaken so that the defense–industrial base can meet future challenges. The use of spiral development and acquisition is likely to be critical in the years ahead. Beyond these efforts, the defense–industrial base will have to possess new capabilities for force constitution and reconstitution: innovative defense research and development; the ability for rapid prototyping of weapons and support systems; flexible, adaptive production capabilities (such as lean manufacturing and small runs); and surge production capability for weapons and support systems. Some of these issues were considered in the 1980s in the debate over reconstitution, but little was done to create a rapidly expansible ability to add weapons to the U.S. inventory quickly. A key issue for the success of this initiative will be developing and implementing the mechanisms needed to secure adequate funding for these capabilities.

Nuclear Weapons Complex/Stockpile Stewardship

A revitalized weapons complex will make an important contribution to achieving the assurance, dissuasion, and deterrence objectives assigned to the new triad. A more capable nuclear infrastructure also will address the ongoing nuclear weapon requirements called for by the Stockpile Stewardship Program.

From a Department of Energy (DoE) perspective, stockpile stewardship involves ensuring the safety, reliability, and performance of the enduring stockpile. Stockpile stewardship also must guarantee that scientists and engineers can respond to future stockpile surprises, to changes in the international security environment, and to new military requirements. As DoE officials and the national nuclear weapon laboratories' directors have pointed out, the ultimate success of the Stockpile Stewardship Program cannot be guaranteed. In the long term, it will be necessary to replace existing weapons with new characteristics. The NPR provides a framework for thinking about the new types of weapons that should be developed and the mission they will be assigned in the decades ahead.

To implement the NPR, U.S. policy makers eventually will have to decide to modernize their nuclear weapons production capabilities, including creating expanded capabilities at certain research and production sites. To date, it appears that insufficient attention has been given to preserving the R&D and technology base to make sure the United States is prepared to preserve or modernize its nuclear forces in the years ahead.

SUPPORTING THE NEW TRIAD

Central to the new strategic framework is an adaptive global command and control capability that is able to conduct rapid and effective operations across the full range of possible contingencies. The strategic deterrent described by the NPR requires an integrated, interactive, real-time picture of the battlespace. This new command and control capability must be able to accommodate the emerging technologies and tools that are produced by an ongoing information revolution. To capitalize on these developments, there is a need for command systems that allow greater integration, interoperability, cost-effectiveness, and efficiency.

Although there are political and technical drivers both for a national system and for joint command and control capabilities, these capabilities are developed independently by the services or combatant commanders, with insufficient coordination and attention to joint and national-level capabilities. Service stovepiping has thus become a roadblock in the overall process of transforming command, control, and intelligence networks. A national-level command, control, and intelligence network dedicated to implementing the strategic deterrent described by the NPR might prove to be a useful vehicle when it comes to designing a modern and efficient national command network.

Intelligence, Surveillance, and Reconnaissance

The intelligence requirements for the triad may be difficult to meet. Intelligence analysts will have to provide strategic and tactical warning and better target location, characterization, and effects-based analysis. As one senior defense official put it, the new strategic deterrent creates a need to see, move, and strike very quickly; intelligence, surveillance, and reconnaissance (ISR) must be improved if the new triad is to become an effective force. To improve target location and target identification, accelerated efforts to integrate special operations forces, unattended ground sensors, and space-based and air-based sensor platforms by information technologies are needed. These efforts, however, are complicated by the need to address multiple targets, states with vastly different strategic personalities, and non-state actors. To meet new requirements and understand a potential adversary's capabilities, doctrines, and weapons employment plans will require improved surveillance and information extraction technologies, different collection strategies, more resources (as well as redistributed resources), greater reliance on human intelligence (HUMINT), and information sharing across several intelligence organizations.

Planning

Capabilities-based planning is the approach to strategic planning adopted in the QDR and the NPR. It replaces the threat-based approach used during the Cold War, an approach that still dominated military thinking and planning throughout the 1990s. Rather than focus on the threat posed by a specific adversary, which is not deemed useful in today's fluid threat environment, capabilities-based planning focuses on the range of potential capabilities that potential adversaries may deploy against the U.S. homeland, its forces, and interests, along with those of U.S. allies. It also provides policy makers and senior military commanders a "toolbox" of capabilities they can use in time of crisis to devise an appropriate U.S. response.

This new way of planning is expected to guide the development of capabilities and the allocation of resources. In principle, it will have the potential to expand the military, diplomatic, economic, psychological, and social instruments of U.S. national security. In practice, extant and emerging threats of special concern will be used to bound future U.S. requirements.

The military is charged with developing its capabilities to undertake prewar and intra-war adaptive planning to support global and regional targeting requirements. In addressing future threats, a range of flexible, preplanned nonnuclear, nuclear, and mixed military options are needed. In the event of an unanticipated contingency, the military must be able (based on preplanned options) to rapidly create new options from existing capabilities.

Capabilities-based and adaptive planning techniques thus increasingly depend on modeling and simulation capabilities, including large-scale mathematical models, to conduct war-gaming and training exercises to understand better the range of effects that can be produced by the military and diplomatic instruments available to policy makers.

Integrating and Transforming the Triad

The new triad concept is only a road map for future deterrence and defense forces and strategy. Analysis and debate about the new triad have been limited. The capabilities embodied in the triad and the issues it raises, however, are critical and are likely to endure for the foreseeable future. The capabilities provided in the new triad will provide the United States with meaningful options to address emerging as well as unexpected contingencies.

Integration of the new triad will have to build on existing plans and capabilities to create a process that brings in new capabilities (e.g., advanced conventional, missile defenses, information operations, or better ISR) as they become available. The elements of the new triad range from mature nuclear forces to limited or developmental capabilities in information operations and missile defenses. Moreover, the prospects for transformation for each leg of the new triad differ. There will be a need to address new capabilities as they emerge, to bring them into the force mix, and to take the necessary steps to fully integrate these new capabilities with the old in new operational contexts. There is a requirement for diverse and flexible forces, and it is anticipated that the elements of the triad will complement each other. Nonetheless, for budgetary and other reasons, tradeoffs certainly will be required among legs of the triad. As new capabilities emerge, it is anticipated there will be opportunities to reduce old capabilities, including massive Cold War–era conventional forces and large numbers of nuclear warheads. But clearly there is a need to develop greater capabilities in all areas, which will increase flexibility and adaptability in the future.

Although some elements of the old triad may be unwisely reduced before new weapons can be developed that provide similar capabilities, there is a recognition that existing forces must be sustained, modernized, and kept operationally ready until they can be replaced. The evolving force thus should be stronger at even less-than-optimized levels of integration. But this positive effect may be outweighed by emerging capabilities of possible adversaries, so net assessments will have to be undertaken to identify critical transition points that opponents might exploit—such as times when old U.S. systems are being retired and new replacement systems are slowly becoming operational.

Integration itself does not necessarily increase U.S. military strength dramatically. To bolster U.S. capability, integration must produce synergies created by the melding of offensive and defensive capabilities, dissuasion created by defenses, information operations, space-based ISR, and new concepts of operations. Information technology is the thread that ties this emerging system of systems together in a seamless web of joint military operations, protecting U.S. capabilities, and enabling direct kinetic and non-kinetic strikes against an adversary with decisive impact.

The benefits of integration must be viewed in the context of specific threats. The force mix required to address a genuine peer competitor in the future will be different from that required, for example, to address residual Russian nuclear threats or emerging proliferant and terrorist threats. Different adversaries also will require different concepts of operations, which will have implications for the way forces are utilized. It might be possible to develop integration "portfolios" based on a range of possible threats and validated by capabilities-based planning and experimentation in an iterative process. Planning scenarios also would have to specify intelligence, surveillance, and reconnaissance requirements and integrate homeland security into the mix of planning concerns.

At an operational level, integration portfolios may be carved into what have been called "mission capabilities packages." These packages will reflect the reality that integration is dependent on specific threats, even though some of these threats remain uncharacterized at present. The relationship between strategic and regional conflict in the future is blurred by the changing nature of the threat and by overlapping jurisdictions and mission areas among competing bureaucratic entities.

CONCLUSION

In many respects, the new triad is evolutionary. Even its more revolutionary elements are rooted in the past. In the new strategic framework, deterrence no longer holds its central Cold War position, and it is no longer expected to be based exclusively (or even primarily) on nuclear weapons. The new strategic objectives of the United States must be met in a dynamic environment. The new triad is designed to meet the full range of possible requirements. Developing and possibly prototyping a range of adaptable conventional and nuclear weapons concepts and defenses is necessary if U.S policy makers are to be confident of their ability to respond to a changing world. To meet future needs, a modernized, reinvigorated, and revitalized conventional and nuclear defense infrastructure is needed.

NOTES

1. For a discussion of options, see Kurt Guthe, *The Nuclear Posture Review: How is the "New Triad" New?* (Washington, D.C.: Center for Strategic and Budgetary Assessments, 2002), 9–14.
2. See *The National Security Strategy of the United States of America*, September 2002, 13–16.
3. As the war with Iraq demonstrated, adversaries will attempt to exploit the U.S. interest in reducing collateral damage in their strategy.
4. A subset of these capabilities was previously known as "nonlethal defenses" or "disabling technologies." See Joseph F. Pilat, "Responding to Proliferation: A

Role for Nonlethal Defenses?" in Mitchell Reiss and Robert Litwak, eds., *Nonproliferation After the Cold War* (Washington, D.C.: Woodrow Wilson Center, 1994).

5. See United States Department of Defense, "Missile Defense Operations Announcement," News Release, no. 642-02, December 17, 2002.

5

Conventional Force Integration in Global Strike

Dennis M. Gormley

It should not have come as any surprise that the Bush administration's 2001 Nuclear Posture Review (NPR) was greeted largely as evidence that U.S. policy makers intended to rely increasingly on nuclear weapons. Until very recently, nuclear deterrence formed the foundation of U.S. national security strategy. Nuclear weapons were expected to deter strikes not only on the American homeland but also on allies in Europe and Asia. Within the growing community of nuclear abolitionists, the end of the Cold War and the nuclear equilibrium that defined it represented a rare turning point in the long-standing quest to eliminate nuclear weapons globally. Many observers expected nuclear arsenals to dwindle in size and importance in the new strategic circumstances, and they remain sensitive to changes in U.S. nuclear weapons policy that portend the persistence of these weapons. Thus, the fact that the NPR mentions the potential need for new types of nuclear weapons to deal, for example, with targets that may not be susceptible to increasingly effective nonnuclear strike forces provoked a firestorm of criticism.

Amid the uproar, few scholars or commentators have paid appropriate attention to the truly revolutionary features of the NPR, most notably the continuing marginalization of nuclear weapons and the corresponding increase in U.S. dependence on non-nuclear solutions to form the basis of a new national security strategy.[1] Critical to implementing this decidedly nascent strategy—and the focus of this chapter—will be the capacity of global non-nuclear strike capabilities to meet the demanding objectives of denying potential adversaries the capacity to do America and its allies harm, especially by using weapons of mass destruction (WMD).

ANTECEDENTS

Truly revolutionary change is rarely without important antecedents, especially when it comes to national security strategy. Nearly two decades ago, during the height of the Cold War, Marshal Nikolai Ogarkov, then Chief of the Soviet General Staff, wrote persuasively about a qualitative leap in conventional weapon effectiveness. In Ogarkov's view, this improvement in conventional weapons was sufficient to suggest that long-range conventional strike capabilities might begin to approximate the terminal effectiveness of nuclear weapons.[2] Of course, Ogarkov was referring to a technological and conceptual revolution in military thinking then largely occurring in the United States, which began to take form during Operation Desert Storm. Although virtually all the weapons used during this conflict were decades old, and no new doctrinal or organizational innovation was on display, in one key aspect the war was tellingly different: The U.S.-led coalition had unprecedented access to precise information, while Iraq was denied access to such information by virtue of the coalition's precision strikes. Equally important, while less than ten percent of the weapons employed were precision-guided munitions (PGMs), they demonstrated at least an order-of-magnitude increase in effectiveness over unguided air-delivered bombs.[3]

Coming on the heels of the collapse of the Soviet Union and the dissolution of the Warsaw Pact, the performance of PGMs during the first Gulf War prompted a reassessment of nuclear weapons policy within the defense community. The notion that "smart" conventional weapons might represent a far more credible and usable instrument of deterrence and warfighting found expression among many military officers. In a series of war games held between 1991 and 1993 sponsored by RAND, a U.S. think tank specializing in defense studies, military participants generally found nuclear weapons to be largely unnecessary because smart conventional weapons were deemed capable of destroying virtually every military target that was once assigned to nuclear weapons.[4] The most profound statement of this new perspective came from Paul Nitze, one of America's principal architects of Soviet containment and nuclear deterrence policy. In an article written in January 1994, Nitze suggested that the time had come for the United States to reexamine its long-standing reliance on nuclear deterrence. He reasoned that the threat of nuclear retaliation would be unlikely to deter aggression by regional powers. More important, the U.S. government would be unwilling to use nuclear weapons to punish such aggression. Thus, Nitze recommended converting the principal U.S. strategic deterrent from nuclear weapons to precision guided conventional weapons. Believing that such a conventional strategic force would furnish the United States with a more credible and flexible deterrent, Nitze argued: "It may well be that conventional strategic weapons will one day perform their primary mission of deterrence immeasurably better than nuclear weapons if only because we can—and will—use them."[5]

THE CHALLENGES OF A DENIAL STRATEGY

The NPR posits a fundamental shift from the historic emphasis on deterrence and a corresponding reliance on offensive nuclear forces to a new strategy, one that assures allies, dissuades potential adversaries from mounting military challenges to the United States, deters adversary use of WMD, and defeats those adversaries decisively should deterrence fail. Although the new strategic triad is intended to mesh missile defenses, nuclear weapons, and nonnuclear strike forces into a truly integrated capacity to achieve challenges of assurance, dissuasion, deterrence, and denial, the most demanding challenge lies in denying potential enemies—most notably, WMD-armed ones—their military objectives.

In his 1994 article, Nitze wrote that it was imperative first to conduct a serious debate about the performance of smart weapons. If nothing else, the 2001 NPR has served to draw valuable analytic attention to questions surrounding the performance of nuclear and conventional weapons against particularly challenging targets.

Any discussion of integrating nuclear and smart conventional weapons must begin with an investigation of the chief demands of any denial targeting strategy. In 1993, Secretary of Defense Les Aspin drew attention to the need to improve capabilities to locate, identify, and attack hardened and deeply buried targets (HDBT) and WMD-armed mobile missiles, and to shoot down enemy missiles that survived these counterforce attacks.[6] These issues remain important because America's adversaries are investing heavily in WMD mobile missiles and HDBTs to shelter their precious investments from U.S. attack. According to the Central Intelligence Agency, there are "well over fifty states of proliferation concern as suppliers, conduits, or potential proliferants" of WMD.[7] While media attention focuses for the most part on North Korean and Iranian nuclear developments, there is a growing awareness of the importance of non-state outlets for furnishing the necessary equipment and technology once thought to emanate exclusively from nations with established capabilities. Developing countries involved in domestic chemical production of pesticides have the necessary dual-use basis to produce chemical weapons, while rapid growth in biotechnology research is fostering an increasing concern that the barriers to producing biological warfare agents are imperiled. Short- and medium-range ballistic missiles already threaten regional American interests and can be used as the foundation to develop intercontinental-range delivery systems.

As the quantitative missile threat expands, the prospect of defending against such threats becomes correspondingly more difficult. This is particularly the case in regional settings when the threat of land-attack cruise missiles and weaponized unmanned air vehicles (UAVs), which are much cheaper to acquire, are added to the missile-defense picture.[8] Numerous countries also are constructing HDBTs. The NPR reveals that more than 1,400 exist today and are suspected of housing WMD, missile bases, and their supporting leadership cadres.[9]

The strike element of the new triad must deal with two of the three most challenging of the foregoing WMD targeting challenges. As the NPR indicates, the conventional component of the new triad is particularly attractive because its use can limit collateral damage and the prospect of conflict escalation to nuclear use. But nuclear weapons may well have to be employed against those targets capable of withstanding nonnuclear strikes.[10]

The Intelligence Requirement

Regardless of whether conventional or nuclear weapons are used, however, the critical factor affecting targeting success is the quality of intelligence about the intended target. Donald Rumsfeld's cover letter to the NPR refers to "exquisite" intelligence about the intentions and capabilities of adversaries, hardly the adjective merited by the poor quality of intelligence before the second Gulf War about Iraq's WMD holdings. Nevertheless, proponents of the revolution in military affairs like to say that what we can see we can hit, and what we hit we will destroy. Certainly, the U.S. military's twenty-one-day march to Baghdad in early 2003 demonstrated an extraordinary capacity to employ ubiquitous sensors and to orchestrate tightly integrated offensive firepower in the pursuit of a decisive battlefield victory. Yet, aside from the Iraqi WMD mystery, which raises questions about detecting and characterizing HDBTs, the emerging lessons learned from Operation Iraqi Freedom suggest that problems also remain with respect to finding and attacking so-called time-critical targets—most notably, in future, WMD-armed mobile missiles.

Several countries are going underground to protect their WMD and other critical assets. No country is more adept at this tactic than North Korea, which, like Iran, Libya, and many others, buries many of its WMD production, storage, and delivery capabilities to protect them from attack. Of course, digging deep underground facilities is nothing new. What is new in the current instance is that modern tunneling equipment—in contrast to tried-and-true explosive techniques—makes the construction process quieter and more efficient. Greater excavation efficiency increases the chances that the HDBT will not be detected by U.S. intelligence, or will be detected only after the facility has become operational. Commercially available boring equipment can now dig a tunnel eighteen meters in diameter at the rate of seventy meters per day, which means that facilities buried beneath hundreds of meters of rock can be constructed much more readily than in the past. Many of these deeply buried underground facilities include an array of distributed tunnel complexes. Some are set into rock at depths ranging from twenty meters to more than a kilometer.[11]

Early detection offers some prospect of understanding the nature and characteristics of the HDBT facility. Such a detailed characterization is crucial to the success of destroying (or literally sterilizing) biological warfare agents with nuclear earth penetrating weapons (EPW). Reinforced concrete will greatly attenuate neutron radiation—the primary radiation kill mechanism—from a nuclear EPW. Otherwise, the EPW must penetrate the structure within which the biological agent is contained to permit the device's fireball, aided by the contained structure, to destroy the agent. Therefore, having detailed information about the precise characteristics of the HDBT—size, depth, construction—is critical to the success of a nuclear or conventional attack on the facility.[12]

Agent Defeat Weapons

Indeed, if nuclear devices are problematic with respect to attacking HDBTs, so too are current and near-term options to destroy HDBTs with conventional weapons. Only within the last three years has the Pentagon commenced in earnest an effort to improve conventional capabilities against such targets. Several concepts are under exploration, the most intriguing of which is an agent defeat weapon called Vulcan Fire, under development by the U.S. Navy. The fill inside the penetrating warhead used on the 2,000-pound GBU-24 laser-guided bomb and the BLU-109 Joint Direct Attack Munition (JDAM) would be designed to produce intense heat sufficient to destroy biological and chemical agents.[13] But, here again, the key challenge is knowing precise details about where the agent is stored in any HDBT. Because such conventional penetrators are theoretically limited to perhaps around thirty meters of penetration capability through hard rock, they would likely have most success against simple, shallow bunkers. Of course, increasing the impact speed of the penetrator—for example, by adding propulsion or launching the penetrator from space—would increase penetration by at least 50 percent in the former case, and much more in the latter.[14] Nevertheless, the overall challenge of targeting the already large and growing population of HDBTs will remain dependent on the quality of intelligence. Even assuming HDBTs can be found and characterized, the best hope may lie in some form of persistent harassment, consisting of precise and repeated attacks designed to prevent the facility from being used.[15]

Improved Targeting

Any application of conventional global strike capability also must contend with locating and attacking fleeting targets, the most important of which are WMD-armed mobile missile launchers. The challenge is no less daunting than effectively prosecuting attacks against HDBTs. America's unparalleled capacity to deliver offensive conventional firepower in a tightly integrated fashion largely assumes attacks on fixed, above ground targets. One of the few notable failures during the first Gulf War was the inability of coalition forces to destroy a single Iraqi mobile missile launcher. More recently, during Operation Allied Force in Kosovo, NATO forces were unable to identify and strike moving Serbian targets operating under thick cloud cover or targets that were camouflaged or well concealed. While Operation Enduring Freedom in Afghanistan did not involve mobile missile threats, U.S. troops there did have to contend with Taliban and al Qaeda forces concentrating in compounds, caves, and other sanctuaries that afforded some protection from air strikes. However, such concentration permitted airpower to bring devastating fire against these fixed locations and related lines of communications with great success. Also, auguring potentially important improvements in counterforce capability were Operation Enduring Freedom's imaginative fusion of targeting on the ground with precision air strikes. Air combat controllers on the ground rapidly furnished target coordinates to loitering aircraft, allowing airborne weapons officers to insert near-real time target coordinates into on-board joint direct attack munitions (JDAM). This nearly instantaneous relay greatly reduced the amount of time between identifying a target and attacking it (from hours in Kosovo to minutes in Afghanistan).

Counterforce Requirements

Although the execution phase of attack operations has shown progress, the process of searching for the target and making the decision to attack it are quite another matter. During Operation Iraqi Freedom, very few so-called time-critical targets were struck, in part because such critically important targets required the approval of the commander of U.S. Central Command. This extra target approval process imposes latency in execution that virtually precludes effective counterforce operations.[16] Effective search seemed problematic too, as the Iraqis managed to continue firing both ballistic and cruise missiles throughout the brief campaign, and thirty-three cruise missiles along with two launchers were found intact after the war ended.[17]

Much of the time between the first and second Gulf Wars was squandered with respect to improving counterforce capabilities; only modest sums were allocated among an array of poorly managed, piecemeal programs, resulting in only marginal improvements in capability.[18] Such a dismal record was not the result of any lack of appreciation for the importance of the task. Counterforce operations (or "attack operations" in Pentagon parlance) stand in joint military doctrine as coequal with the other principal means of coping with missile threats: active and passive defenses and related command and control. Indeed, logically, joint doctrine calls attack operations the preferred method for countering enemy missiles; success means that WMD payloads are destroyed on enemy territory before countermeasures (like decoys) are employed to complicate the task of active missile defense.

As the U.S. military struggles to make improvements in counterforce capability, its adversaries are not standing still. The war in Kosovo demonstrated skilled Serbian use of denial and deception techniques, which also were in evidence during the second Gulf War. Moreover, today's mobile missile launchers carry large ballistic missiles, making them relatively distinguishable from smaller military and civilian vehicles to overhead sensors. But as smaller land-attack cruise missiles enter more arsenals—the second Gulf War represented only a glimpse of this emerging threat—the difficulty of identifying missile launchers will increase. This is because the percentage of civilian and military vehicles of roughly the same length as WMD-armed missile launchers will more than double as smaller cruise and ballistic missile launchers are deployed.[19] As this "look-alike" population grows, airborne and space-based sensors will be more prone to misidentify targets. Striking the wrong target not only wastes attack assets, but also has political costs should the false target prove to be a civilian target. Concern over misidentifying and striking such targets further exacerbates the problem of command latency, that is, the time it takes to decide on striking the target in the first place.

Shortening the Kill Cycle

Improving overall counterforce performance against WMD-armed mobile missiles depends on compressing the time required to search for the target, to decide on prosecuting the attack once the target is confirmed, and to execute the attack with precision. Given that decisions to strike such time-critical targets are the responsibility of senior officers and elected officials, perhaps the search and execution areas are the best places to compress the overall strike cycle. Effective search is contingent on gaining so-called comprehensive battlespace awareness, or the capacity to develop a near-real-time picture of the locations of an adversary's mobile missile units in peacetime, conceivable crisis-deployment locations for these forces, and unit readiness to execute strikes. Achieving such a comprehensive picture requires a seamless connection among peacetime, crisis, and wartime intelligence collection and analysis. It assumes related improvements in radar technology (foliage penetration, most prominently), data fusion, exploitation, and communications. For example, to improve swift and effective filtering of false targets from real ones, automated target recognition algorithms must keep pace with the changing signature characteristics of adversary missile launch systems. In light of the brief exposure times of mobile missiles and their frequent movement cycles, the search function must become virtually continuous. To be sure, the military's increasing employment of UAVs for intensive reconnaissance missions is a positive development, but continuous wide-area surveillance of mobile missile peacetime facilities and crisis and wartime operating and concealment areas will require a large constellation of space-based radar satellites capable of imaging both fixed and moving targets.[20] Current DoD plans call for launching the first space-based radar satellites by 2010 and the full constellation of perhaps as many as twenty satellites by 2012–2013.

Achieving near-ubiquitous surveillance and reconnaissance systems, together with improvements in ancillary imagery exploitation, represent only a part of the quest to improve searching for high-priority time-critical targets such as WMD-armed mobile missiles. True transformation also dictates changes in organizational structures and operational concepts. To conduct effective counterforce attacks against WMD-armed mobile missiles, a truly joint-force organization must have responsibility for conducting these operations roughly on the model of the approach taken by the U.S. Navy in its conduct of antisubmarine warfare operations—that is, internetted forces providing continuous, long-duration surveillance and strike capability over a wide area.

Besides greatly improving the speed and effectiveness of searching for WMD-armed mobile missiles, corresponding improvements are likely to occur in the execution phase and possibly even the decision phase of counterforce operations. The full cycle of detection to strike should be reduced to less than five minutes, or the time it takes to break down a missile launcher and move it to a new hiding spot or launch position. New approaches to gain an exceptionally fast global strike capability (hypersonic missiles, for example, capable of traveling more than five times the speed of sound) foretell a reduction in the time to execute strikes. And should automated target recognition software prove to be half as robust as its proponents predict, perhaps even the time it takes to make a decision to execute a strike will shrink. Still, the challenges posed by counterforce will remain enormously demanding and subject to a never-ending give and take between American technological excellence and highly adaptive adversaries.

GLOBAL STRIKE FORCES

Achieving the NPR's goal of reducing dependence on nuclear weapons hinges on substantial increases in the capacity to deliver conventional weapons over global ranges in times very similar to current strategic nuclear strike forces. The notion of global strike has many facets, not least because of the bureaucratic impulse to wrap large acquisition programs around a compelling strategic concept.

The U.S. Air Force's quest to establish global reach has its inherent limitations, governed by the reality that forward-deployed and -deployable air forces are few in number and very expensive. They also face regional adversaries willing to confront them with anti-access strategies, most notably threatening forward bases with growing numbers of ballistic and cruise missiles. Moreover, the increasingly problematic nature of basing and overflight rights coupled with the lengthy timelines and limitations associated with moving air expeditionary forces and carrier battle groups into unpredictable trouble spots has led to an array of formal requirements for prompt global strike capabilities originating from the continental United States. Predicated on a Defense Planning Guidance requirement, the U.S. Air Force Space Command (AFSPC) established a Mission Need Statement in 2001 for a prompt global strike capability that entailed the ability to strike specific difficult-to-defeat targets (HDBTs, strategic relocatable targets, and targets requiring agent defeat weapons) with conventional means from beyond the range of an adversary's ability to respond. One can find similarly articulated doctrinal, strategic, and study-related statements reflecting the need to deliver precision conventional weaponry anywhere around the globe within hours of a decision to execute such an attack.[21]

The most important organizational manifestation of the need to integrate the various legs of the new triad came in January 2003 when President George W. Bush made changes to the U.S. military's Unified Command Plan. These changes specifically assigned the U.S. Strategic Command (USSTRATCOM) four new responsibilities: global strike, missile defense integration, DoD information operations, and command, control, communications, computers, intelligence, surveillance, and reconnaissance (C^4ISR).

Thus far, USSTRATCOM has acknowledged the inchoate nature of its efforts to integrate these new responsibilities. Admiral James Ellis, USSTRATCOM's commander at the time, told Congress that the transformational shift from predominately nuclear to nonnuclear strike options will require "much laboratory research and development, detailed analytical study, and advanced simulation efforts." Despite the ongoing need for developmental work, Admiral Ellis's top-listed strategic goal was to implement the NPR's guidance "to meet the president's goal of reducing our reliance on operationally deployed strategic nuclear weapons."[22]

Global Strike in the Near Term

Air Force planners have outlined an implementation strategy for global strike comprising three time periods: near-term (2000–2007), mid-term (2008–2013), and far-term (2014–2025). During the near-term time period, the prompt delivery of global firepower will reside chiefly in a highly ready force of twelve B-2 bombers and forty-eight F-22 stealth fighters, complemented by B-1 bombers, sea- and air-launched cruise missiles, and a variety of armed and unarmed UAVs. To underscore the complementary role that such a Global Strike Task Force (GSTF) would perform, Air Force officials refer to the GSTF's goal as "kicking down the door," by which they mean clearing the way for the safe introduction of follow-on forces that depend on forward basing. Thus, F-22s would be expected to eliminate enemy aircraft and advanced anti-aircraft launchers, opening the way for bombers to deliver an intense amount of firepower principally aimed at destroying targets that threaten follow-on forces, particularly WMD-armed ballistic and cruise missiles, related WMD storage areas, and any remaining air defenses.

All of the challenges of prosecuting HDBTs and fleeting targets must be met by a truly effective global strike agenda, but it appears highly doubtful that such demanding tasks are within reach during the near-term. Air Force officials point out the importance of knowing where threat targets are located by virtue of integrating reconnaissance and command functions now performed separately by such platforms as the Airborne Warning and Control System (AWACS), the Joint Surveillance Target Attack Radar System (Joint STARS), Predator UAVs, and special-operations forces behind enemy lines. Current Air Force plans call for this information integration to occur on a centralized platform called the Multi-Sensor Command and Control Aircraft (MC2A), slated for deployment by 2011. MC2A would be one of several component elements contributing to "predictive battlespace awareness," or a "microscopic all-encompassing understanding of the battlespace in all four dimensions," which merits the Rumsfeld characterization of "exquisite" intelligence.[23] MC2A is particularly important to the future ability of detecting land-attack cruise missiles and furnishing fire-control-quality information to ground- and air-based interceptors. Civilian Pentagon budget officials, however, have threatened to cancel the program altogether or delay its fielding by two to three years.[24] Affordability issues undoubtedly will affect the extent to which the Air Force can simultaneously deploy several high-cost systems (Space-Based Radar, MC2A, the Joint Unmanned Air Combat System), not to mention refurbishing an aging air tanker fleet and several other expensive modernization requirements. Thus, only a small part of the GSTF's ambitious goals appears within reach by the end of this decade. They might even be beyond reach into the mid-term.

The U.S. Air Force is not the only service contributing forces to the Global Strike Task Force. Assuming steady funding from Congress, by the end of the near-term phase (2008), the U.S. Navy's program to refuel and convert four Trident ballistic missile submarines (SSBNs) into cruise-missile-carrying and special operations forces (SOF) support submarines (SSGNs) would add substantial precision firepower and SOF support to America's capacity to deliver military force anywhere on earth rapidly. The original idea of converting four Trident SSBNs grew out of the Clinton administration's 1994 NPR, which called for a reduction of Trident boats from eighteen to fourteen. Given that each Trident boat is certified for a forty-two-year life, converting even the oldest boats (dating from 1981) provides an advanced cruise-missile carrier capable of another twenty years of service. Each converted Trident would carry as many as 154 Tomahawk cruise missiles, or possibly the new Tactical Tomahawk, which will include a launch-to-loiter capability with in-flight retargeting, a capability not unlike retargeting JDAMs as bombers or attack aircraft loiter above a conflict awaiting precision attack coordinates from a SOF ground controller. In addition, each SSGN could carry sixty-six Navy SOF personnel and two mini-subs or dry deck shelters. Various other mixes of firepower and SOF capability are conceivable. At least two SSGNs will operate covertly in forward-deployed locations at one time, and each vessel could conceivably satisfy a substantial portion of a regional combatant commanders' in-theater Tomahawk missile requirements, which would free up Navy surface combatants and attack submarines (SSNs) to perform other missions.[25]

Global Strike in the Mid-Term

Considerably more robust and promptly delivered global strike forces are envisioned for the mid-term (2008–2013). Prompt global strike received a surprising endorsement by the U.S. Congress in late 2003, when a provision was written into the 2004 Defense Authorization Act and passed by both the House and the Senate without debate. The defense bill's language instructs the secretary of defense to "establish an integrated plan for developing, deploying, and sustaining a prompt global strike capability in the armed forces," the first one of which was due in April 2004, with annual updates thereafter.[26] While Congress recognizes the difficult integration challenges facing implementation of prompt global strike (largely C⁴ISR ones requiring joint solutions, as well as integrating intercontinental attacks with regional attack plans), the central challenge is to produce viable strike options that truly merit the appellation "prompt." In that regard, the Defense Advanced

Research Projects Agency (DARPA) and the Air Force have teamed to produce a common set of technologies that are designed to produce prompt strike capability along an evolutionary path. The overall project technology development and demonstration project is dubbed FALCON, for Force Application and Launch from CONUS (the continental United States).

By 2010, FALCON is expected to deploy a low-cost small launch vehicle (SLV), capable of boosting a common aero vehicle (CAV) into its required position in space to undertake an unpowered flight to the target region. One additional advantage of the SLV, assuming its projected low cost—some $5 million per vehicle—can be met, is that such a launch vehicle could place small satellites in sun-synchronous orbit rapidly during a crisis or war. The unmanned CAV would be highly maneuverable and capable of attaining hypersonic speeds gliding toward to the target. CAVs would carry 1,000 pounds of payload, in various optional arrays: one rigid penetrator for HDBTs; six wide area autonomous search munitions for land targets; four small smart bomb systems for facility destruction; or six small UAVs for intelligence gathering or bomb damage assessment. After being placed in its required position in space, the CAV would be capable of 3,000 nautical miles of unpowered flight in less than fifteen minutes. More advanced versions, available after 2010, called Enhanced CAV (ECAV), would achieve even greater range and maneuverability, flying 9,000 nautical miles in fifty minutes or so. Both the CAV and ECAV will be capable of turning off a straight trajectory to hit targets up to 800 and 3,000 nautical miles away, respectively.[27] In either case, the reentry speeds of these vehicles suggest that a rigid penetrator (say, a titanium rod) would be capable of penetrating more than twenty meters of solid rock while producing a shock wave with significant destructive force. Current planning calls for the first CAV flight demonstration to take place by mid-2006; the first SLV flight the following year; a test of the two systems together in late 2007; and a prototype demonstration sometime in 2009.

Global Strike in the Long Term

Building on the SLV and CAV programs, and key to meeting the far-term (2014–2025) objectives of Air Force planners, the FALCON program will develop a reusable hypersonic cruise vehicle (HCV). Such an autonomous aircraft will be capable of taking off from standard runways and striking targets 9,000 miles away in less than two hours. The HCV's 12,000-pound payload would permit it to deliver CAVs, cruise missiles, small-diameter bombs, and other weapons or intelligence-gathering systems.

HCVs and CAVs depend on lightweight and durable high temperature materials and thermal management techniques to cope with hypersonic speeds. This is particularly the case for CAVs, which require a thermal protection system capable of preventing their payloads from melting at reentry speeds of as much as Mach 25 (twenty-five times the speed of sound). By contrast, HCVs will be designed to return to their bases at Mach 3 to Mach 4.

CONCLUSION

A truly revolutionary implication of the 2001 NPR is the quiet transformation now taking place to achieve nonnuclear solutions to what have previously been nuclear missions in support of U.S. national security strategy. Thus far, however, there is little analytic rigor underlying the nation's increasing dependence on precision conventional strike capability and plans to reduce operationally deployed strategic nuclear warheads to 1,700–2,200 by 2012. Moreover, little if anything tangible has occurred with respect to integrating the nuclear and nonnuclear components of the new triad. The 2012 objective force of 1,700–2,200 nuclear warheads comes closest to being a strategic hedge against not only geopolitical uncertainty, but also the inherent uncertainty surrounding mid- and long-term future plans for deploying global strike forces. The same holds true for corresponding and essential improvements in missile defenses and C^4ISR capabilities. Yet, to the extent that U.S. national security is now firmly predicated on a strategy of denial rather than punishment, perhaps the best approach to judging the probable effectiveness of emerging global strike forces is to consider the specific challenges of denying adversaries the achievement of their military objectives—particularly their capacity to deliver WMD.

Where residual or improved nuclear capability and prospective nonnuclear forces intersect most conspicuously is in the requirement to destroy HDBTs housing an adversary's WMD. To be sure, tailored nuclear earth penetrators achieve better performance than any of their current or prospective conventional alternatives. Nonetheless, there remain some HDBTs that have highly uncertain characterizations or are so deeply buried that neither nuclear nor conventional weapons can hold them at risk. The best strategy to attack these facilities involves the employment of overwhelming conventional force, especially as it becomes more prompt and precise in delivery. In combination with SOF, intensively and precisely delivered conventional strikes promise to harass such facilities to such an extent as to make them virtually impotent.

Having some small number of reduced collateral damage or earth-penetrating nuclear weapons in the new triad's mix possibly would make declaratory policy more credible, especially in regard to nonnuclear states brandishing biological threats. Yet, there is the undeniable reality—confirmed by the memoirs of former presidents and their top advisers—that retaliatory nuclear use is a decidedly difficult and dubious form of retaliation.[28] The recent words of Secretary of Defense Donald Rumsfeld underscore this point well:

> We have [sixty] years since nuclear weapons have been fired in anger and that's an impressive accomplishment on the part of humanity. . . . I don't know of any other time in history where there has been a significant weapon that has not been used for that long a period and these are not just larger weapons; they are distinctively different weapons.[29]

These words track remarkably well with Paul Nitze's 1994 logic calling for converting the nation's strategic deterrent from nuclear weapons to precision conventional ones.

Implementing the truly revolutionary transformation of global strike capabilities discussed here will depend as much on conceptual and organizational agility as it does on technological achievement. Certainly, the far-term task of developing hypersonic strike systems represents what insiders call a "DARPA-hard problem," at least as demanding as the development of stealth aircraft. But equally demanding will be implementing necessary conceptual and organizational changes, both of which are critical to true revolutions in military affairs. Deploying a space-based radar constellation of twenty satellites in low-earth orbit with near-continuous coverage of moving targets is difficult enough; in some respects it will be even more difficult to adopt new dynamic collection management strategies that fairly arbitrate the competing needs of national and regional command authorities. There will be the additional challenge of instituting new conceptual approaches to prosecuting attack operations against high-priority moving targets, which may require the meshing of intelligence-gathering and operational-targeting duties of the several services into a single joint entity.

In the end, deterrence by denial, using conventional weapons, is markedly more definitive than the mere threat of stirring fears of global destruction by employing nuclear weapons. The diverse considerations that comprise prompt global strike capability will be subject to microscopic examination over the next two decades, the product of which will define in large measure the quality of the new triad's ultimate effectiveness.

NOTES

1. One notable exception is Kurt Guthe, *The Nuclear Posture Review: How Is the "New Triad" New?* (Washington, D.C.: Center for Strategic and Budgetary Assessments, 2002).
2. N. V. Ogarkov, *Krasnaya Zvezda*, May 9, 1984, trans. BBC Monitoring Service, SU/7639/C/10.
3. Thomas A. Keaney and Eliot A. Cohen, *Gulf War Air Power Survey: Summary Report* (Washington, D.C.: GPO, 1993), 243.
4. Mark Dean Millot, "Facing the Emerging Reality of Regional Nuclear Adversaries," *Washington Quarterly* 17, no. 3 (Summer 1994): 50–51.
5. Paul H. Nitze, "Is it Time to Junk Our Nukes?" *Washington Post*, January 16, 1994. For an assessment of the post-Cold War debate over the future role of nuclear weapons, see Dennis M. Gormley and Thomas G. Mahnken, "Facing Nuclear and Conventional Reality," *Orbis* 44, no. 1 (Winter 2000): 109–125. And for an analysis that presaged many features of the development of the NPR's new triad, see Andrew Krepinevich and Robert Martinage, *The Transformation of Strategic-Strike Operations* (Washington, D.C.: Center for Strategic and Budgetary Assessments, March 2001).
6. Les Aspin, "The Defense Department's New Nuclear Counterproliferation Initiative," address to the National Academy of Sciences, Washington, D.C., December 7, 1993.
7. See the April 30, 1999, testimony of John Lauder, CIA special assistant to the director of Central Intelligence for Nonproliferation, at <http://www.usembassy-israel.org.il/publish/press/cia/archive/1999/may/ca1503.htm>.

8. Dennis M. Gormley, "Missile Defence Myopia: Lessons from the Iraq War," *Survival* 45, no. 4 (Winter 2003/2004): 61–86.

9. Nuclear Posture Review [Excerpts] (hereafter NPR), 15 (all page references according to original indicated in excerpts posted at <www.globalsecurity.org/wmd/library/policy/did/npr.htm>).

10. Ibid., 4.

11. Eric Miller and Willis A. Stanley, *The Future of Ballistic Missiles* (Fairfax, Va.: National Institute for Public Policy, 2003), 44.

12. Jonathan Medalia, *Nuclear Weapon Initiatives: Low-Yield R&D, Advanced Concepts, Earth Penetrators, Test Readiness* (Washington, D.C.: Congressional Research Service, 2003), 30–33.

13. Ibid., 35.

14. For a critical treatment of both nuclear and nonnuclear options, see Michael A. Levi, "Fire in the Hole: Nuclear and Non-Nuclear Options for Counterproliferation," Carnegie Endowment for International Peace, Working Papers, no. 31, November 2002. For a proponent's view, see Bryan L. Fearey et al., "An Analysis of Reduced Collateral Damage Nuclear Weapons," *Comparative Strategy* 22, no. 4 (October-November 2003): 305–324.

15. For a comprehensive treatment of the challenge of finding, characterizing, and attacking HDBTs, see *Report to Congress on the Defeat of Hard and Deeply Buried Targets*, submitted by the secretary of Defense in conjunction with the secretary of Energy, July 2001 <http://www.nukewatch.org/importantdocs/#HDBT>.

16. Based on author interviews in November 2003.

17. Gormley, "Missile Defence Myopia," 72.

18. "USAF Theater Missile Defense Attack Operations, Briefing to Mr. Dennis Gormley," HQ USAF/XORT, January 21, 1999, mimeo.

19. The results of one such study of these changes in targeting signatures are found in Dennis M. Gormley, "Counterforce Operations," a presentation made at the Royal United Services Institute for Defence Studies, conference on Extended Air Defense and the Long-Range Missile Threat, September 17–18, 1997, London, England.

20. For one suggested strategy and operations architecture to respond to this problem, see James J. Wirtz, *Counterforce & Theater Missile Defense: An ASW Approach to the SCUD Hunt* (Strategic Studies Institute, U.S. Army War College, March 1995).

21. For details on the origins of global strike, see Matt Bille and Major Rusty Lorenz, "Requirements for a Conventional Prompt Global Strike Capability," briefing presented to the NDIA Missile and Rockets Symposium and Exhibition, May 2001, <http://www.dtic.mil/ndia/2001missiles/bille.pdf>.

22. Statement of Admiral James O. Ellis, USN, Commander, United States Strategic Command Before the Senate Armed Services Committee, Strategic Subcommittee on Command Posture and Strategic Issues, April 8, 2003.

23. Master Sgt. Terry Somerville, "Global Strike Task Force-'Kicking Down the Door,' " <http://www/af.mil/news/Aug2001/n20010810_1100.shtml>.

24. David A. Fulghum, "USAF E-10 Could Be in Jeopardy," *Aviation Week & Space Technology* (December 15, 2002): 25.

25. Ronald O'Rourke, "Navy Trident Submarine Conversion (SSGN) Program: Background and Issues for Congress, CRS Report for Congress <www.thememoryhole.org/crs/more-reports/RS21007.pdf>.

26. William Matthews, "U.S. Lawmakers Push 'Prompt Global Strike,' " *Defense News* (November 24, 2003), 4.

27. Northrop Grumman Corporation makes these performance estimates. See <http://www.capitolsource.net/press_releases/ngpress112503.html>. Also see the DARPA program description, <http://www.darpa.mil/body/NewsItems/pdf/falcon_fs.pdf>.

28. See George Bush and Brent Scowcroft, *A World Transformed* (New York: Knopf, 1998) and Colin L. Powell, *My American Journey: An Autobiography* (New York: Random House, 1995). Bush privately ruled out a nuclear response in the 1991 Gulf War and then acknowledged this stance in his book. Powell, like most of his military peers, dismisses the utility of nuclear use.

29. Secretary of Defense Donald H. Rumsfeld, Joint Press Conference with British Secretary of State for Defence Geoffrey Hoon, June 5, 2002.

6

IMPLEMENTING MISSILE DEFENSE

Kerry M. Kartchner

On December 17, 2002, President George W. Bush directed Secretary of Defense Donald Rumsfeld "to proceed with fielding an initial set of missile defense capabilities" to protect the United States and its allies.[1] Once fully deployed, this system will be composed of: (1) ground-, air-, sea-, and space-based sensors to provide early warning, characterization, and tracking of missile launches anywhere in the world; (2) ground-, air-, and sea-based interceptors to destroy enemy missiles or their warheads on impact; and (3) redundant fire control centers for battle management, command, and control. Missile defense will represent the most significant milestone achieved so far in implementing the third leg of the new triad introduced in the 2001 Nuclear Posture Review (NPR).

This is not the first time the United States has decided to proceed with deploying a missile defense system. In the late 1960s and early 1970s, the United States made similar decisions to deploy the Sentinel and later the Safeguard anti-ballistic missile (ABM) systems. But it was not the most auspicious beginning. The Safeguard system was actually fielded, only to be deactivated less than a year later. Given the episodic and apparently futile history of missile defense in the United States, is there any reason to believe that the current incarnation will fare any better than its predecessors? Like all major defense acquisition programs, the answer will depend on political support, particularly from Congress. This political support, in turn, will be a function of a continuing perception of an emerging missile threat, the degree to which the Missile Defense Agency (MDA) is able to overcome identified technical hurdles and convert a successful test regime into a reliable fielded system, the affordability of such a system, and the strength of international cooperation and support in developing, fielding, and operating a missile defense system that protects not only the United States, but its allies, as well.

This chapter examines the roles and missions prescribed for missile defense by the NPR. It summarizes the substantial progress to date in implementing the NPR's vision for missile defenses. It then reviews the technical, cost, and diplomatic challenges facing the NPR's missile defense recommendations, and concludes with some observations on the long-term prospects for missile defense's staying power.

MISSILE DEFENSE AND THE NPR

The NPR reiterated the basic mission parameters for the U.S. missile defense program as previously established by presidential guidance, called for a broad, layered series of system components to fulfill those parameters, and set a modest threshold for evaluating the system's effectiveness. These initiatives represented a bold departure from previous U.S. missile defense policy.

According to the NPR, missile defenses can contribute to the goals for a new U.S. security strategy in several ways:

- Missile defenses will *assure* friends and allies that the United States is committed to their defense and security. Ballistic missile threats will not coerce the United States to draw back from its security commitments nor allow aggressors the means to undermine the cohesiveness and political stability of a coalition or alliance.
- Missile defenses will *dissuade* potential adversaries from developing offensive ballistic missile programs and their associated nuclear, chemical, and biological warheads by reducing the value of such weapons.
- Missile defenses will *deter* others from using ballistic missiles to attack U.S. territory, its forces deployed abroad, or its allies by reducing an adversary's confidence in the possible success of its missile attack and by denying the political-coercive or military benefits associated with threatening an attack.
- If deterrence and dissuasion fail, missile defenses will help *defeat* attacks by ballistic missiles, defend the population of the United States, contribute to limiting damage, and promote the achievement of U.S. wartime objectives.[2]

The NPR called for initially developing an emergency capability that could be deployed quickly against very small-scale missile attacks. The Department of Defense (DoD) would then build on these near-term emergency capabilities to develop improved variants "leading to more robust, operational systems" in the mid- to long-term.[3]

The NPR defined the near- to mid-term period as 2003 to 2008 and identified some elements of a system that could provide an emergency missile defense capability. These were to consist of a single airborne laser for boost-phase intercepts; a rudimentary ground-based mid-course system, consisting of a small number of interceptors taken from the test program, plus an upgraded Cobra Dane radar in Alaska; and a sea-based Aegis system, which could be available to provide basic midcourse capability against short- to medium-range threats. The NPR further noted that, based on progress achieved in validating the technical feasibility of these near-term "emergency capabilities," the United States could proceed to deploy mid-term operational capabilities by 2008. These mid-term systems would include two to three airborne laser aircraft; additional ground-based midcourse sites (i.e., silo-launchers); four sea-based midcourse intercept ships; terminal systems able to defend against shorter-range threats, including additional Patriot Advanced Capability (PAC-3) units (which began deployment in 2001); and Theater High-Altitude Air Defense (THAAD) missiles, which could be available by 2008. The NPR also directed the DoD to develop a low-orbit constellation of Space-Based Infrared Systems satellites (SBIRS-Low) to support the missile defense system, to track enemy ballistic missiles, and to assist in the discrimination between reentry vehicles and other objects in flight.

INITIAL DEPLOYMENT

Upon taking office in January 2001, the Bush administration set a radically new course for missile defense, distinct from that of its predecessor in four ways. First, the Bush administration did not dispute the validity of the four criteria considered by the Clinton administration, but officials believed that each of these criteria had been or could be met. The threat was imminent; the technology was available (or could be developed given freedom from Anti-Ballistic Missile (ABM) Treaty constraints); it was affordable; and the diplomatic and arms control ramifications could be managed. Second, the Bush administration took a more hostile stance toward the ABM Treaty. Rather than thinking of the treaty as the "cornerstone of strategic stability," it was viewed more as an outdated millstone around the neck of American national security. In this connection, the administration soon dropped the "N" from "NMD" (national missile defense) and began referring to "missile defense" more generically. This change recognized that the distinction between theater missile defense (TMD) and NMD was becoming technologically blurred, and that for some U.S. allies, "tactical" missile defenses could in fact mean "national" missile defenses. The administration announced that it would seek the necessary amendments to the ABM Treaty to allow more robust testing of missile defense systems and their possible deployment in ways then prohibited by the ABM Treaty. Officials also made clear that should Russia refuse to grant such amendments, the United States was prepared to exercise its right under Article XV of the treaty to withdraw from the treaty after a six-month advance notification. Third, President Bush began laying the conceptual basis for missile defense by stating in a speech on May 1, 2001, that the United States needed new approaches to deterrence, approaches that relied on both offensive and defensive means of deterrence. These new approaches also were part of a push for a new strategic framework for U.S.-Russian relations that would reduce the centrality of nuclear weapons and formal arms control agreements in the relationship. Finally, the administration restructured the Ballistic Missile Defense Organization, upgraded it to the Missile Defense Agency, and sought funding increases from Congress for a range of missile defense programs.

Diplomatic consultations began in earnest with Russia over amending the ABM Treaty. Russia warned, however, that U.S. missile defense deployments would provoke a renewed arms race, obligate Russia to withdraw from the Strategic Arms Reduction (START) Treaty, lead to the utter collapse of the whole international arms control regime, undermine international efforts to combat the proliferation of weapons of mass destruction, and lead to a new Cold War between Russia and the United States.

In the fall of 2001, several factors forced a resolution of the impasse between the United States and Russia over amending the ABM Treaty.[4] The administration believed that a long-range ballistic missile threat to the United States could emerge at any time and was determined not to wait until such a threat had actually materialized to begin preparing for it. The longest lead-time item in the administration's missile defense program involved the construction of a new ABM radar on the island of Shemya, Alaska, where the short construction season mandated pressing ahead with an early decision to start construction. It was not clear when such construction plans would cross the line of noncompliance with the ABM Treaty. If the United States wanted to avoid outright violation of the treaty, it would have to provide the requisite notice of withdrawal six months before the beginning of the 2002 construction season in Alaska, or early in the fall of 2001. Furthermore, the administration wanted to begin exploring other technological approaches to missile defense then banned by the ABM Treaty, and it wanted to test certain theater missile defense assets, such as the radars on Aegis cruisers, against strategic ballistic missile threats. Such testing was also banned by the ABM Treaty.

On December 13, 2001, President Bush announced that the United States had given Russia formal notice of U.S. withdrawal from the ABM Treaty, stating that "the ABM Treaty hinders our government's ability to develop ways to protect our people from future terrorist or rogue state missile attacks."[5] Within just a few hours of this announcement, the Russian government released a statement by President Putin characterizing the U.S. decision as a mistake but stating that it was not a security threat to Russia (thus, there would be no arms race response), that Russia was determined to sustain improvements in U.S.-Russian relations (thus, there would be no return to the Cold War), and urging the United States to enter into a legally binding agreement on further reductions in strategic offensive arms (thus, there would be prospects for further arms control arrangements between the United States and Russia).

This announcement amounted to a de facto *quid pro quo*, whereby the United States reversed its earlier opposition to a legally binding strategic offensive arms reduction agreement. The two states signed such an agreement in Moscow on May 29, 2002, apparently in return for Russian acquiescence in U.S. withdrawal from the ABM Treaty, which became effective on June 14, 2002. But before then, DoD began putting into place plans to test TMD systems against long-range ballistic missile targets, reaching out to allies and calling on them to participate with the United States in the development of a missile defense system, and developing ideas for deploying missile defenses outside the limits previously allowed by the ABM Treaty that would be presented to the president later in the summer of 2002. These proposals to the president led to a second announcement from the White House almost exactly a year later, on December 17, 2002, that the United States would proceed to deploy an "initial defense capability" by the end of 2004. Less than a year after the NPR was released, the Bush administration moved to accelerate its proposed deployment schedule by establishing a more ambitious missile defense program than the one envisioned by the NPR. This capability was to be in place by October 31, 2004, at least two years ahead of the NPR's proposed schedule.

Having secured virtual acquiescence from the Russian Federation in its break from the ABM Treaty, the MDA conducted a series of tests that incorporated heretofore prohibited activities, including notably the participation of ship-based radar in two successive missile interceptor tests. Meanwhile, the DoD began drafting plans to deploy some form of defense against long-range missiles by the end of the president's first term in office. On December 17, 2002, President Bush announced that he had directed the secretary of defense to proceed with fielding "an initial set of missile defense capabilities" by 2004.[67]

Echoing the format of the NPR, this announcement provided two tiers of capabilities. The first set of systems would be deployed in the near-term. Future capabilities would be a product of the "spiral development" approach to evolving the system architecture, whereby new components would be evaluated for incorporation into the operational force at two-year intervals. The capabilities planned for operational availability in 2004 and 2005, or the first block, according to this announcement, would include twenty ground-based interceptors, of which sixteen would be located at Fort Greely, Alaska, and four at Vandenberg AFB. There were also up to twenty sea-based interceptors (using the Standard Missile 3—at that time still in development) on three existing Aegis ships, whose radar and data processing systems would be accordingly upgraded to accommodate these missiles. Additionally, the plan called for increasing the number of deployed PAC-3 units, and upgraded sensors based on land, at sea, and in space, including improved radars at Shemya, Alaska, Fylingdales, U.K., and at Thule, Greenland. The administration also seeks to expand the Pacific Test Bed to provide greater flexibility in testing geometry (allowing, for example, launches of interceptors on a more realistic west-to-east trajectory, instead of the existing restriction of launching from Vandenberg in an east-to-west trajectory).

FUTURE PROSPECTS

The chances that the Bush administration's initiatives will lead to a lasting missile defense capability will be enhanced by the fact that U.S.-Russian relations have weathered U.S. withdrawal from the ABM Treaty and that the United States faces a greater number of missile-armed and potentially hostile states than during the Cold War—even if, in absolute terms, fewer long-range ballistic missiles are aimed at the United States or its interests. Current missile defense systems also benefit from advances in key technologies, and they have more modest objectives than did earlier U.S. ABM systems, whose effectiveness was judged by how well they could defend against thousands of sophisticated Soviet ballistic missiles. Nevertheless, the future of missile defense as a component of U.S. national security strategy will depend on how well the program deals with several challenges: overcoming remaining technical hurdles and cost burdens, garnering international cooperation and support, sustaining domestic political support, and integrating missile defense into military doctrine and operations.

Challenge 1: Technical and Budgetary Feasibility

While considerable skepticism still exists regarding the technical feasibility of missile defense,[8] progress across a broad range of technical disciplines is making effective missile defense increasingly feasible and affordable. (See table 6.1.) According to congressional testimony and other reports, advances have taken place in computing technology and telecommunications; thrust and rocketry; materials science; miniaturization and solid-state electronics; visible, infrared, and ultraviolet sensors; and the weaponization of laser systems.[9] Some believe that these developments will alter the offense–defense relationship. For example, in a statement provided to the

Table 6.1 Midcourse missile defense segment test results

Test designation	Test date/Planned date	Results
IFT-3	October 2, 1997	Successful intercept
IFT-4	January 18, 1999	No intercept
IFT-5	July 8, 2000	No intercept
IFT-6	July 14, 2001	Successful intercept
IFT-7	December 3, 2001	Successful intercept
IFT-8	March 15, 2002	Successful intercept
IFT-9	October 14, 2002	Successful intercept
IFT-10	? December	No intercept
IFT-11	Planned for 2003	Cancelled
IFT-12	Planned for 2003	Cancelled
IFT-13	Originally planned for 2003	Reprogrammed as 13A and 13B
IFT-13A planned test of first new booster	Originally planned for January 2004	Booster integration test. No intercept attempted
IFT-13B planned test of second new booster		Booster integration test. No intercept attempted
IFT-14 first intercept test incorporating new booster	Originally planned prior to October 2004 IDO. Conducted December 15, 2004	Interceptor Booster failed to launch due to software problem
IFT-16A radar characterization flight	Planned prior to October 2004 IDO	Delayed
IFT-17	Planned prior to October 2004 IDO	Delayed
IFT-18	Planned prior to October 2004 IDO	
IFT-19	Planned prior to October 2004 IDO	Delayed
IFT-20	Planned prior to October 2004 IDO	Delayed

IDO, Initial Defensive Operations; IFT, Integrated Flight Test.

House Armed Services Committee, William R. Graham, former White House Science Adviser, said, "[A]s missile defense technologies have improved, the advantage has shifted from the offense to the defense."[10] Nevertheless, more realistic testing must be undertaken to validate issues of basic physics associated with intercepting ballistic missiles.

In April 2003, the General Accounting Office (GAO) published a report at the request of the ranking member of the Senate Armed Services Committee, Carl Levin (D-MI), examining the MDA's acquisition strategy and assessing the level of its budgetary and technological risk. It concluded that, for the most part, "MDA has adopted practices that offer the best opportunity to develop a complex weapon system successfully."[11] The report cautioned, however, that MDA has had "mixed results" in achieving a reliable "hit-to-kill" capability, and that the development of some components of the overall system needed to detect and track a missile in all phases of its flight had not yet been completed. It noted that significant uncertainties remained in terms of estimating the total projected cost for developing and deploying the system. The GAO report then assessed progress in ten of the most critical technologies that would be necessary to field the ground-based midcourse intercept segment (GMD) of the system. It concluded that two of the ten critical GMD technologies were mature enough to have demonstrated their "expected functionality in an operational environment." (See table 6.2.) The GAO report further assessed that, if development and testing proceed as planned by MDA, seven of the ten critical technologies will have achieved this level of maturity upon completion of IFT-14, scheduled for the second quarter of FY2004, prior to the October 31 deadline for initial defensive operations (IDO).[12]

Table 6.2 Technology readiness levels of GMD critical technologies (as of August 2003)[13]

Critical technology	Maturity status/Date expected to mature
Exoatmospheric kill vehicle	
Infrared seeker	Mature
On-board discrimination	(2nd quarter FY2004)
Guidance, navigation, and control subsystem	(2nd quarter FY2004)
Boosters	
BV+	(1st quarter FY2004)
OSC Lite	(1st quarter FY2004)
Battle management command, control, and communications	
Fire-control software	Mature
In-flight interceptor communications system	(2nd quarter FY2004)
Radars	
Cobra Dane radar	Unknown
Beale upgraded early warning radar	(1st quarter FY2005)
Sea-based X-band radar	(4th quarter FY2005)

While technology has been changing opinions on missile defense, there also has been an important shift in how cost issues related to missile defense are debated and evaluated. Traditionally, the costs of a missile defense program have been assessed in terms of their relationship to the cost of equivalent offensive weapons programs. That is to say, for much of the last fifty years, missile defense was considered cost-prohibitive if it cost less to acquire an offensive ballistic missile than to buy a defensive interceptor missile. As the U.S. missile defense program has changed its focus from defeating thousands of ballistic missiles to fending off a few missiles—which probably represent the culmination of huge resource expenditures on the part of the actors building and fielding the weapons —the principal criteria for assessing cost now has become affordability.

Additionally, with less confidence in the adequacy of traditional offense-dominant deterrence, defensive contributions to deterrence assume greater priority. This is coupled with the fact that the need for offensive strategic forces is declining, thus freeing up resources for missile defenses.

There are still other ways of looking at the costs associated with developing and fielding a missile defense capability.[14] Investments in missile defenses may, for example, be considered a form of insurance premium. Rather than comparing the costs of a missile defense system to an equivalent offensive system, it may be useful to consider the prospective cost to replace defended assets that might otherwise be destroyed in an attack if left unprotected. Compared to other defense programs, the total program costs of the U.S. missile defense effort are not exceptional. The Department of Defense has reportedly estimated the cost of acquiring the planned missile defense system at around $50 billion over the next twenty years. By comparison, the cost of developing the F-35 Joint Strike Fighter is now estimated to be $40.5 billion, a sum that simply buys a new generation of a system with significant precedents, and not a wholly new weapon system.[15]

Challenge 2: International Cooperation and Support

International support is the second most important challenge that will help determine the future of the U.S. missile defense program. Allies can provide intelligence, technology, supplemental research, and development funding; they also can allow access for forward basing. For example, while the ABM Treaty banned forward-deployed radars from having early warning and inter-ceptor guidance functions, now both functions can be combined in the same radar. The upgrades planned by the United States will significantly improve the early warning capabilities of these two radars, giving them the ability to hand off data regarding tracking offensive missiles to other components of the U.S. missile defense system or to cue other radars with narrower search capabilities. The United Kingdom granted permission to the United States to perform this upgrade to the early warning radar at Fylingdales in April 2003, and the government of Denmark approved the upgrade to the early-warning radar located on the territory of Greenland in May 2004.

In June 2003, the United Kingdom signed a memorandum of understanding (MOU) providing a legal framework for participating in the U.S. missile defense program as a full partner. The United States and Japan also have engaged in cooperative missile defense research since the early1990s. These efforts have focused on sea-based missile defense efforts (Japan has acquired several Aegis ship platforms), including an evolutionary development upgrade to the U.S. Navy's Standard Missile 3 (SM-3). The United States and Japan are scheduled to conduct joint flight tests of the SM-3 before 2006. In December 2003, the government of Japan also announced a decision to fund the acquisition of additional land-based Patriot missile defense systems (PAC-3), and to acquire Aegis missile defense systems for its existing Aegis cruisers.[16] It signed an MOU on missile defense cooperation with the United States in December 2004.[17] Also, in early December 2003, the government of Australia announced a decision to begin participating in the U.S. missile defense program. It signed an MOU to that effect in July 2004.

These joint programs will build on existing cooperative agreements that date back several years. The governments of Germany, Italy, and the United States have been pursuing a multilateral research and development program to field a new mobile air and missile defense system capable of protecting deployed military forces on the move, called the Medium Extended Air Defense System (MEADS). MEADS is expected to replace the U.S. Army's Patriot system in the next decade and has the potential to become the core short-range missile defense capability for the North Atlantic Treaty Organization (NATO). Both Germany and Italy support MEADS and have programmed funding for the next phase of activities. The United States also has been working with Israel since the late 1980s to design and develop missile defense systems. U.S. and Israeli cooperative programs include sharing U.S. missile launch warning information and co-production of Arrow missile components in the United States.

NATO has been part of the renewed international interest in cooperating with the United States in the development of missile defenses. In 1998, for example, NATO ministers agreed to undertake a feasibility study of theater missile defenses to protect NATO forces that might have to be deployed into regions under threat of missile attack. The most important milestone in NATO's consideration of missile defense to date, however, was the unanimous decision by NATO ministers at the Prague Summit in November 2003 to examine the feasibility and role of missile defenses designed to protect NATO populations and territory, to create a "national missile defense" on a multinational scale.[18] Although past missile defense feasibility studies only examined missile defenses against ballistic missile threats of less than 3,000 kilometers in range—reflecting a desire to respect the ABM Treaty distinction between theater and strategic missile defenses—this new study will examine threats from longer-range ballistic missiles. Theoretically, this development places NATO on a track toward a missile defense capability that is much more compatible with U.S. missile defense systems that are designed to respond to long-range threats.

The United States continues to cooperate with the Russian Federation in missile defense. The Joint Declaration signed by Presidents Bush and Putin in May 2003 called for missile defense cooperation and reflects a new level of maturity in the U.S.-Russian relationship. To fulfill the U.S. and Russian presidents' commitment to strengthen confidence, increase transparency, and study areas for missile defense cooperation, a U.S.-Russian Missile Defense Working Group has been established under the auspices of the Ministerial-level Consultative Group on Strategic Security. In this venue, the United States has proposed to begin voluntary and reciprocal information exchanges and visits and encouraged Russian interaction with U.S. corporations working on missile defense. The United States also has conducted three successful TMD exercises with the Russian Federation. A fourth exercise is planned in Moscow in the spring of 2005. These unclassified, computer-based exercises are designed to establish procedures for independent but coordinated operations in the event that U.S. and Russian missile defense forces are deployed together against a common adversary.

Challenge 3: Operational Integration

New weapon systems are not proven fully effective until they have been integrated into the operations and doctrine of the armed forces. Missile defense is not intended to be a stand-alone system; it will operate hand-in-hand with other units and systems. For example, the SM-3 interceptor missile will be only one of several types of missiles carried by Aegis cruisers selected to fulfill a missile defense role. And missile defense will not be these cruisers' sole mission. Juggling these various missions will necessitate an operational doctrine and procedures. To cite another example, although the Patriot missile defense system was highly effective in Operation Iraqi Freedom, there were also three tragic instances of "friendly fire," in which British and American fighter jets were shot down. It appears that some of these instances were the result of Patriot radars operating too close to other radar units. In future operations, Patriot units will have to be spaced sufficiently far from other radar units, which is an issue of operational doctrine.

Current planning for missile defense operations is taking place at two levels. The first level is "integrated missile defense," and refers to the interaction of active defense systems, passive defense systems, and attack operations, as well as the battle management, command, control, communications, and intelligence systems required to support them.[19] Referred to in the past as "offense-defense integration," this planning involves the overall integration of missile defenses into the operational force. It is necessarily highly theoretical at this point. Planning at this level explores the role and requirements for pre-positioning missile defense assets (both shooters and sensors) in a potential theater of operations before a conflict erupts. It also explores how missile defense activities will interact with other diplomatic and intelligence requirements in pre-, trans-, and post-conflict phases. It examines how offensive attack operations would be used to enhance the contributions of active missile defenses and how best to include missile defense capabilities in air and space expeditionary force packages.

The second level involves planning for actual missile defense intercept operations. The stages of such an operation are described in table 6.3. This level of planning explores the actual employment of individual components of a future, layered missile defense system. For example, Air Combat Command has developed an initial "concept of employment" for how the Air Force would employ the Airborne Laser (ABL) aircraft in combat situations, based on the timeframe in which the first aircraft is expected to be delivered by the Missile Defense Agency. This preliminary concept of employment is necessarily drafted in general terms, because the precise number of aircraft— or even their final airframe configuration—is not known yet. But the initial planning calls for up to seven aircraft to cover two theaters of combat. This concept of employment specifies the requirements involved in transitioning the aircraft from its research and development phases to its operational fielding.[20] Such plans also will address the full spectrum of a deployment operation, from pre-activation, activation, deployment, redeployment, and sustainment, and it will specify the steps to be taken before, during, and after an operation involving the ABL.

Training soldiers to man the fielded system is another aspect of preparation for the transition to operational deployment of missile defenses. The Army has activated a ninety-soldier Ground-Based Midcourse Defense Brigade, which includes both National Guard and active-duty personnel.[22] The Alaska National Guard also has stood up a unit to prepare to operate the system to be deployed at Fort Greely, near Fairbanks.

Table 6.3   Notional GMD concept of operations[21]

1. Enemy missile is launched.
2. Space-based satellites detect and report launch to the GMD fire-control component; GMD element transitions to alert state.
3. Fire control begins engagement planning based on initial track data from satellites.
4. Primary radars (for example, Cobra Dane) are cued to track enemy missile.
5. Radars provide high-quality track data to fire control, which then develops battle plans to engage the threat.
6. Human operator grants engagement authority to launch interceptors.
7. Interceptor is launched; exoatmospheric kill vehicle deployed to engage the threat.
8. Radars continue to provide updated track data to the fire control.
9. In-flight interceptor communications system (IFICS) of the fire control component sends updated targeting information to the kill vehicle while in flight.
10. Radars classify or discriminate objects of target complex; associated data are communicated to the interceptor via the in-flight interceptor communications system.
11. Kill vehicle acquires, tracks, and discriminates threat complex.
12. Kill vehicle makes final target selection and steers itself for a "hit-to-kill" impact of the designated target.
13. Kill assessment is made from radar data.
14. If threat from attack has been eliminated, GMD element returns to normal state.

Challenge 4: Political Sustainability

Success in implementing the NPR's vision for an effective missile defense will depend on continued support and funding from the U.S. Congress. Congress, in turn, must be convinced that missile defense is needed, a function of how perceptions of the threat evolve. If the threats that precipitated the program in the first place (Iran, Iraq, North Korea) are eliminated militarily or resolved diplomatically, the perceived need for missile defense may subside. What happens to the U.S. missile defense program under these circumstances? As one former Bush administration official told the author, "In that case, our missile defense program will have succeeded even before it is deployed."[23]

Over the last couple of years, missile defense has enjoyed unprecedented bipartisan support in Congress, although significant skepticism remains in some quarters. Two significant events have shaped recent congressional attitudes toward missile defense. First, since the terrorist attacks of September 11, 2001, President Bush has received considerable political latitude in defense and security matters, including funding for the missile defense program. Some members of Congress continue to cite the terrorist attacks as evidence that resources for missile defense would be better spent elsewhere, for example on homeland defense, counter-proliferation, or the war on terrorism. The administration has responded that the budget for missile defense represents a much smaller portion of the overall defense budget than that for homeland defense—and further, missile defense forms one essential element of a robust homeland defense. Nevertheless, even many of the most skeptical members of Congress have suppressed their opposition to missile defense in favor of promoting a unified front on behalf of the nation's security.

The second event was the December 13, 2001, U.S. decision to exercise its Article XV right to withdraw from the ABM Treaty—and the surprisingly moderate Russian response to this announcement. Much of the criticism of missile defense had been predicated on the allegation that any U.S. deployment of missile defense (even a deployment that complied with the limited defenses allowed by the ABM Treaty) would spark a renewed arms race with Russia. When this dire consequence failed to transpire, much of the wind was taken out of the skeptics' sails, both in Congress and among America's allies.[24] Nevertheless, congressional critics continue to argue that:

- Attack by ballistic missile is much less likely than attack with chemical, biological, or nuclear weapons by non-missile means of delivery, such as by truck, ship, or plane.
- The ballistic missile technology developed so far by the United States does not have the ability to defeat even relatively simple countermeasures.
- Existing missile defense technology has not been adequately tested under operationally realistic conditions.
- Despite official Russian and Chinese statements to the contrary, deployment of missile defenses will be seen as threatening by both Russia and China.

- The emerging threat so far does not justify the resources devoted to missile defense, which could be better spent elsewhere.[25]

As the missile defense program matures and enters initial operational deployment, these congressional views and concerns will have to be taken into account by the managers and operators of the U.S. missile defense program.

CONCLUSION

To some, it may seem that even if the formidable task of developing and mastering the complex technologies needed to deploy an effective missile defense is accomplished, and even if such a system were somehow integrated into other aspects of U.S. military power and strategy, it may not be politically sustainable. In the absence of a clear and present danger of missile attack, missile defense could lose political endorsement and funding, leading either to reliance on a minimal system of sensors and a few interceptors or to being shut down altogether, only to be revived again if a missile threat suddenly materialized. U.S. allies are particularly concerned about this possibility, fearing that once they have made substantial investments in the systems and have linked their own security plans to available U.S. missile defenses, the United States will then pull the rug out from under them by canceling or abandoning the program.

Two factors will prove decisive when it comes to the future of missile defense. If the United States and its allies realize verifiable and enduring success in disarming states like Libya, continued diplomatic progress will diminish the priority assigned to missile defense. But if missile defense proves itself in actual combat, beyond the handful of lower-range missiles intercepted in Operation Iraqi Freedom, by intercepting a long-range missile destined for the United States or one of its allies, missile defense will be transformed into a key component of the U.S. global military posture, as the NPR envisions it.

NOTES

1. "Statement by the President on Progress in Missile Defense Capabilities," December 17, 2002 <http://www.whitehouse.gov/news/releases/2002/12/20021217.html>.
2. "United States Missile Defense Policy," statement by J. D. Crouch II, Assistant Secretary of Defense for International Security Policy, before the Senate Armed Services Committee, March 18, 2003 <http://www.globalsecurity.org/space/library/congress/2003_h/crouch.pdf>.
3. Except for the public admission that the test launchers to be deployed at Fort Greely would have an "emergency" operational capability allowing them to be used operationally in a crisis, such a system arguably would have been compatible with the ABM Treaty, which did not limit the number of test ranges either side could declare. However, announcing that this system would have some latent operational capability ran afoul of the ABM Treaty's prohibition on basing of operational ABM systems outside established and declared ABM sites.

4. For a good discussion of this timeline and the associated pressures for an early decision to withdraw from the ABM Treaty, see Bradley Graham, *Hit-to-Kill: The New Battle Over Shielding American From Missile Attack* (New York: Public Affairs Publishing, 2001), 73–100.

5. "Remarks by the President on National Missile Defense," December 12, 2001 <http://www.whitehouse.gov/news/releases/2001/12/20011213-4.html>.

6. Nevertheless, the goal of having this initial capability achieve operational status by the end of 2004 proved problematic, due to unforeseen delays in the system's test schedule, the failure of a long-delayed full test of the interceptor booster on December 15, 2004, and the challenges associated with the transition of the system from a research and development program to an operational component of the U.S. armed forces.

7. "Statement by the President on Progress in Missile Defense Capabilities."

8. For a coherent argument regarding the technological hurdles still facing missile defenses, see Forrest E. Morgan, "Ballistic Missile Defense: Flying in the Face of Offensive Technological Dominance," paper prepared for the International Studies Association annual convention, March 27, 2002.

9. Ballistic Missile Defense Organization, *Harnessing the Power of Technology: The Road to Ballistic Missile Defense from 1983 to 2007* (Washington, D.C.: U.S. Department of Defense, September 2000). This report cites the miniaturization of advanced inertial measurement units as a key example. "What had been a state-of-the-art, lightweight ring laser gyro unit in the 1980s (replacing the earlier mechanical gimbaled gyro), evolved into a solid-state fiber-optic gyro, then to a quartz tuning fork gyro, to a micro-mechanical gyro. By the mid-1990s, the instrument's size had shrunk from 0.47 to 0.17 cubic inches and its weight had dropped from about 4 ounces to less than half an ounce— about the size of a grain of rice." Also see Dennis M. Ward, "The Changing Technological Environment," in James J. Wirtz and Jeffrey A. Larsen, eds., *Rockets' Red Glare: Missile Defenses and the Future of World Politics* (Boulder, Colo.: Westview Press, 2001).

10. William R. Graham, statement to the House Armed Services Committee, Hearing on U.S. National Missile Defense Policy and the Anti-Ballistic Missile Treaty, 106th Cong., October 13, 1999.

11. U.S. General Accounting Office, *Missile Defense: Additional Knowledge Needed in Developing System for Intercepting Long-Range Missiles*, GAO-03-600, August 2003, p. 3, <http://www.gao.gov/new.items/d03600.pdf> (hereafter "GAO Report").

12. Ibid., 10–11.

13. Ibid., 11.

14. The foregoing discussion draws on, *inter alia*, David E. Mosher, "The Budget Politics of Missile Defense," MCIS Paper Number MP4/3, prepared for the Missile Proliferation, Missile Defences, and Space Security Conference, held at Wiston House, Sussex, England, June 1–4, 2003; and Congressional Budget Office, *Estimated Costs and Technical Characteristics of Selected National Missile Defense Systems*, January 31, 2002.

15. The estimate for the F-35 Joint Strike Fighter was given in the *Washington Post*, January 6, 2004.

16. David Pilling, "Japan and U.S. Set for Joint Work on Missiles," *London Financial Times*, December 19, 2003.

17. "Japan, US Sign Missile Defense Agreement," China Daily, December 17, 2004. http://www.chinadaily.com.cn/english/doc/2004-12/17/content_401196. htm.

18. "Prague Summit Declaration—Issued by the Heads of State and Government participating in the meeting of the North Atlantic Council in Prague on 21 November 2002," <http://www.nato.int/docu/pr/2002/p02-127e.htm>.

19. Note the use of this term in Lt. Col. Merrick E. Krause, USAF, "Attack Operations: First Layer of an Integrated Missile Defense," *Air Power Journal* XVII, no. 1 (Spring 2003): 101–112.

20. "Air Combat Command Unclear How ABL Will be Used Operationally," *Inside Missile Defense* July 23, 2003.

21. U.S. General Accounting Office, *Missile Defense: Additional Knowledge Needed in Developing System for Intercepting Long-Range Missiles*, GAO-03-600, August 7, 2003. http://www.gao.gov/new.items/d03600.pdf.

22. Erin Emery, "Missile Defense Soldiers Deploy," *Denver Post*, October 17, 2003.

23. A high level Bush administration official made this comment to the author during a missile defense conference in London, November 2004.

24. An informal survey of leading senators' websites revealed that few have used such a forum to express opposition to missile defense, while some, such as Democrat Joseph Leiberman actually have posted statements in support of missile defense. See <http://lieberman.senate.gov/newsroom/release.cfm?id = 208160>.

25. See statements by Levin and Biden given or summarized at, respectively, <http://levin.senate.gov/issues/missile.htm>; and, <http://www.clw.org/ coalition/biden050201.htm>.

7

A RESPONSIVE NEW TRIAD INFRASTRUCTURE

Steve Maaranen

A responsive defense research, development, and production infrastructure for U.S. strategic forces has been designated as one of the three legs of the new triad, and therefore has (in principle) equal status with strategic strike and defense capabilities. The responsive infrastructure, however, is the least well-defined, most poorly understood, and arguably the least effectively implemented component of the new triad. The function of the responsive infrastructure is to provide flexibility needed to address threats successfully, especially unexpected strategic challenges to U.S. interests. It is meant to add a powerful element of dissuasion to U.S. strategy by demonstrating America's technological superiority. A responsive strategic infrastructure is also intended to provide technically superior forces to deter, defend against, and defeat any threat that actually arises.

The responsive new triad infrastructure includes the defense research and development (R&D) base and the production plants for nuclear and nonnuclear strike forces and active and passive defenses. Many changes to the defense infrastructure have occurred since the end of the Cold War, in particular the contraction and consolidation of the Department of Defense (DoD) industrial base and the downsizing and deterioration of the Department of Energy's (DoE) nuclear weapon infrastructure. The 2001 Nuclear Posture Review (NPR) suggested that the nuclear weapons complex is in need of modernization and improvement. Additionally, the current DoD strategic force infrastructure cannot provide the flexibility, adaptability, and responsiveness that the NPR strategy requires.

Transforming the existing defense–industrial base for strategic forces into a responsive R&D and production infrastructure that can achieve the goals of the NPR will require intellectual innovation, changes to long-standing practices and policies, and sustained political and budgetary support. None of these prerequisites is assured. This chapter examines the requirements of a responsive infrastructure, as well as the bureaucratic, historical, and technical situation of the infrastructure.

THE QUADRENNIAL DEFENSE REVIEW
STRATEGY AND THE
DEFENSE INFRASTRUCTURE

The Quadrennial Defense Review (QDR) highlighted the diversity and unpredictability of possible threats to U.S. interests. To prepare for this uncertainty, the QDR introduced the concept of "capabilities-based planning." Capabilities-based planning entails the development of military technologies and forces to counter the military capabilities that diverse adversaries might bring to a future conflict. This planning approach is clearly a departure from the Cold War convention of preparing to defend against a well-known adversary with predictable, slowly changing military forces. Achieving the QDR's capabilities-based approach requires shaping the U.S. force posture and defense–industrial base to respond to different threats, to unexpected developments, and to known threats that may worsen rapidly.[1]

The capabilities-based approach requires an enhanced defense R&D effort. To be responsive, the defense infrastructure must conduct well-conceived programs of defense research, develop new weapon system designs, in some cases build prototypes, and have the capacity for rapid, serial production of weapons that meet emerging needs. A well-planned, responsive defense–industrial base would enable the United States to anticipate, foreclose, or counter technological avenues by which adversaries might try to steal a march. In particular, the ability to demonstrate a potent defense infrastructure that is able to upgrade existing weapons, rapidly produce additional weapons, or develop and field entirely new systems strengthens dissuasion of potential adversaries. The NPR applies the concept of a responsive infrastructure to the new triad of strategic forces, giving the infrastructure added prominence by designating it the third leg of the triad.[2]

Even before the NPR, several R&D programs were underway to strengthen the strategic force capabilities base.[3] To expand strategic strike capabilities, for example, DoD is currently pursuing R&D programs to identify and develop improved nonnuclear weapons. For long-range, precision global strike, there are many possible technical avenues: ballistic missiles, traditional bombers, hypersonic aircraft, and aerospace vehicles.[4] Such nonkinetic strikes as computer network attack and high-powered microwave weapons also could contribute to long-range strike. In addition to these nonnuclear weapon programs, the National Nuclear Security Administration (NNSA) is exploring improved nuclear strike capabilities, including the Robust Nuclear Earth Penetrator and the Advanced Concept Initiative.[5]

The NPR confirms that safe, secure, and effective nuclear weapons will, for the foreseeable future, remain a key element of U.S. national security strategy and an important part of the new triad. Accordingly, an effective nuclear weapon infrastructure will remain essential. The NPR also indicates that changes to current U.S. nuclear weapon capabilities may be required: "[A]djustments may be needed to match capabilities of the remaining nuclear forces to new missions . . . A need may arise to modify, upgrade, or replace portions of the extant nuclear force or develop concepts for follow-on nuclear weapons better suited to the nation's needs."[6]

The nuclear weapon infrastructure must be able to certify, sustain, and refurbish current weapons; research, develop, and certify modified or new weapons to meet new requirements (using nuclear testing if that is required to ensure confidence); manufacture all components and assemble required types of weapons in the quantities and timeframes needed; and dismantle excess weapons. The current nuclear weapon infrastructure falls short of these requirements. A responsive infrastructure would be able to improve the understanding of physical principles, nuclear weapons engineering, and manufacturing expertise, and it would transfer this knowledge to the next generation of nuclear weapons designers. It also would guarantee that the United States could conduct cutting-edge nuclear weapon research, development, and design, while maintaining the capacity to analyze foreign nuclear weapon developments and countermeasures. A responsive infrastructure would facilitate U.S. nuclear weapons life-extension programs. NNSA also would have to provide production capacity for weapon assembly and disassembly, nuclear weapon secondaries, new pits, and tritium production and processing.

The U.S. Strategic Weapons Arsenal

Operationally deployed strategic nuclear weapons should be capable of dealing with immediate threats and meeting plausible unexpected threats that might arise quickly. For potential threats, downloaded warheads will be placed in storage. They could be placed back on nuclear missiles and bombers (reloaded), should it become necessary to expand the arsenal.[7] Some additional warheads are likely to be retained as replacements for warheads that develop serious technical problems. In the past, technical problems have been detected in stockpile warheads—sometimes affecting all weapons of a given type. The past practice of continuous development, testing, and production of warheads is no longer available. In their absence, NNSA developed a different methodology—the Stockpile Stewardship Program (SSP)—to detect technical problems, then design a fix and carry out a repair. It is not yet clear if this approach will fully succeed.

Complementing the SSP, the NPR's hedge against failing warheads is to retain a pool of warheads of various types that can replace any warheads that fail. Several factors bear on the size and scope of this warhead pool, including the degree of capability that would be lost in the event of a technical failure, the risks that can be tolerated, and improvements in NNSA's ability to produce new or refurbished warheads. NNSA might seek to retain a large number of warheads to hedge against the failure of one type of warhead that may make up a large part of the stockpile.[8] The NPR did not finally determine the total nuclear stockpile, but it did set some parameters. It calls for retaining enough weapons to upload much or all of the United States' planned nuclear delivery systems (fourteen Trident nuclear-armed ballistic missile submarines (SSBNs), 500 single warhead Minuteman III intercontinental ballistic missiles, seventy-six B-52H bombers, and twenty-one B-2 bombers). Other warheads are designated for the reliability pool. Still others will be retired. For the near- to mid-term, the stockpile to be retained will be much larger than the 1,700 to 2,200 operationally deployed warheads permitted under the Moscow Treaty. That number will be further reduced, however, when the nuclear weapon complex is fully operational.

TODAY'S NUCLEAR WEAPONS INFRASTRUCTURE

The present-day nuclear weapons infrastructure falls far short of what would be needed to meet NPR requirements. The NPR's assessment was that underinvestment in the infrastructure—in particular the production complex—has increased the risks that if substantial problems in the stockpile are discovered, future options to refurbish or replace existing designs will be inadequate. For example, although an interim pit production capability will be established later in this decade, no current capability exists to build and certify plutonium pits, certain secondary components, or complete warheads.[9]

What caused this deterioration? The nuclear weapons complex was built to support a large Cold War stockpile of as many as 30,000 warheads. By the end of Cold War, the complex was made up of sixteen separate sites.[10] To meet Cold War demands, the complex conducted continuous R&D and built new warheads as a matter of routine. Warheads stayed in the stockpile for an average of only ten years before they were replaced with new designs. U.S. nuclear weapons met exacting standards of size, weight, and nuclear materials for increasingly stressing missions (e.g., the development of small, light warheads for missiles with multiple independently targetable reentry vehicles (MIRVs) to attack growing numbers of hardened silos). Underground nuclear testing provided confidence that designs would work as intended.

The collapse of the Soviet Union and the diminished nuclear threat from Russia made it clear that this large nuclear weapon stockpile and complex were obsolete. Moreover, the complex was showing its age, and it did not meet new and more exacting safety and environmental standards. A systematic downsizing process commenced (see figure 7.1). The Rocky Flats Plant, near Denver, Colorado, was the only place where nuclear pits were produced. It was closed to nuclear activities in 1989 because of safety and environmental concerns[11] Nuclear weapon-related facilities at Hanford, Washington, Savannah River Site, South Carolina, Mound, Ohio, and Pinellas, Florida, were closed and their missions were transferred within the remaining sites. Some were left temporarily in abeyance. The nuclear test moratorium of 1992 indefinitely suspended nuclear testing activities at the Nevada Test Site.

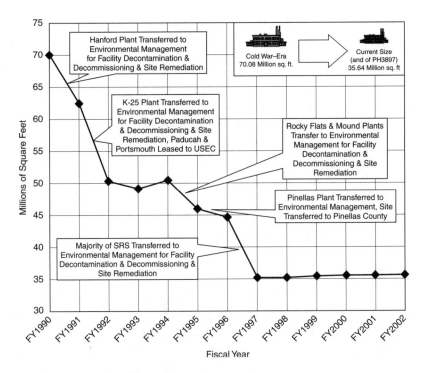

Figure 7.1 Downsizing of the nuclear weapon complex.

Policy did call for retaining a "residual" production capability. In 1996, the Department of Energy reduced the nuclear complex in place rather than design a new, smaller complex. The complex was reduced to its present eight sites (four production plants, three laboratories, and the Nevada Test Site), and its footprint cut by half from Cold War levels. The nation's nuclear weapons production capability now consists of several "one-of-a-kind" facilities: the Pantex Plant in Amarillo, Texas, which conducts warhead assembly, disassembly, and disposal, and manufactures high-explosive components; the Y-12 Plant at Oak Ridge National Laboratory, Tennessee, which fabricates uranium and other components; the Kansas City Plant, which manufactures nonnuclear components; and the remaining parts of the Savannah River Plant, which undertakes tritium extraction and handling. Additional component production occurs at two R&D laboratories: Sandia National Laboratories, Albuquerque, New Mexico, works on neutron generators, and Los Alamos National Laboratory, New Mexico, manufactures plutonium and beryllium parts, detonators, tritium targets for neutron generators, and runs a small-scale, interim pit fabrication facility.

The reduction in the size and capability of the weapons infrastructure was accompanied by sharply lower funding that seemed permissible with the end of the Cold War. Larger fractions of the remaining budgets were required to clean up the sites and improve their safety and security.

Stockpile Stewardship Program

In combination, these decisions and the higher priority given to the Stockpile Stewardship Program resulted in deferred maintenance and reduced investment in production facilities and equipment.

With the end of nuclear testing and with no requirements foreseen for new nuclear weapons design or production, DoE developed a new approach to its R&D programs and facilities: the SSP.[12] Because national policy was to retain "legacy" weapons in smaller numbers—indefinitely—the SSP was designed to ensure that remaining weapons continued to be safe and reliable. This decision to rely on physics knowledge and simulations without underground nuclear testing was a major change from past practices, entailing substantial programmatic risk. SSP sought to improve dramatically the basic understanding of the physics of nuclear explosions, including the effects of aging or remanufacture on warhead performance, by using nonnuclear experiments, computer simulations, examination of information from the nuclear test database, improved stockpile surveillance, peer review by the two laboratory design teams, and independent assessments. It also required a major expansion of computer simulation capabilities and the construction of a number of new experimental facilities for hydrodynamics testing, materials science, and high-energy density physics. Using information gathered by the SSP, existing weapons are systematically evaluated and, when necessary, refurbished to eliminate problems that were discovered and to extend the life of the stockpile. Much of the SSP is underway today.

The Situation at Century's End

In congressional testimony in 2002, John Gordon, the first administrator of the new National Nuclear Security Administration, evaluated the state of the complex in the following terms: "How far along are we in creating a 'responsive nuclear weapons enterprise?' The answer is: 'We're making progress, but we have a ways to go.' " Gordon admitted that the results of DoE's efforts had been mixed. DoE had been able to certify stockpile safety and reliability without underground nuclear testing, but Gordon was uncertain about DoE's ability to do so in the future, especially as the stockpile ages. Gordon also noted that no advanced warhead concept development was underway; meanwhile, under-investment in the production complex would limit future options. Gordon noted that "restoring lost nuclear weapons capabilities, and modernizing others, will require substantial investment over the next several years both to recapitalize laboratory and production infrastructure, and to strengthen our most important asset: our people."[13]

NNSA PLANS FOR CREATING A RESPONSIVE NUCLEAR WEAPONS INFRASTRUCTURE

The NPR's flexible and responsive nuclear weapons complex will include the ability to design and develop weapons to dissuade nuclear competitors, to respond to emerging major adversaries, and to understand any nuclear weapon developments by current and potential adversaries. The SSP was planned in the 1990s, at a time of a different security context, and it must be reviewed and perhaps adjusted to meet emerging security challenges.[14] The goals of maintaining current weapons and assuring the capability to undertake new designs without nuclear testing will demand further improvements of SSP projects: for example, improved physics knowledge, more detailed models with greater fidelity, nonnuclear experiments to help develop and verify models, and advanced engineering capabilities, including development of modern microelectronics. NNSA has laid plans for enhancing science, engineering, inertial confinement fusion, and advanced simulation and computing as part of the evolution of the SSP.[15]

New or emerging threats of weapons of mass destruction (WMD) make it difficult to predict future nuclear deterrence requirements. For the flexibility to meet unexpected developments, NNSA must be able to provide nuclear warheads appropriate to changing strategic conditions. This need may require adapting and modernizing warheads or developing new ones. The NPR called for the creation of advanced concepts teams at the design laboratories to reinvigorate the design process and develop concepts for modified or new warheads. The NNSA has programmed an Advanced Concepts Initiative (ACI), but competing pressures on the NNSA budget and concerns about the political implications of new design activity has severely restricted funding for ACI to date. DoD must define specific nuclear weapon requirements before design work can move beyond the ACI. Currently, only one weapon design program, the modification of an existing warhead to serve as an earth penetrating weapon (the Robust Nuclear Earth Penetrator) has been authorized and funded beyond the conceptual development stage. Moving a design into full-scale development requires an additional vote by Congress. Other concepts emerging from the design laboratories include warheads that would be intrinsically easier to maintain and certify—conceivably without nuclear testing—and designs that would reuse existing pits (the fissile core of nuclear weapon primaries) to build weapons, thereby postponing the need for the new pit production facility. In the area of weapons design, NNSA has set a responsiveness goal, "to maintain sufficient R&D and production capability to be able to design, develop, and begin production on the order of five years from a decision to enter full-scale development of a new warhead."[16]

The NNSA's program to update the nuclear weapon complex and create a responsive nuclear warhead infrastructure will, if successful, satisfy all the requirements in the NPR.[17] The main elements of the NNSA plan are: (1) to examine, sustain, repair, or replace weapons in the legacy stockpile; (2) to provide and maintain ready weapons to meet DoD needs; and (3) to provide a responsive nuclear weapon R&D system; sustain active, knowledgeable nuclear weapon design, engineering, and manufacturing personnel; provide the capability to test nuclear weapons should that become necessary; and provide a fully capable production complex. We will examine each of these three elements.

Examine, Sustain, Repair, Replace, or Refurbish Stockpile Weapons

With a large nuclear weapon stockpile and active infrastructure, the United States has several options for restoring the military capability that would be lost should a warhead type develop a serious technical fault. For instance, planners could adjust the number or types of warheads assigned to targets or increase warhead loadings on some delivery vehicles (e.g., bombers). The ultimate hedge against warhead failure, however, has always been the nuclear weapon complex's capability to repair faulty warheads quickly or to replace them with new warheads. Under the SSP, NNSA aimed to replace this old paradigm with the high-confidence capability to sustain legacy weapons for the long term. The SSP approach contains several steps. The surveillance program verifies the safety and reliability of nuclear weapons and the effects of aging on them. Aging effects have become even more important because weapons are expected to remain in the stockpile well beyond their planned life expectancy. There has been particular concern about plutonium pits because they undergo aging processes that are not fully understood. With a very limited ability to produce new pits until at least 2020, nuclear planners must predict when new pits will be needed. This information will help determine needs for future pit production—either the large Modern Pit Facility that is being planned or some lesser capability, probably in Los Alamos National Laboratory. There have been schedule slippages and missed milestones in the Enhanced Surveillance Campaign. An April 2004 report from the DoE Inspector General found that "NNSA experienced delays in completing certain Enhanced Surveillance Campaign milestones and is at risk of missing some future milestones."[18] These delays "may deprive NNSA of the information it needs to make informed decisions on such topics as weapon refurbishment schedules and building a new pit facility." The complex also must be able to design, develop, implement, and certify remedies to problems that are detected in weapons. When a decision is made to refurbish a weapon in order to extend its lifetime or to repair a technical problem, the design laboratories must design the rebuild or repair, and certify that the refurbished weapon will still satisfy all safety, reliability, and effectiveness requirements. The SSP is designed to make certification possible without nuclear testing. To date, the laboratories have been able each year to certify all U.S. weapons. Questions remain, however, about whether technical problems will arise that require fundamental design changes that cannot be certified without nuclear tests.

The NPR also reaffirmed a stockpile refurbishment plan using "block upgrades," which segment major life extension programs into five-year blocks. This approach provides the flexibility to refurbish only a portion of the warheads of a given type, and to shift schedules if refurbishment priorities change. It also provides opportunities to introduce modified or new weapons into the production line. Current plans envision refurbishment of eight warhead types over the next twenty-five years.

Provide and Maintain Ready Weapons

The 1,700 to 2,200 operationally deployed warheads allowed under the Moscow Treaty must be ready for use at all times. To check on warhead reliability, NNSA removes warheads from deployed systems and conducts numerous inspections and tests. NNSA also periodically replaces such limited life components as tritium on weapons in the active stockpile.

Another task is to make sure that augmentation warheads will be available if needed and that they can be ready for transport to deployment sites in time to meet the DoD's upload schedule. Some augmentation warheads will be required quickly. Others can be in the inactive stockpile. Now that DoD and NNSA have determined the required size and makeup of the stockpile, including deployed, augmentation, and reliability replacement warheads, NNSA can begin to eliminate excess weapons.

Provide a Responsive Nuclear Weapon R&D System

To meet the demands of the NPR, the nuclear infrastructure's remaining production plants must be ready, able, and flexible enough to produce any design that may be required, and in required quantity. Some observers believe that in addition to large programs to refurbish or build weapons in quantity, the complex should be prepared to build small numbers of weapons that are optimized to accomplish specific missions, such as destroying chemical or biological agents. Some suggest that it may be desirable to produce a few prototype weapons of different designs as a means to exercise key production skills and to prove that a design could be produced in quantity if it were ever needed. In response to internal planning and the NPR, NNSA has developed plans to restore and improve many elements of its production infrastructure. These include renovations of several key facilities to be able to "meet the anticipated Nuclear Posture Review workload with a reserve capacity to fix unanticipated problems in the stockpile, respond to new warhead production requirements, or handle a potentially increased dismantlement workload."[19] The current capacity of the Pantex plant in Amarillo for warhead assembly and disassembly will be expanded by refurbishment activities and construction of new facilities. Currently, the Y-12 Plant in Oak Ridge cannot produce a new nuclear weapon secondary. NNSA plans to restore that capability, with expanded capacity, in about ten years. The most prominent weakness in the nuclear weapons production infrastructure is the inability to fabricate and certify weapon pits. The NNSA plan is to expand the small capacity at Los Alamos to build pits,[20] and then design and build a Modern Pit Facility (MPF) that would begin operations in about 2020, with a capacity of producing between 125 and 450 pits per year.[21]

After many years without the ability to produce tritium, a Tennessee Valley Authority reactor has begun to irradiate fuel rods to produce tritium and a new Tritium Extraction Facility is being built at Savannah River to separate tritium from the fuel rods.[22] It is scheduled for completion in 2006.

Some additional special materials and parts, not available commercially, are required for modern nuclear warheads. NNSA has laid plans to build modern facilities at the Y-12 Special Materials Complex at Oak Ridge for manufacturing unique components and materials.

Enhanced Test Readiness

The U.S moratorium on nuclear testing continues despite the Senate's refusal to consent to a binding Comprehensive Nuclear Test Ban Treaty (CTBT). The Bush administration says it currently has no plans to resume testing. When the Clinton administration was arguing for the CTBT, it established a set of domestic safeguards in the event the United States could not sustain its stockpile without testing. Safeguards included the SSP program to ensure the reliability and safety of the stockpile, and explicitly reserving the right to resume testing. Views differ on the likelihood that the stockpile can be kept healthy and whether nuclear testing will be required again. The NNSA has aimed to be able to test within two to three years, but the NPR calls for NNSA to shorten this to eighteen months. NNSA has initiated a program to reduce their response to eighteen months, as called for in the NPR.

Retaining Nuclear Weapon Expertise

Crucial aspects of nuclear weapon research, design, engineering, and production are unique to the NNSA complex, partly because there is no need for those capabilities outside the nuclear weapons program, and partly because many of these areas are a closely held, highly classified, government monopoly. Some aspects of the essential skills and knowledge are acquired from coworkers and hands-on training. Passing on this expertise and experience is particularly important for the very sophisticated designs in the current stockpile, which have little margin for error. Accordingly, NNSA and the laboratories are working to transfer accumulated experience from one generation to the next and catalog what has been learned over the years. This exercise is particularly urgent because much of the expert workforce is retiring. In addition, recently established recruitment and training programs at the labs and plants are helping to rejuvenate the workforce.[23]

Issues with the Nuclear Weapons Infrastructure

Important issues remain about the prospects for a responsive nuclear weapons infrastructure. The first is the future role of nuclear weapons themselves. The NPR's new strategic triad concept combines nuclear weapons, in smaller numbers, with nonnuclear strike weapons and defenses in order to make the strategic forces more relevant to regional WMD threats as well as larger-scale nuclear threats. This strategy has been criticized on the grounds that it reduces the firebreak between conventional and nuclear weapons, expands the role of nuclear weapons rather than reducing it, requires an unnecessarily large and costly nuclear weapons infrastructure, and provokes nuclear proliferation. Some favor an alternative strategy that would limit the role of nuclear weapons to the deterrence of large-scale nuclear threats. This alternative strategy, they argue, would keep the nuclear threshold very high, set a good example to other states, reduce the pressure for those states to acquire nuclear weapons, and reduce the size and cost of the U.S. nuclear stockpile and infrastructure.

Although there would be differences between a nuclear weapons complex designed to support the NPR strategy and one focused only on major nuclear threats, there would likely also be a number of common requirements. A capable infrastructure that could manufacture both types of weapons would be needed to ensure an effective nuclear deterrent for the foreseeable future. A better understanding of nuclear weapon science and technology would be needed in either case to provide confidence in the stockpile without nuclear testing. Both would need similar design and engineering expertise to diagnose technical problems and design remedies; both would require a substantial plant capacity to refurbish and dismantle weapons.

There would be important differences between the two infrastructures, as well. A limited deterrence strategy would allow for a simpler complex and a smaller R&D capability that would be focused on maintaining the health of the remaining stockpile (with only a modest capability for work on new or modified warheads). The size of the augmentation and the inventory of replacement components of the stockpile probably would be considerably smaller; some weapon types might be eliminated to reduce costs. These changes would likely allow for a smaller weapon production capacity and, depending on the assessed lifetime of plutonium pits, a pit production plant smaller than that envisioned for the Modern Pit Facility.

Additional challenges must be overcome to create a responsive infrastructure. These include the delays and cost overruns of several SSP projects. Most of these problems have been resolved, but they have increased the cost and delayed the availability of important components of the R&D complex. They also have raised concerns among the military "customers" and program funders about NNSA's ability to realize its plans. The NNSA plans for a responsive infrastructure will be expensive and take more than a decade to complete. In an era of constrained defense budgets and with nuclear weapons playing a less conspicuous role in national defense, it will be difficult to sustain the needed funding year after year.

A RESPONSIVE DoD INFRASTRUCTURE

The DoD industrial base and infrastructure for strategic forces is the second component of a responsive infrastructure for U.S. strategic forces. It includes the traditional, well-established DoD infrastructure for nuclear delivery systems; the infrastructure for long-range nonnuclear strike including both kinetic and non-kinetic weapons; the R&D and production infrastructure for missile defense; and the base for DoD's homeland defense forces. The challenge for DoD is to guide each element of its strategic force infrastructure and to coordinate or integrate planning to optimize the value of the infra-structure for the combined strategic force.

The DoD's task is quite different from redirecting the NNSA nuclear weapon infrastructure. NNSA essentially owns the nuclear weapon complex, operating it through government-owned, contractor-operated (GOCO) arrangements. Hence, NNSA can exercise considerable control in planning and implementing the transformation of its infrastructure. DoD, on the other hand, operates primarily by setting requirements and purchasing goods and services from defense-oriented private industry. These for-profit indus-tries often undertake commercial as well as defense development and pro-duction, and they plan according to their own business calculations. DoD does fund its own R&D labs and allows contractors to invest a fraction of their contract funds in research and development. Thus, DoD's control over the decisions of private defense industries is mostly indirect.

The deep budget reductions that affected the NNSA nuclear weapons program cut across the DoD budget as well. In the 1990s, the department initiated a plan to encourage and support the rationalization and consoli-dation of the defense R&D and industrial base. While doing so, it made efforts to identify and support those (few) companies and technologies that were truly unique and essential to important defense capabilities. In the area of nuclear delivery systems, the 1994 NPR concluded that new nuclear deliv-ery systems were not required. Instead, DoD would fund the industrial base primarily to sustain and modernize existing forces and develop technical upgrades. This approach, it was hoped, would keep many of the key suppli-ers active with funded work and focused on R&D for improved capabilities. The department did identify some unique and vulnerable industrial capabil-ities that were in danger of being lost. Crucial elements of the ballistic missile industry, for example, were to be kept healthy through continuing D-5 pro-duction and major subsystem improvements to the D-5 and Minuteman III missiles. The existing military and civil aircraft industries were judged capa-ble of meeting future bomber requirements without direct assistance. The nuclear submarine industrial infrastructure, on the other hand, was judged to be unique to military needs, and DoD decided that keeping two subma-rine shipyards operating by low-production builds of the Seawolf nuclear-powered attack submarine (SSN) and planning for a follow-on attack submarine would sustain the industrial capabilities needed for a future ballis-tic missile submarine (SSBN).[24] The R&D and industrial base for conven-tional weapons, defenses, and generic technologies received similar scrutiny and, in some cases, direct support.

Many elements of this post–Cold War approach continue in U.S. policy toward the defense industrial base. While current policy is to reduce govern-ment controls and regulations where possible, DoD still guides, evaluates, and assesses the health of the defense industrial base. It provides input to decisions on mergers and acquisitions, it uses acquisition policies and decisions to direct industry programs, and it assesses specific sectors of the defense industry to identify areas that require financial support.[25]

Current policy continues to support defense industry consolidation in order to eliminate unwanted redundancies, to yield cost savings, and to create defense contractors with new capabilities and synergies needed to produce future defense systems. The DoD Industrial Policy Office, while generally favoring contractor control over subcontractors, is willing to intervene to protect an industry when there is a risk that a critical defense capability will be lost. The Department of Defense uses several mechanisms to identify weaknesses in the R&D and production infrastructure. The services review technology capabilities and needs within their areas of responsibility. The deputy undersecretary for Advanced Concepts oversees the ManTech program, which supports the services and the Defense Logistics Agency, to look at the health of crosscutting technologies and subcontractors.

Nuclear Weapon Delivery Systems Infrastructure

DoD has a long-established relationship with its primary suppliers of nuclear weapon delivery systems. The department makes long-range plans for future nuclear weapon systems and workss closely with its contractors to guide their research and development to identify future requirements.[26] In terms of intercontinental ballistic missiles (ICBMs), plans call for 500 single-warhead Minuteman IIIs in the 2012 force. Minuteman III missiles have been operational since 1970, with major overhauls and upgrades in recent years to extend their service life through 2020. A comprehensive set of sustainment programs are planned or underway, including replacement of the guidance system and propellant, life extension of the rocket motor, improved retargeting capabilities, and a new reentry vehicle to carry the warheads removed from the Peacekeeper missiles as they are deactivated.

The Air Force believes that a replacement for these missiles is needed, to come on-line as the Minuteman III's extended service life ends. Air Force studies have identified longer range, trajectory shaping, and attack of strategic relocatable targets and deeply buried targets as desirable characteristics for the next generation missile. Air Force Space Command now plans to begin an analysis of alternatives for a "land-based strategic deterrent" in FY 2006, with an anticipated IOC for the new system in 2018.[27]

The planned 2012 force of nuclear-armed submarines will contain fourteen *Ohio*-class ballistic missile submarines carrying D-5 (Trident II) missiles. The remaining four boats will be converted to carry special operations forces and cruise missiles. The Navy estimates that the *Ohio* class's service life will be forty-two years, with retirements not beginning until 2029. Current studies identify either a variant of the *Virginia*-class attack submarines or a new SSBN as an eventual replacement for the *Ohio* class, with early development beginning about 2016.

A program is needed to extend the life of the D-5 missiles. Plans call for continued, low-rate production of the D-5 until 2013 to keep the production line alive, and to provide upgrades to guidance and electronics systems. The Navy has begun to study a follow-on to the D-5. It is likely that any new land- or sea-based missiles will share sub-systems (including guidance, reentry vehicle technology, propulsion technology, and sustainment technology).

Current plans call for keeping B-52 and B-2 strategic bombers operational for thirty-five to forty more years. No new aircraft design and production is underway today, although the NPR suggests that these bombers need improved communications, avionics, processors, radar systems, displays, and navigation systems.

The B-52s lack reliable, secure, survivable communications with the National Command Authority; they also are burdened with aged and outmoded situational awareness and electronic countermeasures and old avionics that cannot meet NPR demands for worldwide tasking and nuclear weapons delivery. They require major upgrades to fulfill their strategic and tactical missions. The B-2s, more modern aircraft, are being upgraded to sustain their stealth qualities, improve their communications equipment, and expand their weapon delivery options.

Because of the long projected lifetime of current bombers and the reasonably good health of the military and civil aircraft industries, the Air Force has decided that the private sector will continue to provide an effective infrastructure for bombers without DoD intervention. There could be a need for a follow-on bomber after 2040; there is analysis and initial R&D on a spectrum of long-range strike platforms that could lead to greatly improved and more flexible aerospace capabilities, which could serve as a basis for nuclear delivery systems.[28]

In terms of air-launched cruise missiles (ALCM), the Air Force believes that it can sustain its current systems until 2030, and currently it is not planning for a follow-on nuclear ALCM. Advanced conventional cruise missiles, however, are being developed that could probably be modified for an improved nuclear ALCM, if it is required.

Nonnuclear Strike Force Infrastructure

R&D and production of nonnuclear systems for strategic forces piggybacks on development and infrastructure for the conventional forces. Offices within the Air Force and Navy staffs have been the primary advocates for nuclear weapon systems, although their influence over budgets has diminished with the growing emphasis on advanced conventional forces. In some areas—for example, long-range strike systems—the needs for strategic forces and service requirements overlap, which helps to support strategic force requirements. The defense infrastructure for information warfare seems to have its own features. Nondefense companies, many with little historical connection to DoD, are technology leaders in this rapidly changing field; however, several national security agencies, including DoD, have a long history in promoting and using information technologies. The services all have information warfare programs of their own, focused on their respective operational needs.

Missile Defense Infrastructure

There has been substantial funding for the development of missile defenses since President Ronald Reagan's Strategic Defense Initiative in 1983. A fairly well-defined set of industrial contractors has grown up with special expertise and capabilities for missile defense weapons, sensors, and command and control. This industrial base responds to the specific needs of missile defense systems, but the inclusion of companies with a broader range of defense technology expertise allows for drawing upon R&D and technologies in related defense fields. The need for command and control, intelligence surveillance, and reconnaissance is in many ways similar for the offensive and defensive strategic forces. This realization may allow the different parts of the triad to borrow technologies developed by the others.

NPR INFRASTRUCTURE ISSUES AND THE WAY AHEAD

Transforming the new triad into an effective force will be expensive and difficult. Transforming the nuclear weapon infrastructure and spiral development of an increasingly effective set of layered missile defenses will require large and continuing investments. The strategic force, although given new breadth and importance by the NPR, must compete with a host of other defense needs, from personnel costs and operations and maintenance (e.g., paying for Operation Iraqi Freedom), to funding new capabilities for the conventional forces, counterterrorism, and counterproliferation. Budgets for strategic force improvements have fared well since the NPR, but it will require considerable top-down pressure from the White House, the secretary of defense, U.S. Strategic Command, and the Navy and Air Force to prevent incremental reductions in new triad budgets. In addition, funding for a responsive infrastructure must compete with the more glamorous strike and defense weapon systems within the new triad. Some analysts believe defense budgets have reached a plateau, and that future investment in particular capabilities such as strategic forces will have to be paid for by reductions in other programs, rather than budget plus-ups.

Since the NPR, the new triad has benefited from top-level political support. There has been only a modest effort, however, to convince the public and Congress of its virtues. In light of very uneven public perceptions about the principles and objectives of the NPR, renewed high-level political support may be needed to assure further progress in the program. On the other hand, U.S. Strategic Command has been given responsibility for the entire strategic force, allowing it to become a strong advocate for its success. Still, Strategic Command must contend with strong traditional advocates of competing military needs within DoD.

CONCLUSION

Creating an effective, coordinated new triad R&D program and responsive infrastructure will require a compelling and reiterated case for the NPR strategy, a broad, comprehensive planning process for the strategic forces, altering deeply embedded roles and responsibilities within DoD, and a significant investment of political influence and scarce dollars for more than a decade. This is true for both the DoD's industrial base and the DoE's nuclear weapons complex. Historically, however, the United States has found it difficult to sustain investment in capabilities that do not meet clear, near-term requirements.

Finding a way to develop and sustain an integrated responsive defense base is one of the key challenges for the new triad concept. Improving the condition of the nuclear weapon R&D and production infrastructure is mandatory if the United States intends to rely on nuclear deterrence for the foreseeable future. NNSA has developed a promising plan to transform its infrastructure to meet NPR requirements. Bringing a responsive infrastructure to reality, however, will require occasional reaffirmation of the NPR strategy, and considerable tenacity in procuring the necessary funding over another decade and more.

NOTES

The views expressed in this chapter are the author's own and do not necessarily reflect the official position of Los Alamos National Laboratory, the Department of Energy, or the United States government.

1. Department of Defense, *Report of the Quadrennial Defense Review* September 30, 2001, 13–14, <http://www.defenselink.mil/pubs/qdr2001/pdf>.
2. Ibid., 14
3. See e.g., "information superiority" and "precision engagement" in *Joint Vision 2010* and *Joint Vision 2020.* <http://www.dtic.mil/jointvision/history.htm>.
4. Office of the Under Secretary of Defense for Acquisition, Technology, and Logistics, *Report of the Defense Science Board Task Force on Future Strategic Strike Forces*, (February 2004).
5. In 2000, Congress legislated the creation of the semiautonomous National Nuclear Security Administration within the Department of Energy in an attempt to provide greater attention to, accountability for, and focus on resolving the shortcomings of the nuclear weapons program.
6. GlobalSecurity.org, *Nuclear Posture Review Report*, 23.
7. Many of the warhead reductions from now to 2012 will be accomplished by removing operationally deployed warheads from strategic nuclear delivery systems, but retaining the capability to upload them if that becomes necessary.
8. Testimony of Ambassador Linton R. Brooks, Administrator, National Nuclear Security Administration, Department of Energy, before the subcommittee on strategic forces, House Armed Services Committee, United States Houses of Representatives, March 18, 2004.
9. *Nuclear Posture Review* [excerpts], January 8, 2002, <http://www.globalsecurity. org/wmd/library/policy/dod/npr.htm> (hereinafter NPR).
10. These sites included three research and development laboratories, twelve production plants, and the Nevada Test Site.
11. National Nuclear Security Administration, *NNSA Infrastructure Plan for the NNSA Nuclear Complex*, April, 2003, 6.

12. U.S. Department of Energy Office of Defense Programs, "The Stockpile Stewardship and Management Program," May 1995.
13. Statement of John A. Gordon, Undersecretary for Nuclear Security and Administrator, National Nuclear Security Administration, U.S. Department of Energy, before the Committee on Armed Services, U.S. Senate, February 14, 2002.
14. NNSA, "NNSA Strategic Planning Guidance for Fiscal Years 2006–2010," April 2000.
15. The combined FY2004 budget for these programs is $1.77 billion. See *DOE FY2005 Congressional Budget*, 52–53.
16. The development of designs or prototypes, put "on the shelf," would greatly reduce the lead time between a decision to produce a weapon and the availability of a design for full-scale development.
17. "NNSA Strategic Planning Guidance for Fiscal Years 2006–2010."
18. The U.S. Department of Energy, Office of Inspector General, "Audit Report: the National Nuclear Security Administration's Enhanced Surveillance Campaign, April 2004."
19. *Infrastructure Plan for the NNSA Nuclear Complex*, 14.
20. With a nominal capacity of twenty pits per year, which might be expanded to fifty per year.
21. Jonathan Medalia, CRS Report for Congress, "Nuclear Warhead 'Pit' Production: Background for Congress," (updated March 29, 2004).
22. Tritium decays at a known rate. The tritium in warheads must be replenished periodically.
23. This approach could be used deliberately to provide on-the-shelf designs that could be rapidly put into production if the need arose, and thus contribute to national security goals of dissuasion and deterrence.
24. See Paul G. Kaminski, Undersecretary of Defense for Acquisition and Technology, "Sustaining the U.S. Nuclear Deterrent in the 21st Century," August 30, 1995 <http://www.acq.osd.mil/ip/docs/5000_60h.pdf.> <www.fas.org/nuke/guide/usa/doctrine/dod/di1099.htm>. The methodology DoD used to sift through the defense industrial base, in "Assessing Defense Industrial Capabilities," appears at <www.acq.osd.mil/ip/docs/5000_60h.pdf>.
25. Suzanne D. Patrick, Under Secretary of Defense (Industrial Policy), "Statement before the House Armed Services Committee Subcommittee on Military Procurement," March 19, 2002.
26. Amy Wolf, Congressional Research Service, "U.S. Nuclear Weapons: Changes in Policy and Force Structure," Penny Hill Press, (updated February 23, 2004).
27. A collection of documents on the next generation of U.S. land-based strategic deterrent can be found at <http://www.wslfweb.org/space/spacedocs.htm>.
28. U.S. Air Force, "Future Strategic Strike Forces."

Controlling the Strike Complex

8

COMMAND, CONTROL, AND THE NUCLEAR POSTURE REVIEW

Nathan Busch

In a series of high-level reports in 2001 and 2002, the U.S. government outlined its future strategic posture. These documents made it clear that the U.S. military would be transformed to meet the the military threats of the next century. Although the Cold War was long over, the United States still retained a Cold War-level force structure, doctrine, and outlook. According to these reports, the U.S. military had to abandon its "threat-based" approach to planning and adopt a "capabilities-based" approach to antici-pating future conflict.[1] U.S. military planners would no longer focus on major threats from a few specific countries but would instead develop a flexible system that could address conflicts in a number of countries, includ-ing combat situations that were not previously foreseen. A striking example of this new need in the military was seen in Operation Enduring Freedom, the effort to destroy al Qaeda operatives and their Taliban supporters in Afghanistan. On September 10, 2001, U.S. officials and planners had no idea that the armed forces would soon be engaging in a major military oper-ation in Afghanistan. And yet, less than a month later, the United States began air strikes, which were followed quickly by the introduction of ground forces, in a successful campaign to remove the Taliban from power.

Proposed changes in U.S. military doctrine and force structure were iden-tified by the Quadrennial Defense Review (QDR) of September 2001 and were supported by the 2002 National Security Strategy of the United States and the 2001 Nuclear Posture Review (NPR). Both the QDR and the NPR outlined four primary objectives for the military: assure allies and friends; dis-suade other nations from future military competition with the United States; deter threats and coercion against U.S. interests; and if deterrence fails, decisively defeat an adversary.[2]

Changes in the size and force structure of the U.S. military are necessary to achieve these objectives, but many observers ignore the fact that the implementation of the NPR also will require changes in U.S. command and control (C^2) procedures and capabilities. Because modern military opera-tions rely heavily on technology, including communications systems and computers, the concept of command and control has been expanded to include these elements. As a result, this notion is often referred to as command, control, and communications (C^3), or command, control, communications, and computers (C^4). The Department of Defense (DoD) defines a "command and control system" as "the facilities, equipment, communications, procedures, and personnel essential to a commander for planning, directing, and controlling operations of assigned forces to the missions assigned."[3] To be effective, a command and control system must have a clear chain of authority for directing a mission and secure, reliable, and rapid communications systems to relay operational commands. Well-defined procedures, state-of-the-art equipment and launch platforms, and well-trained personnel also facilitate effective command and control.

To address the command and control requirements imposed by the NPR, this chapter will first describe the call for improved strategic command and control contained in Bush administration policy documents. Second, it will describe shortcomings in current command and control networks, especially in light of the NPR's new requirements. Third, the chapter describes the current command and control network and how it might serve as the basis of a new approach to strategic command and control. Fourth, it outlines several significant objectives the Bush administration already has undertaken to transform existing command and control to meet emerging demands outlined in the NPR. The chapter concludes with a brief summary of the steps that remain to be taken to create the command and control network needed to backstop the strategic vision outlined in the NPR.

New Demands for Command and Control

To meet the four primary objectives outlined by the NPR, the Bush administration has called for a "new triad" to replace the old triad of intercontinental ballistic missiles, submarine launched ballistic missiles, and long-range bombers. The new triad will consist of (1) nuclear and conventional offensive forces; (2) defensive forces, including such passive defenses as warning systems, and active defenses such as missile defenses; and (3) the military–industrial infrastructure to support these systems.[4] The QDR also calls for a "flexible, reliable, and effective joint command and control architecture" to carry out global operations that cross over traditional regional combatant commands.[5] These requirements set the stage for modifications to the Unified Command structure that occurred in 2002 and 2003 (described below). According to the QDR, future military responses will require "rapid movement and integration of joint and combined forces in battlefield situations" as well as a coordination of communications systems, not only among various branches of the U.S. armed forces, but also "with government agencies and allies and friends."[6]

U.S. command and control systems must allow allies access to a common information picture, or to some portion of the depiction of a battlefield situation used by commanders, to maximize combined operations on the battlefield. The lessons of the 2003 Iraq War, however, will not be lost on military planners: if key allies do not allow U.S. forces to operate from their territory or fail to participate in coalition operations, does it make sense to provide them insights into the operational "picture?" U.S. C^2 thus faces a three-fold challenge. It must be capable of including allies, limiting information to allies, and carrying out unilateral long-range "global strikes" anywhere in the world from either the continental United States or forward-based forces.

The NPR further highlights new command and control requirements for the United States. It states a requirement to integrate nuclear and conventional forces to create a "strategic deterrent." This requirement suggests that nuclear command and control procedures and systems that currently are dedicated to maintaining the nuclear deterrent would somehow have to be integrated into existing conventional command and control and war planning to make this proposed nuclear-conventional strategic deterrent a reality. Furthermore, because the proliferation of weapons of mass destruction (WMD) will likely be a central security concern for the United States in the future, U.S. forces should have the ability to eliminate WMD stockpiles and related WMD facilities, and they could potentially use nuclear weapons (or a combination of conventional and nuclear weapons) for this purpose.[7] This will require an ability to respond rapidly to a changing peacetime or wartime intelligence picture.

The NPR emphasizes that the threat environment has become increasingly unpredictable since the end of the Cold War. The strategic deterrent no longer can be based on large, deliberately planned nuclear strikes, but will instead require planners to devise responses to rapidly evolving crises. The NPR therefore calls for a more flexible planning system that moves away from "deliberate planning," which prepares detailed war plans in advance to address anticipated contingencies, to "adaptive planning," which would allow for war plans to be generated quickly during crises.[8]

This transition to adaptive planning requires a more centralized C^3 structure. To underscore the necessity for such an integrated C^3 system, the NPR cites a study by the Federal Advisory Council (FAC), which was created by the secretary of defense to review all activities involved in nuclear weapons safety, security, control, and reliability. The FAC found that there was an urgent need to expand the military's command and control architecture to allow for a "true national command and control conferencing system."[9]

The NPR also notes that the effectiveness of the new triad depends on improved and integrated command and control, "exquisite" intelligence on the intentions and capabilities of adversaries, and the ability to flexibly and rapidly plan the employment of strike and defense forces.[10] These command and control systems will include expanded and improved communications links among decision makers, command centers, and operational forces, and they will allow authorized, combined, and effective use of offensive and defensive forces.[11] Strike options will require intricate planning, flexibility, and interface with decision makers during potential engagements. Command and control will become more complex and the supporting systems and platforms "will require augmentation, modernization, and replacement."[12] These will be very demanding objectives to meet.

CURRENT C^2 FOR GLOBAL OPERATIONS

Current C^2 systems were designed to operate in specific theaters of operation, with separate C^2 systems for the various legs of the old triad (air-, land-, and sea-based strategic weapons). Moreover, each regional combatant command (e.g., U.S. Pacific Command, U.S. Central Command, etc.) had a distinct and incompatible C^2 system.[13] Historically, the Army, Navy, and Air Force also have developed their own C^3 systems to meet their particular needs, and these systems are not always integrated and compatible. As a result, some requirements simply are not satisfied by current C^2 systems. In the old triad, for example, U.S. Strategic Command (USSTRATCOM) was charged with "planning, targeting, and wartime employment" of strategic nuclear forces, but it played little role in planning or carrying out conventional strikes.[14] Regional combatant commands were tasked with planning and, if necessary, executing tactical nuclear strikes within their respective theaters. USSTRATCOM would have provided support for the planning stage, and the authorization and launch codes for these weapons would still need to come from the president.[15] Effective command and control thus would have to bridge this operational and planning gap between USSTRATCOM and regional combat commanders. In addition, traditionally there has been a sharp distinction between nuclear and conventional weapons planning and employment in U.S. military doctrine. The NPR's call to integrate nuclear and conventional strategic weapons will force an end to this distinction.[16]

Other practical issues make it difficult to create a seamless command and control architecture for the new strategic deterrent. For example, there has never been an infrastructure in place for strategic missile defense as an emerging capability. Currently, each combatant command is responsible for missile defense within its own area of responsibility (AOR). USSTRATCOM now has a coordinating role, integrating all missile defense elements. Without a template to integrate disparate commands and operating procedures, debate about command responsibilities and architecture likely will be long and acrimonious. Currently, an attack on a global scale that crosses regional boundaries would precipitate significant C^2 difficulties. To be effective, new mechanisms and procedures to permit all the combatant commanders to have access to the same information in real time, as well as mechanisms for coordinating actions that span across traditional regional boundaries, must be devised to make the new strategic deterrent a reality.

Current plans call for using missile defense to bolster strategic deterrence; deterrence will no longer depend solely on offensive forces. U.S. Northern Command (USNORTHCOM) is tasked with the missile defense of North America. Beginning in late 2004, initial missile defenses are supposed to be guided by deliberate employment plans or rules of engagement that are coordinated with initial strike plans. But as defenses become more capable, it would be advantageous to be able to alter defense tactics to meet battle-field circumstances. Then senior decision makers could call for a change of tactics to protect a particularly important target, to conserve interceptor missiles, or to coordinate with counterforce operations. To make clear and effective tactical changes, civilian leaders and military commanders must have a clear picture of the unfolding offensive and defensive battle. They will require a planning system that can quickly modify tactics in the course of the engagement, and finally, they will need a communications system that allows decision makers to relay their decisions to the missile defense commands.

CURRENT STRATEGIC C³ SYSTEM

The current strategic C^3 system is designed to detect and launch intercontinental nuclear strikes using the Cold War triad. This system relies on a highly centralized structure for detecting, authenticating, and ordering these strikes. The data from all early-warning sensors is fed to Cheyenne Mountain, Colorado, which serves as the primary missile attack warning center for North American Aerospace Defense Command (NORAD) and USSTRATCOM. If the early-warning center at NORAD determines that an attack might be headed toward the United States or its allies, it notifies the commander-in-chief of NORAD (CINCNORAD) at nearby Peterson Air Force Base. If CINCNORAD assesses indicators of an attack as significant, he convenes a "threat assessment conference" with more senior personnel, such as the chairman of the Joint Chiefs of Staff.[17] If the threat persists, the final action is to convene a "missile attack conference," which brings in all senior personnel including the president to decide on U.S. options.[18] This assessment process transpires very rapidly—in the course of, perhaps, fifteen minutes.

According to the procedures, the president or his designated successor is the only person authorized to order the use of nuclear weapons. If the president decides to use nuclear weapons, he transmits the decision down the chain of command, through the secretary of defense, to the appropriate and specified regional combatant commanders.[19] The president then transmits the launch code after consulting the "football," which follows the president at all times. The football is a briefcase that contains authenticating codes which identify the launch command as emanating from the president, and options for launching U.S. nuclear weapons. If the president wanted to issue a launch command, he would gain access to the contents of the football after consulting a code card that he carries on his person.[20]

After the president makes the decision to employ nuclear weapons, this decision is relayed to USSTRATCOM, which passes the order to the U.S. alert forces. In the event that the underground USSTRATCOM center at Offutt Air Force Base, Nebraska, became inoperable, operational control of strategic forces would be transferred either to Mobile Consolidated Command Centers (MCCCs), consisting of a series of electrically shielded shelters mounted on semitrailers, or to the USSTRATCOM Airborne Command Post, which is ready to become airborne twenty-four hours a day.[21]

The Air Force and Navy provide intercontinental-range nuclear forces to USSTRATCOM and shorter-range nuclear strike aircraft and submarine-launched cruise missiles to the regional combatant commanders.[22] All nuclear weapons in the U.S. arsenal contain use-control devices, such as permissive action links or their equivalent, which require an authenticating code to be entered before the weapon can be used.[23]

The changes called for in the QDR and NPR raise significant questions about how the new C³ system will integrate the strategic nuclear and conventional forces into the existing chain of command. Will this rigid chain of command stay in place, or must it be modified if conventional forces are used in conjunction with nuclear ones to carry out strategic attacks? Will the ultimate authority for ordering nonnuclear strategic strikes still pass through the president? In any case, the nuclear weapon command chain is unlikely to be as separate and rigid as it was, if there is a closer integration of nuclear and conventional forces. Military planners will have to struggle with this issue as they move forward with the structural changes called for in the NPR.

ADDRESSING THE NEW C³ OBJECTIVES

The requirements outlined in the QDR and the NPR will place significant demands on U.S. C³ systems. DoD has made C³ modernization and unification one of its top priorities. Funding for these objectives has increased significantly in recent years, and such organizations such as the Office of the Secretary of Defense (OSD), the Assistant Secretary of Defense for Networks and Information Integration (ASD/NII), and USSTRATCOM are working to meet these new objectives.

Unified Command Plans and USSTRATCOM

On October 1, 2002, the United States implemented the 2002 Unified Command Plan (UCP), following the directions of the president. The subsequent UCP, Change 1 (UCP-1), created United States Northern Command, eliminated United States Space Command (USSPACECOM), and combined the missions of USSPACECOM with USSTRATCOM, thereby creating a new USSTRATCOM with greatly expanded responsibilities.[24]

The newly created Northern Command is now tasked with providing the military elements for supporting the defense of the U.S. homeland. It is the military organization responsible for defending against any future terrorist attacks on U.S. territory, as well as defending the United States from ballistic missile attacks. The unification of USSPACECOM and the old USSTRATCOM allows for the streamlining of strategic operations involving the use of outer space, including global missile defense, command and control systems, and Global Positioning System (GPS)-guided missiles.

Because USSPACECOM was critical in coordinating attacks with conventional weapons (by providing communications links and space-based intelligence, surveillance, and reconnaissance), the unification of USSPACECOM and USSTRATCOM will facilitate the integration of conventional and nuclear strike capabilities.[25]

On January 10, 2003, the president signed Change 2 to the Unified Command Plan (known as UCP-2). Under UCP-2, USSTRATCOM received four primary responsibilities: global missile defense; global strike; DoD information operations; and global command, control, communications, computers, intelligence, surveillance, and reconnaissance (C^4ISR).[26]

As part of its global strike responsibilities, USSTRATCOM will play a central role in planning and executing nuclear, conventional, and information operations worldwide.[27] As Admiral James O. Ellis, the commander of USSTRATCOM put it, USSTRATCOM's "objective is to provide the means to integrate, synchronize, coordinate, and convey information to support superior decision making and tasking at any level from the president to the front-line warfighter."[28] An effective C^3 system is essential for achieving this objective, and USSTRATCOM is the primary organization tasked with developing a C^3 system capable of carrying out the new U.S. strategic assignments. USSTRATCOM is working closely with several partners, including U.S. Joint Forces Command, the Defense Information Systems Agency (DISA), and the ASD/NII to craft a new C^3 system that will provide "improved information flow, rapid decision making, and dramatic improvements in the current U.S. bandwidth capability."[29] Because USSTRATCOM already has a command system with global reach, its current C^3 system will form the core of the new C^3 system that will be used for global operations, though significant expansion and improvement is required to provide a seamless command structure, especially with conventional forces.

Missile Defense Integration

Previous plans for missile defense called for a stand-alone system to defend the continental United States and regional defenses to protect allies and deployed U.S. forces. New operational plans call for a layered global missile defense system that can defend against a missile attack anywhere in the world and support tactical battlefield situations. Thus, "missile defense has evolved from an effort focused on mid-course intercept of ballistic missiles to an integrated, multilayered, cross-AOR approach."[30]

Although each regional combatant command is responsible for missile defense within its AOR, USSTRATCOM has been given responsibility for developing a global missile defense system capable of defeating a missile strike anywhere in the world. USSTRATCOM will serve as the primary advocate in the development of a worldwide missile defense operational architecture.[31] In meeting these missile defense objectives, USSTRATCOM must integrate its efforts with the combatant commands, particularly with

USNORTHCOM, which has the responsibility of defending the United States. Because the global missile defense system must defend U.S. forces and U.S. allies throughout the world, however, USSTRATCOM must integrate closely with all the combatant commands. A key element of global missile defense capability would be to provide detailed and effective tactical warning to national leaders and combatant commanders. USSTRATCOM will be one of the primary organizations providing that information.[32]

Communication Networks

The primary approach to emerging real-time global communications will be network-based. This system will allow all combatant commanders to access the same information, allow communication within and between commands, and allow allies access to relevant information. This network will need to be capable of transmitting large amounts of information. It also must be protected to prevent unauthorized access or attacks on the system.

Global Information Grid

A key element in the global communication network is the creation of a Global Information Grid (GIG) which "will provide all forces a seamless network to provide the uninterrupted exchange of information necessary to achieve decision superiority."[33] Because vast amounts of information necessarily will be transmitted extremely rapidly on this communications network, one of the primary challenges facing the military is how to create sufficient bandwidth to accommodate the transfer an ever-increasing flow of data. Indeed, the military is already reportedly encountering shortfalls in available bandwidth. According to some reports, the military had insufficient bandwidth to simultaneously fly all available Predator and Global Hawk unmanned aerial vehicles during Operation Enduring Freedom.[34] To implement the NPR, higher-capacity information and communications grids will have to be constructed.

To achieve this objective, USSTRATCOM is overseeing the development of Global Information Grid-Bandwidth Expansion (GIG-BE). According to Admiral Ellis, this program "is key to enabling the vision of situational awareness for the warfighter. GIG-BE is scheduled to provide a fiber connection to more than 100 sites by the end of FY05, providing much-needed wideband terrestrial connectivity. Once completed, GIG-BE will provide a robust Internet Protocol Network so that the war fighter can post and access information at multiple levels of classification."[35] According to DISA, a key partner in GIG-BE, this program will connect sites in the continental United States, as well as the Pacific and European theaters. In particular, it will "connect key intelligence, command, and operational locations with high-bandwidth capability over physically diverse routes, and the vast majority of these locations will be connected by a state-of-the-art optical mesh network design."[36]

Information Assurance

Ensuring security for computer and communications systems is essential for any modern military, but information assurance (IA) will be all the more critical in the new information system required by the U.S. military—particularly since the information systems are moving to a network-based approach. For this reason, the QDR establishes the operational goal of "assuring information in the face of attack and conducting effective information operations."[37]

To help identify and correct vulnerabilities throughout the defense complex, in 1998 DoD established the Information Assurance Vulnerability Management (IAVM) program. In conjunction with IAVM and DISA, USSTRATCOM is "working to improve [its] ability to automatically apply software patches across large networks, correct vulnerabilities identified through the IAVM process, and automatically patch compliance."[38]

As DoD transitions to the GIG system it will be faced with increased opportunities and challenges in the area of information assurance. Information will be less stratified and more generally accessible to critical decision makers, but this development presents unique challenges, particularly the prevention of unauthorized access. As Admiral Ellis put it in his 2004 congressional testimony,

> The warfighter of today accesses information by sifting through networks stratified by classification and membership. The GIG-BE will result in a more easily accessible network providing multi level security information to authorized users. Enforcing need-to-know while enabling need-to-share presents DoD IA personnel the challenge of moving from a defense-in-depth mindset to an IA-throughout approach.[39]

To secure the GIG-BE networks, the military is moving to adopt a new approach to network defense. Under the previous system, efforts were focused on defense-in-depth, with a layered defense to keep intruders from breaching information networks. In contrast, the GIG focuses on defense throughout the entire communication network. This GIG concept incorporates a model that recognizes that intrusions may occur and allows the network to remain functional even as an "infection" is cured.[40] This new approach will require an increased ability to detect, identify, and characterize the nature of attacks on the system, to formulate and coordinate effective responses to attacks on both communication software and hardware, and to execute rapidly appropriate and authorized responses to attack across a global infrastructure.[41]

Transformational Communications System

In his 2004 congressional testimony, Admiral Ellis also outlined DoD's efforts to create a Transformational Communications System. In his explanation of this new system, Ellis cited the "power to the edge" vision of John Stenbit, the former assistant secretary of defense for Networks and Information Integration, which calls for replacing "top-down operations with distributed operations—and [using] information technology to empower whomever is in need of a solution, regardless of where that individual is."[42] This new paradigm shifts power from the center (headquarters) to the edge (warfighters), by enabling the warfighters "to 'pull' from DoD, other U.S. agencies, and allied powers the information the warfighters determine they require to complete their mission."[43] As Ellis explained, "identity management must focus on end users, applications, and services. This will enable distributed computing between allied components using applications able to securely communicate with other applications."[44]

Creating this new management paradigm is an ambitious objective. It will require an expansion and integration of communications capabilities. In early fiscal year 2002, DoD initiated a Transformational Communications Study to "outline a vision for a joint integrated communications network that included both laser and radio frequency communication capabilities."[45] The study confirmed that the defense establishment needed to transform its communications architecture and "suggested that we now have a window of opportunity to provide an architectural framework for a compatible communications system across the Department of Defense and the intelligence community that could increase our capabilities by a factor of 10." The architecture itself would be a single, integrated communications network that utilizes satellite and fiber-optic capabilities[46] to increase "intersystem connectivity via optical crosslinks, greater reliance on ground fiber where possible, and the use of commercial assets as appropriate."[47]

To help implement the changes called for in the Transformational Communications Study, DoD created the Transformational Communications Office in September 2002 to coordinate, synchronize, and direct execution of the Transformational Communications Architecture. Its mission is "to assure that we have communications compatibility across the Department of Defense, the intelligence community, and NASA."[48] The Transformational Communications Architecture (TCA) is a joint effort with full involvement by the ASD/NII and DISA.[49] The office will "coordinate the acquisition [and] implementation of the various system elements of the architecture under the existing program offices, using established authorities and budgets," though each service or agency will remain responsible for managing its individual programs within the framework of the TCA.[50]

FUTURE CHALLENGES AND DIFFICULTIES

DoD is making progress in addressing several difficult objectives outlined by the QDR and NPR. Key transitions have been made, including the creation of USNORTHCOM, the elimination of USSPACECOM, and the establishment of a new USSTRATCOM that will serve as the centerpiece for C^2 support to the Unified Command. In many areas, the conceptual frameworks are in place for the significant work that lies ahead. There is little open-source information on how much technical, as opposed to organizational and conceptual, progress has been made in critical areas, so it is impossible at this moment to gauge how long it might take for planners to create new information networks.

As defense planners move forward, however, they will need to devise solutions to several important issues. First, planners must define the roles of the combatant commands and the role of USSTRATCOM in the overall command and control network. Second, policy makers must create an information and command system that allows the combatant commanders as well as U.S. allies to access information and command channels. Whatever system is devised, it also must provide security for information. Third, a compelling plan must be devised to integrate U.S. strategic nuclear forces with conventional forces. It is critical to clarify early on how the chain of authorization and command will work. Policy makers will have to determine if the new strategic deterrent will require the same system of authorization and use-control devices that were utilized by the old nuclear triad. Fourth, policy makers will have to devise a system to allow the global missile defense system to work in conjunction with regional combatant commands. It appears that a central role for USSTRATCOM will be to provide early-warning information about incoming missile attack, but it remains unclear exactly how missile defense command and control will eventually extend to U.S. conventional forces worldwide.

NOTES

The author would like to thank Steven Maaranen, Bradley Martin, Joseph Pilat, and the panelists at the Implementing the Nuclear Posture Review conference, September 2003, Monterey, Calif., for their comments and advice on this paper. The views expressed in this paper are the author's own.

1. Department of Defense, *Quadrennial Defense Review Report* September 30, 2001, 13–14 <www.defenselink.mil/pubs/qdr2001.pdf>. (Hereinafter referred to as QDR.).
2. Ibid., 11–16.
3. Department of Defense, *Dictionary of Military and Associated Terms*, Joint Publication (JC)-102, December 17, 2003 <www.dtic.mil/doctrine/jel/new_pubs/jp1_02.pdf>.
4. For a discussion of these active and passive defensive measures, see Kurt Guthe, *How Is the "New Triad" New?* (Washington, D.C.: Center for Strategic and Budgetary Assessments, 2002), 15–18, www.csbaonline.org/4Publications/Archive/R.20020729.Nuclear_Posture_Review/R.20020729.Nuclear_Posture_Review.pdf.
5. QDR, 33.
6. Ibid.
7. Because many WMD facilities throughout the world are contained in hardened, underground structures, new nuclear weapons may be required to eliminate these threats. U.S. intelligence networks estimate that there are more than 1,400 underground facilities throughout the world that are associated with WMD or their delivery vehicles (*Nuclear Posture Review*, 46). For a detailed study of this issue, see *Report to Congress on the Defeat of Hard and Deeply Buried Targets*, submitted by the secretary of defense in conjunction with the secretary of energy in

response to section 1044 of the Floyd D. Spence National Defense Authorization Act for the Year 2001, PL 106–398, July 2001. The unclassified content of the report can be found at <www.nukewatch.org/facts/nwd/HiRes_Report_to_Congress_on_the_Defeat.pdf>.

8. Department of Defense, *Nuclear Posture Review* January 8, 2002, foreword. The majority of *Nuclear Posture Review* remains classified, though the foreword to the report has been declassified and is available at <www.defenselink.mil/news/Jan2002/d20020109npr.pdf>. Much of the rest of the Nuclear Posture Review was leaked to the *New York Times* and is available at <www.globalsecurity.org/wmd/library/policy/dod/npr.htm>. References to the foreword of the NPR will be to the former source, while references to the actual report will be to the Globalsecurity.org website.

9. *Nuclear Posture Review*, 26.

10. Ibid., 29.

11. Guthe, *How Is the "New' Triad" New?* 3.

12. *Nuclear Posture Review*, 15.

13. The "combatant commanders" were previously referred to as "Commanders in Chief" (CINCs) of the various regions (e.g., CINC, U.S. Pacific Command, etc.), but in October 2002, Secretary of Defense Donald Rumsfeld announced that only the president would have the title of CINC and the other commanders (with the exception of the CINC of NORAD, a binational command) would be referred to as "combatant commanders." See Jim Garamone, " 'CINC' Is Sunk," *DefenseLink.mil* October 25, 2002 <www.defenselink.mil/news/Oct2002/n10252002_200210252.html>.

14. Guthe, *How Is the "New' Triad" New?* 32.

15. Ibid. There is some evidence that U.S. presidents, beginning with Dwight D. Eisenhower, delegated to key military commanders the authority to use nuclear weapons under certain circumstances. This "predelegation" of launch authority would enable the United States to respond with nuclear weapons if the president was unable to order their use in a timely manner (such as in the event of a surprise attack that "decapitated" the civilian command authority). For details on the predelegation of launch authority, see Nathan E. Busch, *No End in Sight: The Continuing Menace of Nuclear Proliferation* (Lexington, Ky.: University Press of Kentucky, 2004), ch. 2.

16. Admiral James O. Ellis, testimony before the Senate Armed Services Committee on the Nuclear Posture Review, 107th Congress, February 14, 2002, 6.

17. Senator Gary Hart and Senator Barry Goldwater, *Recent False Alerts from the Nation's Missile Attack Warning System*, U.S. House of Representatives, Committee on Armed Services, 96th Cong., 2nd session, October 9, 1980, 3.

18. Ibid., 5. For additional information on the integrated U.S. early-warning system, see "PAVE PAWS Radar System"; "North American Aerospace Defense Command," <www.spacecom.af.mil/norad/noradfs.htm>; TSgt. Pat McKenna, "The Border Guards: NORAD: The Eyes and Ears of North America," *Airman Magazine* 40, no. 1 (January 1996) <www.af.mil/news/airman/0196/border.htm>.

19. "Strategic Command Command Center," <www.stratcom.mil/factsheets/cmdctr.html>; Peter D. Feaver, *Guarding the Guardians: Civilian Control of Nuclear Weapons in the United States* (Ithaca: Cornell University Press, 1992), 30.

20. Feaver, *Guarding the Guardians*, 38.

21. "CINC Mobile Alternate Headquarters (CMAH)," Federation of American Scientists <http://www.fas.org/nuke/guide/usa/c3i/cmah.htm>; "Strategic Command Command Center."

22. Guthe, *How Is the "New' Triad" New?* 32.

23. For a more detailed discussion of the U.S. chain of command, authorization and use-control procedures, and launch procedures, see Busch, *No End in Sight*, chap. 2.

24. For details on some of these changes, see Donald H. Rumsfeld, Special Briefing on the Unified Command Plan, April 17, 2002 <www.defenselink.mil/news/Apr2002/t04172002_t0417sd.html>; General Richard B. Myers, U.S. Air Force Chairman of the Joint Chiefs of Staff, posture statement before the 108th Congress, House Armed Services Committee, February 5, 2003 <www.house.gov/hasc/openingstatementsandpressreleases/108thcongress/03-02-05myers.html>.

25. Guthe, *How Is the "New' Triad" New?* 33.

26. General Richard B. Myers, U.S. Air Force Chairman of the Joint Chiefs of Staff, posture statement before the 108th Congress, House Armed Services Committee, February 5, 2003 <www.house.gov/hasc/openingstatementsandpressreleases/108thcongress/03-02-05myers.html>.

27. Ibid.

28. Ibid.

29. Admiral James O. Ellis, statement before the Senate Armed Services Committee, Strategic Subcommittee on Command Posture and Space Issues, 108th Congress, March 12, 2003, 8.

30. Ibid., 10.

31. Ibid., 8.

32. Ibid., 10.

33. General Charles R. Holland, statement before the Senate Armed Services Committee, Emerging Threats and Capabilities Subcommittee, on the State of Special Operations Forces, March 12, 2002, 107th Cong., 23.

34. Greg Jaffe, "Military Feels Bandwidth Squeeze as The Satellite Industry Sputters," *The Wall Street Journal* April 10, 2002. For an excellent discussion of this "bandwidth gap," see Major David G. Erhard (USAF), "Standing in the Strategic Bandwidth Gap: A View of Military Communications in 2012," *Air and Space Power Chronicles* March 9, 2004 <www.airpower.maxwell.af.mil/airchronicles/cc/ehrhard.html>.

35. Admiral James O. Ellis, testimony before the Strategic Forces Subcommittee of the Senate Armed Services Committee on National Security Space Programs and Management in Review of the DoD Authorization Request for FY2005, 108th Congress, March 25, 2004, 9–10.

36. "GIG Bandwidth Expansion," Defense Information Systems Agency <www.disa.mil/main/gigbe.html>.

37. QDR, 30.

38. Ellis, 2004 Congressional Testimony, 10.

39. Ibid.

40. Ibid.

41. "Information Assurance," Defense Information Systems Agency <http://www.disa.mil/main/infoops.html>.

42. John P. Stenbit, cited in Ellis, 2004 Congressional testimony, 11.

43. John P. Stenbit, "Moving Power to the Edge," *CHIPS—The Department of the Navy Information Technology Magazine* Summer 2003 <www.chips.navy.mil/ archives/03_summer/web%20pages/stenbit.htm>.

44. Ellis, 2004 Congressional testimony, 11.

45. Peter Teets, Undersecretary of the Air Force, "Special Briefing on the Opening of the Transformational Communications Office," *Defenselink.mil* September 3, 2002 <www.defenselink.mil/news/Sep2002/t09042002_t03teets.html>. See also "Transformational Communications Study," *Globalsecurity.org* <http:// www.globalsecurity.org/space/systems/tcs.htm>.

46. Teets, "Special Briefing on the Opening of the Transformational Communications Office."

47. Teets, "Transformational Communications Office," *Globalsecurity.org* <www. globalsecurity.org/space/agency/tco.htm>.

48. Ibid.

49. "Transformational Communications Office Formed," press release, National Reconnaissance Office, September 3, 2002 <www.nro.gov/PressReleases/ prs_rel63.html>.

50. Teets, "Special Briefing on the Opening of the Transformational Communications Office."

9

INTELLIGENCE AND THE NPR

Charles Ball

The 2001 Nuclear Posture Review (NPR) elicited even more than the usual amount of *Sturm und Drang* associated with the public articulation of nuclear strategies and doctrines. A careful reading of the NPR, however, reveals that many of the inferences drawn from the Bush administration's new nuclear thinking reflect the predispositions of the interpreters rather than the intent of the authors. To be sure, the NPR recommends pursuing research on "improved nuclear earth penetrating weapons (EPWs) to counter the increased use by potential adversaries of hardened and deeply buried facilities, and warheads that reduce collateral damage."[1] Still, these modest recommendations constitute neither a radical departure from past U.S. nuclear practice nor the most significant aspect of the 2001 NPR. What truly distinguishes this NPR from earlier nuclear policy reviews is its espousal of a reduced reliance on nuclear weapons alone and its focus on the threat posed by weapons of mass destruction (WMD) that are proliferating to a number of state and possibly even non-state actors that are hostile to the United States.

The NPR explicitly states that in order to reduce reliance on nuclear weapons and to address concerns prompted by WMD proliferation, the United States will require significantly better intelligence capabilities than it currently possesses. Secretary of Defense Donald Rumsfeld stated in his introduction to the NPR that its success will require "exquisite intelligence."[2] The perceived requirement for intelligence of such an extraordinarily high caliber is a reflection of the extent to which the Bush administration believes that the geopolitical environment confronting the United States has been transformed in an extraordinary way. Indeed, the Bush administration believes that the threat of terrorists and rogue states armed with weapons of mass destruction "make today's security environment more complex and dangerous" than it was during the Cold War. According to President Bush, in this new security environment "intelligence—and how we use it—is our first line of defense against terrorists and the threat posed by hostile states."[3]

The primary reason that the Bush administration deems the new security environment to be so dangerous and complex is the specter of terrorist adversaries who are undeterrable. Emerging adversaries, while lacking the huge nuclear weapons arsenal of the Soviet Union, are in many respects more dangerous because, unlike the Soviet Union, they value the results they believe they can achieve through violence more than they value their own lives. Moreover, unlike the leaders of the Communist Party of the Soviet Union, who believed that history was on their side, U.S. policy makers now confront adversaries animated by an ideology that openly promises rewards in the hereafter for the perpetrators of terrorist attacks. The Bush administration has therefore concluded, "traditional concepts of deterrence will not work against a terrorist enemy whose avowed tactics are wanton destruction and the targeting of innocents; whose so-called soldiers seek martyrdom in death; and whose most potent protection is statelessness."[4]

Nor is the Bush administration sanguine about the deterrablity of rogue states. Implicitly ascribing a reduced measure of rationality—or an illogical decision calculus—to rogue-state adversaries, the Bush administration contends that "deterrence based on the threat of retaliation is less likely to work against leaders of rogue states more willing to take risks, gambling with the lives of their people, and the wealth of their nations."[5] Even if we were to ascribe higher levels of rationality and caution to the decision makers in rogue regimes, their possession of weapons of mass destruction is deemed by the Bush administration to confer a measure of power that, coupled with their aggressive intentions, could redound to the profound strategic disfavor of the United States.

Should adversary regimes acquire weapons of mass destruction, it could significantly complicate the ability of the United States to come to the aid of allies threatened by rogue regimes. The United States may be deterred from confronting the conventional or nuclear aggression of rogue states, fearing such action risks having weapons of mass destruction used against U.S. forces or the homeland. The Bush administration explicitly states that "[f]or rogue states these weapons are tools of intimidation and military aggression against their neighbors. These weapons may also allow these states to attempt to blackmail the United States and our allies to prevent us from deterring or repelling the aggressive behavior of rogue states."[6]

This conclusion indicates the extent to which the Bush administration fears not only the potential undeterrability of rogue regimes but, even more significantly, their ability to deter the United States from defending its allies and its interests because U.S. officials would fear attack from opponents' nuclear weapons should they decide to respond to some provocation.

Even relatively modest arsenals in the hands of these regimes raise the dilemma that pervaded most of the Cold War: how to project American power in defense of its interests or allied interests under circumstances in which the exercise of that power could expose the U.S. homeland or its forces to devastating attack by weapons of mass destruction. This problem is further complicated by the potential relationship between rogue states and terrorists. There is a possibility that state actors might employ WMD against the United States through terrorist affiliates, reducing the likelihood of certain traceability and thereby greatly complicating the likelihood or perceived international legitimacy of ensuing U.S. retaliation. The Bush administration believes the confluence of terrorism, WMD, and rogue states has created radically new circumstances that are not safely addressed by reliance on deterrence alone. In this strategic setting, exquisite intelligence may be just as important.

INTELLIGENCE: THE NEED TO PREVENT PROLIFERATION

Rather than react to the myriad dilemmas posed by rogue states' possession of WMD, the Bush administration clearly seeks to prevent such states from acquiring weapons of mass destruction in the first place. This desire to prevent proliferation constitutes the crux of the new strategy, leading to the unique and significant demands placed on U.S. intelligence. While the Bush administration's strategy for dealing with the rogue states has been dubbed preemptive, it is in fact preventive: "We must be prepared to stop rogue states and their terrorist clients before they are able to threaten or use weapons of mass destruction against the United States and our allies and friends. Our response must take full advantage of modern technologies . . . and increased emphasis on intelligence collection and analysis."[7] Or as President Bush remarked, "History will judge harshly those who saw this coming danger but failed to act. In the new world we have entered, the only path to peace and security is the path of action."[8]

This approach goes far beyond the traditional conception of preemption, in which states attack other states upon receiving information that an attack is imminent. The Bush administration views the mere possession of WMD by hostile regimes as a dire threat. Accordingly, the Bush administration has suggested that the traditional concept of imminent threat, which historically was used to justify preemptive measures, be transformed to meet the implications of technologies not contemplated when the doctrine of imminent threat was first formulated: "We must adapt the concept of imminent threat to the capabilities and objectives of today's adversaries."[9]

Defeating the objectives of proliferant countries logically leads the United States and its allies to rely on preventing these states from acquiring the materials, technologies, and know-how necessary to produce weapons of mass destruction. The administration is therefore intent on augmenting the ability of the United States to interdict the transfer of weapons-related material or precursors. It has implemented major initiatives toward this end, including the Proliferation Security Initiative (PSI), which has already contributed significantly to interdicting WMD trafficking.

The type of intelligence required to execute such an ambitious undertaking as PSI will require a far greater appreciation of the transnational nature of the proliferation threat. As demonstrated by the case of A. Q. Khan, the potential for transnational networks to bypass much of the research and development that proliferants previously pursued raises the real specter that America's enemies may purchase "turnkey" WMD production facilities, if not the weapons themselves.[10] Trade in this deadly contraband is apparently escaping control of state actors as criminal entrepreneurs traffic in chemical, biological, and nuclear weapons for profit.

To combat this danger, the U.S. intelligence community must develop a far more sophisticated understanding of how seemingly benign technologies apply to WMD production and what procurement networks supply these dual use technologies. Given the difficulty of tracking equipment and material once they have left their manufacturing sites, as well as the difficulty of tracing the front companies, it will be important to provide decision makers with better intelligence regarding where some of these technologies are being manufactured so that they have the option to disrupt shipments before they leave the manufacturing site.

The authors of the NPR were cognizant of the shortcoming of U.S. intelligence in the WMD realm: "Significant capability shortfalls currently exist in: finding and tracking mobile and re-locatable targets and WMD sites and in locating, identifying, and characterizing hard and deeply buried targets (HDBTs); [and] providing intelligence support to Information Operations and federated intelligence operations."[11] This step will require enhancements in U.S. human intelligence (HUMINT), signals intelligence (SIGINT), and measurement intelligence (MASINT).

The Central Intelligence Agency's Directorate of Operations has yet to recover from the personnel cuts and restrictions on its HUMINT capabilities that were implemented in the late 1970s. While recent years have seen an increased appreciation for the indispensability of HUMINT, as former CIA Director George Tenet recently stated in Congressional testimony, it will take at least five more years to bring U.S. HUMINT capabilities to a point where they can support policy makers and military planners, especially in the realm of tracking key proliferation targets. Essential to achieving "exquisite" human intelligence is a recognition that U.S. agencies must take a long-term approach to the recruitment of human assets, a willingness to utilize fully the vast émigré community in the United States, and a sustained and significant increase in the Directorate of Operations budget. The intelligence community must also recognize that the type of HUMINT required is changing. While it remains vital to understand the plans, motivations, and strategies of U.S. adversaries' leadership, what was previously often seen as lower level, tactical HUMINT now must be regarded as information of strategic importance.

While in the past the main threats to the United States emanated from large-scale, overt deployments by large states that were relatively risk-averse, U.S. policy makers now confront small-scale, covert (yet highly lethal) deployments by smaller states and potentially by non-state actors. Whereas the threat was more easily observed in the past—it was comprised mainly of vast fields of intercontinental ballistic missiles (ICBMs) and large fleets of submarine launched ballistic missiles (SLBMs)—intelligence analysts now must be more concerned with WMD production that is being concealed underground or in dual-use facilities. Moreover, it is these very capabilities that, though modest by comparison to the Soviet nuclear weapons arsenal, are in possession of leaders who are less risk-averse or who may transfer these weapons to terrorists. The terrorist or criminal threat that was previously regarded as a tactical problem is now strategic.

WHAT'S MISSING FROM THE INTELLIGENCE PICTURE?

A major impediment to achieving the objectives outlined by the NPR is that the United States currently lacks the ability to conduct around-the-clock collection and surveillance of suspect areas. The U.S. intelligence community is overly reliant on space-based satellite collection capabilities that operate in known ephemera, leading to significant gaps in its coverage as proliferant countries (and other actors) conduct activities when they know the United States cannot watch them. Most of the United States' airborne collection assets are vulnerable to enemy air defenses and lack the ability to provide persistent and sufficiently intrusive coverage of suspect activity. Thus while space-based and aerial collection and surveillance assets will continue to play a vital role, they must be supplemented by other means of collection in order to realize their true potential.[12] These space-based assets need to be "cued" by other types of intelligence sources so they can focus at the right time on targets of greatest interest.

The United States must accelerate development of ground-based sensors that can be placed close to suspicious targets. There are many revealing signatures that can only be collected from short distances. The intelligence community can glean significant insights into WMD activities by more fully utilizing the ability to analyze small traces of biological material, chemicals, and radionucliedes.[13] Samples often reveal the presence of materials whose only known use is in the production of weapons of mass destruction. Usually, the ability to collect such samples requires getting closer to suspect sites than can be achieved by satellites or aircraft. Thus, the ability to deploy sensors covertly and retrieve the data gleaned in a timely and covert manner is the heart of the intelligence collection challenge when it comes to preventing the spread of chemical, biological, and nuclear weapons. Unattended ground sensors (UGS) are ideally suited for such missions, and it is vital that this technology be pursued to its fullest because it offers the intelligence community the best hope of obtaining "close-in" data.[14]

In addition to their ability to glean MASINT, UGS can contain a variety of transducers designed to detect "acoustic, seismic, radio-frequency" signatures. These sensors can be deployed by unmanned aerial vehicles (UAVs). Today, UAVs have enough on-board data processing capability to require only low-bandwidth transmission rates to supply partially analyzed data to intelligence agencies. Cellular telephone technology also can permit clusters of UGSs to be networked, providing wide coverage of suspicious areas. If information from multiple UGS networks is combined and compared with data from other parts of the intelligence architecture, the intelligence community can better avoid false positives from its remote and robotic sensor systems.

Much also can be gleaned at further distances from effluents escaping from smokestacks. Specialists can interrogate such effluents with lasers and then analyze what is "backscattered" to reveal information about the composition of the plume and thus the activities underway within a suspicious facility.[15] Tagging is another promising technology that can greatly enhance the intelligence community's ability to ascertain where WMD production may be underway at suspicious sites and to track WMD (and other objects) after they have left production facilities. Tagging involves the covert emplacement of identifying features, transmitters, or chemical markers on objects destined for WMD laboratories or production facilities, and then remotely monitoring the tag. While the tagging of actual chemical, biological, or nuclear weapons warheads or bombs is difficult (though not impossible), tagging the equipment or transportation vehicles associated with these weapons is a more realistic option for special operations forces or CIA operatives. If pursued with sufficient energy, tagging technologies could enable the intelligence community to begin solving one of the most vexing problems it confronts: determining where actual weaponized agent or nuclear weapons are stored or transported.

Improvements in intelligence collection and surveillance will enable the United States to reduce its reliance on nuclear weapons. "Accurate and timely targeting information," according to the NPR, "can increase both the lethality of strike capabilities and the possibilities for nonnuclear strike capabilities to substitute for nuclear weapons."[16] Moreover, detailed intelligence about WMD production facilities and other key targets could enable the United States to decrease its reliance on the kinetic option altogether (whether nuclear or conventional). The authors of the NPR fully appreciate this possibility and devote significant attention to the increasingly important arena of information operations (IO) and the extent to which these operations depend on excellent intelligence: "Information [o]perations targeting, weaponeering, and execution requires intelligence collection of finer granularity and depth than is currently available. The intelligence community lacks adequate data on most adversary local area networks and other command and control systems. Additionally, there is limited analytical capability to exploit these networks using IO tools."[17]

To facilitate information operations, the intelligence community will have to exploit the revolution underway in close-in signals intelligence. It will have to develop ways to exploit cell phones, laptop computers, local area networks, and other information infrastructure so that targeted WMD programs can be penetrated.[18] Gaining access to these networks is clearly essential to potential IO missions. However, without detailed knowledge of operating systems within research facilities or production plants, the intelligence community's ability to exploit the access gained through this "revolution" in close-in-signals intelligence will be severely limited. An enhanced ability to understand and characterize how in-house operating systems are used is thus critically important to commanders who wish to make full use of the promise of IO actionable intelligence.

To exploit the powerful collection capabilities offered by close-in emplacement of sensors (whether for nuclear, conventional, or IO targeting), operators and analysts must be sure that they are correctly cued by other intelligence such as HUMINT. The proper exploitation of HUMINT and strategic SIGINT dramatically increases the likelihood of the intelligence community determining where suspicious activities may be occurring—activities that, in turn, warrant deployment of the type of intrusive, close-in collection that will provide the required granularity to identify what is taking place within closed or clandestine facilities. To realize the full promise of such sensors, however, they will have to be integrated into a system that includes the gamut of collection capabilities from space-based, airborne, and ground-based sensors. Only through this type of integration can the full potential of each sensor tier be exploited fully.

This systems and analytic integration necessitates a far more concentrated effort to combine databases, cue existing assets correctly, and mine already collected data. According to the Defense Science Board, "crosscutting signal processing and data mining algorithm initiatives across the various intelligence programs are essential to implement effectively the pull of 'knowledge' from 'data.' "[19] This vertical and horizontal integration will help break down the traditional stovepipes, enabling all-source intelligence to be collected and, more importantly, analyzed to form a coherent whole that fully exploits the synergies that can be achieved by all-source analysis. All of this will require better tools for exploiting new and existing data and doing as much real-time analysis as possible.

To achieve these goals, the current task, process, exploit, and disseminate (TPED) system must be revamped. At present, it cannot track the volume of data that even the current surveillance systems provide. It also cannot task and retask sensors quickly enough to prosecute time-sensitive targets.[20] Unless the shortcomings of this system are addressed, the intelligence community will be unable to exploit sensor improvements or to provide operationally useful intelligence to support the strategic strike decision loop.

INTELLIGENCE AND TRADITIONAL THREATS

While the NPR gives far greater attention to the threats posed by the proliferation of WMD than past nuclear posture reviews, these are by no means the only threats that it identifies as confronting the United States. Within the context of shifting from the "threat-based approach of the Cold War" to a "capabilities-based approach" in dealing with the nuclear weapons arsenal of Russia, the NPR states: "Russia's nuclear forces and programs, nevertheless, remain a concern. Russia faces many strategic problems around its periphery and its future course cannot be charted with certainty. U.S. planning must take this into account." The NPR also highlights concerns about China, stating: "Due to the combination of China's still developing strategic objectives and its ongoing modernization of its nuclear and non-nuclear forces, China is a country that could be involved in an immediate or potential contingency."[21]

Both Russia and China have expressed opposition to U.S. deployment of ballistic missile defenses (BMD), and both states evidence a desire to develop countermeasures to overcome U.S. defenses. Because the NPR explicitly states that missile defenses constitute an important component of the new triad that will permit a reduced reliance on nuclear weapons, the U.S. intelligence community must train significant collection assets on the type and extent of countermeasures that Russia and China might develop or deploy to overcome U.S. BMD. Such intelligence is particularly important in view of the likelihood that Russia and China could share the fruits of their countermeasures research with the rogue state adversaries of the United States.

While Russia's own BMD efforts appear to have waned in conjunction with its other defense-related activities, its BMD research continues. It would be prudent for the United States to devote significant assets toward understanding Russia's progress in BMD research. Significant uncertainties also remain about the extent of Russia's strategic nuclear programs, manifested most prominently in the enduring mystery surrounding activities at Yamata Mountain, for which Russia has yet to offer convincing explanations. Yamata Mountain has been the subject of extensive media speculation. Most commentators believe that this vast underground facility was built into the side of a mountain for some "strategic purpose." However, while speculation has centered on nuclear weapons, ICBMs, and new types of weapons, neither the Boris Yeltsin nor Vladimir Putin administrations have been willing to reveal the nature or scope of the activities that are occurring there.

Indeed, guarding against technological surprises that we may currently have difficulty envisaging remains one of the most important—and most neglected—tasks of the U.S. intelligence community. These problems most properly fall under the category of the proverbial unknown unknowns. Yet given the enormous importance of ensuring the credibility of the U.S. nuclear deterrent, the intelligence community must remain on guard against the tendency to think that U.S. offensive delivery systems will retain their penetrability in perpetuity. Indeed, the United States has developed a limited BMD capability that is likely to grow in capability, but it is regarded, particularly by China, as at least partly directed against potential adversaries' ability to deliver nuclear weapons against the United States. The intelligence community also should assume that China and other countries will one day be capable of mounting a ballistic missile defense. How they propose to do this and whether they will use means different from what we use is a topic that should be of the highest interest to the U.S. intelligence analysts, even if these developments are far off in the future. While analysts should plan for surprise, they should nevertheless take precautions to avoid it, particularly when surprise can have such severe consequences for U.S. security as the undermining of U.S. nuclear credibility. Obviously, the sooner the United States can discover its adversaries' plans the more quickly it can take appropriate countermeasures, a salient consideration given the large lead times required to develop new delivery systems.

Not only should the intelligence community be more concerned with potential technological breakthroughs that render delivery systems obsolete, but it also should guard against complacency regarding the ability of U.S. nuclear-armed ballistic missile submarines (SSBNs) to remain relatively undetectable. The majority of U.S. nuclear weapons are deployed on submarines, and they constitute an even greater percentage of warheads available for rapid launch. As U.S. nuclear forces are drawn down, the total number of U.S. SSBNs is being reduced to fourteen, and at any given time only about half of them are at sea. This represents a relatively small target set. In the future, new ways to detect and destroy submarines that do not rely on traditional naval units may be possible. For instance, very long-range, "smart" torpedoes could be developed with breakthrough detection capabilities that would place the U.S. SSBN force at risk. Moreover, China is embarking on a long-term program to develop a more formidable submarine force, a project that might provide the technological wherewithal to create a more capable, blue ocean force. Thus, if U.S. adversaries were to achieve breakthroughs in the techniques and technologies for discovering the U.S. submarine force, the strategic implications would be significant. To conduct this type of strategic anti submarine warfare campaign would be extraordinarily challenging, but potential adversaries have a strong incentive to use novel or asymmetric methods to neutralize the U.S. submarine-based deterrent. The potential significance of such a discovery not only increases the incentive to pursue such a research program, but it should also increase the U.S. intelligence community's effort to detect high-payoff breakthroughs that can place U.S. strategic assets at risk.

DENIAL AND DECEPTION

To fulfill the intelligence requirements generated by the NPR, increased emphasis must be placed on overcoming sophisticated efforts at denial and deception practiced by U.S. adversaries. Over time, rogue states and other targets of U.S. intelligence collection have become increasingly knowledgeable about the collection methods employed by the intelligence community. This knowledge has in turn greatly enhanced their ability to frustrate U.S. collection efforts.

While the intelligence community already recognizes the problems created by denial and deception, far more needs to be done to take into account an opponent's ability to prevent key data and information from reaching analysts or misdirecting their attention along unproductive pathways. Successful denial efforts by U.S. adversaries tend to limit the information available to the intelligence community, which in turn leads to a tendency to place relatively greater emphasis on the scant intelligence information that is collected. Yet, a reduction in available sources of information renders the United States more vulnerable to deception because the targeted country or entity surmises that analysts are gleaning little and are thus perhaps overly eager for any information that they can obtain. This situation creates an opportunity for the release of misinformation that the intelligence community is less able to verify using other sources (because they may not exist). This problem is particularly acute where little information is available on an issue or facility of vital significance to U.S. policy makers or military planners. Under these circumstances, the tendency is to rely on the information that is available and to downplay the likelihood that this information is false.

While the pitfalls of denial and deception are well understood by the intelligence community, more can be done to integrate this knowledge into the day-to-day work of analysts. Institutional checks and balances also can be developed to increase the likelihood that efforts at denial and deception do not succeed. To avoid denial and deception, an environment within the intelligence community must be fostered to encourage analysts, when appropriate, to tell policy makers and planners "We simply don't know," or "Our level of knowledge is such that it would be imprudent to even speculate on this question." This option is not always possible or desirable, given the need in certain operational situations to provide the best assessment almost irrespective of one's level of confidence in the information. Nevertheless, a more systematic approach to denial and deception must be incorporated into intelligence assessments of chemical, biological, and nuclear proliferation.

CONCLUSION

When Secretary of Defense Rumsfeld articulated the need for exquisite intelligence in the introduction to the NPR, he was giving voice to the conviction that the new security environment confronting the United States, characterized by the dangerous union of radicalism and technology, presents unique dangers. The widely available means of producing chemical and biological weapons, coupled with actors imbued with suicidal hatred of the United States, means that the United States faces a high likelihood of suffering a WMD attack. If the U.S. intelligence community fails to stop even a small percentage of plots to use WMD against the United States, the consequences could be catastrophic. Ergo, the need for exquisite intelligence.

It is tempting to conclude, therefore—and it may in fact be correct to assume—that the requirements for intelligence of this fidelity will prove to be sufficiently difficult to obtain that policy makers will conclude that it cannot be done, thereby reinforcing the belief that the mere existence of regimes with potential WMD capabilities and ties with terrorists poses a threat so inherently dangerous that it constitutes an immediate challenge to U.S. security. This insight provides the most powerful impetus for the Bush administration's doctrine of preemption.

NOTES

The views expressed in this chapter are the author's own and do not necessarily reflect the official position of Lawrence Livermore National Laboratory, the Department of Energy, or the United States government.

1. Nuclear Posture Review January 8, 2002, 11 (all page references according to original indicated in excerpts posted at <www.globalsecurity.org/wmd/library/policy/did/npr.htm>), henceforth referred to as "NPR excerpts".
2. Ibid., 16–17.
3. Ibid., 30.
4. *The National Security Strategy of the United States of America* September 2002, 15 <www.whitehouse.gov/nsc/nss.pdf>.
5. Ibid., 15.
6. Ibid., 15.
7. Ibid., 14.
8. Ibid., introduction.
9. Ibid., 15.
10. A. Q. Khan, the father of the Pakistani nuclear bomb, was pardoned in 2004 by Pakistan's President Musharraf after admitting that he had been trading nuclear secrets, some stolen from European sources, to Libya, Iran, and North Korea for fifteen years.
11. NPR excerpts, 28.
12. U.S. Department of Defense, *Report of the Defense Science Board on Future Strategic Strike Forces*, February 2004, 3–2 <http://www.acq.osd.mil/dsb/fssf.pdf>.
13. "Overhauling Counterproliferation," statement of Ashton B. Carter before the Committee on Foreign Relations, United States Senate, March 10, 2004 <http://foreign.senate.gov/testimony/2004/CarterTestimony040310.pdf>.
14. Ibid.
15. Ibid.
16. *NPR* excerpts, 15.
17. Ibid., 28.
18. Carter testimony.
19. *Defense Science Board Study*, 3–3.
20. Ibid., 3–4.
21. *NPR* excerpts, 5.

10

The New Strategic Framework, the New Strategic Triad, and the Strategic Military Services

James M. Smith

All organizations adapt to changes in their particular operating or task environment. Often the environmental changes are evolutionary, and the resulting process of organizational change can be limited to adaptation and accommodation. However, fundamental—even revolutionary—changes in the environment demand appropriately fundamental changes in the organizations that carry out operations in the new threat environment. This situation today presents itself to the U.S. military services that are tasked with preparing and presenting forces and systems—strategic capabilities—to realize the objectives outlined in the 2001 Nuclear Posture Review (NPR). Chief among these objectives is making the new strategic triad a reality.

This chapter addresses the impacts and implications of the changed U.S. strategic policy and posture on the military services charged to carry out these changes. It begins with a brief overview of the military services as unique organizations and how they adapt to change. This theoretical discussion is followed by an equally brief explanation of why and how the dictates of the NPR created significant impetus toward fundamental organizational change. Finally, the chapter describes several specific implementation issues, along with recommended actions to help the services adapt to the new threat and operational environment that the NPR describes.

Strategic Culture and Cohesion in the Military Services

Military organizations, which traditionally correspond to the military services in the United States, develop their core cultural essence around their central, defining operational mission sets. Those service members with the most critical roles in carrying out the central missions define their service's "battlespace" in terms of these mission sets. They exercise control over their respective services and their Title 10 "organize, train, and equip" functions to further the accomplishment of these mission sets. They also manage the service systems (personnel, acquisition, resourcing) to institutionalize excellence in operations within their battlespace and in carrying out these mission sets.[1]

To the extent that there is uniformity and cohesion across the mission sets, each service also exhibits cohesion and uniformity in its purpose and culture. Members share a sense of mission and operational essence. Services faced with a complex battlespace—a large and diverse universe of mission sets—develop subcultures around each relatively distinct mission segment. The subcultures then display their own sense of essence and cohesion, develop their own leadership and professional competence, and even compete with other subcultures within their service for status, resources, and control of the overall organization.

The relative cohesion of the service mission sets and the singularity of focus of its operational essence go far in explaining the organization's institutional behavior. Services compete with one another for both budget share and mission preeminence, with the hardest fights reserved for mission competition. But the same conflicts also take place within each service—among the subcultures representing diverse mission elements—before it can take its resulting priorities to the joint table. The relative unanimity of the service's position coming out of this internal competition influences its ability to present a united front and compete in the joint arena.

In reaching this internal consensus, however, services undervalue what they see as peripheral mission sets. They seek to marginalize or even expel noncore mission elements that are believed to reduce resourcing of and attention to the central, core mission elements. This internal and joint competition can be assessed as functional, in that it creates incentives to excel through competition. But it can also be seen as dysfunctional and divisive, with very negative consequences for overall mission accomplishment. In some cases, internal, bureaucratic "warfare" can take precedence over preparations to meet foreign adversaries on the battlefield.

Concern about mission accomplishment is most often associated with the processes of organizational change beyond simple adaptation and accommodation. Major changes in either the task environment—the focal point, scope, and nature of the battlespace itself—or in operational direction dictated by political oversight can demand fundamental transformation of the organization. Military organizational change of this magnitude involves a multistage process: recognition of the changed environment that makes transformation imperative; formulation of a revised operational strategy to fit the new environment; modification of the organizational structure around the new tasks and priorities; and institutionalization of the change in terms of transformed organizational culture and performance.[2] Although proponents of "transformation" often highlight the need to adopt and utilize new weaponry, the real transformational process involves the need to break down old cultures and organizations and to create new institutions that can capitalize on the advances offered by new technologies.

THE CHANGING STRATEGIC CONTEXT OF UNITED STATES DEFENSE POLICY

For the U.S. military services that retain nuclear weapons responsibilities, the changed environmental imperatives and strategic concepts that have slowly emerged in the aftermath of the Cold War were formalized in the new strategic framework outlined in the NPR. The new strategic triad reflects the strategic guidance and organizational transformation called for by the NPR. These new strategic tasks create several imperatives that are pushing the military services to accelerate an already painful process of transformation.

New Strategic Framework

The extent of the fundamental change outlined by the NPR is reflected in the new strategic framework that underlies U.S. nuclear policy. The Cold War strategic framework serves as a point of comparison to underscore the change called for by the NPR.

The Cold War was characterized by a single strategic threat—the Soviet Union and its strategic nuclear arsenal. Key to this relationship, from the United States' point of view, was that even though the Soviet Union was an adversary, it came to be seen as fairly reasonable and rational within an acceptable set of strategic parameters. The Soviets also were knowledgeable about weapons, strategy, and arms control, and this common experience lent a certain degree of predictability to U.S.-Soviet strategic relations. All of these factors, as they became generally accepted within the U.S. strategic community, meant that the United States could trust to some extent Soviet acceptance of American concepts of deterrent postures and policies. Even though U.S. strategic offensive forces remained capable and vigilant, buttressing any diplomatic initiatives, the United States focused its policy on containing and deterring the Soviets. These were coercive rather than brute-force objectives.

Thus, the central military dimension of Cold War U.S. policy was to maintain and present a credible offensive nuclear posture to ensure unacceptable nuclear retaliation in the face of certain defensive impotence. This force structure and employment policy was supplemented by significant diplomatic efforts to involve the Soviets in multilateral nonproliferation initiatives and bilateral arms control to bound the nuclear threat within the "comfort zone" created by the deterring and containing military posture. The United States also extended this comfort zone from North America to key European allies and Japan, placing them under the U.S. nuclear deterrent umbrella. It seems somehow illogical, but maintaining this relatively stable and manageable "balance of terror" became an accepted role for U.S. strategic forces, and any departure from it could (and did, with the end of the Cold War) produce discomfort. As a result, policy, force structure, and institutions that were involved in maintaining nuclear deterrence were slow and somewhat reluctant to accept the imperative to change.

The new strategic framework for the post–Cold War era is virtually the polar opposite of the mature Cold War framework (see table 10.1). First, the successor state to the Soviet Union is now seen as a potential partner, not as an enemy, and U.S.-Russian relations now focus on cooperation and competition, not conflict. The new threat is not unitary, but lies in the uncertainty of the "new world disorder." No longer bounded by great-power strategic restraints, the world's developing regions today are home to states with aspirations of regional supremacy—some of which seek strategic weapons capabilities to further this aim. These regions also include failed and failing states, circumstances that spawn chaos, warlordism, and extreme disorder. This environment, too, is conducive to strategic weapons proliferation by aspiring factions of non-state groups that utilize areas of disorder for sanctuary and support. These actors enjoy a world situation ripe with assets and opportunities for proliferation; they are anything but "rational" within a Western perspective and are, therefore, not wholly predictable in terms of their acceptance of U.S. policy initiatives. They may not be deterrable when faced with traditional and accepted military postures and policies.

This uncertainty, especially when coupled with vehement anti-Western or anti-American rhetoric and action, has caused U.S. officials to shift their focus away from concepts of containment or deterrence to an imperative to disarm strategic threats. If disarmament fails, they also are increasingly prepared to defeat regimes and groups arming with weapons of mass destruction. This readiness includes the use of preemptive military means if there is a perceived threat of opponents contemplating the use of nuclear, chemical, or biological weapons. Cooperative diplomatic approaches are seen as both hopeless and inappropriate in the face of the threats posed by rogue regimes or non-state actors armed with weapons of mass destruction. America's

Table 10.1 The new strategic framework

	Cold War strategic framework	New strategic framework
Threat	USSR	Proliferant states, failed/failing states, and non-states
	reasonable, rational, informed predictable deterrable	different, uncertain rationality unpredictable? undeterrable?
Strategic focus	Contain/deter	Disarm/prevent/preempt Deter/defeat/dissuade/assure
Diplomatic imperatives	Arms control, Nonproliferation	Counterproliferation (active and passive), prevention/preemption
Military imperatives	Credible nuclear offense (defense uncertain)	Effective strategic offense and defense (deterrence uncertain)
Allies	U.S. nuclear umbrella	Theater missile defense

policy focus has shifted to creating credible counterproliferation and strategic defenses, which are now seen as possible with the smaller scale of the strategic threat, as compared to the Cold War and the threat created by the Soviet nuclear arsenal.

During the Cold War, deterrence seemed certain and defense was impractical. Today, the opposite view now dominates official thinking in Washington. Without a sure and trusted deterrent umbrella, the United States seeks allied cooperation in this more active counterproliferation stance, offering strategic defenses in lieu of deterrent umbrellas. The goals of this turn to strategic defenses are to deter where possible and decisively defeat (perhaps preemptively) where necessary. U.S. policy makers also hope to dissuade future potential proliferants and adversaries from challenging the United States in either the military or diplomatic realm. They also aim to assure allies about U.S. capabilities, making cooperative action increasingly likely in the future. This fundamentally different strategic environment demands significant organizational change within the U.S. strategic posture.

New Strategic Triad

Changes in the strategic environment are reflected in the NPR guidance on creating a new strategic triad. The old strategic triad of the Cold War consisted of a three-legged mix of strategic offensive weapons: manned bombers, land-based intercontinental ballistic missiles, and submarine launched ballistic missiles. Each of these systems brought distinct advantages to the overall capability of the U.S. strategic deterrent in terms of survivability, accuracy, flexibility, and responsiveness. While these nuclear offensive forces were supplemented by a significant conventional force structure and by theater nuclear capabilities, the strategic force was distinct in terms of organization, planning, command and control, and operations. The United States had a dual military structure: one for its nuclear/strategic arsenal and one for its conventional forces. Nuclear forces were postured around the direct, physical effects of their weapons—nuclear strike—with the ultimate goal of achieving the psychological effect of deterrence while posing a credible physical threat of catastrophic destruction. These offensive nuclear forces were maintained on alert and operated under a sophisticated and integrated strategic warning and command and control structure. The planning for their employment was based on a sustained, deliberate planning and target selection and validation process.

While the old strategic triad was a single-purpose, single-threat deterrent force, the NPR's new strategic triad is designed to create a wide array of both discrete and complementary strategic effects against a range of threats and targets. As shown in table 10.2, the new strategic triad is made up of offensive global strike capabilities (including all three legs of the old nuclear strategic triad, and nonnuclear precision strike forces), active and passive defenses, and a defense infrastructure to sustain and advance U.S. strategic capabilities. The new strategic triad proceeds from the belief that defenses enhance and

Table 10.2 The new strategic triad

	Cold War strategic posture	New strategic triad posture
Force structure	Strategic nuclear offense (old triad) Theater nuclear offense Conventional offense (largely distinct)	Strategic nuclear offense (old triad) Theater nuclear offense Strategic conventional offense Strategic defense Theater defense (blended/overlapped)
Weapons mix	Kinetic	Kinetic and Non-Kinetic
Intent of use	Nuclear weapon effects Physical application for physical and psychological effects	Strategic effects Physical and psychological applications and effects
C^2	Strategic warning and C^2	Strategic warning, nuclear C^2 homeland defense warning and strategic C^2 Conventional C^2
Planning	Threat-based nuclear targeting	Integrated effects-based/ capabilities-based/multi-system

actively contribute to deterrence. It follows, then, that a wide mix of conventional offensive capabilities, including strategic information operations and special operations employed for strategic effects, can reduce or even replace some of the former reliance on nuclear weapons to hold certain targets at risk. This blended force posture relies on both kinetic and non-kinetic strategic weapons, with even more emphasis on the psychological dimension of force than the traditional deterrent maintained during the Cold War. This broadened deterrence construct must integrate traditional strategic warning and command and control (C^2), homeland defense warning and command and control, and global conventional command and control into one package. It also must develop a multipurpose planning system based not on threats and targets, but on a range of capabilities to create a quiver of "effects arrows."

The new strategic framework and the new strategic triad will produce several significant effects. First, they will create new organizations and capabilities with a completely recast concept of threat and response that reflects the realities of a fundamentally different strategic environment. Second, they will create a broadened mission set and more generalized strategic guidance for the strategic deterrent that will require new planning, operations, and command and control concepts. Third, implementing the NPR will require a completely different approach to capabilities conceptualization and organization—indeed, a fundamental redefinition of the foundational concept of "strategic" for the United States. And while these changes were, in fact, underway for a decade before their formalization in the NPR, the net effects of this changed reality—as codified in the new strategic framework and the new strategic triad—represent a fundamental imperative to transformation for the services and organizations designated to provide the new strategic strike and deterrent force.

IMPLEMENTATION ISSUES AND CONCERNS

The U.S. military faces a battlespace that is changing from a single and known survival-level threat to a wide range of significant dangers involving states and non-state challengers potentially armed with weapons of mass destruction and the means to deliver them against U.S. interests, citizens, and territory. This change has led to a redefinition of what constitutes a "strategic" threat and to a search for a range of responses to produce several strategic effects across a broad deterrent and defense posture. For the military services, this changed task environment, new operating and planning concepts, and a new alert posture all require significant organizational change and new forms of technical and human-resource development.

Organization

U.S strategic forces and commands already have undergone significant reorganization. The end of the Cold War ushered in some of these changes, although the initial decline of traditional strategic organizations was seen as part of a general downsizing of the U.S. military. Several events at the time seemed to herald the beginning of the end of the U.S. nuclear deterrent: the demise of Strategic Air Command (SAC); the concurrent transfer of the manned bomber force to Air Combat Command (ACC), an organization dominated by fighter pilots; and the transfer of land-based strategic missiles to Air Force Space Command (AFSPC), an organization focused on space launch and satellite operations. These moves were seen by many as the clear death knell for the nuclear deterrent maintained by the United States military. The oft-heard question asked: Which command or service would assume advocacy for the now-legacy strategic mission, forces, warheads, and systems? Today, one can sense the relief among advocates of a strong deterrent because they believe that the NPR promises to reverse the decline of U.S. nuclear forces by underscoring the national importance of the strategic mission of U.S. Strategic Command (USSTRATCOM—the successor unified command to SAC).

Significant organizational issues, however, remain unresolved by the NPR. The question of who will be the primary advocate for strategic matters—particularly nuclear—within the U.S. military remains to be answered. USSTRATCOM has the primary operational tasking in this arena; however, as a unified command it does not have the "organize, train, and equip" (OT&E) role which is reserved for the military services. There is precedent for a unified command to have partial OT&E responsibility and assets for a specialized, unique mission set. The United States Special Operations Command has some OT&E authorization to supplement service efforts in the special operations realm. USSTRATCOM is unlikely to gain more than supplemental OT&E authority and resources for the strategic mission because responsibility for the strategic missions still reside within a service. USSTRATCOM also has absorbed U.S. Space Command, and while the Air

Force is the executive agent for OT&E for military space, USSTRATCOM cannot become the multi-role advocate for both space and strategic forces and capabilities without diluting the punch of this advocacy. The services—and particularly the Air Force—must begin to take the new strategic missions outlined by the NPR seriously.[3]

The problem with Air Force advocacy is demonstrated by the current organizational placement of strategic assets. The manned bomber force (as well as Air Force information operations and warfare) is assigned to Eighth Air Force, which in turn reports to the Air Combat Command. The logic behind this organizational structure holds that because both the bomber force and information warfare units have concurrent strategic and operational-level missions, placing them within one command ensures a broad operational and strategic focus in their training and preparation. While this logic has merit, the Eighth Air Force is in ACC, and ACC is the primary Air Force component, or includes the primary Air Force component, of five unified commands. The diversity of the ACC mission and the split taskings created by the range of its component responsibilities dilute ACC's ability or interest in assuming the role of advocate for the new strategic mission. At the same time, the bomber force is multitasked under the ACC banner, and the bomber force's strategic mission is only one of its mission sets. In a conventional role, the bomber force is primarily prepared to produce strategic (or at least "theater strategic") effects. Operationally, the bomber force is placed under the operational command of USSTRATCOM for actual nuclear operations. But a three-star numbered Air Force commander (Eighth Air Force) cannot be an effective advocate—within the Air Force or within the competitive joint community—for strategic forces and systems.

Similarly, the land-based intercontinental ballistic missile (ICBM) force is located within Twentieth Air Force, a subordinate unit to AFSPC, for preparation to chop to USSTRATCOM for nuclear operations. While this force has only the nuclear mission to prepare for, it still lacks an effective service advocate because of its relatively low-ranking commander (a two-star position) and its subordination to an Air Force command with a wide-ranging portfolio, the central focus of which is military space, not strategic systems. None of this is to say that the commanders of ACC or AFSPC ignore or undervalue their assigned strategic forces. It is simply to recognize the fact that neither has a single focus or primary purpose of ensuring full support to the strategic mission.

The primary advocate for strategic issues in the Air Force is a staff directorate at the Air Staff in the Pentagon, for the past several years the Nuclear and Counterproliferation Directorate (XON). An ongoing reorganization placed that function within an expanded Strategic Security Directorate (XOS). This nuclear advocate, under the Deputy Chief of Staff for Air and Space Operations (XO), is a two-star billet with only one three-star between it and the Chief of Staff, so it does have some significant advocacy potential. In fact, today the Air Staff has formed and chairs a committee of all of the Air Force generals who have nuclear responsibilities (including the commanders of both Eighth and Twentieth Air Forces) to provide group advocacy and ensure a powerful voice for strategic assets and systems. Similarly, submarine-launched ballistic missile (SLBM) systems in the Navy are dispersed in the fleet but enjoy some significant visibility through the Navy staff Submarine Warfare Division. These Air Force and Navy headquarters advocates can ensure that strategic programs and systems survive, but it remains to be seen whether such non-line command arrangements can help them thrive. This organizational and advocacy arrangement probably was the inevitable successor to SAC, but headquarters committees and directorates do not foster the development of a powerful subculture necessary for the long-term advancement of strategic forces and outlooks within the U.S. military.

Operations

Adjustments to the new battlespace, especially those produced by the creation of the new strategic triad, will significantly affect U.S. military strategic operational concepts and assets. New issues and concerns revolve around the blending of what were distinct mission sets and systems—deterrence and defense; nuclear and conventional. They seek to ensure both an integrated posture and distinct attention to the unique and special nature of specific weapons, particularly nuclear weapons.

One impetus to change comes from the prospect that a new generation of "conventional strategic" weapons systems might be developed. There are suggestions and studies on converting ICBMs that are currently tipped with nuclear weapons or adapting new space-launched missiles to conduct conventional strategic strikes. Similarly, the Navy is studying the use of Trident ballistic missile submarines to carry and launch a new generation of conventional submarine-launched ballistic missiles (SLBM). Any of these changes would require the services to operate with much greater transparency. For instance, it might be necessary in the future to alter missile launch profiles to allow third parties to distinguish among launches for each purpose. It might be necessary to designate specific bases and regions as launch or operating areas for specific systems, allowing others to verify that weapons only contain conventional payloads. Increased transparency in missile operations, deployments, and systems is likely.

The NPR also has focused interest in the development of a modified small nuclear weapon or a new generation of small nuclear weapons for use against hardened and deeply buried targets. During the Cold War, delivery of small, so-called tactical, theater, or nonstrategic nuclear weapons was treated as a secondary mission for "dual capable" (primarily conventional) forces, and the services neither fully supported nor embraced it. Depending on the design of any new system and the delivery platform selected for it, the same risk persists. Without primary mission status and advocacy from a powerful organization within the service, new weapons could become a neglected and unwanted sidebar to the "real" mission set of the service. The deterrent, dissuasion, or assurance effects of weapons will be diminished if they are employed by organizations that treat them as a subordinate concern to their primary mission.

Conversely, there also is a danger that a new, small, and relatively clean generation of nuclear weapons might be perceived by policy makers or military planners as "just another weapon"—a usable, even a preferred, option for achieving particular strategic effects against specific targets. Blending weapons and integrating planning and operations around strategic effects can, over time, blur even the distinction between nuclear and conventional weapons in the minds of the people who develop and recommend options to policy makers. Certainly any decision on the employment of nuclear weapons—regardless of size or target—will ultimately include the full range of political as well as military considerations. There is a possibility, however, that a new small nuclear penetrator might come to be viewed by operators or planners as simply another military option for achieving a particular strategic effect.

Given the development of more "usable" nuclear weapons and conventional strategic weapons, the process of creating strategic effects will have to be reconceptualized, especially as regards the ideas of deterrence, dissuasion, and assurance. Traditional notions of deterrence by punishment must be supplemented with concepts and operations to create deterrence by denial. Planners must articulate the synergies made possible by the combination of effective strategic offenses and defenses. Credibility must be rethought for new target actors and a wide range of coercive strategies. And the results of this new thinking must feed into the newly integrated warning, planning, and command and control structures and processes if the new strategic triad will achieve its intended effects.

As it was with the advent of strategic nuclear weapons, the development and fielding of new systems will likely prove to be easier than the evolution of the conceptual and organizational framework necessary to make the new strategic triad a reality. The advent of the nuclear age required the birth and development of a new field of thought and new generation of thinkers to make sense of the new strategic reality. Today the United States faces a tougher task developing new thinking while concurrently altering old thought, all in an environment of fading expertise and uncertain advocacy.

Resourcing

The services must sustain legacy strategic systems well into the twenty-first century, even while studying and perhaps developing new weapons and systems. This national imperative was recognized in the NPR in the third leg of the new strategic triad, which outlines a revitalized defense infrastructure including the nuclear weapons complex. With a formal place in the NPR and direct attention in the past several editions of the National Security Strategy, the defense and nuclear weapons infrastructure should be able to command resources for modernization and sustainment, although this process will not occur without vigilance and hard work on the part of advocacy groups within service staffs and at the level of the unified command.

Over the long term, the human-resource issues represent the weakest link in maintaining a viable strategic deterrent. The services have seen a precipitous decline in technical expertise required to support and maintain nuclear weapons and their associated delivery systems. The services have recognized this problem, and some steps have been initiated to address it. For example, finding a decline in direct missile launch experience in a non-dedicated "space and missile officer" career field within the Air Force, the service reestablished its "Top Hand" missile launch program at Vandenberg Air Force Base, California, to ensure that personnel will be able to cultivate experience and expertise in missile testing and launches. Personnel assigned to the program do actual testing and are involved in live missile launches, which enhances and sustains expertise—or creates this expertise for personnel whose background does not include maintaining or operating missiles.[4]

The number of people with experience and expertise in maintaining nuclear weapons and their associated infrastructure is also on the decline. The Air Force began a partnership program with the national laboratories in 1999 that has grown into today's Air Force-National Laboratories Technical Fellowship Program (AF-NLTFP). Under AF-NLTFP, three mid-ranking officers enter the program annually under the auspices of the Air Force Intermediate Developmental Education Program, and one comes from the Senior Developmental Education Program. Selectees become nuclear weapons fellows at Sandia, Los Alamos, or Lawrence Livermore Laboratories in lieu of attending the traditional command and staff college or war college (though they would still receive in-residence credit through the fellowship). The Air Force also has created other senior and junior civilian billets for AF-NLTFP and related programs to increase technical expertise across the total force. The service must monitor this program along with retention and accession rates to ensure that sufficient numbers of personnel attain the expertise necessary to operate and sustain the nuclear weapons inventory.

The most subtle and yet most critical aspect of the dwindling strategic expertise in the services is in the area of policy expertise—such fields as nuclear strategy, deterrence, and arms control. The nuclear mission may still be primary for certain bomber pilots and missileers, but for many flyers today, it is a secondary mission. For space and missile officers it is but one part of a multiple mission set. Even for nuclear submariners it often is rotational duty. No single, dedicated nuclear career track exists, nor do parallel tracks on nonnuclear strategic operations. Further, Army personnel come to the nuclear operations field for the first time at mid-career without any dedicated experience leading up to that assignment. This expertise deficiency also extends into the civilian academic community, where young doctoral students see no incentive to focus their career research interests on strategic policy or nuclear weapons-related areas (assuming that any senior faculty remain at their institutions who have the background to guide such research and study).

The decline in strategic studies and expertise has been recognized, and several efforts have been made to develop a strategic perspective and thinking both inside and outside of the services and military organizations. For example, Dr. John Hamre, president of the Center for Strategic and International Studies (CSIS) and former deputy secretary of defense, has launched the CSIS Project on Nuclear Issues as a network to help develop a new generation of young professionals from across the policy community (government, military, academic, contractors, and national laboratories). This project is a start, but the measure is not enough to develop the cadre of expertise needed within the strategic services.

One option would be to bolster and enlarge the strategic studies program at the Naval Postgraduate School, which currently has mid-ranking graduate students from all of the military services. A dedicated number of Air Force slots should be designated as part of the existing Intermediate Developmental Education Program, tackling the same issues as does AF-NLTFP on the technical side. A number of Navy students also should be designated for this graduate curriculum in strategic policy issues, including nuclear strategy, deterrence theory, and strategic coercion. The resident intermediate and senior service schools of both the Air Force and the Navy also should require a block of study that surveys this body of knowledge and serves as a departure point for more in-depth self-study or follow-on study should other programs be developed (such as a USSTRATCOM Strategic Officer Orientation Course or an equivalent service course).

CONCLUSION

Carl Builder, observing the immediate transition period following the end of the Cold War, fretted that the Air Force, now lacking a central and primary strategic mission, was floundering for a new vision, which put the service in jeopardy of internal dissention and decline. He later wrote that the loss of the strategic Air Force presence put at risk the continued strategic focus for the military as a whole, and he called for rekindling the strategic flame.[5] Whether or not one agrees with the Builder analysis, the fact is that the strategic mission, including the traditional and, perhaps, a new nuclear component, is a national tasking to the military services. The strategic landscape has changed—indeed, it has broadened—and the clear imperative is for the military services to transform to embrace and prosecute this revised mission set. The NPR process has pointed the way in terms of defining the new strategic framework and outlining the new strategic objectives and an expanded posture in the new strategic triad. But those points are guide posts on a continuing journey of change and transformation; they are waypoints in the process, not endpoints.

The strategic services, in conjunction with USSTRATCOM, must embrace this guidance and develop institutions to achieve the new strategic mission. They must understand what strategic threats and effects mean today; they must develop effective organizational structures and advocacy channels to organize, train, and equip forces for these mission sets; and they must develop the systems and personnel with the required technical and policy expertise—and with sustainable career opportunities—to keep the strategic flame burning bright. These efforts mark the minimum requirement to sustain an effective subculture to ensure expertise and advocacy to serve the national interest; they may also be the seed from which a renewed and recast strategic profession might someday grow.

NOTES

The views expressed in this chapter are those of the author and do not necessarily reflect the official policy or position of the United States Air Force, the Department of Defense, or the U.S. government.

1. The classic and best basic discussions of U.S. military service culture, subcultures, and cohesion are: Carl H. Builder, *The Masks of War: American Military Styles in Strategy and Analysis* (Baltimore: Johns Hopkins University, 1989); Morton H. Halperin, *Bureaucratic Politics and Foreign Policy* (Washington, D.C.: Brookings, 1974); Arnold Kanter, *Defense Politics: A Budgetary Perspective* (Chicago: University of Chicago, 1975); Frederick C. Mosher, *Democracy and the Public Service* (New York: Oxford University, 1982); and James Q. Wilson, *Bureaucracy: What Government Agencies Do and Why They Do It* (New York: Basic Books, 1989).

2. For two clear overviews of this change process particularly suited to U.S. military services, see Wallace Earl Walker, *Changing Organizational Culture: Strategy, Structure, and Professionalism in the U.S. General Accounting Office* (Knoxville: University of Tennessee, 1986); and Stephen Peter Rosen, "New Ways of War: Understanding Military Innovation," *International Security* (Summer 1988): 134–168. The voluminous recent literature on defense "transformation" develops various steps in this process in exhaustive detail, but does not alter the basic process.

3. This analysis focuses primarily on U.S. Air Force issues and programs. This focus is not meant in any way to devalue the central and vital place of the U.S. Navy beside the Air Force as a strategic service. It simply reflects the author's Air Force background and knowledge.

4. For details on these human development programs see the U.S. Air Force "Arms Control Bulletin" series at www.xo.hq.af.mil/xos/xosp/xospi/.

5. Carl H. Builder, *The Icarus Syndrome: The Role of Air Power Theory in the Evolution and fate of the U.S. Air Force* (New Brunswick, N.J.: Transaction Publishers, 1994); and Carl H. Builder, "Keeping the Strategic Flame," *Joint Force Quarterly* (Winter 1996–1997), 76–84.

EFFECTS AND IMPLICATIONS

11

The Bush Administration's New
Approach to Arms Control

Jeffrey A. Larsen

In the first years of this century, the word coming out of the White House has seemed particularly discouraging for the arms control community. In short, the message was that arms control is dead. The series of national security papers that have been published since George W. Bush took office have reflected this perspective. The administration shifted its foreign relations focus away from cooperative instruments (such as arms control) to an approach that emphasizes active self-help and coalitions of the willing.

Rather than critically analyzing these new policies for threads of traditional arms control and its past success, however, the arms control community reacted on a more instinctive and emotional level. The community's general response has been to position itself in fervent opposition to virtually everything the Bush administration has done or stands for, rather than adapting its policies to their own use and mutual benefit.

Jeffrey Knopf argues in chapter 12 that the Nuclear Posture Review (NPR) and the direction currently being taken by the Bush administration in terms of U.S. national security are fundamentally incompatible with the goals of nonproliferation and, by implication, arms control in general. But I argue that the Bush approach to world affairs *is*, in fact, arms control, albeit an approach that many in the traditional arms control and disarmament community—as well as members of the current administration—find difficult to accept.

This chapter argues that the current emphasis on self-reliance, preemption, and preventive war against terrorism reflects a different, activist approach to arms control that seeks many of the same objectives that were sought by the traditionalists in the heyday of arms control during the late Cold War. More than forty years ago, Thomas Schelling and Morton Halperin put forward three criteria for determining whether a policy fell under the rubric of arms control. According to the Schelling–Halperin taxonomy, an arms control agreement or approach must lessen the chances of war, reduce the consequences should war occur, and decrease the cost of preparing for war. As this chapter shows, the Bush administration's preemptive policy and the

NPR's recommendations all meet these criteria. They represent a new, radically different means of handling international challenges formerly dealt with through arms control. In short, the NPR *is* arms control.

One analyst recently wrote that, "You would think the arms control community would be grateful [for the NPR]. After all, they have championed such ideas for decades. . . . Instead, they are denouncing the NPR. What's going on here?"[1] It is a good question, which this chapter attempts to answer.

A DECADE OF CHANGE

The NPR and its associated documents—including the National Security Strategy (NSS), the Quadrennial Defense Review (QDR), and the draft National Military Strategy (NMS)—all represent a fundamental shift in the U.S. view of the world. The current administration believes that the world is different that it was during the Cold War; we face new threats from new adversaries; traditional deterrence may no longer work; traditional arms control will not suffice; the country is weary of long, drawn-out negotiations leading to formal treaties; and there is a new requirement for offensive counterproliferation efforts.

The first Nuclear Posture Review, in 1994, was conducted at a time of considerable optimism about arms control and its future central role in international relations. The early to mid-1990s represented the high-water mark for arms control. The first Strategic Arms Reduction Treaty, START I, provided the parameters of options and changes that would be acceptable for the NPR. In particular, the NPR had to justify its findings and recommendations by calling on the United States to lead the world toward a reduced prominence for nuclear weapons, while at the same time keeping a hedge against surprises. This hedge included a stockpile of warheads that had been withdrawn from service and removed from their delivery systems, though they remained in storage and available to the military on short notice.

There are no such arms control considerations restricting the 2001 NPR. Instead, the participants pursued more radical thinking about the future and the use of nuclear weapons in U.S. military policy. The primary authors of the 2001 NPR came from the nuclear community. Most were conservative in political orientation, and nearly all had prior government experience in earlier presidential administrations. They had one other factor in common: Few of them had any appreciation for arms control or its supposed achievements over the previous decades. The Bush administration was filled with neoconservatives who believed in a strong military and an America that could take care of business—unilaterally if necessary. They distrusted or discounted multilateral negotiations and arms control treaties that hampered the United States' ability to meet its security goals. While not all of them necessarily opposed arms control in principle, many members of the new administration were concerned with the way previous arms control treaties had been enforced. If the enforcement and verification mechanisms were good enough, perhaps arms control could play a role in U.S. foreign policy—but Cold War history had given them serious doubts about the efficacy of such mechanisms.

The U.S. view of the post–Cold War world shifted fundamentally in the first years of the new century as the George W. Bush administration came to Washington. The new government looked out at the world and perceived many new threats from previously unseen sources, as well as a more benign Russia that could become a great-power partner of the United States in its international endeavors. These new views were strengthened by the September 11, 2001, terrorist attacks on the United States.

All of the major policy papers published by the administration since 2001—including the NSS, the NPR, the QDR, the NMS, the National Security Strategy for Homeland Defense, and the National Strategy for Combating Weapons of Mass Destruction—reflect this new view. In fact, the concordance of the language among all of these documents is striking. Rarely has an administration put forth such a focused perspective of its place in the world. And never in living memory has there been less mention of the role arms control measures could play in achieving these national interests. The QDR, for example, contained four major categories of discussion and recommendations that parallel the defense policy objectives discussed by other chapters in this volume: assuring friends and allies, dissuading competitors, deterring aggressors, and defeating enemies. None of the sub-bullets in any of these four categories were related to traditional arms control.[2]

The Bush administration's key policy positions were first previewed in a report by the National Institute for Public Policy that was published January 2001. Many of the participants in this study became leading members of the administration following the November 2000 election. The report's bottom line concerning arms control was summed up in the following sentence: "Strategic adaptability . . . weighs heavily against continuation of the traditional bipolar Cold War approach to strategic arms control."[3] Secretary of Defense Donald Rumsfeld has publicly stated "arms control treaties are not for friends."[4] In 2003, Thomas Barnett, deputy director of the Department of Defense's Office of Transformation, bluntly said "arms control is dead. . . . The answer to dealing with nations that harbor terrorists is not arms control; it is to go in there and disarm them."[5] At the press briefing when the NPR was released, Assistant Secretary of Defense J. D. Crouch said, "One of the things to come out of the NPR is that there is not a single solution to the problem of weapons of mass destruction. It is not entirely a military problem; it is also a diplomatic problem. It is also a problem that will involve other aspects of national power . . . We are trying to achieve these reductions without having to wait for Cold War arms control treaties."[6] And Loren Thompson of the Lexington Institute has written of the NPR: "The new stance is an effort to maximize the incentives of other countries to avoid using such weapons, . . . an overdue response to shifts in the global security environment."[7]

The NPR has few specific phrases that provide linkage to arms control concepts and existing treaties. It discusses a new relationship with Russia, and calls for future deals between the United States and Russia that minimize negotiations and result in less-detailed treaties. It also calls on the United States to develop strategic defenses at the earliest opportunity, which would require withdrawal from the 1972 Anti-Ballistic Missile Treaty—a step the United States took in May 2002. The United States currently has no plans to resume testing its nuclear weapons, but it will keep that option open— hence the NPR recommends that the United States not ratify the Comprehensive Test Ban Treaty (CTBT). Rather than create a new verification regime for the 2002 Moscow Treaty (the Strategic Offensive Reductions Treaty, or SORT), the NPR suggests using the existing verification regime put in place for START I monitoring and compliance as the basis for this new agreement. And it calls on the United States to store its warheads that are removed from the active delivery inventory, rather than destroying them. This position is evident in the SORT treaty, too.

"Neo"-Arms Control

Despite the publicly reiterated positions of the Bush administration and its critics, the White House does have an approach to arms control—whether planned or fortuitous. The Bush administration's unilateral decisions and actions to further U.S. national security have direct and indirect supporting effects on existing arms control regimes. For example, the United States has made it clear that it wants to stem the proliferation of weapons of mass destruction (WMD), to prevent such weapons falling into the hands of terrorists or rogue states, and to make examples of such groups or nations when they do attempt to acquire WMD. The new approach emphasizes dissuasion as well as deterrence. All of these positions support the basic precepts of the 1968 Nuclear Non-Proliferation Treaty (NPT).

The Bush administration's foreign and security policy reflects a new way of approaching arms control. The Bush way is unilateral and self-sufficient, and it attempts to stem proliferation by making examples of proliferants. It seeks to end the adversarial, Cold War relationship with Russia, which was based on mutually assured destruction, and to develop and exploit advances in nonnuclear strategic strike forces that can reduce the dependency on nuclear forces. The approach seeks continued unilateral or multilateral reductions in nuclear forces, but without lengthy negotiated treaties; it sees no need for codification or irreversibility. Administration officials also have an aversion to binding legal constraints that might hinder the U.S. ability to adjust to unforeseen changes in the strategic environment, including the development of new weapons. It also maintains the negative security assurances made at the 1995 NPT Review Conference.

The U.S. desire to continue reductions in the U.S. and Russian strategic nuclear arsenals, carrying forward the efforts codified in both START treaties and the SORT treaty, reflects a core objective of traditional arms control and

Table 11.1   Progressive decreases in superpower strategic nuclear weapons

Treaty	Year	Allowable deployed strategic nuclear warheads
End of Cold War status	Approx. 1990	10,000–12,000 on each side
START I	1991	6,000
START II	1993	3,000–3,500
START III	Discussed 1997	2,000–2,500
SORT	2002	1,700–2,200

another primary purpose of the NPT; to proceed toward nuclear disarmament by the nuclear weapons states. While the new focus is on quicker results with less hassle, the goals remain the same. The new approach focuses on close consultation, coordination, and transparency among the states parties to the agreement, rather than on strict, legally binding inspections or monitoring. It avoids locking in specific numbers of weapons or specific types of technologies. In this sense the new approach is, in fact, much different from traditional arms control, yet again, its goals and results are in accord with the old approach. New treaties are not overturning the old agreements; they are building on past experience and precedent, while avoiding built-in constraints on the nation's flexibility.

The Bush administration's new foreign and defense policy remains surprisingly in line with the traditional tenets of arms control. In terms of nuclear force reductions, for example, the NPR dismisses arms control as outmoded and unworkable. Yet, the fifteen-year tradition of ever-increasing cuts in the strategic nuclear arsenals of Russia and the United States continued in the 2002 Moscow Treaty, which the Bush administration proposed and signed. Table 11.1 shows this trend.[8]

APPLYING SCHELLING'S DEFINITION: IS NEO-ARMS CONTROL REALLY ARMS CONTROL?

One can consider the Bush national security strategy in light of three well-known criteria to see if it meets the definition of arms control measures. In 1961, Thomas Schelling led a group of academics and policy makers who came up with a definition of arms control that has been generally accepted as the *sine qua non* for determining if an agreement or treaty is valid. Schelling's three rules are still valid today. Any agreement must: (1) reduce the chances of war occurring; (2) reduce the consequences should war occur; and (3) reduce the costs of preparing for war.[9]

The original goal of arms control was to promote national security by making the country safer. It was originally conceived as a multilateral process. Many political leaders and the media seemed to keep the definition limited to a set of activities dealing with specific steps to control a class or related classes of weapon systems. These activities were then codified in formal agreements or treaties. Over time, however, other thinkers began to broaden the definition of arms control to include goals in addition to constraining arms competition or proliferation—punitive disarmament of aggressor states, for example. They also sought to use arms control negotiations to improve communication and relations among antagonists. As one writer put it, "We define arms control as a process involving specific, declared steps by a state to enhance security through cooperation with other states. These steps can be unilateral, bilateral, or multilateral. Cooperation can be implicit as well as explicit."[10] Using this broadened definition allows us to see many of the recent U.S. policy pronouncements, decisions, and diplomatic and military actions in a new light.

Reducing the Chances of War

The first rationale for arms control, reducing the chances of war, has been strengthened in the NPR. Its call for a mix of strategic options, including an offense–defense mix and advanced conventional strike capabilities, should convince potential opponents that they have nothing to gain by attacking the United States or its global interests. There has never been a nation-state as singularly powerful as the United States is today, and the provisions called for in the Nuclear Posture Review will only add to this strength. Deterrence and dissuasion, whether through the threatened use of nuclear weapons, modern precision conventional forces, or any of the multiple other means of national power, can achieve the goal of avoiding war in the first place.

Reducing the Consequences Should War Occur

By enhancing conventional strike capabilities, the NPR provides a way to reduce reliance on nuclear weapons for some missions, thereby reducing the prospects of collateral damage. The NPR also calls for a parallel effort to develop smaller, more precise, more discrete nuclear weapons that hold out the prospect of further reducing collateral damage. In fact, a host of new technologies promise to reduce collateral damage in war: precision guided munitions, including deep earth penetrating warheads; the Global Positioning System to improve targeting, including the Joint Direct Attack Munition; improvements in the targeting cycle, including intelligence, surveillance, and reconnaissance capabilities and more flexible command and control arrangements to react to time-critical targets; and the development and use of more sophisticated computer programs for determining and minimizing collateral damage and casualties. Being able to conduct a strategic attack using minimal force, applied in a precise way on a specific target, while minimizing the collateral damage associated with that attack, makes a measurable difference in the consequences of war for both sides. Gone are the days of the early Cold War, when war plans mirrored all-out, counter-value attacks that relied on manned bombers releasing huge thermonuclear weapons on the unprotected population of a major city.

Of equal importance is the development and deployment of active defenses, particularly missile defenses, to protect the homeland, and the rehabilitation of air defenses over North America since September 11. During the Cold War, a misguided belief in the value of mutually assured destruction drove U.S. perceptions about the best way to protect its society and citizenry. This approach meant eliminating missile defenses, minimizing air defenses, and leaving the country open and vulnerable to any attack. Today we have tasted in small measure what such openness can bring—and found it bitter. Hence, the Bush administration has decided to mount modest air and space defenses against incoming threats to reduce the consquences of a small attack should diplomacy, dissuasion, and deterrence fail.

Reducing the Costs of Preparing for War

The direct and immediate cost savings of changes called for by the NPR and associated documents are readily identifiable. The 1991 Presidential Nuclear Initiatives already removed most tactical nuclear weapons from the Army and Navy and cancelled all future tactical nuclear development programs, saving untold millions of dollars in direct (e.g., systems development and maintenance; warhead storage) and indirect (e.g., training and readiness) costs. The continuing reductions in strategic arsenals, exemplified most recently in the SORT Treaty's call for 1,700 to 2,200 deployed warheads by the year 2012, have the same positive fiscal impact with respect to land and sea-based strategic systems. While modern advanced conventional weapons are not inexpensive, they are still less costly than the huge and far-flung nuclear infrastructure that the United States built and maintained during the Cold War. Moving toward the changes called for in the NPR holds out the prospect of long-term savings, even with the modest increase in spending needed to bolster the nuclear infrastructure.

CRITICAL RESPONSE FROM THE ARMS CONTROL AND DISARMAMENT COMMUNITIES

Rather than looking at the NPR in light of Schelling's three rules for arms control, traditional arms control and disarmament advocates decry the NPR for its warlike tone and practical approach to enhanced national security. They seem to miss the point that the NPR and other Bush administration policies advance common goals of greater security at less risk and smaller cost. Ironically, the arms control community has chosen to take the Bush administration's leading figures at their word when the latter claim that they do not like arms control, that there is no place for such an outmoded approach to international relations in the new world, and that their policies have no arms control component. If the arms control community had thought through the implications of these new positions, rather than merely reacting in a stereotypical anti-Republican, antimilitary fashion, they might have been able to steer the debate along parallel tracks, thereby lessening the acrimony of the debate over the NPR and its negative effect on arms control.

Criticisms of the Bush administration's defense policy by the arms control community are fairly well known but worth reiterating here:[11]

- The prescriptions of the NPR will lead to greater reliance by the United States on nuclear weapons in future conflicts.
- The development of new designs for nuclear weapons, as called for in the NPR, will increase the likelihood of their use and lower the nuclear threshold.
- The NPR expands the set of countries targeted by nuclear weapons, thereby hurting diplomatic relations with these and other states and potentially undermining the concept of negative security assurances (whereby the United States promised not to target or use nuclear weapons on nonnuclear states).
- Relying on long-range, precision conventional weaponry will increase the proliferation of weapons of mass destruction as other states and groups seek asymmetric responses to American military might.
- Recent nuclear reductions, as called for in the SORT Treaty, are a sham because the warheads will be placed in reserve rather than destroyed. This practice will be potentially destabilizing and could lead Russia to follow suit rather than destroying its large arsenal.
- Current nuclear reductions are still not deep enough and are not in keeping with the commitment of the nuclear weapon states to pursue nuclear disarmament under Article VI of the Non-Proliferation Treaty.
- China will react to the deployment of missile defenses with a strategic arms buildup of its own, thereby triggering another arms race.
- The retention of U.S. nuclear weapons and a nuclear development and testing infrastructure justifies other states' efforts to acquire similar capabilities. It also increases the possibility of a nuclear accident.
- The actions recommended by the NPR and other recent policy papers threaten to undermine two generations of norm building: specifically, the taboo against nuclear use, and more generally, the rules of international cooperation (often achieved through arms control venues).

The disarmament community differs somewhat from more traditional arms control advocates. Its position was best exemplified by the 1996 Report of the Canberra Commission, with its calls for deeper force reductions and eventual nuclear abolition. According to the members of that commission, the mere existence of nuclear weapons greatly increases the likelihood and potential destructiveness of conflict.[12] Calls for disarmament in the 1990s rested on the belief in a benign future, one that would have greater international cooperation and no need for nuclear weapons. Disarmament advocates typically advance three objectives: nonproliferation of WMD; the creation of international norms to guide behavior; and the development of improved operational safety measures until such time as nuclear weapons can be eliminated. While all worthy goals, realists might respond that these objectives ignore three other factors of equal or greater importance: the requirement of deterring a potential adversary; the wartime military utility of particular weapons in specific circumstances; and the fact that there are other U.S. foreign policy goals beyond disarmament.

As one leading advocate of the disarmament school recently wrote, when linking these disarmament beliefs to the NPR:

> The recent Nuclear Posture Review tells us that U.S. policy-makers are still thinking that nuclear weapons make us safer, when, in fact, they remain weapons capable of destroying us. Their desire to retain flexibility is in reality a recipe for ending four decades of arms control. Their push for ballistic missile defenses is a formula for assuring that U.S. taxpayers enrich defense contractors while diverting defense expenditures from protecting against very real terrorist threats. The Bush promise of nuclear weapons reductions turns out to be a policy for missing the real opportunities of the post–Cold War period to not only shelve these weapons but eliminate them forever.[13]

This attitude summarizes the view of many members of the arms control and disarmament communities, but it also shows their unwillingness to see how the NPR contributes to the battle against WMD proliferation, large nuclear arsenals, and unprotected societies. The arms control and disarmament communities need to remove their ideological blinders and take to heart such positive elements as they can find in the NPR and its related documents.

THE NPR'S IMPACT ON NUCLEAR ARMS CONTROL TREATIES

Arms control treaties are vested with normative value and are seen as evidence of the good will and peaceful intentions of the states that sign them. As such, it is difficult for Western societies to change or withdraw from treaties, even when the documents have served their purpose or no longer seem to enhance national security. The Bush administration recognized this dilemma and chose to reverse the course of previous administrations by extricating the United States from outdated treaties, refusing to enter new agreements that did not seem to offer enhancements to U.S. security, and suggesting changes to existing treaties to reflect American security needs better. The NPR might thus have an impact on existing nuclear arms control treaties and regimes.

Nuclear Non-Proliferation Treaty

The NPT was signed in 1968 and has formed the cornerstone of nonproliferation efforts for thirty-five years. Among its principle clauses (reiterated in its Program of Action agreed to at the 2000 NPR Review Conference) are the nuclear taboo, the concept of negative security guarantees, the principle of irreversibility, the goal of a comprehensive test ban treaty, reduced nuclear planning for military contingencies, and the eventual elimination of nuclear weapons by those states that have them. In all but the last objective, as Jeffrey Knopf points out in the next chapter, the NPT is under assault by the recommendations of the NPR. As the arms control community pointed out in their list of concerns above, the nuclear taboo is challenged by the possibility that the classified version of the NPR may have included a list of countries specifically targeted by U.S. nuclear weapons; the fact that some of these countries may not be nuclear powers undermines the negative security guarantees made by the United States; the United States wants to retain its option for future testing, so it will not ratify the CTBT; and the NPT specifically calls for enhanced flexibility and the option to reverse recent decisions to build and test new nuclear weapons. In other words, the NPR can be seen as a major assault on the NPT, or it can be seen as a new way to look at arms control, nonproliferation, and national security. Either way, Knopf is correct when he says that it will be a tradeoff—either the United States follows the road laid out by our fathers in the NPT, or it pursues the new road offered by the NPR. It will be nearly impossible to maintain both simultaneously.

START I

The Strategic Arms Reduction Treaty was signed in 1991, and it entered into force in 1994. It remains in effect, and both the United States and Russia achieved the reductions necessary to reach the limits called for in the treaty by December 2001. The NPR has no major impact on START I.

START II

The START II treaty was signed in 1993 but never ratified. It was allowed to lapse, although both sides have agreed in principle to abide by its provisions, including continued reductions in the nuclear arsenals. Those lower limits were surpassed by the Moscow Treaty of 2002, in which both sides agreed to even lower levels in the number of deployed strategic nuclear weapons.

SORT

The Strategic Offensive Reductions Treaty (or Moscow Treaty) was signed in May 2002 and ratified in March 2003. It continues the reductions in strategic nuclear reductions codified over the preceding twelve years, lowering the arsenals of both major powers to levels undreamed of—even by disarmament advocates—until recently. The SORT Treaty reflects a new approach to arms control and national security strategy with its short, pointed, and practical style. Only two pages long, and relying on existing START enforcement mechanisms to ensure compliance, it is a low-key agreement between partners, rather than a traditional arms control treaty between adversaries. But it still accomplishes the common arms control and disarmament goals of seeking lower levels of strategic nuclear forces.

Comprehensive Test Ban Treaty

The Bush administration wishes to keep its options open in terms of future nuclear weapons requirements, including testing new nuclear weapons or verifying the reliability of the nuclear stockpile. This means that while the CTBT was signed in 1996, it has not yet been ratified, and it is unlikely that the current U.S. government will send it back to the Senate for further consideration. The permanent constraints it would impose on U.S. policy makers are simply too great, given current security threats. Nonetheless, according to the NPR, the United States merely wants to retain the option of future testing, and has no current plans to resume testing or develop new warhead designs that would require testing.[14]

Fissile Material Cutoff Treaty

The Fissile Material Cutoff Treaty is not in force, and negotiations have not begun officially within the United Nations Conference on Disarmament. The United States has for many years been among the leading advocates for such a treaty. But given the NPR's recommendation that the United States consider future requirements for new, small, tailored nuclear warheads, it is now less likely that it would be interested in signing such a treaty. New warheads may require new sources of fissile material, which could possibly be manufactured in the existing nuclear infrastructure or might require the creation of new facilities.

Cooperative Threat Reduction Program

Elements of the Nunn-Lugar Cooperative Threat Reduction (CTR) Program can be used to reduce the number of Russian forces to the limits imposed by the SORT Treaty. It also can continue to support the broad goal of nonproliferation through enhanced security of those weapons. In this sense, the CTR program neither directly supports nor contravenes anything in the NPR. The Bush administration would be wise to continue funding the CTR at current or enhanced levels.

Chemical Weapons Convention and Biological and Toxin Weapons Convention

Both of these regimes—the Chemical Weapons Convention, signed in 1993, and the Biological & Toxin Weapons Convention, which was signed in 1974—could be strengthened by the NPR's call for a more robust conventional strike force structure, one that would enforce these regimes by punishing infractions and breaches of the treaties by military strikes, if necessary.

Convention on Certain Conventional Weapons

The Convention on Certain Conventional Weapons entered into force in 1983. Its purpose is to limit weapons with effects that have been declared to be indiscriminate or to produce unnecessary suffering. The NPR and the U.S. military's new approach to warfighting are in accord with this regime, as the development of new conventional strategic strike capabilities protects noncombatants by reducing collateral effects and allowing the use of smaller, more discrete weapons than have been used in the past.

Intermediate-Range Nuclear Forces Treaty

The Intermediate-Range Nuclear Forces Treaty entered into force in 1988 and eliminated an entire category of weapons—missiles with a range of 500 to 5,000 kilometers. It remains in effect. Nothing in the NPR will affect this treaty, as the United States has no plans to develop new intermediate-range missiles with nuclear warheads.

Anti-Ballistic Missile Treaty

The Anti-Ballistic Missile (ABM) Treaty signed in 1972 was one half of the first Strategic Arms Limitation Treaty. Its success led to the subsequent series of arms control initiatives undertaken by the United States and the Soviet Union. It limited the development or deployment of ballistic missile defenses in the Soviet Union and the United States, and in effect drove the United States out of the strategic defense business when it closed its sole operational ABM site in North Dakota in 1976. The NPR addresses the requirement for active defenses to enhance U.S. security as one leg of the "new triad." The U.S. withdrawal from the ABM Treaty in May 2002 allowed the deployment of modest ballistic missile defenses planned for Alaska, California, and aboard Aegis ships off the coast of North America. The first element of this defense system was supposed to be operational by late 2004 (although delays pushed this date back into 2005). The end of the ABM Treaty has changed the basis of security relations between the United States and Russia; the Bush administration hopes that future relations will be based on cooperation if not outright coordination typical of allied relations.

Presidential Nuclear Initiatives

The 1991 Presidential Nuclear Initiatives (PNIs) and the December 2001 Crawford Summit decisions that led to the Moscow Treaty were clearly a means of accomplishing arms control objectives without the formality, expense, posturing, or challenges of traditional negotiations. The 1991 PNIs addressed tactical nuclear weapons, a category of weaponry that is still not covered by any formal arms control treaty. The NPR did nothing to address that shortcoming in Russian–American strategic relations. In fact, one could argue that the Moscow Treaty, for all its success in reducing the level of strategic warheads, actually hurt the chances for eventually developing a framework to deal with tactical weapons because it obviated the need for a START III treaty. In the 1997 Helsinki Agreement, Presidents William Clinton and Boris Yeltsin had agreed to include tactical (or nonstrategic) nuclear weapons as a separate venue in any future START III negotiation, but the SORT treaty meant that there would be no START III talks—and no discussion of nonstrategic nuclear weapons.

CONCLUSION

The NPR was not written with arms control in mind. Yet, it and related national security documents put forth by the George W. Bush administration can achieve many of the same effects as formal arms control treaties. The nuclear reductions that the Moscow Treaty calls for further the goal of eventual disarmament that the Nuclear Non-Proliferation Treaty seeks. There has been more progress in reducing the chances of mutually assured destruction in the past fifteen years than in the previous forty. The ability to conduct conventional and information operations as strategic strikes, something that could previously only be done using nuclear weapons, may actually raise the nuclear threshold, making the use of nuclear weapons less likely than in the past.

The key challenge for arms control advocates today is the same challenge facing defense planners: policies, strategies, and institutions must be adapted to changing world conditions. Both communities must minimize chances that they will make the wrong choices; they must minimize the "regret factor."

In reality, the new strategies of the Bush administration, with their emphasis on preemption, preventive war, enhanced national military capabilities, and a willingness to undertake unilateral actions, are simply a different, more effective means of handling challenges formerly dealt with by arms control. The arms control community must accept, adapt, and embrace these new approaches if it wants to avoid becoming marginalized.

NOTES

1. Frank Gaffney, "Alternative Arms Control Reality," *National Review* on-line, January 21, 2002 <www.nationalreview.com/contributors/gaffney012201.shtml>.
2. For details of these categories, see slide 7 from "Special Briefing on the Nuclear Posture Review," U.S. Department of State, International Information Programs, January 9, 2002 <www.defenselink.mil/news/Jan2002/t01092002_t0109npr.html>. Or see the full QDR report at Donald Rumsfeld, *Report of the Quadrennial Defense Review*, September 30, 2001 <www. defenselink.mil/pubs/qdr2001/pdf>.
3. National Institute for Public Policy, *Rationale and Requirements for U.S. Nuclear Forces and Arms Control*, volume 1, executive report, January 2001, iii.

4. Donald Rumsfeld quoted in Ivo Daalder and James Lindsay, "A New Agenda for Nuclear Weapons," The Brookings Institute, policy brief no. 94, February 2002, 2.

5. Thomas Barnett quoted in Amy Svitak, "A Decades-Long Policy Shifts," *Armed Forces Journal*, September 2003, 12.

6. J. D. Crouch, quoted in "Special Briefing on the Nuclear Posture Review," U.S. Department of State, International Information Programs, January 9, 2002 <http://usinfo.state.gov/topical/pol/arms/stories/review.htm>.

7. Loren Thompson, "How to Stop Worrying and Love the Bomb," *Wall Street Journal*, March 13, 2002.

8. For an expanded and detailed look at these treaties and associated numbers, see Anthony H. Cordesman, "U.S. and Russian Nuclear Forces and Arms Control after the U.S. Nuclear Posture Review" (Washington, D.C.: Center for Strategic and International Studies, January 10, 2002). Also see Rose Gottemoeller, "Beyond Arms Control: How to Deal with Nuclear Weapons," Carnegie Endowment for International Peace, policy brief no. 23, February 2003.

9. See Thomas C. Schelling and Morton H. Halperin, *Strategy and Arms Control* (New York: Twentieth Century Fund, 1961). For similar sets of rules and definitions that were promulgated during this fertile period for arms control, see Hedley Bull, *The Control of the Arms Race* (London: Bradbury Agnew Press, 1961), and Donald G. Brennan, *Arms Control, Disarmament, and National Security* (New York: George Braziller, 1961).

10. Gregory J. Rattray, "Introduction," in Jeffrey A. Larsen and Gregory J. Rattray, eds., *Arms Control Toward the 21st Century* (Boulder, Colo.: Lynne Rienner Publishers, 1996), 7–8. See also Thomas C. Schelling, "Foreword," in Jeffrey A. Larsen, ed., *Arms Control: Cooperative Security in a Changing Environment* (Boulder, Colo.: Lynne Rienner Publishers, 2002).

11. Expanded discussion of most of these points can be found in Mark Bromley, "Planning to Be Surprised: The U.S. Nuclear Posture Review and its Implications for Arms Control," BASIC Papers, no. 39, April 2002, <www.basicint.org/pubs/Papers/BP39.htm>.

12. "The Canberra Commission on the Elimination of Nuclear Weapons," August 14, 1996 <www.prop1.org/2000/canbrp01.htm>.

13. David Krieger, "Nuclear Age Peace Foundation Press Release Regarding the January 9 Nuclear Posture Review," Waging Peace.org: Website of the Nuclear Age Peace Foundation <www.wagingpeace.org/articles/02.01/02111napfnprpressrelease.htm>.

14. This perspective was reiterated by Linton Brooks, Under Secretary of Energy and Administrator of the National Nuclear Security Administration, in Congressional testimony on March 24, 2004. He stated that "We have no plan to resume testing; our efforts to improve test readiness are a prudent hedge against the possibility of a problem arising in the stockpile that cannot be confirmed, or a fix certified, without a nuclear test." "Statement of Ambassador Linton F. Brooks before the Senate Armed Services Committee, 24 March 2004" <http://armed-services.senate.gov/statemnt/2004/March/Brooks.pdf>.

12

Nuclear Tradeoffs: Conflicts between U.S. National Security Strategy and Global Nonproliferation Efforts

Jeffrey W. Knopf

The Nuclear Posture Review (NPR) and the larger trends in U.S. national security policy of which the NPR is a part are in significant ways incompatible with existing international nonproliferation arrangements—arrangements that are commonly called the "nonproliferation regime." The net effect of U.S. national security policies on nuclear nonproliferation is likely to be negative; in other words, the NPR could actually increase the likelihood of nuclear proliferation. There are several policy measures that could mitigate the potential damage the NPR might inflict on global nonproliferation efforts, but these measures are likely to have only a modest effect. The tradeoff between the NPR and traditional nonproliferation approaches cannot be entirely eliminated.

The Nuclear Nonproliferation Regime

Specialists in international relations use the term *regime* to describe international arrangements intended to govern a particular issue area in world politics.[1] Regimes have both formal and informal elements. The formal foundations of regimes typically involve treaties and international organizations. In functioning regimes, there also are informal, shared understandings of the norms and principles that guide a regime's official elements.

There are several global regimes concerning nuclear, biological and chemical (NBC) weapons. The NBC regimes share the basic informal underlying idea that there is an important distinction between conventional and unconventional weapons. NBC weapons are characterized as unconventional weapons because most observers believe that such weapons are more horrific in their effects than their conventional counterparts.[2] Reflecting this understanding, the various weapons of mass destruction (WMD) regimes seek to create and strengthen norms to preclude the use of NBC weapons, in part by delegitimizing even the possession of such arms.

The treaty provisions related to possession of NBC weapons are more complicated for nuclear arms than for chemical or biological arms. The heart of the nuclear nonproliferation regime is the Nuclear Non-Proliferation Treaty (NPT). The NPT, which was opened for signature in 1968, represents an unusual bargain. It allows five states that already had a nuclear weapons capability to retain their nuclear arms for an indefinite time. (The five NPT "nuclear weapon states" [NWS] are the United States, Russia, China, Great Britain, and France). The 180 other signatory states are categorized as nonnuclear weapon states (NNWS), meaning they legally forswear any effort to acquire nuclear arms.

To get the NNWS to accept such an unequal bargain, the NWS had to make several concessions. Three were especially important. First, NPT Article IV promised that the NWS would provide technical assistance to the NNWS on the peaceful uses of nuclear technology.[3] Similarly—although this second concession was not part of the original NPT text—the nuclear-armed states have given negative security guarantees in which they pledge not to use or threaten to use their nuclear weapons against nonnuclear states that sign the NPT, unless those states are engaged in military action in alliance with one NWS against another. Such negative security assurances were later recognized in the formal part of the regime by the final document from an NPT review conference in 1995.[4] Most relevant to the present discussion is the final key concession, contained in NPT Article VI. Article VI begins: "Each of the Parties to the Treaty undertakes to pursue negotiations in good faith on effective measures relating to cessation of the nuclear arms race at an early date and to nuclear disarmament. . . ." Article VI confirmed that the ultimate goal of the NPT was to eliminate nuclear weapons, and it reassured the NNWS that their unequal status in the regime would not be permanent. Article VI, however, did not establish a specific timetable for reaching its objectives.

The NNWS have long expressed dissatisfaction at the slow progress on Article VI. As a result, the final documents approved at NPT review conferences in 1995 and 2000 specified concrete measures that would show movement on nuclear arms control and disarmament. The 1995 conference agreed to a three-step program of action. It gave first priority to negotiation of a Comprehensive Test Ban Treaty (CTBT), which would prohibit all test explosions of nuclear devices. The second step called for was a Fissile Material Cutoff Treaty (FMCT), which would ban new production of plutonium or highly enriched uranium suitable for use in nuclear weapons. The third step set the more general goal of "systematic and progressive efforts to reduce nuclear weapons globally."[5]

The 2000 conference agreed to thirteen "practical steps" to implement Article VI. The first three reiterated goals concerning nuclear testing and a fissile materials ban. Although negotiation of a CTBT was completed in

1996, the treaty has not entered into force. The U.S. Senate voted against ratification in 1999, and several other countries whose accession is required for the treaty to enter into force have either not signed it (e.g., India and Pakistan) or signed but not ratified (e.g., China). The United States has been observing a moratorium on testing since 1992, and the other NWS recognized by the NPT also have joined the moratorium. The 2000 review conference agreed on the importance of maintaining the moratorium and bringing about the CTBT's entry into force. Another step, carefully negotiated with the NWS, was especially important to many NNWS. It pledged "[a]n unequivocal undertaking by the nuclear-weapon States to accomplish the total elimination of their nuclear arsenals," thereby forcing them to reiterate their commitment to Article VI. Another noteworthy step announced a principle of irreversibility, meaning that arms reductions should not be reversed by subsequent buildups. One other relevant step promised "[a] diminishing role for nuclear weapons in security policies to minimize the risk that these weapons ever be used." This made it explicit that one goal of the nonproliferation regime is to prevent nuclear weapons from being used in war.[6]

The nuclear nonproliferation regime thus comprises underlying norms against the possession and use of nuclear arms. It also reflects agreements on specific measures designed to prevent the spread of nuclear arms and growth of existing arsenals. Over the long run, it works to bring about global nuclear disarmament. The United States has officially agreed to the NPT and the specific steps embraced at subsequent review conferences.

In a world where events such as the attacks of September 11, 2001 can happen, however, the United States has also seen reason to embrace policies that are not compatible with these nonproliferation commitments. Certainly there have been important nonproliferation failures, including states that never signed the NPT and then developed nuclear weapons, such as India and Pakistan, and, more problematically for the regime, states such as Iraq, Iran, and North Korea that joined the NPT but then cheated, at times without being detected.

Although nonproliferation clearly has not been 100-percent successful, it is a mistake to think in all-or-nothing terms when it comes to stopping the spread of nuclear weapons. A policy can enjoy less than complete success without thereby being a complete failure. The nonproliferation regime has been largely successful. If the nonproliferation regime were weaker or nonexistent, nuclear proliferation would almost certainly have been more widespread. A recent tally estimates that thirty-four countries in the past had an interest in developing nuclear arms and the possibility to do so. Yet, out of these potential proliferators, many more decided to join the NPT as nonnuclear states than decided to defy the regime, including some states that actually had nuclear weapons for a time. States that decided to abandon the possibility of acquiring or keeping nuclear weapons include Germany, Argentina, Brazil, South Africa, and Ukraine.[7]

In sum, even though the regime is not perfect, it does make a positive contribution to slowing proliferation. The regime has serious shortcomings, but it has not collapsed. Thus, it will make a difference if the U.S. nuclear posture further weakens the regime.

CONFLICTS BETWEEN U.S. POLICY AND THE NONPROLIFERATION REGIME

Several elements of the NPR and related developments in U.S. national security strategy contradict U.S. commitments under the NPT. There are conflicts with general principles of the regime concerning both disarmament and nuclear nonuse as well as with specific policy objectives agreed to at the two most recent NPT review conferences.

Conflicts with Disarmament Principles

The Article VI objective of early cessation of the arms race has generally been taken to proscribe continued efforts to develop new types of nuclear weapons, based on the idea that arms buildups can be qualitative as well as quantitative. For example, NPR proposals to research and possibly develop relatively low-yield "mini-nukes" and a new high-yield device for an earth-penetrating warhead are inconsistent with the idea of halting further qualitative nuclear arms development.

The NPR also seems to defer indefinitely the goal of nuclear disarmament. The publicly leaked portions of the NPR do not mention the NPT at all, nor do they specify eventual elimination of nuclear weapons as a desired objective.[8] Instead, the NPR emphasizes the need to prepare to replace existing nuclear weapon systems. The leg of the "new triad" dealing with defense infrastructure includes provisions to revitalize the U.S. nuclear weapons complex, in part to reduce the lead time to produce new nuclear weapons. The NPR also anticipates that the United States will require follow-on intercontinental ballistic missiles (ICBMs), submarine launched ballistic missiles (SLBMs), and strategic bombers.[9] The NPR thus plans continued reliance on nuclear weapons for many decades to come.

On the other hand, the NPR also envisions reducing the operationally deployed nuclear force to 1,700–2,200 warheads by 2012, an objective that the 2002 Moscow Treaty formalized. The NPR also describes the rationale for the new triad as an effort to create nonnuclear options that would permit the United States to reduce its reliance on offensive nuclear forces for achieving its strategic goals. Although these aspects of the NPR are compatible with NPT mandates, they do not derive from an intent to conform to NPT obligations. In fact, the NPR never relates these proposals to Article VI. Rather, the chief motivation is to shift away from a force structure designed to meet the old Soviet threat to one that is better suited for anticipated future threats. This is a reasonable motivation, but the fact that meeting NPT obligations is not included in the list of official policy objectives sends a signal that the United States attaches little priority to these commitments. Because these objectives are never listed as policy goals, the

NPR creates ambiguity about whether U.S. officials still see a nuclear-free world as a desirable goal.

Given this ambiguity, some have questioned how real the reductions envisioned by the NPR will turn out to be. The Moscow Treaty does not mandate any restrictions on force size after it expires in 2012, and the NPR calls for creating an open-ended "responsive force," meaning that some percentage of the warheads taken off operational deployment might be available for redeployment on short notice. These hedges against "locking in" reductions have created doubts about whether the envisioned cuts actually will prove permanent. The NPR leaves considerable room for uncertainty about whether the United States supports NPT norms favoring eventual elimination of nuclear arsenals.[10]

Conflicts with Nonuse Principles

The NPR, in combination with other statements of U.S. strategy, challenges not only general understandings regarding possession but also the potential use of nuclear arms. Suggestions that the United States will consider using nuclear weapons in preemptive strikes against a range of nonnuclear targets contradict the nuclear taboo that has been developing since 1945. The threat of nuclear strikes against chemical or biological weapons (CBW) facilities has received the most attention. The reasons for considering this option are easy to comprehend. First, nuclear arms are more destructive than chemical and biological arms, so restraining nuclear weapons has generally been the top nonproliferation priority, and other WMD threats do not reverse that priority. Second, while the regime has tolerated threats to use nuclear weapons in retaliatory strikes as a means of deterring attacks by others, the new U.S. national security strategy does not restrict nuclear weapons primarily to a deterrent role. Because of fears that deterrence might fail, official U.S. statements now envision possible preventive nuclear strikes in situations where the other side has not attacked or possibly even threatened an attack on the United States.

Furthermore, the NPR discusses possible nuclear use in situations beyond preempting potential CBW attacks. It identifies command, control, and military infrastructure, including those elements that might be in hardened, underground sites, as potential targets.[11] While the motivations behind all these shifts are entirely understandable, suggestions that the United States would consider nuclear weapons use as an option in contingencies other than responding to the threat of a nuclear attack are hard to square with the goal of maintaining a taboo against nuclear use.

Conflicts with Specific Commitments

The NPR and associated developments also seem to repudiate specific commitments made in connection with the NPT. For example, if threats to use nuclear weapons against biological or chemical weapon sites apply to states that do not have nuclear weapons and are party to the NPT, such threats—and, obviously, any actual nuclear strikes—violate existing negative security guarantees.

The NPR also calls into question commitments regarding nuclear testing. It recommends maintaining the current testing moratorium for the time being, but also confirms the Bush administration's opposition to seeking CTBT ratification. The NPR also strongly implies the possible future resumption of testing. It calls for reducing the lead time required to resume testing at the Nevada Test Site; it states that it might not be possible to maintain the existing moratorium indefinitely and that the need for testing will be reassessed annually; and it observes that decisions about whether to produce new types of warheads will entail "assessments of whether nuclear testing would be required to field such weapons."[12]

The NPR also ignores the principle of irreversibility adopted at the 2000 review conference. The nuclear force reductions envisioned in the posture review, which were formalized in the Moscow Treaty, do not involve any steps to make the reductions permanent, such as dismantling warheads removed from operational deployment.[13] On the contrary, the concept of a responsive force explicitly holds open the possibility of reversing reductions by redeploying warheads that were previously removed from missiles or bombers.

Conflict with the Underlying Idea of
Unconventional Weapons

Finally, the NPR is at least partly in tension with one of the deepest underlying understandings behind the various nonproliferation regimes: the distinction between conventional and unconventional weapons. Aspects of the new triad reduce this sense of differentiation between nuclear and conventional weapons. In particular, the NPR combines nuclear and nonnuclear strike forces in a single leg of the triad and suggests that both nuclear and nonnuclear options should be available for a wide range of contingencies. On the one hand, this could reduce reliance on nuclear weapons by creating nonnuclear alternatives, which would be consistent with the regime's goal of preventing nuclear use. On the other hand, this suggests that all weapons types should be equally available for use, with the choice dependent upon which option will best accomplish the mission at hand—implying that the United States should not limit its options due to some sense that nuclear weapons are "different." On balance, the NPR tends to "conventionalize" nuclear forces more strongly than it implies a desire to preclude their ever being used. This tendency to think about nuclear arms in conventional terms underlies much of what brings the posture review into conflict with existing nonproliferation arrangements.

THE NET EFFECT ON PROLIFERATION
WILL BE NEGATIVE

The conclusion that the NPR is incompatible with the nonproliferation regime does not automatically mean the U.S. nuclear posture will exacerbate the proliferation problem. Indeed, as Jeff Larsen points out in chapter 11, any prediction about the impact of the NPR must consider how the NPR and other Bush administration initiatives might make positive contributions to combating WMD proliferation. On balance, however, the counterproductive effects of the NPR for nuclear nonproliferation are likely to be stronger than its impact on restricting proliferation. The new directions in U.S. strategy could actually make nuclear proliferation more likely by weakening support for the NPT, by affecting perceptions of the utility of nuclear weapons, and by creating direct incentives for nuclear proliferation.

Consequences of Weakening the NPT

According to the NPT "bargain," most states agreed never to seek nuclear weapons in return for commitments by existing NWS to reduce their nuclear arsenals and not to target NNWS with their nuclear weapons. If other states perceive that the United States is not upholding its end of the bargain, their commitment to the regime is likely to slacken. In most cases, this will not lead to withdrawal from the NPT or an effort to develop nuclear arms. Rather, other countries will become less willing to invest in maintaining the regime. This could arise from pique that their trust has been violated, from a belief that "defections" of their own will pressure the United States to comply with its NPT obligations, or from loss of confidence in the regime's viability if they perceive the United States as no longer committed to the NPT. [14]

As a result, other states might give less support to the regime's institutions, such as the International Atomic Energy Agency (IAEA). They also may become less inclined to cooperate with the United States in collective enforcement efforts against suspected regime violators. Any perception that the NPT is unraveling will lessen the inhibitions against initiating new nuclear weapons programs. For all these reasons, U.S. policies that chip away at the foundations of the current nonproliferation regime could make future proliferation more likely.

Effects on Perceptions of the Value of
Nuclear Weapons

Because the United States is the world's sole superpower, what it seeks to do with its nuclear arsenal is likely to influence how other countries view such weapons. The NPR could increase the perceived utility of nuclear weapons. The NPR does not treat nuclear weapons as weapons whose sole use is to deter existential threats. By grouping together nuclear and conventional strike forces and contemplating possible nuclear first strikes against certain nonnuclear targets, the NPR projects an image of nuclear weapons as usable military instruments. If the United States suggests that it regards nuclear weapons as both useful and usable in a range of contingencies, other countries will be more likely to identify military contingencies in which nuclear weapons might be useful to them. This could give them new reasons to seek nuclear arms.

Because the NPR suggests NPT Article VI will not be implemented any time soon and points to possible new missions for nuclear arms, it could enhance beliefs that to become a great power it will be necessary for a state to deploy a nuclear arsenal. This perception creates incentives for proliferation beyond the usual rogue-state suspects. This perceived association of major-power status and possession of nuclear arms was an important factor in India's development of nuclear weapons.[15] Nationalist sentiment in rising regional powers, such as Brazil, Indonesia, or South Africa, or in former great powers such as Japan or (less likely) Germany, could create pressures to develop a nuclear arsenal as a way to join (or rejoin) the great power club.

Direct Effects on Other States' Proliferation Incentives

Apart from their effects on the nonproliferation regime and on perceptions of the utility of nuclear weapons, the U.S. nuclear posture and related policies could directly affect the security calculations of other states. The question is whether the U.S. posture is more likely to dissuade or to encourage proliferation. Recent U.S. policy provides some incentives in both directions, which makes it difficult to predict the net effects with confidence. There are grounds, however, for expecting that U.S. national security efforts will be a spur to proliferation in at least some cases.

The NPR and other aspects of U.S. strategy seek to enhance the U.S. ability to respond to WMD proliferation. These counterproliferation aspects of U.S. strategy might reduce other actors' incentives to proliferate in the first place. For example, new offensive strike capabilities that could destroy chemical or biological weapon sites, especially when combined with a doctrine that threatens preventive attacks, could convince rogue states that they will be denied any chance to benefit from developing NBC weapons. This extends the familiar logic of "deterrence by denial" into what recent defense planning documents have labeled the "dissuasion" mission. While deterrence typically seeks to convince countries not to use existing forces to launch an attack, dissuasion seeks to convince them not to develop certain military capabilities in the first place. The Iraq war of 2003, moreover, showed U.S. willingness to act preventively in response to perceived WMD threats. This could make the threat to act elsewhere more credible, thereby increasing U.S. ability to compel other states to give up existing NBC development programs.

Although the new U.S. posture creates some disincentives for proliferation, there are also factors that could limit the effectiveness of dissuasion. While it is easy to believe the United States would retaliate against a chemical or biological attack, other countries might doubt that the United States would use nuclear weapons in a "bolt from the blue" first strike against sites related to chemical or biological weapons programs. If they did fear such strikes, they might also believe they could design around U.S. strike capabilities, for example by building their facilities even deeper underground, by increasing the mobility of their weapons, or by deploying a large number of weapons. Highly motivated proliferants are still likely to believe they can get away with developing and deploying NBC weapons (but U.S. strike and defense capabilities should still exercise a traditional deterrent effect against *use* of such weapons).

In addition to the intended dissuasive effects, the NPR and related aspects of U.S. strategy might add to the motivations to obtain NBC weapons. Apparently the NPR explicitly names several states as possible nuclear targets, and U.S. policy statements as a whole suggest that nuclear weapons might be used, even preemptively, against chemical and biological weapons sites and command and control centers (including a state's leaders). U.S. actions in Iraq add the threat of invasion by conventional forces to impose a regime change. These threats to target other states' weapons and leaders, without necessarily waiting to see if those states first attack the United States, might encourage rogue regimes to embrace good behavior. At the same time, though, the U.S. stance will create fear in other capitals about regime survival, which could lead them to focus on increasing their security against possible U.S. threats. The more explicitly the United States declares it might launch nuclear strikes in scenarios other than responding to a nuclear attack, the more incentive other countries have to think about how they might deter such a nuclear strike upon themselves. Realistically, the most effective deterrent against a potential nuclear attack is to have a nuclear retaliatory capability. Thus, the NPR creates added incentives for certain other countries to develop an indigenous nuclear capability.

Developments since President George W. Bush took office provide mixed evidence on how rogue regimes will react to hard-line U.S. policies. On the face evidence of their behavior, Libya appears to represent a success for the new approach; Iran is a mixed outcome; and North Korea appears to demonstrate how the new posture can make matters worse.

In December 2003, Libya's Colonel Qaddafi agreed to give up his country's NBC weapon programs. Fear that Libya could be the next Iraq likely played a role but was not alone decisive. Libya had been making efforts to rejoin the international community and get economic sanctions lifted since before the Bush administration came to power. The costs of sanctions and the existence of a diplomatic track that offered the possibility for Qaddafi to improve his regime's situation thus also mattered. Countries that are not experiencing international isolation, or that do not care about ending such isolation, or that do not believe the United States will respond positively to their diplomacy might not respond as favorably to U.S. coercive tactics. In addition, the importance of the Iraq example suggests Qaddafi reacted mainly to the threat the United States might use conventional forces. This example thus provides little evidence as to whether the threat of offensive nuclear strikes would prove equally credible and productive.

Iran and North Korea, in contrast, suggest that the threatening posture conveyed by U.S. statements can prove counterproductive. Both countries had clandestine nuclear weapons programs before 2001 and governments that were quick to proclaim their implacable hostility to the United States. Once the policy views of the Bush administration became clear—as symbolized by the inclusion of both countries in the "axis of evil"—it appears both countries intensified their drives toward nuclear weapons. In October 2003, following diplomatic efforts by European governments, Iran agreed to certain steps that, if implemented, would have put much of its nuclear weapons activity on hold. But by June 2004, the IAEA was reporting that Iran had failed to abide by its NPT obligations and had been actively pursuing nuclear capabilities. Given the mix of coercion and diplomacy involved and the switches back and forth in Iranian policy, Iran cannot be considered either a clear success or a clear failure for the Bush approach.

North Korea, however, is at the time of this writing still moving toward development of a functional nuclear arsenal. Since Bush became president, North Korea has withdrawn from both the NPT and the 1994 Agreed Framework and begun reprocessing plutonium that had previously been under IAEA safeguards. In December 2003, North Korea announced that it had one or more nuclear weapons in its arsenal. Rather than dissuading North Korea, the NPR and other aspects of Bush policy seem to have heightened Pyongyang's insecurities and thereby increased the urgency the regime felt about nuclear weapons development. The North Korean case suggests that, confronted with U.S. threats to take action against them, countries with a gradual development program might decide to increase the program's pace and make their nuclear ambitions more open, in hopes of being able to deter a perceived new threat from the United States. In this way, the NPR could end up contributing to proliferation.[16]

If some states, fearing their WMD option could soon be preempted, choose to cross the nuclear threshold openly and as quickly as possible, they will in turn affect the security calculations of other states. For example, North Korean deployment of a nuclear arsenal would force Japan and South Korea to consider acquiring their own nuclear deterrents. Each new state that goes nuclear will further weaken the nonproliferation regime and could lead additional states in the region to perceive new security threats, possibly triggering a proliferation chain reaction. The net results of the conflicting incentives and disincentives created by the U.S. posture are difficult to predict, but if even a single country responds by moving from development efforts to deployment of a nuclear arsenal, this development would be a serious consequence.

OPTIONS FOR MITIGATING THE NEGATIVE IMPACT ON NONPROLIFERATION

On balance, current trends in U.S. national security strategy, including its nuclear component, are likely to damage nonproliferation efforts more than they bolster them. Five possible policy actions exist, however, that could lessen the conflict between the U.S. nuclear posture and the nonproliferation regime. The effectiveness of these measures is likely to be limited. The core premises of the emerging U.S. nuclear doctrine and those of the nonproliferation regime are too different to be easily reconciled.

The first two policy options I list would be most effective measures to reduce the tension between U.S. strategy and the NPT. They also are the least likely to be adopted, however, because they would require foreclosing some options that the posture review seeks to keep open. I therefore add three further policy suggestions. Even though these are not likely to do as much to reduce the negative effects on nonproliferation, they are also not directly incompatible with the NPR and thus stand a better chance of being implemented.

Ratify the CTBT

The single most effective step the United States could take to reduce international criticism of the NPR's consequences for nonproliferation and to impart new momentum to the regime would be to ratify the comprehensive test ban and then work to secure the signatures and ratifications of other countries needed to bring about the treaty's entry into force. Whether or not a CTBT would actually be an effective nonproliferation measure, it has come to have great importance as a symbol of states' commitments to stop both vertical and horizontal proliferation. Ratification and active efforts to promote entry into force would send a clear signal that the world's sole superpower is still willing to put its weight behind the original NPT bargain. This would be an effective way to blunt criticism of U.S. nuclear weapons policy and create political space for some of the other controversial elements of the NPR.

Ratifying the CTBT also would make it more difficult for the United States to pursue certain objectives envisioned by the NPR. It would foreclose or make harder the possible development of a new, low-yield earth penetrating warhead, add to uncertainty about the long-term reliability of the existing nuclear stockpile, and limit the options for a future generation of nuclear delivery systems. Unless current priorities change, therefore, the proposal to seek CTBT ratification is unlikely to be accepted.

Adopt a No-First-Use of WMD Policy

The best chance to reconcile the conflicting principles behind the posture review and the nonproliferation regime would be to adopt a no-first-use policy with respect to all WMD—and to invite other countries to make the same pledge. A no-first-use pledge covering nuclear, biological and chemical weapons would help reinforce the norms seeking to delegitimize these weapons. It would thus make U.S. policy more compatible with the norms of the nuclear nonproliferation regime. At the same time, though, by linking the three types of weapons of mass destruction more closely, such a posture would help legitimize threatening to use nuclear weapons in response to a chemical or biological attack. Seeking a global no-first-use regime could thus make it seem more acceptable to threaten to retaliate with nuclear weapons after a CBW attack or to include a damage-limitation mission in the nuclear posture, provided that the posture specified that such strikes would only be launched after an initial attack by another state.

A no-first-use posture would also require renouncing the possibility of using nuclear weapons in preventive strikes—including the implication in the NPR that nuclear preemption might be acceptable. For this reason, there is little chance this recommendation will be adopted. If it were, this would require accepting a serious tradeoff, because the threat to use nuclear weapons in preemptive first strikes is the feature of emerging U.S. strategy that places the most strain on international efforts to restrain proliferation.

Change the Tone of Diplomacy and Rhetoric on Nuclear Weapons

Although CTBT ratification and a no-first-use policy would have the greatest potential to minimize conflicts between U.S. nuclear strategy and the nonproliferation regime, it is unlikely that these measures will be adopted at the present time. Much could be gained, however, by adjusting the language of U.S. diplomacy. Although people elsewhere genuinely object to some of the content of the NPR, their negative reactions have been made sharper because the posture review emerged amid rising unease about U.S. rhetoric and policy actions on other issues. Taking steps to reduce the friction in relations with other countries would help lessen the resistance to U.S. policy plans, including the NPR. Implementation of the NPR could thus be smoothed by improving the tone of U.S. diplomacy, making a greater effort to consult with allies, showing more responsiveness to the policy concerns of other countries, and seeking more often to work with the United Nations— and by cutting back on the number of prominent statements that emphasize U.S. intentions to act alone when necessary.

The benefits of adjusting foreign policy rhetoric apply specifically to the nuclear weapons realm as well. The leaked portions of the NPR do not once mention the NPT or list eventual nuclear disarmament as a goal. This suggests some simple ways to mitigate the negative consequences of the NPR for the nonproliferation regime. In official policy documents and statements, the United States could more regularly acknowledge the NPT, including the nuclear disarmament goals of Article VI and the U.S. commitment to meet its Article VI obligations. The president and other officials could also emphasize in their public statements the global nature of WMD threats and the shared aspirations of all people to see these weapons eliminated. Framing U.S. policies as part of a common, worldwide fight against WMD proliferation, rather than talking about nonproliferation only as it relates to purely U.S. national interests, would invite others to support new U.S. initiatives to fight proliferation.

A historical precedent shows that such rhetorical adjustments can be effective. In the early 1980s, the Reagan administration helped dissipate widespread opposition to its nuclear weapon policies by consciously changing the language it used.[17] Administration officials stopped discussing in public the possibility that a nuclear war could be won. Instead, officials, including the president, began emphasizing that a nuclear war must never be fought. If President Bush and other U.S. officials began speaking publicly of a desire to reduce reliance on nuclear weapons and make progress toward a nuclear-free world, they could similarly reduce some of the suspicion about U.S. motives aroused by the NPR.

Strengthen Positive Security Guarantees and Cooperation

If nuclear proliferation continues, the new nuclear nations will pose potential security threats to other countries, including U.S. friends and allies. In the past, the United States has sought to diffuse such pressures by offering positive security guarantees, which involve a promise to assist nonnuclear states that confront a possible nuclear weapon threat from another country. In the Cold War, the United States provided positive guarantees mainly in the form of extended deterrence: it provided a "nuclear umbrella" that helped convince other states not to seek their own nuclear deterrent.

The United States could reduce the chances that the new global security environment will trigger nuclear development programs by reinvigorating its use of positive security guarantees. This could take several forms. The United States could publicly restate and repeatedly emphasize its existing extended deterrence commitments. This might be especially important in reassuring Japan and South Korea in light of the continuing crisis with North Korea. The United States could initiate efforts to work out new forms of security cooperation designed to address alllies' security concerns. This could involve new consultation procedures to assure regional allies they will have real input into relevant U.S. policy decisions. In addition, the United States could accelerate efforts to assist key allies in the deployment of missile defenses. Helping other states develop and deploy ballistic missile defenses would give them an alternative defense measure to pursuing an independent nuclear deterrent.

Further Cut the U.S. Nuclear Arsenal

The United States could counteract some of the criticism that the NPR is inconsistent with Article VI and help reinforce norms that favor moving toward eventual nuclear abolition by committing itself to reduce nuclear weapons even more than called for by the posture review. As established in the Moscow Treaty, the United States currently plans to reduce operationally deployed weapons to between 1,700 and 2,200 by 2012, while moving an unspecified number of weapons into a responsive force. The only scenario in which the United States could find that many targets for nuclear weapons is a U.S.-Russian nuclear war. The NPR and the Moscow Treaty, however, start from the premise that the prospect of Russian–American nuclear hostilities is very unlikely. Furthermore, even if this assumption about U.S.-Russian relations proves to be overly optimistic, Russia lacks the wherewithal to catch the United States by surprise with a sudden nuclear arms buildup. There is no pressing reason to retain an arsenal as large as the NPR envisions; the United States could maintain a credible nuclear deterrent at lower force levels.

The United States could therefore increase both the speed and depth of its nuclear arms reductions. It could announce plans to reach the Moscow Treaty limits much earlier than 2012, and it could declare a lower ceiling as the end goal. Aiming for a posture of 1,000 to 1,200 deployed warheads, for example, would still leave the United States well ahead of China and with ample ability to target the potential rogue state threats emphasized in the current national security strategy. Yet cuts of this size also would be dramatic enough to demonstrate a serious commitment to nuclear arms reductions.

Equally if not more important, the United States should identify a specific number for the size of its responsive force, which should be kept modest, probably no more than 200 to 300 weapons. This would be large enough to let the United States respond to any sudden surge by a more adversarial China or Russia, but small enough to relieve suspicions that the United States plans to use the responsive force as a loophole to avoid significantly reducing its nuclear stockpile. If the United States expressed its long-term objective as reducing and eventually eliminating nuclear weapons—and took actions that represent progress along this path—it could create greater political space to make adjustments to its nuclear posture in the short term.

CONCLUSION

Many people think of themselves as members of something they call "the international community." As with any community, members of the international community have endeavored to create standards of right and wrong and to develop customs and conventions that help each member form expectations about how other members will behave. The international community has developed norms of these types with respect to nuclear weapons, norms that have been largely formalized in the nonproliferation regime. The nonproliferation regime rests on widely shared beliefs that nuclear arms are unconventional weapons, the use of which should be taboo, the proliferation of which—both vertically and horizontally—should be stopped in the short term, and the abolition of which should be pursued in the long term.

A handful of states and non-state actors reject and defy the norms of the international community, including nonproliferation norms. The U.S. government calls these actors rogue states and terrorists, respectively, and has for good reasons grown increasingly concerned about what might happen if these actors acquire WMD. These concerns have been a driving force in the formulation of a new national security strategy, including the new nuclear posture.

Unfortunately, the proposals for how the United States should respond to the increased urgency of threats from rogue states and terrorists include several elements that are themselves incompatible with the principles and rules of the nonproliferation regime. Proposals to consider developing new nuclear weapons, especially if they lead to resumption of testing, and suggestions the United States might use or threaten to use nuclear weapons preemptively against nonnuclear targets pose the sharpest challenges to previous nonproliferation understandings.

These contradictions can be finessed up to a point, but they cannot be avoided altogether. The United States can reduce some of the friction over nonproliferation by altering the language it uses so as to give greater recognition to the NPT and U.S. obligations under that agreement, by pursuing additional cuts in strategic weapons, and by emphasizing other forms of security cooperation. If the United States is willing to step back from some aspects of the new posture, then CTBT ratification and a no-first-use pledge would be even more helpful in limiting possible harm to the nonproliferation regime.

The U.S. government still sees value in maintaining and, if possible, strengthening the nonproliferation regime. It also wants to create new options for the United States to deal with emerging threats. Greater sensitivity to existing international norms could help the United States reconcile these objectives. The tradeoffs between them, however, are real. The NPR and national security strategy are based on the principles that the United States should be willing to act on its own if necessary, using military force preventively, including nuclear options. The nonproliferation regime is based on the principle that every effort should be made to avoid the use of nuclear weapons, including serious efforts to eliminate the possession of such weapons. In short, the tendency to conventionalize nuclear weapons that underlies the new U.S. strategy diverges greatly from the basic understanding that underlies the nonproliferation regime: that nuclear arms are different. This puts U.S. policy on a collision course with regime principles against the use and possession of nuclear weapons. Because the underlying principles of the NPR and the NPT are so divergent, the United States cannot fully achieve both its new defense objectives and its objective of strengthening the existing nonproliferation regime. Before the United States implements a new posture, it must make a choice about where to set the balance between alternative policy approaches and priorities in this area.

Notes

1. Stephen D. Krasner, ed., *International Regimes* (Ithaca, N.Y.: Cornell University Press, 1983). For the standard definition of a regime, see page 1.
2. In practice, the three types of weapons differ considerably in their effects, to the extent that some people argue only nuclear weapons are truly weapons of mass destruction. For a comparison of the relative effects, see Steve Fetter, "Ballistic Missiles and Weapons of Mass Destruction: What is the Threat? What Should be Done?" *International Security* 16, no. 1 (Summer 1991).
3. Nuclear technical assistance has been an issue in U.S. disputes with Iran, however. The United States opposes Iran's construction of nuclear power plants at Bushehr, while Iran defends its nuclear energy program on the grounds that it is a peaceful application of nuclear power and hence legally consistent with Iran's NPT obligations.
4. 1995 Review and Extension Conference of the Parties to the Treaty on the Non-Proliferation of Nuclear Weapons, Final Document, Part I, Decision 2: "Principles and Objectives for Nuclear Non-Proliferation and Disarmament," NPT/CONF.1995/32 (Part I), 10.
5. Ibid.
6. Final Document Issued by 2000 *NPT* Review Conference, May 20, 2000, as reproduced in U.S. Department of State, Washington File <usinfo.state.gov/topical/pol/arms/stories/finaldoc.htm>.
7. The estimate that thirty-four states had an interest in nuclear weapons comes from James Walsh, Executive Director of the Managing the Atom Project, Kennedy School of Government, Harvard University, "Nonproliferation, Persuasion and Peace," *The Philadelphia Inquirer* December 12, 2003 <www.ksg.harvard.edu/news/opeds/2003/walsh_atom_pi_121203.htm>. Among the states listed as examples of nuclear renunciation, South Africa and Ukraine both had nuclear weapons on their soil before they joined the NPT.
8. Jean du Preez, "The Impact of the Nuclear Posture Review on the International Nuclear Nonproliferation Regime," *The Nonproliferation Review* 9, no. 3 (Fall/Winter 2002): 70, 75.
9. *Nuclear Posture Review* (January 8, 2002): 41–44 (all page references according to original indicated in excerpts posted at <www.globalsecurity.org/wmd/library/policy/dod/npr.htm>).
10. See du Preez, "The Impact of the Nuclear Posture Review," for examples of statements by officials of other governments and the United Nations that express skepticism on precisely these points.
11. *NPR*, "Sizing the Nuclear Force," 16.
12. Ibid., "NNSA Initiatives for Nuclear Weapons Programs," 35.
13. The administration has said this is an unfair criticism because no prior arms control treaty explicitly mandated dismantling warheads. All previous treaties were negotiated before the 1995 and 2000 review conferences, however, and acceptance at these conferences of such goals as progressive reductions and irreversibility implied a commitment that new arms control treaties would have to satisfy these new criteria.
14. On the importance of such reciprocity in sustaining international cooperation, see Robert Axelrod, *The Evolution of Cooperation* (New York: Basic Books, 1984); Robert O. Keohane, *After Hegemony: Cooperation and Discord in the World Political Economy* (Princeton, N.J.: Princeton University Press, 1984).

15. George Perkovich, *India's Nuclear Bomb: The Impact on Global Proliferation* (Berkeley and Los Angeles, Calif.: University of California Press, 1999). See, e.g., 400.

16. This should not be taken to imply the NPR somehow *caused* North Korea to go nuclear; North Korea was already working covertly on a nuclear weapons program before President Bush took office, so its decision to seek nuclear weapons has other roots. My point is rather that, having inherited a bad situation, the Bush administration, through its hard-line diplomacy and the NPR, initially made this situation even worse. Since the ultimate outcome has yet to be determined, however, no final judgment is yet possible. (At the conference where we first presented these papers, Charles Ball pointed out that my initial presentation could be interpreted as implying the NPR caused North Korea's proliferation. I thank him for drawing my attention to the need to clarify this point.)

17. For details, see Jeffrey W. Knopf, *Domestic Society and International Cooperation: The Impact of Protest on U.S. Arms Control Policy* (Cambridge, U.K.: Cambridge University Press, 1998), ch. 7.

INTERNATIONAL REACTIONS

13

The NATO Allies

David S. Yost

The most recent U.S. Nuclear Posture Review (NPR), completed in December 2001, has received little sustained attention in North Atlantic Treaty Organization (NATO) countries outside expert circles in governments, research institutes, and nongovernmental organizations. Popular and, to some extent, governmental and expert impressions of the NPR remain marked by critical news coverage in early 2002. Views of the NPR are influenced by aspects of U.S. policy that have rightly or wrongly become closely associated with it, including President George W. Bush's description of Iran, Iraq, and North Korea as an "axis of evil" in January 2002; the administration's elevation of the option of preemptive military action to the status of a doctrine; and the administration's comparatively explicit language concerning the possibility of nuclear retaliation for the use of chemical or biological weapons against U.S. interests.

Given that all decision making in NATO is based on consensus building, it is impossible to discuss NPR implementation and the alliance without considering allied views on associated issues, even if these issues are not strictly elements of the NPR. This essay discusses the brief reference to NATO that reportedly appears in the NPR before turning to allied views on the NPR's main implications.

NATO in the NPR

The nuclear capabilities considered in the NPR were strategic forces—that is, U.S. long-range nuclear forces such as bombers, intercontinental ballistic missiles (ICBMs), and submarine launched ballistic missiles. The NPR deferred attention to the nuclear gravity bombs and dual-capable aircraft remaining in Europe after the United States completed extensive reductions in its nuclear presence in the early 1990s.[1] However, the NPR reportedly included the following paragraph:

Dual-capable aircraft and nuclear weapons in support of NATO. DoD will not seek any change to the current posture in FY02 but will review both issues to assess whether any modifications to the current posture are appropriate to

adapt to the changing threat environment. A plan is already underway to
conduct a NATO review of U.S. and allied dual-capable aircraft in Europe and
to present recommendations to Ministers in [the] summer of 2002. Dual-capable
aircraft and deployed weapons are important to the continued viability of
NATO's nuclear deterrent strategy and any changes need to be discussed
within the alliance.[2]

NATO evidently completed a review of dual-capable aircraft, because in
June 2003, the Nuclear Planning Group (that is, the defense ministers of all
the allies except France) "noted with satisfaction that, based on our guidance
issued in June last year, NATO's dual-capable aircraft posture has been further adapted and readiness requirements for these aircraft have been further
relaxed."[3] In December 2000, the allies had noted that, "At the height of
the Cold War, quick-reaction alert capable of launching within minutes
was maintained for a portion of these aircraft, whereas nuclear readiness is
now measured in weeks and months. There are no longer any NATO sub-
strategic nuclear forces in Europe on alert."[4] The allies have evidently
expanded the proportion of dual-capable aircraft that are maintained at
lower levels of readiness. The relaxation of readiness requirements for dual-
capable aircraft has provoked little discussion or controversy in NATO.

Allied observers have assessed the NPR's broader significance from various perspectives. Bruno Tertrais, a prominent French expert, has suggested
that the NPR represents three noteworthy aspirations: ending "Russo-
centrism" in U.S. nuclear planning, which has important implications for
force sizing; endorsing a new comprehensive concept of deterrence, in
which nuclear forces are supplemented with missile defenses and high-
technology conventional means; and stopping the decline of the U.S. nuclear
infrastructure.[5]

Allied experts recognize that the NPR affects America's strategic posture
in at least three significant ways. They note that the NPR will reduce operationally deployed U.S. strategic nuclear warheads by almost two-thirds over
the decade ending in 2012. They acknowledge that the Bush administration
is emphasizing the development and/or improvement of capabilities other
than nuclear forces, including missile defenses, nonnuclear strike forces,
C4ISR, and a responsive infrastructure—and integrating these capabilities,
together with nuclear forces, in a new triad. They also realize that the NPR
places U.S. nuclear force policy within the conceptual framework of the
2001 Quadrennial Defense Review, with new concepts such as "dissuasion"
and "capabilities-based" planning.

REDUCING OPERATIONALLY DEPLOYED U.S. STRATEGIC NUCLEAR WARHEADS

The main findings of the NPR reflect President Bush's November 2001
decision to reduce operationally deployed U.S. strategic nuclear warheads by
almost two-thirds by 2012. Allied observers have to date expressed little

concern about the implications of these reductions for extended deterrence, but they may do so in some circumstances. The reductions foreseen in the NPR furnished the basis for the May 2002 Moscow Treaty. Allied observers have generally welcomed the treaty as a political substitute for the Anti-Ballistic Missile (ABM) Treaty and Strategic Arms Reduction Treaty negotiations, but have found it disappointing as an arms control measure. Moreover, some allied observers regret that the United States has concluded that it is not practical to pursue negotiated arms control regarding Russian nonstrategic nuclear forces.

Implications for Extended Deterrence

Perhaps partly because of the improved relations with Russia, allied observers have expressed no noteworthy concerns about the effects of the NPR-mandated reductions in operationally deployed U.S. strategic nuclear warheads on extended deterrence. This is consistent with a long-standing pattern in which most allies have deemed strategic nuclear matters a U.S. responsibility and have deferred to U.S. judgment about the appropriate structure and size of U.S. strategic nuclear forces.

Exceptions to this pattern have arisen historically, however, and further exceptions could occur in some circumstances. Ever since the Soviet Union launched Sputnik in 1957 and developed the world's first ICBMs, NATO has been subject to periodic crises of confidence—in essence, European doubts about America's will to defend its allies, given the risk of prompt intercontinental nuclear retaliation from Moscow. These doubts have been aggravated whenever Americans have expressed anxieties about U.S. strategic capabilities—as during the "bomber gap" and "missile gap" controversies in the late 1950s and early 1960s, and the debates about the second Strategic Arms Limitation Treaty (SALT II), ICBM vulnerability, and "gray area" systems such as the Backfire bomber in the late 1970s and early 1980s. If a debate emerged in the United States about the adequacy of the U.S. strategic force posture for national security (without the U.S. debate necessarily featuring extended deterrence for allied security), allied experts and officials would probably ask questions about the implications for NATO, Japan, and other beneficiaries of U.S. nuclear guarantees. In this event, the perceived political commitment of the United States—including its manifest intentions and its apparent confidence in the adequacy of its strategic nuclear posture—would probably matter more in reassuring allies than the size of the force and its specific characteristics.

Short of a grave crisis in which the resolve and operational capabilities of the United States would be tested, the U.S. strategic nuclear force posture is significant for extended deterrence in Europe mainly on a political level. Moreover, many allied observers have long regarded the numbers of U.S. strategic nuclear warheads as disproportionate to the requirements of the post–Cold War world, in which the most immediate threats are terrorists and regional powers armed with weapons of mass destruction (WMD) and in which Russia (it is hoped) may increasingly become a reliable partner of the alliance.

Critical Assessments of the Moscow Treaty

The Moscow Treaty, the May 2002 U.S.-Russian treaty on strategic nuclear arms control, is much less elaborate than previous bilateral nuclear arms control treaties. It is therefore in keeping with the NPR's call to move beyond the intricate, lengthy, and inflexible accords of the Cold War. The Moscow Treaty also is consistent with the NPR in restating the U.S. level of operationally deployed strategic nuclear warheads for 2012 envisaged by the NPR. This force level was defined as a function of America's global strategic requirements rather than requirements for targeting Russia. A certain link to Russian strategic nuclear force levels remains, however, not only because of the Moscow Treaty terms, but also because of the NPR's "second to none" principle concerning operationally deployed strategic nuclear forces. That is, to satisfy the U.S. defense policy goal of assuring U.S. allies about the reliability of U.S. security commitments, the United States must maintain operationally deployed strategic nuclear capabilities that are "second to none."

Allied observers have praised the Moscow Treaty as a political substitute for the ABM Treaty and a means to avoid a U.S.-Russian confrontation undercutting the whole structure of treaty-based arms control. Some allied observers consider the fact that the Moscow Treaty was signed in May 2002—before the U.S. withdrawal from the ABM Treaty took effect in June 2002—as positive and significant. Despite general political relief in allied circles that the U.S.-Russian agreement was articulated in the form of a treaty, some dissatisfaction with the Moscow Treaty persists.

Allied critics attribute what they consider the treaty's deficiencies to the Bush administration's original interest in pursuing non-treaty-based arms control, which seems to these detractors to have been translated into a treaty generating few obligations or constraints. According to the critics, the Moscow Treaty suffers from several deficiencies. They note that the relatively short three-months'-notice withdrawal clause diminishes the predictability that, in their view, arms control treaties should provide. They judge that the treaty's verification mechanisms, including how START I procedures will be used and what counting rules will apply, are vague, and in fact constitute a U.S. failure to seek greater transparency regarding Russia's nuclear arsenal and infrastructure, including production and dismantlement facilities, with steps toward nuclear disarmament. Critics also charge that the treaty, like the Moscow–Washington nuclear arms control treaties during the Cold War, fails to provide for the destruction of warheads withdrawn from operational deployment and, in fact, tacitly permits their storage for possible redeployment. Some observers regret that the treaty fails to ban Russia's ICBMs equipped with multiple independently targetable reentry vehicles (MIRVs), enabling Moscow to retain its SS-18s and MIRV the Topol M, and generally providing Russia with more options at lower costs than it would have had under START II. Critics also assert that because the Moscow Treaty allows Russia to maintain its intercontinental nuclear capabilities by MIRVing ICBMs, it encourages Russia to maintain strategic nuclear parity and a mutual assured destruction (MAD) relationship with the United States at an affordable price, despite the Bush administration's declared interest in going beyond MAD in U.S.-Russian strategic relations. Many observers also are concerned about the "reversibility" of the entire agreement. The treaty obliges Russia to respect the ceiling of 2,200 operationally deployed strategic nuclear warheads only on December 31, 2012, after which Moscow will be at liberty to deploy additional warheads.

U.S. supporters of the Moscow Treaty have argued that it preserves the flexibility and adaptability called for in the NPR, including the "responsive force" options. Under the Moscow Treaty, the United States will be able to reduce its operationally deployed strategic nuclear warheads while retaining force structure and protecting vital conventional capabilities. Furthermore, they note that the Moscow Treaty approach to arms control steps away from an adversarial Cold War relationship with Russia. Allied critics have replied that the goal of maintaining flexibility for the U.S. nuclear posture has been pursued at the expense of what might have been an opportunity to gain better transparency and control over the Russian nuclear arsenal. Aside from the practical problems of effective warhead transparency and verification, Russia's willingness to agree to greater transparency and control is in fact doubtful, in view of the years of failure during the William Clinton administration to achieve these objectives in the START III consultations with Moscow.

Some allied critics have expressed bewilderment and skepticism at how the U.S. government's emphasis on uncertainty and preparedness to meet unexpected threats appears to be joined with confidence in Russia's future democratization and reliability as a partner in international security. In their view, by failing to seek a more comprehensive and binding treaty, the United States has neglected the risk that Vladimir Putin or a future Russian leader could preside over an economic recovery, pursue more authoritarian and assertive policies within and beyond Russia, and make his country a powerful adversary of the United States and the Atlantic alliance as a whole. How any negotiable treaty could provide protection against such a contingency, however, remains unclear.

Continuing Concerns about Russian Nonstrategic Nuclear Forces

Some allied observers have expressed regret that the United States has concluded that it is impractical to go beyond the Moscow Treaty to pursue negotiated arms control regarding Russian nonstrategic nuclear forces (NSNF), despite the fact that many of these weapons could be applied to "strategic" purposes. At the same time, allied experts recognize both the inherent obstacles to arms control for NSNF and Russia's unwillingness to pursue arms control for NSNF.

The inherent obstacles to arms control for NSNF include the baseline or initialization problems (such as determining the numbers and locations of Russian NSNF) and the difficulties of verification and geographical scope. The baseline numbers on the Russian side could not be easily established, at least in the eyes of cautious and responsible officials in alliance governments. The verification difficulties, especially regarding NSNF warheads, raise questions about whether arms control gains could be reliably realized. The problems of defining "Europe" and hedging against Russian options for covert redeployments could, moreover, argue for global limitations. This would evoke issues not only of territorial scope, but also of the participants—for example, it might include China, India, and Pakistan as well as the four nuclear powers in Europe (Britain, France, Russia, and the United States), as opposed to a bilateral U.S.-Russian or NATO–Russian negotiation.

Russia's aversion to pursuing arms control measures that would constrain its NSNF has been evident in Moscow's lack of transparency in the NATO–Russia dialogue and its rejection of the confidence and security building measures, including those for NSNF, proposed by NATO.[6] Russia's participation in the seminars, information exchanges, and other NATO–Russia confidence and security building measures for NSNF has appeared to be *pro forma*, and Moscow's unwillingness to provide greater transparency has disappointed allied observers. Whether the readiness to consider greater transparency expressed by some Russian officials in late 2003 will lead to substantial results at the negotiating table remains to be seen.

Some allied observers have accepted as well-founded the U.S. tendency to discount the political and operational relevance of Russia's large arsenal of nonstrategic nuclear forces. According to Secretary of State Colin Powell, "we're concerned . . . with them more from the standpoint of we really don't want these nukes loose anywhere, and as a proliferation problem more so than a war-fighting problem; it's almost a disposal problem more so than a war-fighting problem."[7] Similarly, Secretary of Defense Donald Rumsfeld has said that he "would be perfectly comfortable" with Russia's superiority in this category of nuclear weapons, owing to the distinct geostrategic circumstances of the two countries: "So I'm not looking for symmetry, but I am looking for greater transparency."[8]

In contrast to Secretary Rumsfeld's view, some allied observers would prefer more than greater transparency about Russian NSNF. Their preference would not necessarily be U.S.-Russian symmetry in NSNF, but they would favor drastic reductions in Russian NSNF and some sort of binding verification regime. Some hold that even an unavoidably flawed treaty verification regime might furnish greater knowledge and confidence about the safety and security arrangements for Russian NSNF than Moscow has to date provided in NATO–Russia exchanges. It is difficult, however, to see how such a regime could provide increased confidence in the absence of effective warhead control.

THE NEW TRIAD

The "new triad" under the NPR consists of three legs: nuclear and nonnuclear strike capabilities; active and passive defenses; and a responsive infrastructure. While allied observers have expressed reservations about combining nuclear and nonnuclear strike forces in a single notional leg of the new triad, they have endorsed unprecedented steps in the defensive area, notably with respect to ballistic missile defense. The third leg of the new triad, the responsive infrastructure, has attracted much less attention in allied circles, except in reference to possible nuclear testing.

Combined Nuclear and Nonnuclear Strike Forces

The NPR concept of nonnuclear strike forces encompasses not only "kinetic" systems such as missiles with high-explosive munitions, but also "non-kinetic" capabilities such as information operations assets capable of electronic or computer network attacks. U.S. authorities have noted that the combining of nuclear and nonnuclear strike forces in the same leg of the new triad is a way to substitute nonnuclear explosives for nuclear weapons. Still, it evokes concern because of an impression that this could increase the likelihood that nuclear weapons will be used operationally.

The September 2002 National Security Strategy expressed doubts about the reliability of deterrence and a readiness to engage in preemptive action when threats are immediate and dire.[9] Some allied observers have gone beyond declared U.S. policy and have inaccurately linked U.S. discussions of preemption to the interest in investigating the potential need for (and feasibility of constructing) low-yield and earth-penetrating nuclear weapons and increasing readiness for nuclear testing.[10] The potential new nuclear arms have been portrayed in some circles as part of U.S. preparations for preemptive attacks against WMD proliferants or "rogue" states that support terrorism. Most allied observers strongly object to any doctrine conveying the impression that nuclear weapons could be more readily employed. Like Americans, Europeans and Canadians are committed to deterrence doctrines intended to make actual use of nuclear weapons (indeed, any weapons) increasingly remote. While allied observers understand the decades-old argument that more operationally usable weapons would in fact enhance deterrence by making a threatened nuclear response appear more feasible and hence more credible, many refuse to endorse it.

The NATO allies share the predominant U.S. view that it is imperative to avoid any operational use of nuclear weapons if allied security interests can be defended without their use. They also agree that it is essential to improve conventional nonnuclear capabilities. The allies endorsed this objective in the Prague Summit Declaration in November 2002, notably in the Prague Capabilities Commitment and in the decisions to organize a NATO

Response Force and to devise a more operationally oriented command structure.

Missile Defense

The end of the ABM Treaty—U.S. withdrawal became effective in June 2002—has changed the political and practical context for missile defense in North America and NATO Europe. Allied observers for years had expressed various anxieties about this prospect—above all, that U.S. withdrawal from the ABM Treaty would lead to U.S.-Russian confrontation, provoke an arms race, undermine strategic stability, and terminate nuclear arms control. These fears seemed to have been proven groundless when the Russians expressed only muted regrets about the end of the ABM Treaty, and when Russia and the United States signed the Moscow Treaty in May 2002. Indeed, NATO and Russia agreed in May 2002 to pursue enhanced consultations and cooperation in theater missile defense, and in the same month Russia and the United States announced that they would seek increased transparency in missile defense and examine possible fields for missile defense cooperation.

Moreover, the end of the ABM Treaty rendered irrelevant the distinction between national missile defense (NMD) and theater missile defense (TMD) that derived from respect for ABM Treaty limitations on defenses against "strategic ballistic missiles." Well before the NPR was completed, the Bush administration abandoned the terms NMD and TMD in favor of simply "missile defense." According to Lord Robertson, then the secretary general of NATO, "taking the 'N' out of 'NMD' has changed perceptions on that and encouraged a more rational debate."[11] Some allied observers interpreted the U.S. abandonment of the NMD/TMD distinction as motivated in part by a desire to address longstanding allied concerns about the "decoupling" that hypothetically might derive from asymmetries in vulnerability caused by U.S. missile defenses.

The ABM Treaty ruled out the deployment of U.S. defenses against strategic ballistic missiles in Europe or elsewhere, other than the sole site in the United States permitted after the 1974 amendment of the treaty. With the end of the ABM Treaty, the United States is free to work with its allies to construct such defenses, with no ABM Treaty-imposed restrictions on deployments abroad to protect U.S. allies, air- or sea- or space- or mobile land-based defenses, or transfers to allies of U.S. missile defense technology. Although ending the ABM Treaty eliminated the artificial distinction between theater and strategic missile defenses for some purposes, the term "theater missile defense" is still employed in the alliance to refer to systems to protect deployed forces against shorter-range missiles—as opposed to "full spectrum" defenses against missiles of all ranges for the safety of national homelands.

In weighing the utility of missile defenses, European allied observers have tended to focus less on the capabilities of WMD proliferant states pursuing long-range missile programs than on their intentions. Allies have emphasized the possibility of improving relations with proliferant states through economic and diplomatic measures. Allied skepticism about the utility of missile defenses for the protection of national homelands has been weakening since the late 1990s, however, for various reasons, including impressive Iranian and North Korean missile tests, the terrorist attacks against the United States on September 11, 2001, and the more recent terrorist attacks in Spain and elsewhere. The U.S. and NATO deterrence posture was not designed to prevent terrorist attacks. These attacks nonetheless have been viewed as an indicator of the fallibility of deterrence based on threats of retaliation; the willingness of fanatical adversaries to strike civilian targets; and the potential value of missile defense options, especially when they become technically feasible, effective, and financially affordable. The fact that the United States may be prepared to pay for a disproportionate share of the research and development expenses related to missile defense may help the allies surmount the cost obstacle. Some allies might offer basing sites for sensors, interceptors, or command, control, and communications nodes in lieu of funding. In November 2002, the NATO allies decided to:

> Examine options for addressing the increasing missile threat to Alliance territory, forces and population centres in an effective and efficient way through an appropriate mix of political and defence efforts, along with deterrence. Today we initiated a new NATO Missile Defence feasibility study to examine options for protecting Alliance territory, forces and population centres against the full range of missile threats, which we will continue to assess.[12]

This decision, taken at the Prague Summit, reflects NATO's acceptance of missile defense as an area of increasing importance to the alliance.

Responsive Infrastructure

Few allied observers have commented on the "responsive infrastructure" leg of the new triad. Some have interpreted defining the new triad in this fashion as an attempt by the U.S. government to reverse the long-standing neglect of the nation's nuclear infrastructure. The part of the responsive infrastructure that seems to have raised most apprehension in NATO concerns the plan to improve nuclear testing preparations, so that tests could be conducted more promptly in the event of a decision to resume testing. This apprehension involves multiple anxieties, including the possible development of new nuclear warhead designs and the potential consequences of a collapse of the current informal moratorium on nuclear testing. France, Russia, and the United Kingdom have ratified the Comprehensive Test Ban Treaty (CTBT), unlike China, the United States, and other (non-NPT-recognized) nuclear weapons powers. Some allied observers fear that a U.S. decision to resume testing could provide a pretext for other established nuclear weapons states and nuclear proliferants to test. They believe that U.S. testing could lead to the development of more sophisticated nuclear arms in various national arsenals and further nuclear proliferation. Allied experts acknowledge, however, that the CTBT does not constitute an effective bar to nuclear proliferation in that crude but workable nuclear weapons can be designed and built without testing.

NEW CONCEPTS

Allies have reacted to the new U.S. strategic concepts that have become associated with the NPR in three ways. First, some concepts have been relatively uncontroversial because they represent continuity. For example, the idea of deterrence by threat of punishment remains widely accepted among the allies. Second, certain U.S. concepts are often regarded by allied experts as speculative and yet to be proven—or their validity is deemed hard to prove. These include the theory of dissuading potential adversaries from entering an arms competition by developing specific types of superior military capabilities and the idea of deterring enemies from attacking through missile defenses and other capabilities intended to deny operational success. Third, some of the new U.S. ideas have been highly controversial. The most controversial of the new U.S. concepts in NATO circles has no doubt been that of preemptive action.

Preemption is controversial partly on definitional grounds. The U.S. government has chosen to call "preemptive" what many Americans, Europeans, and others would call "preventive" war. Many observers would make the following distinction: *Preemptive attack* consists of prompt action on the basis of evidence that an enemy is about to strike. In contrast, *preventive war* involves military operations undertaken to avert a plausible but hypothetical future risk, such as an unacceptable balance of power, a position of increased vulnerability, or even potential subjugation—or the possibility of a transfer of WMD to a terrorist group. The latter risk was one of the main justifications advanced by the U.S. government for the military intervention in Iraq in March–April 2003.

Allies do not rule out the idea of preemption on the basis of evidence that an enemy is about to attack. In fact, that principle appears explicitly in a recent and authoritative expression of French security policy, the military program-law for 2003–2008.[13] But allied (and American) critics of U.S. policy argued that there was no evidence that Saddam Hussein was about to attack the United States or to transfer WMD to terrorists, so this was not a preemptive war but a preventive war—a war waged on the basis of a hypothetical future threat. Furthermore, some European observers argued that the U.S. approach amounted to a prescription for permanent war against all WMD proliferants and terrorists unless the United States could somehow dominate the entire world.

The purpose of dissuasion is to convince potential adversaries that it would be pointless to compete in the acquisition of certain military capabilities. Secretary of Defense Rumsfeld described the logic of the concept by giving an example. "[D]eployment of effective missile defenses may dissuade others from spending to obtain ballistic missiles, because missiles will not provide them what they want: the power to hold U.S. and allied cities hostage to nuclear blackmail."[14] By this logic, the NATO allies clearly have a role in dissuasion; and the allied role in dissuading potential adversaries from seeking ballistic missiles will grow as the alliance develops and deploys missile defenses and other advanced military capabilities.

Allied observers who have commented on the American theory of dissuasion have generally expressed skepticism about the concept. With regard to Rumsfeld's specific example, critics have asked: to what extent will U.S. or NATO missile defenses discourage missile-builders and missile-buyers who are interested in being able to launch missiles against non-NATO countries? If the immediate targets of their missiles are regional antagonists outside NATO territory, the strike capability that could be redirected on command against NATO is a bonus. By this logic, for NATO, greater utility resides in the capacity of missile defenses actually to defend against missile attacks than in their potential effect on missile acquisition decisions. The U.S. government is, however, interested in operational effectiveness as well as in trying to achieve dissuasion, if possible. Indeed, achieving dissuasion depends on deploying effective capabilities. Even if those capabilities fail to prevent military competition, they may complicate the adversary's planning and shape the competition in directions advantageous to the alliance.

As various U.S. and allied observers have pointed out, other activities could contribute to the aim of discouraging arms competitions. Export controls, legal norms, and nonproliferation regimes may help to prevent arms competitions. Cultivating positive political relations may improve the chances that no motive for military competition with the United States or NATO will arise. Promoting regional political stabilization and security also may reduce motives for competition with neighbors; and nation building and state building, notably to support democratization and free-marketization, may lower the likelihood military competitions.

The United States has been engaged in all of these activities, which have been pursued mainly for reasons other than dissuasion. While such cooperative activities have not been highlighted in some U.S. strategy documents, they figure significantly in the National Security Strategy. Moreover, the United States is increasingly disposed to accept an expanded definition of how to achieve dissuasion. The clearest signs of this include the interest in nation building and state building in Afghanistan and Iraq.

U.S. strategists for years have advocated supplementing the Cold War's dominant form of deterrence—deterrence by threat of punishment—with deterrence by denial. Deterrence by denial means persuading the enemy not to attack by convincing him that the attack will be defeated—that is, that he will not be able to achieve his operational objectives. In other words, if the missile defenses do not discourage an enemy from acquiring missiles (the goal of dissuasion), they might discourage an enemy from using them (the goal of deterrence by denial). Some of the experts and officials in NATO countries that have endorsed ballistic missile defense for the protection of populations and territories have done so on grounds other than confidence in the theory of deterrence by denial. Like many Americans, they have taken a more operational perspective—that is, that defenses could actually defend, and that they could thereby make effective intervention against WMD proliferants armed with ballistic missiles operationally safer and politically less risky. Some allied experts support complementing deterrence by threat of punishment with deterrence based on limited missile defenses that would add to the uncertainties facing WMD-armed regional powers.

The deterrence-by-denial theory is not limited to missile defenses. The theory applies to any capability that can deny an enemy success in achieving its objectives. For example, passive defenses such as decontamination equipment and suits and gas masks for protection might help to convince an enemy not to use chemical or biological weapons. Allied experts have often expressed doubts about the effectiveness of deterrence by denial and deem it less reliable than deterrence by threat of punishment. However, allied observers generally endorse the U.S. view that deterrence by denial capabilities could in principle complement deterrence by threat of punishment.

Finally, the Bush administration has argued for "capabilities-based" planning in addition to a "threat-based" approach. Capabilities-based planning appears to be inspired by genuine uncertainty about the future security environment, although it might also reflect a reluctance to specify openly certain potential adversaries out of concern for the political consequences. In 1991, at the end of the Cold War, a decade before the QDR and the NPR popularized the phrase "capabilities-based," NATO's nuclear policy departed from a threat-based approach and appeared to move toward a capabilities-based approach to planning. At that time, owing mainly to President George H.W. Bush's initiatives, the U.S. nuclear presence in Europe was drastically reduced. An element of the capabilities-based approach was announced in the 1999 Strategic Concept: "NATO's nuclear forces no longer target any country."[15]

CONCLUSION

America's NATO allies have but a secondary role in NPR implementation if it is defined solely in terms of U.S. strategic nuclear forces, which are based at sea or in the United States. The NPR, however, also involves advanced nonnuclear capabilities and improved defenses, notably against missile attacks, as well as concepts such as dissuasion and deterrence by denial. The full scope of the NPR makes clear the prospectively significant role of the allies, if they choose to participate in implementing key initiatives that fall within the same broad strategic framework. For example, if the allies decided to construct a missile defense architecture capable of protecting the territories and populations of all the allies in North America and Europe (the subject of a feasibility study called for at the Prague Summit in November 2002), this would require far-reaching allied cooperation and contributions.

Similarly, the establishment of a more flexible and promptly responsive military posture, with enhanced nonnuclear capabilities, as foreseen in the Prague Capabilities Commitment and the NATO Response Force, can only be achieved through multinational allied efforts.

The successful pursuit of these constructive initiatives will not be possible without an improved understanding of national policies among NATO allies. Partly because U.S. public information efforts concerning the NPR have been inadequate and ineffective, allied criticisms are often aimed not at the NPR and related U.S. policies, but at inaccurate accounts of them. Some of the criticisms have made the NPR a platform for vigorously relaunching long-running debates about deterrence, nonproliferation, and other fundamental issues. These debates often have been unproductive, owing in part to mistaken impressions about the content of the NPR but also to differing assessments of the urgency of adopting new strategic approaches and of the utility of certain arms control measures in dealing with new forms of terrorism and WMD proliferation.[16]

The interdependence and shared interests of the NATO allies have helped to sustain the alliance through many post–Cold War disputes, and the NPR offers examples of that mutual dependence as well as discord. This discord has been expressed within an alliance that continues to serve as a privileged forum for dialogue and consultation among democratic nations with common security interests. Moving beyond current disagreements will not be easy, but it is a shared imperative.

NOTES

The views expressed are the author's alone and do not represent those of the Department of the Navy or any U.S. government agency.

1. For background, see David S. Yost, *The US and Nuclear Deterrence in Europe*, Adelphi Paper no. 326 (London: Oxford University Press for the International Institute for Strategic Studies, March 1999).
2. *Nuclear Posture Review* (excerpts), submitted to Congress on December 31, 2001, 44 <http://www.globalsecurity.org/wmd/library/policy/dod/npr.htm>.
3. Final Communiqué, Ministerial Meeting of the Defence Planning Committee and the Nuclear Planning Group, June 12, 2003, par. 14 <http://www.nato. int/docu/pr/2003/p03-064e.htm>.
4. Report on Options for Confidence and Security Building Measures (CSBMs), Verification, Non-Proliferation, Arms Control, and Disarmament, Press Communiqué M-NAC-2 (2000) 121 (Brussels, December 14, 2000), par. 77 <http://www.nato.int/docu/pr/2000/p00-121e/rep-csbm.pdf>.
5. Bruno Tertrais, "Polémique déplacée autour de la Nuclear Posture Review," *TTU Europe*, no. 400 (March 14, 2002): 6.
6. For background, see David S. Yost, "Russia's Non-Strategic Nuclear Forces," *International Affairs* 77 (July 2001): 531–551.
7. Secretary of State Colin Powell, testimony to the Senate Foreign Relations Committee on July 9, 2002. Federal Document Clearing House, transcript available at <http://web.lexis-nexis.com.>.

8. Secretary of Defense Donald H. Rumsfeld, testimony as delivered for the Senate Foreign Relations Committee regarding the Moscow Treaty, July 17, 2002 <www.defenselink.mil/speeches/2002/s20020717-secdefl.html>.

9. *The National Security Strategy of the United States of America* (Washington, D.C.: The White House, September 2002), 15.

10. The NPR did not call for new nuclear warhead designs or nuclear testing but identified shortfalls in U.S. capabilities—e.g., concerning hardened and deeply buried targets. Nonnuclear means, if feasible, will probably have priority in addressing such shortfalls; but there are recognized limits to such means.

11. Lord Robertson quoted in Lee Ewing, "Why 'National' Has Been Dropped from 'National Missile Defense'," *Aerospace Daily* March 12, 2001.

12. Prague Summit Declaration, issued by the Heads of State and Government participating in the meeting of the North Atlantic Council in Prague on November 21, 2002, par. 4g <http://www.nato.int/docu/pr/2002/p02-127e.htm>.

13. Loi no. 2003-73 du 27 janvier 2003 relative à la programmation militaire pour les années 2003 à 2008, section 2.3.1., "Les fonctions stratégiques," available at <www.legifrance.gouv.fr>; italics added.

14. Donald H. Rumsfeld, "Transforming the Military," *Foreign Affairs* 81 (May/June 2002): 27.

15. North Atlantic Council, Strategic Concept (April 24, 1999), par. 64 <http://www.nato.int/docu/pr/1999/p99-065e.htm>.

16. For a thoughtful analysis, see Michael Rühle, "America and Europe in the Second Nuclear Age," *AICGS Advisor* February 19, 2004 <http://www.aicgs.org/c/ruhlec.shtml>.

Implementing the Nuclear Posture Review: The Impact on Russia

Alexander G. Saveliev

Russian interest in the 2002 Nuclear Posture Review (NPR) is not just theoretical; it is also based on practical politics. This chapter examines both aspects of the Russian analysis of and response to the NPR. It also describes some of the security concepts and challenges that face Russia today and in the future.

When the NPR was issued, negotiations on the Strategic Offensive Reductions Treaty (SORT) were underway and Russian policy makers were determined to advance their state's security interests. Their main interest was to achieve as deep reductions as possible in Russian and American strategic forces. In November 2002, Russian President V.Putin even proposed cutting both sides' strategic nuclear warheads to about 1,500. The Russians were interested in deep cuts because from an industrial, technical, and financial perspective, Russia is unable to support or modernize its current strategic arsenal of about 6,000 "accountable" warheads. Russian strategists, however, also seek to preserve the strategic stability of the Russian–American nuclear balance, which is considered by Russian military and civilian leaders to be an essential element of the country's security. They are intent on preserving a strategic deterrent that approximates the strategic potential of the United States' deterrent. Thus, Russian leaders could only welcome the Bush administration's proposal to reduce the number of operationally deployed strategic forces to about 2000 nuclear warheads.

Russian Strategic Posture Today

The fact that the United States agreed to sign the SORT Treaty is a real achievement for Russian diplomacy and President Putin. Yet, a spirit of dissatisfaction emerged in Russia following the signing of the treaty, not about the treaty itself, but about the general decline of Russian strategic forces. The reduction of the number of "combat-ready" strategic nuclear warheads over the last few years has not been offset by the production rate of new strategic systems such as the "Topol M" (SS-27) intercontinental ballistic missile (ICBM). Only about eight Topol Ms enter service annually. At the same time, however, hundreds of old systems are withdrawn from active duty each year. Equipping the SS-27 with multiple independently targetable reentry vehicles (MIRVs) is out of the question due to the limitations of the Strategic Arms Reduction Treaty (START I), which counts the SS-27 as a single-warhead ICBM.

The decision to keep existing systems such as the SS-18 ICBM on active duty beyond their planned retirement dates can only help maintain Russian strategic forces for a short period of time. Similarly, the decision to deploy additional numbers of SS-19 ICBMs from storage can only be considered as a stopgap measure. In any event, these systems are suited to relatively large forces, which are scheduled to be phased out in a way that preserves strategic stability.

Over the next decade, Russia will not undertake any serious efforts to modernize its strategic forces. Instead, its primary efforts will be to preserve the number of deployed warheads within the "reasonable" limits of 1,200 to 1,500 warheads, although some skeptics believe that Russian resources will be taxed to the limit in the effort to deploy just 800 nuclear warheads.

THE RUSSIAN POSTURE TOMORROW

In response to the decline in the overall number and capability of Russian strategic forces over the next decade, Moscow is compensating by adopting a more active nuclear strategy. This new doctrine represents partly the Russian reaction to the Bush administration's NPR and partly a critique of the limited financing received by Russian strategic programs The main goal of the new policy is to provide evidence to the Russian public that their security can be protected following the planned deep reductions in Russian strategic offensive forces.[1]

The most important statement of the new Russian doctrine was contained in the report of Russian Defense Minister Sergei Ivanov, which was issued in November 2003. The report was more comprehensive than the Bush administration's NPR because it covered virtually every aspect of the Russian military posture. Its discussion of nuclear issues, however, provides a theoretical critique of the NPR. For example, it takes a dim view of the American attempt to "return nuclear weapons to the category of permissible military instruments" by using breakthrough technologies that are supposedly able to transform nuclear weapons into relatively "clean" systems that produce little collateral damage. Ivanov stated that efforts to make nuclear weapons more "usable" undermine global and regional stability. The development and deployment of a new generation of more usable nuclear weapons, according to Ivanov, will force Russia's new command and control procedures and systems to develop new ways to deter threats that exist at different levels of violence. In particular, Ivanov listed several potential threats that would be of concern to the Russian government: an attack against Russia or its allies; territorial claims against Russia or political or military efforts to seize Russian territory; and the use of weapons of mass destruction by state or non-state actors, including separatist groups.

Ivanov's list of external threats to Russian security remains somewhat vague. It is not clear, for example, exactly which state or non-state actors are seen as the greatest threat. It also is not clear if the North Atlantic Treaty Organization (NATO) is perceived as a potential threat. Indeed, in terms of potential conflicts, the report simply calls for the Russian armed forces to be ready to participate in military conflicts "of any known type."[2] In terms of strategic forces, the most straightforward statements were made in connection with the possible military conflict at "Western strategic direction."

The authors of the report predict that the main characteristics of a future conflict with the West will be comprehensive aerospace, naval and ground operations of very high intensity. In the course of such a conflict, the prediction continues that Rusian armed forces and military infrastructure will be attacked and that Russia's industrial infrastructure and civil population will be subject to attack.[3] In the event of an all-out attack, the mission of the Russian armed forces will be to gain the strategic initiative during the course of the conflict because "passive warfare" will only result in defeat.

These potential facets of a large-scale conflict led the authors of the report to a surprising conclusion. They suggest that Russia must be prepared to win a large-scale nuclear war in the traditional meaning of "victory." They state that Russian military planning, "based on realistic understanding of contemporary resources and capabilities of Russia" provides that the Russian armed forces together with other forces[4] must be prepared to repulse an enemy's attack and to defeat the aggressor under any conditions of war, including the massive use of such modern weapon systems as weapons of mass destruction.[5] To this end, the report identifies several priorities in terms of Russian force modernization: high military and mobilization readiness; strategic mobility; increased military professionalism; and improved technical quality of military hardware.

The primary purpose of the Russian strategic deterrent, according to the report, is to reject coercive actions and aggression against Russia and its allies, and to contain aggression once war breaks out by threatening to deliver unacceptable damage against the attacker. The refusal to adopt a no-first-use pledge also theoretically lowers the nuclear use threshold for Russian officials.

Although policies and programs outlined in the report and other Russian Federation official documents (e.g., the National Security Concept and Military Doctrine of the Russian Federation adopted in 2000) reflect similar themes, they leave several questions unanswered. First, estimates vary of the current and future threats that Russia faces and how best to use available diplomatic, military, and economic instruments to deter these threats. Complicating this uncertainty is the fact that Russia, much like the USSR, has never really offered official statements describing the details of its nuclear policy and strategy. Thus the Russian public and military community lack a clear understanding of how nuclear deterrence is supposed to function during peace and war, and of what measures should be taken to preserve political control over its nuclear arsenal and to avoid escalation and unauthorized use of these weapons.

The end of bipolarity also has made the security challenges facing Russia more comprehensive in nature. On the one hand, the end of confrontation with the United States and NATO dramatically reduced the probability of a global conflict and the use of nuclear weapons, opening the way for deep reductions of nuclear arsenals. On the other hand, the world community now faces several new threats that demand a global response. Nuclear weapons can do little to address most of these emerging security issues.

Acknowledging the limited role of nuclear weapons and the goal of further reducing the nuclear threat, Russian and American officials could state (in a joint declaration or some other official document) that nuclear weapons fail to offer a universal, useful, or generally desirable way to preserve national security. Policy makers in Moscow could make the additional statement that their use of nuclear weapons is unlikely because large-scale aggression against Russia—a situation that might demand a nuclear response—is a remote possibility.

Nevertheless, Russia cannot ignore the possibility that grave threats to national security might emerge. To guard against such extreme but unlikely threats, Russia will maintain and modernize its nuclear deterrent in a way that reflects economic and political constraints and competing military priorities. Thus, over the next ten years, Russian nuclear policy and strategy will probably enter an evolutionary period as officials attempt to bring policy and force structure in line with current international realities.

Soviet versus Russian Security Concepts: Parity versus "Equal Security"

During the Cold War, the modernization and build-up of Soviet strategic forces was based on the principle of "equal security." Calculating this balance required analysts to take into account all the factors that defined the strategic situation. In practice, it meant that the USSR had to create parity in strategic forces not only with the United States, but also to balance the nuclear forces maintain by Britain and France, as well as NATO's nonstrategic (tactical) forward-based nuclear weapons that could reach Soviet territory. Soviet planners also believed that it was prudent to maintain a strategic reserve to hold targets in China at risk. The Soviet approach to security created a need for large numbers of strategic forces. The arms control negotiations undertaken with the United States insisted on basing negotiations on the principle of equality between the two superpowers but never accepted the right of Russia for "compensation" to match the forces of such third states.[6]

Soviet strategic forces were also maintained at extremely high levels for political reasons. Soviet leaders believed that it was important to demonstrate to the world that the U.S.S.R. could compete with the West in the military sphere. The existence of a huge nuclear arsenal was the most high-profile demonstration of Soviet military power.

Today, Russia should abandon the goal of maintaining nuclear parity with the United States. Maintaining a large nuclear arsenal is no longer important in Russian–American strategic relations, especially compared to the situation during the Cold War. Instead of equality, Russian and American policy makers should replace parity with the principle of "equal security" as a more rational basis for mutual relations. Russian officials should recognize that a small nuclear arsenal can provide a strong deterrent against practically any potential aggressor. Russian officials have just about accepted the idea that a minimum nuclear force structure should be the centerpiece of any scheme to revise Russian nuclear policy and force posture. Reducing the size of is nuclear arsenal is probably the most productive and politically acceptable way Moscow can adapt to the new world military–political situation while meeting Russian security needs.

THE NEW RUSSIAN STRATEGIC MISSION

The adjustment of Russian nuclear policy to the new military–political environment requires a reassessment of the missions given to Russian strategic forces. One of the most important tasks is to be able to inflict damage on any aggressor—whether a state or a coalition of states. Yet, policy makers and officials rarely hint at how this damage will be inflicted, what level constitutes a sufficient level of damage, and what kind of criteria should be used to calculate what constitutes a sufficient level of damage on opponents. Official documents also call for Russia to have a strategic force capable of delivering "given damage" under any circumstances, including the worst-case scenario of a massive surprise attack against Russian strategic forces. Russian strategic forces must be able to survive a full-scale nuclear attack and retaliate, delivering "given damage" to the aggressor in retaliation. Despite official rhetoric and force downsizing, Russian strategic planners, as before, must still prepare for the massive use of nuclear weapons to punish the aggressor. Strategic planning is still driven by the least likely strategic scenario facing Moscow today. In addition to providing a nuclear deterrent, the Russian armed forces also are charged with defending against and air and space attack against Russian territory and assets, to defeat the armed forces of opponents, and to destroy an opponent's war-making capability. In Russian military doctrine, these tasks are formulated: repulsion of the aggression, defeat of the aggressor, and the compulsion of the enemy to cease aggression on conditions that meet the interests of Russia and its allies.

Given that doctrine, Russian strategic forces also are assigned the same tasks as conventional forces. This tasking creates a serious contradiction in contemporary Russian nuclear policy and planning. Employment of Russian nuclear weapons in conventional missions would prove to be highly counter productive. Once the Russian president authorizes the use of nuclear weapons, it is unlikely that the president and his civilian staff would be able to interfere in preexisting military plans for making war. To produce a more rational, less risky, and more balanced nuclear policy and strategy, review of the missions given to Russian strategic nuclear forces must be undertaken to limit the military's ability to use these weapons according to its own vision of military efficiency—as opposed to the political constraints of the moment. For example, it might be desirable to increase the time available for Russian officials to make a decision about nuclear use. If a warning of an incoming attack were received today, the president of Russia would have to make a decision about retaliation in a matter of minutes. He must use the "black case" that accompanies him everywhere to delegate launch authority and to release special codes to the military. Under these circumstances the Russian president would lack effective control over Russia's strategic weapons. As a Russian political scientist, Dr. Alexei Arbatov stated, the demand for a quick decision would turn the Russian president into a sort of "trained monkey" that "pulls the handle of the machine after the lamp flashed to get a banana."[7] This quick reaction command posture only makes sense if it is likely that Russia might suffer a massive surprise attack. It is difficult to imagine, however, a set of circumstances that might lead to this scenario, or a possibility that a Russian president might have to choose between using or losing his nuclear force. There is a greater threat that pressure to make a snap decision about nuclear use without serious analysis can lead to catastrophe.

Russia and the United States

The Bush administration's NPR has prompted more independent thinking in Russia about nuclear policy. In the past, Soviet nuclear doctrine, especially during the period of arms control, was influenced by U.S. concepts, negotiating positions, and force modernization plans. Today, it is difficult to predict how Russian nuclear strategy will evolve in the years after START I is no longer in force and the SORT treaty is implemented. Until now it has focused on the traditional objective of "strengthening strategic stability," preserving parity, and equal security. In the future, however, Russia will face a situation in which it is no longer an equal player with its only conceivable nuclear opponent, the United States. Eventually, Russia will become equal with Britain, France, and China in the nuclear field while the United States will continue to pull ahead in terms of nuclear systems and precision-guided conventional technology.

In the near future, Russia will lose its ability to employ its traditional approach to foreign and defense policy, which is based on maintaining a large nuclear force. Russia might undertake several expedient efforts to maintain a large force, but these efforts would prove to be counterproductive in the long run. For example, Russia could replace diminishing numbers of strategic nuclear weapons with nonstrategic nuclear weapons. Instead of trying to maintain a large strategic nuclear force, however, Russian planners should develop new approaches to all types of military modernization to meet a changing strategic environment.

NEW CONCEPTS

Although many ideas might compete for inclusion in a new Russian strategic doctrine, new thinking should reflect several concepts. First, nuclear strategy and the war plans should not be based on suicidal scenarios related to massive nuclear exchanges, although a surprise massive counterforce nuclear attack against Russia might be included in war plans as a remote possibility. Second, nuclear forces should be given unique missions and not be asked simply to undertake or backstop missions assigned to conventional military operations. It is a mistake to give nuclear forces the same functions and the same tasks that are given to conventional forces. Political leaders must understand that nuclear weapons are not just weapons with more destructive power. Nuclear weapons are a deadly dangerous instrument of war, and it is impossible to use them like conventional weapons. Any attempt to incorporate nuclear weapons into conventional war planning and operations can lead to nuclear escalation and the complete destruction of a state that tries to use nuclear weapons in a conventional manner. Nuclear forces and strategic nuclear forces should not be integrated into routine types of military operations.

Strategic nuclear forces should only take on two missions on the modern battlefield: operations that are intended to de-escalate a conflict or operations to punish an aggressor. Punishment is a well understood concept: After suffering a nuclear attack, Russian nuclear forces, for example, must be able to inflict comparable levels of death and destruction in a retaliatory strike. Submarines that carry nuclear armed ballistic missiles (strategic naval forces) are the ideal weapon to complete this mission because a single submarine at sea can easily escape a nuclear strike and go on to inflict massive levels of destruction against an attacker.

The de-escalation mission is more complicated. Russian official documents suggest that de-escalation involves the complete destruction of the attacker, but it might be possible to take an incremental approach to this task. In order to undertake this mission, however, policymakers would have to establish strict negative and positive control over strategic nuclear forces. The strategic rocket forces should be given the de-escalation mission, but they first require modernizaton. The strategic rocket forces must gain more flexibility, especially limited-strike options. Russian planners should also strive to develop nonnuclear strategic options. Modernization will require portions of the Russian ICBM force to be equipped with conventional warheads and kinetic kill vehicles. This force could then be used across a spectrum of operations with a minimal risk of escalation. The use of a nonnuclear strategic missile might be used to signal concern or resolve during a crisis. Professor Andrey Kokoshin has described this nonnuclear option as a type of "pre-nuclear deterrence."[8]

CONCLUSION

There are several new features in Russian nuclear strategy. Strategic forces have been given two missions: de-escalation and punishment. The de-escalation mission has been assigned to the Strategic Rocket Forces; submarines have been given the punishment mission. The Russian president retains overall positive and negative control over these forces. The president also has a spectrum of nuclear and nonnuclear options, and he can exercise limited strategic options without turning over control of the strategic forces to the military.

Politically, Russian officials should declare a general deterrent policy against potential threats, without directing the strategic forces against specific states. They should state that Russian strategic forces will not target other countries on a day-to-day basis and that the Russian Federation only will use its military power to deal with critical situations. Russia should preserve the right to use nuclear weapons first, but the main goal of first use should be to de-escalate conflicts on terms favorable to Russia.

Russian officials do not treat their nuclear arsenal as an instrument of a victory, and they are confident that other nuclear states do not plan to launch a massive strike against the Russian Federaton. In the immediate future, the punishment mission will remain among the tasks assigned to Russian strategic forces, but Russian officials are ready to abandon it in the event of new arms control negotiations that call for further deep reductions of nuclear forces as confidence-building measures.

A multifaceted approach to deterrence that combines negotiations with deterrence measures tailored to the new environment offers a positive and constructive Russian response to the Bush administration's NPR. In any event, U.S.-Russian dialogue about contemporary security threats is a critical first step in addressing the role of nuclear weapons in world politics, a problem that exceeds the framework of U.S.-Russian relations. The United States and Russia should slowly include other nuclear states in this dialogue because nuclear issues can no longer be addressed only on a unilateral or bilateral basis.

NOTES

1. After the U.S. NPR became public, some Russian experts proposed to develop a "Russian NPR" and to present it to the State Duma for approval.
2. The Report of the Russian Defense Minister was published by the Russian MoD under the title "Actual Tasks of the Development of the Armed Forces of Russian Federation" at the end of November 2003 without the names of the authors and even without the year and month of the publication. The referenced quotation appears on page 25.
3. "Actual Tasks," 29.
4. According to present official definition "the other forces" of Russian Federation include the interior troops (MVD), border guards, armed forces of the Ministry of Emergency Situations (MChS), Federal Security Service (FSB), and the forces of some other agencies of the Russian Federation.

5. "Actual Tasks," 39.
6. For more details see A. Savel'yev and N. Detinov, *The Big Five: Arms Control Decision-Making in the Soviet Union* (New York: Praeger, 1995).
7. A. Arbatov, "Delicate Political Instrument" (in Russian), *Independent Military Review* 43 (December 5–18, 2003): 4.
8. A. Kokoshin. *Nuclear Conflicts in the Twenty-First Century* (in Russian), A. Saveliev, ed. (Moscow: Media-Press, 2003).

15

South Asian Nuclear Dynamics and the Nuclear Posture Review

Stephen Burgess

The 2001 U.S. Nuclear Posture Review (NPR) made an impact on both India and Pakistan, the South Asian subcontinent's two nuclear weapons states. As the following analysis shows, the changes in U.S. policy that the NPR expresses have brought about changes in the relationship of the United States with India and Pakistan and in the behavior of each of South Asia's major powers toward one another. On the one hand, the U.S. stance, as described in the NPR, almost automatically ends discussions that urge India and Pakistan to give up their nuclear weapons programs. On the other hand, the new U.S. policy establishes a framework that can encourage greater responsibility and accountability with the recognition of India and Pakistan as nuclear weapon states. In some connections, this changed global nuclear policy situation has already improved the prospects for a peaceable South Asia.

Initial Response to the Nuclear Posture Review

Among students and observers of nuclear policy, comments about the NPR centered on the U.S. intention to develop and test a new generation of nuclear weapons in defiance of the Comprehensive Test Ban Treaty (CTBT) and the threat of attacking nonnuclear states, apparently including Syria and Libya, with nuclear weapons in contravention of the Nuclear Nonproliferation Treaty (NPT).[1] Many in South Asia also were alerted to the possibility of a preemptive attack, as indicated by the NPR's statement that the United States would take action given "a sudden regime change by which an existing nuclear arsenal comes into the hands of a new, hostile leadership group."[2]

Strikingly, the Indian government, headed by Prime Minister Atal Behari Vajpayee and the Bharatiya Janata Party (BJP), actually welcomed President George W. Bush's May 1, 2001, announcement of a "defensive nuclear weapons strategy" and deep reductions in nuclear warheads and missiles coupled with the launching of a ballistic missile defense initiative.[3] As Vajpayee put it, "There is a strategic and technological inevitability in stepping away from a world that is held hostage by the doctrine of MAD [Mutual Assured Destruction] to a cooperative, defensive transition that is under-pinned by further cuts and a de-alert of nuclear forces."[4] On November 9, 2001, in Washington, D.C., Vajpayee spoke of the United States and India as "natural allies" and reiterated his support for Bush's proposal, which included withdrawing from the 1972 Anti-Ballistic Missile (ABM) Treaty. Subsequently, the U.S.-India Defense Policy Group (DPG) met to discuss defense cooperation and nuclear weapons strategy, including the NPR.

The opposition Congress Party (which formed a new government after the May 2004 elections) was critical of the Vajpayee government's embrace of the Bush administration's missile defense proposal and decision to scrap the ABM Treaty. The Congress Party continued to advocate total nuclear disarmament and was less welcoming of the changes in U.S. security policy embodied in the NPR.[5]

An example of Indian press criticism of the NPR came from a lead article for the middle-of-the-road newspaper, *The Hindu*, in which P. S. Suryanarayana criticized the United States for proclaiming its readiness to defy the NPT (by threatening to attack nonnuclear weapons states) and for defying the CTBT (by planning a new generation of nuclear weapons). He rebuked the Vajpayee government for not protesting U.S. plans and intentions, includ-ing a "first-strike" stance:

> Although India has over time expressed serious reservations about both the NPT and the CTBT, New Delhi cannot afford to see with equanimity or unconcern any future American transgressions of these agreements. The reason is not far to seek. Washington's growing disenchantment with the CTBT may catalyse India's own plans, if any, for transforming its notional nuclear deterrence into a reasonably realistic one over time. However, India cannot embrace a morally controversial idea which is implicit in the Pentagon's reported thinking that favours nuclear strikes against those without the proven means to retaliate in a like manner. New Delhi (no less than Beijing) has repeatedly proclaimed adherence to the principle that India will not initiate a nuclear war by being the first to use the atom bomb. From an Indian perspec-tive, therefore, the idea of a first nuclear strike, as distinct from a retaliatory second strike, can only imply a doctrine of nuclear permissiveness.[6]

In Pakistan, reaction to the NPR was more critical, even though the gov-ernment of General Pervez Musharraf had decided to ally itself with the United States after September 11, 2001. The negative reactions focused on perceptions of U.S. unilateralism and the possibility that the United States might decide to attack states that it found objectionable, even Pakistan, especially if the Musharraf regime were to be overthrown by radical Islamist elements.[7]

On March 31, 2002, Pakistan's Foreign Minister, Abdul Sattar, addressed the Conference on Disarmament in Geneva. As reported by *The Frontier*

Post, he joined with the Iranian deputy foreign minister in criticizing the NPR: "Pakistan and Iran have taken umbrage at the recently unveiled U.S. Nuclear Posture Review that envisages new types of nuclear weapons and contingency plans for using them against seven countries, including Iran, Russia and China."[8] *The Frontier Post* report continued with a commentary on how the NPR was part of anti-Pakistan and pro-India policies that the United States was pursuing:

> The spelling out of its nuclear designs as contained in its so-called Nuclear Posture Review is a manifestation of this sinister quest. While the US is persisting with its erroneous pursuit of nuclear hegemony, it has been levelling accusations of nuclear proliferation against every country that provokes its ire. For example, it has been accusing China of facilitating shipments to Pakistan in order to help build its ballistic missiles. And as if to give further proof of its duplicity, it has been looking the other way to implicitly permit India to pursue its missile plans.[9]

In December 2002, the Pakistan newspaper, *Dawn*, pointed to the linkages between the NPR and India's increased hard-line stance toward Pakistan during 2002:

> The timing of the hardening of the Indian stance is highly significant. It has come in the wake of some other unprecedented moves by the US under President Bush, whose unilateralism has grown after a brief interlude of multilateralism necessitated by the need to forge an international coalition after 9/11. The Bush Doctrine, that includes elements derived from the Nuclear Posture Review, claiming the right to use nuclear weapons against a number of potential adversaries and the June 1 declaration at West Point, establishing the right to pre-emption, has encouraged the hawkish regimes in Israel and India to follow suit. The decision to deescalate, taken by the Indian leadership in October, appears to have been overtaken by opportunities that have arisen since then. The Bush doctrine, and signs of a US decision to attack Iraq even if the UN inspectors fail to come up with concrete proof of Iraqi possession of weapons of mass destruction, have encouraged the hard-line regimes in Israel and India to take full advantage of the resultant weakening of international law.[10]

The Pakistan press viewed the NPR as part of a U.S. strategy to encourage India to become more aggressive toward Pakistan.

U.S.-INDIA–PAKISTAN RELATIONS BEFORE THE NUCLEAR POSTURE REVIEW

Before the Bush administration and the 2001 Nuclear Posture Review, the United States had pursued a classic arms control approach toward India and Pakistan, pressuring the two states to renounce their nuclear weapons programs and imposing sanctions as the two cleared successive hurdles on their respective courses to becoming overt nuclear weapons states. In the early 1990s, the United States helped to roll back nuclear weapons programs in South Africa, Ukraine, Belarus, and Kazakhstan. U.S. officials hoped that a similar "carrot and stick" approach would bring disarmament in South Asia.

Clinton administration officials were determined to intensify arms control efforts, including in South Asia. They were particularly concerned about the rapidly escalating arms race, proliferation, and Pakistan's first-strike stance. They helped to bring about the 1993 Chemical Weapons Convention (CWC), the indefinite extension of the NPT in 1995, and negotiations for a Fissile Material Cut-off Treaty (FMCT).[11] The administration was a major promoter of the CTBT, which was under negotiation in the UN Conference on Disarmament in Geneva after approval by the UN General Assembly in 1993. CTBT negotiations coincided with a de facto nuclear test ban by the nuclear weapons states that has now lasted more than a decade.[12]

The United States attempted to bring India and Pakistan into the CTBT, concentrating particularly on India, as the lone holdout against the CTBT among the forty-four Conference on Disarmament member countries with the potential to develop and test nuclear weapons. Pakistan expressed its willingness to sign the CTBT as long as India did. In addition, other states pressured India and Pakistan to sign the CTBT and refrain from testing. The efforts led to debates within India and Pakistan about the CTBT and nuclear testing. Many Indian officials believed that, as long as the NPT's distinctions between nuclear "haves" and "have-nots" were in place, the CTBT would reinforce privileges enjoyed by the nuclear weapons states. Thus in May 1995, the indefinite extension of the NPT—which was approved without any disarmament concessions by the nuclear weapons states—was strongly criticized by India's officials for undermining CTBT negotiations. In 1996, CTBT negotiations concluded in the Conference on Disarmament. The draft was presented to the UN General Assembly and overwhelmingly approved, over the objections of India, Pakistan, China, and Russia.[13] Subsequently, India and Pakistan dropped out of arms control negotiations and prepared to test nuclear weapons.

Nuclear Testing in South Asia

In the 1998 general election campaign, India's BJP campaigned on a platform that included a promise to test nuclear weapons in defiance of U.S. pressure to abide by the CTBT and to join the NPT. The BJP's *realpolitik* and furtherance of India's national interests as a rising great power outweighed the country's long-standing pacifist and nuclear disarmament principles, articulated by the country's first leaders, Nehru and Gandhi.[14] The BJP was determined to make India a great power and nuclear weapons state with defense capabilities that would enable India to compete eventually with China.[15] In March 1998, the BJP came to power and promptly set in motion the process of nuclear testing.[16] The week before the test, Minister of Defense George Fernandes called China "potential enemy number one."[17]

The May 11 and 13, 1998, Indian tests ended the country's three-decade-old stance of nuclear opacity. In a statement to the Lok Sabha (lower house of parliament) after the test, Prime Minister Vajpayee announced that India would not be the first to use nuclear weapons, and he promised to avoid an arms race, which would mean that India would produce just enough nuclear weapons to support a strategy of minimum deterrence. Soon afterward, he announced a unilateral moratorium on nuclear testing.[18] Also, Vajpayee wrote a letter to President Clinton, in which he named China as India's principal security concern.[19]

The Indian test prompted the military and Islamists within Pakistan to pressure Prime Minister Nawaz Sharif for a reciprocal Pakistani nuclear test. The United States sent a team, led by Deputy Secretary of State Strobe Talbott and U.S. Central Command Commander-in-Chief General Anthony Zinni, to offer an aid package and the easing of sanctions if Pakistan would not test. Prime Minister Sharif and the Pakistan government, however, rejected the U.S. overture and ordered a nuclear test, which was conducted on May 28, 1998.

On June 6, 1998, the UN Security Council adopted Resolution 1172, which urged India and Pakistan to restrain their nuclear ambitions.[20] Condemnation came from the United States, the Group of Eight (G-8), the European Union, the Organization of American States, the Association of Southeast Asian Nations regional forum, and a number of concerned states, including several that had given up nuclear weapon aspirations, such as Argentina, Brazil, South Africa, and Ukraine.

The May 1998 tests proved India and Pakistan's nuclear capabilities and eligibility for admission into the "club" of nuclear weapons states. Once they had tested, both India and Pakistan expressed a willingness to renegotiate the CTBT and to continue negotiating the Fissile Material Cut-off Treaty (FMCT)—as nuclear weapons states. If the other nuclear weapons states accepted India and Pakistan's nuclear weapons programs, it might pave the way for their inclusion within the NPT as nuclear weapons states. After the tests, Pakistan continued to offer to disarm if India did, and India pledged not to strike first with nuclear weapons.

A positive consequence of the tests was that India and Pakistan held several bilateral meetings on Kashmir and other security issues. Pakistan, however, continued to keep its first-strike option open.

The nuclear tests and India and Pakistan's security dilemma accelerated the ongoing arms race, especially in missiles and fissile material available for nuclear weapons development. The fissile material race caused considerable concern among nonproliferation experts. India moved ahead in fissile material production more quickly than Pakistan. Today, India possesses more than fifty nuclear weapons, while Pakistan has more than twenty nuclear weapons in its arsenal.[21] On the other hand, India's nuclear weapons have not been deployed on a day-to-day operational status, and no further tests have occurred in the past six years.[22] In addition, doubts arose during the 1998 test about the ability of India's scientists to build and test reliable fusion devices for thermonuclear weapons. Doubts about reliability also persist, because the nuclear testing moratorium continues.[23]

Arms Control Negotiations

After the tests, the Clinton administration intensified sanctions against India and Pakistan. The administration also dispatched Deputy Secretary of State Talbott and other diplomats to reduce tensions and to prevent nuclear war in South Asia. Their diplomatic efforts focused on the promotion of confidence-building measures (CBMs) and nuclear risk reduction measures (NRRMs) that ensured sound command-and-control over nuclear weapons. Starting in July 1998, a series of negotiations between Talbott and Indian Foreign Minister Jaswant Singh dealt with issues of command-and-control, a transparent nuclear doctrine, and export controls.[24] (Similar discussions occurred with Pakistani officials.) The Singh-Talbott discussions led to the reaffirmation of civilian command-and-control and a "minimum deterrent, no first use" doctrine.[25] Singh expressed India's interest in joining the CTBT and a FMCT.[26] U.S. efforts to convince India and Pakistan to adopt the NPT as nonnuclear states, however, were rejected.

U.S. negotiations and diplomatic moves by Prime Minister Vajpayee led to the February 1999 Lahore summit between Vajpayee and Sharif, which covered Kashmir, nuclear weapons, and other issues.[27] The parties agreed to confidence-building measures to stabilize India–Pakistan relations and issued the "Lahore Declaration," which, with its accompanying documents, contained NRRMs to reduce the risks of a nuclear exchange prompted by an accident or misinterpretation of a nuclear or ballistic missile test. The two states agreed to resolve remaining technical details in bilateral agreements by mid-1999 and to take steps to reduce the danger of nuclear war between them.

The first step in this process was to exchange information on nuclear doctrines and security strategies, as well as data on numbers of nuclear warheads and ballistic missiles and deployment information. The memorandum of understanding (MOU) agreed at Lahore called for advance notification of ballistic missile test flights and prompt notification of "any accidental, unauthorized, or unexplained incident" regarding nuclear weapons. It also called for improved control over each side's nuclear weapons. Finally, the MOU recommended reviews of existing CBMs and emergency communications arrangements "with a view to upgrading and improving these links."[28]

The full potential of the Lahore meeting was short-lived, however. The Kargil War of May–June 1999 and General Pervez Musharraf's October 1999 coup ended the promise of the Lahore Declaration and all other confidence-building measures.

On October 13, 1999, the Clinton administration lost a major component of its arms control policy when Republicans in the U.S. Senate led a majority in voting down the CTBT. As a result, it became more difficult to pressure India and Pakistan to sign the CTBT. Even so, U.S officials appealed to India and Pakistan to sign the CTBT as a way of putting pressure on the Senate to reverse its decision.

In spite of the setbacks, the dialogue between Talbott and Singh continued. In a November 29, 1999, interview in *The Hindu Times*, Singh clarified his government's position regarding nuclear weapons.[29] He stated India's willingness to consider signing the CTBT and negotiate a Fissile Material Cut-off Treaty. He reiterated previous statements about a minimum credible deterrent, no first use of nuclear weapons, and civilian control. The foreign minister did not see submarine launched ballistic missiles as feasible in India's foreseeable future and warned against the development of tactical nuclear weapons.

In a January 2000 interview, Talbott indicated that he was satisfied with India's nuclear stance and that he was not pressuring New Delhi to abandon its nuclear weapons. He commented, however, that the United States continued to be concerned about command-and-control issues, particularly given the level of tension and the rise of terrorist groups in the region, such as al Qaeda, that sought weapons of mass destruction.[30] President Clinton's March 2000 trip to South Asia confirmed de facto recognition of India as a nuclear weapons state and emerging great power. His one-day visit to Pakistan demonstrated disapproval for General Musharraf's October 1999 military coup and suspected proliferation activities.

In sum, U.S. arms control efforts in South Asia before 2001 helped India and Pakistan agree to CBMs and NRRMs, which could have led to greater transparency and improved nuclear weapons command-and-control. The administration's failure to keep India and Pakistan from testing in May 1998, however, was a major setback to the nonproliferation regime. In the mid-1990s, the Clinton administration had miscalculated by pushing India and Pakistan to sign both the CTBT and NPT. The Senate defeat of the CTBT also was disappointing, while the FMCT remained stalled in the UN Conference on Disarmament. In spite of these setbacks, arms control prospects in South Asia were still alive when the Bush administration came to power in January 2001.

THE BUSH ADMINISTRATION, THE NPR, AND SOUTH ASIAN DYNAMICS

In January 2001, the Bush administration came to office determined to adopt a markedly different security strategy, including a different approach toward nuclear proliferation, from the preceding Democratic administration's. The new strategy entailed changed U.S. policy toward South Asia, including closer relations with India as an emerging power and more proactive measures to prevent Pakistan from proliferating and supporting radical Islamists. The terrorist attacks of September 11, 2001, brought further dramatic changes, which appeared in the NPR and the 2002 National Security Strategy.

The Bush administration strategy was designed to improve relations with India as a rising power in Asia that could assist in balancing a rising China. The Indian government reciprocated by welcoming a U.S. defensive nuclear weapons strategy, missile defense, and deep reductions in warheads and missiles. After September 11, 2001, India joined the U.S. coalition against terrorism, provided over-flight and port rights, and offered basing rights.[31] The launch of Operation Enduring Freedom against al Qaeda and the Taliban in Afghanistan led the Bush administration to intensify bilateral relations with both Pakistan and India, ease sanctions against both countries, abandon its paternalistic approach to arms control, and work on a more equal footing with both governments.

Organizational politics played a major role in the Bush administration's strategy on nuclear weapons and South Asia. Most Bush administration national security political appointees, especially those in the Department of Defense, were skeptical of the State Department's traditional emphasis on arms control and deterrence and promoted missile defense, especially for India, and counterproliferation as alternatives to arms control.[32] This perspective was reinforced after September 11 by the specter of terrorists obtaining weapons of mass destruction and attacking the United States. Since then, the Defense Department has been building relations with both India and Pakistan with military aid, training, and exercises.

In the area of arms control, the only major initiative that the Bush administration supported was the FMCT. Negotiations on the FMCT in the UN Conference on Disarmament remained suspended because of disagreement among participants. On one side were states, including the United States and India, which had substantial fissile material and wanted the FMCT to merely cap each nation's supply. On the other side were countries such as Pakistan, with less fissile material, which wanted reductions that would bring greater strategic balance. In addition, China and Pakistan demanded consideration of a treaty to prevent an arms race in outer space (PAROS) before agreeing to negotiations on the FMCT. The Bush administration remained cool toward PAROS, which might restrict the development of its missile defense and space-based sensor programs.[33]

On December 13, 2001, Islamist terrorists, who enjoyed the backing of some Pakistani officials, attacked the Indian Parliament. In the next five months, India mobilized 700,000 troops and sent them to confront Pakistan. As during the 1999 Kargil war, India threatened—but did not attack—Pakistan-controlled territory in response to Pakistani threats to use nuclear weapons, in part because of significant U.S. pressure to maintain peace between the two South Asian powers. Any large-scale Indian cross-border action would probably have wrecked Operation Enduring Freedom and hastened the region toward nuclear war.[34]

At the height of the crisis, in late May 2002, the Bush administration sent Deputy Secretary of State Richard Armitage, followed by Defense Secretary Donald Rumsfeld, to South Asia to act as peacemakers. Russian President Vladimir Putin and British Foreign Secretary Jack Straw also visited.

All stressed the gravity of the confrontation and Pakistan's obligation to stop cross-border terrorism. Indian Deputy Prime Minister L. K. Advani, Defense Minister George Fernandes, and other Indian and Pakistani leaders continued to engage in rhetoric about their countries' ability to fight, prevail in, and survive nuclear war.[35] U.S. officials tried to tone down this nuclear bluster by describing the cataclysmic consequences of a nuclear exchange in which millions could be killed.[36]

By October 2002, the confrontation deescalated. Indian troops withdrew, and Pakistan made efforts to stop cross-border terrorist activities. That same month, India managed to hold successful elections in Jammu and Kashmir that brought greater legitimacy to its presence. In the meantime, the United States continued its diplomatic campaign to bring the two countries together to negotiate, and by May 2003, relations had so improved that Prime Minister Vajpayee made an overture to President Musharraf of Pakistan, which was accepted at the January 2004 South Asian Association for Regional Cooperation (SAARC) summit in Islamabad. The thrust of this gesture was restoring diplomatic relations and travel and then striving to negotiate a final settlement regarding larger issues, including the status of Jammu and Kashmir.

INDIA AND THEATER MISSILE DEFENSE

Prime Minister Vajpayee's positive response to President Bush's defensive nuclear strategy proposal led India to begin exploring the acquisition of theater missile defense (TMD).[37] By 2002, the Bush administration was exploring ways of providing missile defenses to India and perhaps Pakistan, which some Bush officials hoped might provide incentives for the easing of tensions and arms control. Pakistani officials, however, have remained concerned about the prospect of the United States providing missile defenses to India alone—possibly nullifying Pakistan's first-strike nuclear deterrent.

Indian strategists studied the probable impact of TMD and concluded that Pakistan's nuclear arsenal would be largely neutralized. China's arsenal would not be affected, however.[38] U.S. experts estimated that China would probably view an Indian missile defense system as intended to defend against China, though China would be able to keep well ahead of India in any subsequent arms race.[39] Issues remained about the effect of an offense–defense arms race on Asian security, especially an arms race involving China and Pakistan.[40] According to some experts, Vajpayee's support for a defensive nuclear weapons strategy was intended to avoid a more expensive strategy of developing intercontinental ballistic missiles.[41] (China is developing such missiles as a deterrent against the United States and Russia.)

India examined the feasibility of converting its Akash surface-to-air missile system into a homegrown TMD system. India also inquired about the purchase of the Israeli Arrow TMD system, the U.S. Patriot Advanced Capability PAC-3, and the Russian S300-V TMD surface-to-air missile. Several unresolved issues complicated this acquisition strategy. Questions remained, for example, about the Russian S300-V TMD system's convertibility to TMD and about the expense and transfer of technology from Israel, which is constrained by the United States and by the Missile Technology Control Regime (MTCR) and other measures from selling certain technologies.[42] India eventually settled on the Arrow 2 and Patriot 3, which were less expensive than the S300. The sale of the Arrow 2 system to India, however, was slowed by concerns raised by the U.S. State Department about the power of the Arrow 2's booster phase rocket, which exceeded MTCR Category I limits.[43] In regard to a joint missile defense development program with the United States involving Patriot 3, the limits to technology transfer have largely been determined, and India can proceed within those limits.[44] The United States is providing some support for India's space program, but there are still restrictions on some high-tech defense and space exports.[45]

In August 2003, the U.S.-India DPG met in Washington, D.C. Under Secretary of Defense for Policy Douglas Feith hosted the meeting, and Defense Secretary Ajay Prasad led the Indian delegation. By this time, the Bush administration had given its approval for Israel to sell India three Phalcon Airborne Warning and Control System (AWACS) aircraft. The press release mentioned that approval for the sale of the Israeli Arrow 2 anti-missile system, jointly developed by Israel and the United States, would soon follow.[46] The two sides reaffirmed the shared view that missile defense enhances cooperative security and stability. Indian and U.S. officials agreed to hold a missile defense workshop in India as follow-on to an international workshop attended by U.S. and Indian delegations at the June 2003 Multinational Ballistic Missile Defense Conference in Kyoto, Japan. The Indian delegation also accepted invitations to the July 2004 Multinational Ballistic Missile Defense Conference in Berlin and the 2005 Roving Sands Missile Defense Exercise.[47]

In the 2004 election campaign, the Congress Party promised to focus on domestic issues, such as poverty alleviation. After the Congress Party victory, it would appear that India will be less open to cooperation with the United States regarding missile defense and more critical of the NPR. Overall relations with the United States, however, should remain positive.

THE NUCLEAR POSTURE REVIEW, PAKISTAN, AND PROLIFERATION

In August 2002, British intelligence agents inside the Pakistan High Commission in London found incriminating documents that showed Pakistan was still helping North Korea develop a highly enriched uranium (HEU) program in exchange for assistance with missile technology.[48] This revelation came after President Musharraf had assured Secretary of State Colin Powell that cooperation with North Korea had ended after the 1999 coup, and it led to a vigorous U.S. interagency debate. Nonproliferation experts in the State Department pressed for punishment, while top officials in the White House and Pentagon argued that admonishment of Pakistan, one of the key U.S. allies in the global war on terrorism, was sufficient. The White House and Pentagon prevailed, and no sanctions were applied against Pakistan. Symbolic sanctions were levied, however, on a North Korean state-owned company that was supplying missile technology to Pakistan. Public revelations of the case led to calls for greater control over Pakistan's nuclear weapons program, including the employment of U.S. monitoring technologies and on-site U.S. inspections of nuclear facilities as part of a cooperative threat reduction (CTR) program, as well as tighter Pakistani export controls.[49]

In January 2004, President Musharraf revealed that the "father of the Pakistan bomb," A. Q. Khan, had headed a ring of scientists, entrepreneurs, and security personnel who had been selling nuclear secrets and HEU enrichment centrifuges. Buyers included North Korea, Iran, and Libya.[50] While the involvement of the Pakistan government in this proliferation remained unclear, the revelations reopened the issue of how to control Pakistan's nuclear weapons program. Once again, U.S. requirements in fighting al Qaeda in Pakistan prevented punishment, and Pakistan was named a "major non-NATO ally" in June 2004.

Nonetheless, the NPR's vision of radical Islamists seizing power and nuclear weapons in Pakistan remains a possibility, and the United States might be compelled to act in the future.

In 2004, the Bush administration launched the Proliferation Security Initiative (PSI) to stop the spread of material for weapons of mass destruction. The PSI came in the wake of revelations about A. Q. Khan and his network, and it led *The Daily Times* of Lahore, Pakistan, to comment on the NPR and the desirability of Pakistan joining the PSI:

The 2002 Nuclear Posture Review of the United States talks about "forward deterrence" based on integrating low-yield mini-nukes into the war-fighting arsenal to take out undeterrable actors. Add to this the U.S. Ballistic Missile Defence [BMD] programme and the concept of pre-emption, which forms the corner stone of the U.S. security doctrine, and we have a new security framework for the coming decades. Additionally, the U.S., in alliance with 10 other countries, is embarked on putting in place the proliferation security initiative (PSI) "which seeks to combat proliferation by developing new means to disrupt WMD trafficking at sea, in the air, and on land." These developments are very significant and should force Pakistan into new thinking.

India has already grasped the significance of the evolving framework. This was clear in its response to the U.S. BMD programme. It became the first state to welcome it, though later it tried to take some of the enthusiasm out of its initial support for a host of reasons. In the February editorial on this issue we wrote that with the peace process it had become easier for Pakistan to talk to India on engaging the five legitimate nuclear-weapon states on the issue of granting legitimacy to the three non-NPT de facto nuclear weapon states. "Since Pakistan and India are embarked on a peace process, part of which also deals with nuclear risk reduction, it would make eminent sense for the two sides to deliberate on a joint draft to this end. India has close relations with Israel and it could get input from that country also before such a draft is finalised and presented to the Club of Five. Movement towards this end would bring the three de facto nuclear states into the legal loop. It would also enhance their commitment to nonproliferation."

It is also time for Pakistan to join the PSI. If Pakistan wants to take advantage of the evolving framework . . . it makes sense for Islamabad to step forward and project its willingness to play its role in preventing horizontal proliferation. This is the paradox of acquiring nuclear capability. While the three non-NPT de facto nuclear-weapon states developed their potential against the nonproliferation norm, they did not accept the legal obligation of the NPT. Being nuclear capable now, it is in their interest not to allow proliferation.[51]

Pakistan remains committed to using nuclear weapons first in case of an Indian attack. Pakistan also asserts that it is dedicated to arms control and reduction and is willing to embrace nuclear disarmament if India also disarms. While rejecting India's mutual "no first use" proposal, Pakistan has stepped away from maximizing threats to use nuclear weapons given any provocation and will now use nuclear weapons as a last resort, exhausting conventional options first.[52]

Pakistan believes that India is not interested in strategic restraint, as evidenced by India's embrace of the Bush administration's missile defense overture.[53] Pakistani officials think that the United States and Israel have been supplying radars to India to help develop missile defenses.[54] A Pakistani strategic expert sees India's interest in missile defense "as an indicator of Indian designs and ambitions to acquire absolute regional superiority in the nuclear domain" and warns that "Pakistan would be compelled to respond to Indian ambitions by increasing military cooperation with China and keeping its nuclear option open as the last resort in a war against India."[55]

CONCLUSION

Major changes in the U.S. approach toward South Asia have been associated with the Bush administration's National Security Strategy and the NPR. Before 2001, the approach was more detached, as diplomats attempted to induce India and Pakistan to join the NPT and CTBT. The Bush administration moved the United States closer to India and Pakistan, especially after September 11, 2001, and eased sanctions for violating arms control measures, which sent a message to both countries that it was acceptable for them to remain as de facto nuclear weapons states. Therefore, the Bush administration recognized that India and Pakistan could not be coaxed as nonnuclear states toward the CTBT and NPT. India would not give up its nuclear deterrent, because leaders have been convinced that a long-term conflict with China is possible. Pakistan has remained determined to keep its nuclear deterrent to guarantee its survival in the event that India launches a massive conventional attack.

It appears increasingly possible that the United States and the other nuclear weapons states might accept India and Pakistan entirely into their club. India and, particularly, Pakistan are being persuaded to adhere more closely to nuclear weapons standards and to be more receptive to intensive and regular on-site inspections by the International Atomic Energy Agency and the United States.

Closer relations with India and Pakistan opened the door to U.S. assisted negotiations on Jammu and Kashmir, arms control, and missile defense. The United States has helped India and Pakistan to recognize the devastating implications of nuclear war and demonstrated that it can help increase stability in South Asia without dramatically changing the balance of power or encroaching on Indian or Pakistani sovereignty.

The United States could achieve further progress through confidence-building measures, such as cooperative aerial monitoring, assisting with a more rigorous "hotline," and a cooperative threat reduction program.[56] The two countries could do a better job of providing data and strategies concerning their nuclear weapons programs and advance notification of ballistic missile test flights. U.S. monitoring technologies and systems for transparency and agreement compliance verification could serve as the basis for a CTR program. Thus it is possible that India and Pakistan could be brought into an arms control process and move toward solving the Kashmir conflict with U.S. assistance.

In terms of missile defenses, India could provide a test for the globalization of such defenses. Pakistan might be persuaded to join a multilateral missile defense community; otherwise, it would have to be reassured, through better air defenses and security guarantees, that India would not exploit a superior missile defense to gamble on attempting to disarm Pakistan in a first strike. India could successfully adapt the Patriot PAC-3 system to South Asia, which would validate the prospects for cooperative missile defense systems among the United States, Israel, India, and other states. In recent months, however, the Congress Party government has slowed the process of developing TMD.

Pakistan will remain a problematic case for some time to come, as demonstrated by HEU proliferation to North Korea, Iran, and Libya, China's exports of missile and nuclear technology to Pakistan, and the presence of al Qaeda and other extremist groups in the country. Closer U.S. relations with Pakistan, however, have provided an opportunity for increased surveillance of proliferation activities and have diminished the chances of Pakistan's disintegration.

Neorealist theory would posit that unipolarity and a U.S. administration that has been prepared to exploit its power, especially after September 11, 2001, in order to forge new relations provides the best explanation for the stabilization of South Asia in the last two years. Also, the bilateral or trilateral approach to resolving crises and negotiating arms control agreements is easier to implement than the multilateral approach. The long-range U.S. plan for South Asia should lead to a U.S.-India partnership and efforts to contain a rising China as the twenty-first century unfolds.

NOTES

1. For example, an article depicted the Nuclear Posture Review as "a report submitted to Congress early this year, [which] had recommended resumption of nuclear tests, producing or modifying new nukes and preparing for nuclear strikes against seven potential adversaries—Russia, China, North Korea, Iraq, Iran, Libya and Syria." "Panel Recommends US to Prepare for Nuclear Testing," *Times of India* March 23, 2002.

2. Nuclear Posture Review (excerpts), submitted to Congress on December 31, 2001, p. 16 <http://www.globalsecurity.org/wmd/library/policy/dod/npr.htm>. See also, Pervez Hoodbhoy and Zia Mian, "The India–Pakistan Conflict—Towards the Failure of Nuclear Deterrence," *Policy Forum Online* Special Forum 48 (Berkeley, Cal.: The Nautilus Institute for Security and Sustainable Development, November 13, 2002) <http://www.gakushuin.ac. jp/~881791/ hoodbhoy/Deterrence.html>.

3. Jim Hoagland, "Rethinking Asia in India's Favor," *The Washington Post* July 1, 2001.

4. C. Raja Mohan, *Crossing the Rubicon: The Shaping of India's New Foreign Policy* (New Delhi: Penguin/Viking, 2003), 19.

5. Shyam Babu, Rajiv Gandhi Institute of Contemporary Studies, interviewed by the author, New Delhi, India, September 3, 2003.

6. P. S. Suryanarayana, "America's Nuclear Hit-list," *The Hindu* April 30, 2002.

7. Nuclear Posture Review, 16. See also, Hoodbhoy and Mian, "The India-Pakistan Conflict."

8. "U.S. Nuclear Duplicity," *The Frontier Post*, Peshawar, Pakistan, March 31, 2002 <http://www.nci.org/02/03f/31-01.htm>.

9. "U.S. Nuclear Duplicity."

10. Maqbool Ahmad Bhatty "Scuttling of Saarc Summit," *Dawn*, Karachi, Pakistan, December 14, 2002, opinion page <http://www.dawn.com/2002/12/14/op.htm>.

11. *A Brief History of the FMCT* (Oxford, United Kingdom: Research Group, 2003), 12, available at <http://www.oxfordresearchgroup.org.uk/publications/books/handbook/ch2.pdf>.

12. Harsh V. Pant, "India and Nuclear Arms Control: A Study of the CTBT," *Comparative Strategy* 21, (2002): 91–105.

13. Ibid., 95.

14. Bharat Karnad, *Nuclear Weapons and Nuclear Security: The Realist Foundations of Strategy* (Delhi, India: Macmillan, 2002). Karnad articulates a *realpolitik* strategy for India, which the BJP moved toward in the 1990s, and which would include the development of a nuclear force to rival and target China and other competitors.

15. Narendra Gupta, "India's Days of Nuclear Ambivalence are Over," *The Times of India* July 16, 1997.

16. Rodney W. Jones and Sumit Ganguly, "Debating New Delhi's Nuclear Decision," *International Security* 24, no. 4 (Winter 2001): 181–189. When the BJP came to office, it soon became apparent that it would not be able to enact any of its election manifesto proposals and that the government would be short-lived. The promise to carry out a nuclear test was the only proposal that was attainable at the time. The fulfillment of the promise helped the BJP in the next round of elections in September–October 1999.

17. John F. Burns, "India Carries Out Nuclear Tests in Defiance of International Treaty," *New York Times* May 12, 1998.

18. Statement by Prime Minister Behari Vajpayee in the Indian Parliament, May 27, 1998.

19. John W. Garver, *Protracted Contest: Sino-Indian Rivalry in the Twentieth Century* (Seattle: University of Washington Press, 2001), 275–342. Since India's defeat by China in 1962, India's strategic thinkers had focused on competition with China, and, in May 1998, many of them concurred with Fernandes and rationalized the nuclear test decision by referring to the need for a nuclear balance. China tested from 1964 to 1995, and India wanted to demonstrate its nuclear capabilities to its strategic competitor.

20. *United Nations Security Council Resolution 1172* June 6, 1998.

21. Joseph Cirincione, *Deadly Arsenals: Tracking Weapons of Mass Destruction* (Washington, D.C.: Carnegie Endowment for International Peace, 2002), 191. Rodney Jones, *Minimum Nuclear Deterrence Postures in South Asia* (Washington, D.C.: Defense Threat Reduction Agency, 2002), 3, estimated more than 100 Indian nuclear weapons equivalents (NWEs) and 50 Pakistani NWEs by the latter half of 2001. However, India has the potential to produce more than 400 NWEs and catch up with China's 450 NWEs. Pakistan has the potential to produce more than 100 NWEs.

22. Tellis, *India's Emerging Nuclear Posture*, 211–225.

23. Karnad, *Nuclear Weapons*, 405–408.

24. Strobe Talbott, "Dealing with the Bomb in South Asia" *Foreign Affairs* 78, no. 2 (March/April 1999), 110–122.

25. Ashley J. Tellis, *India's Emerging Nuclear Posture: Between Recessed Deterrent and Ready Arsenal* (Santa Monica, Calif.: Rand, 2001), 392–398. Tellis lays out a number of scenarios involving India's nuclear weapons program and concludes that a "minimum recessed deterrent" and a "force in being" will be the most likely outcome for the foreseeable future.

26. *A Brief History of the FMCT*, 12.

27. "India, Pakistan Agree on Security, Confidence-Building Measures," *Arms Control Today* (January–February 1999), 21.

28. "India, Pakistan Agree," 21. Data exchanges could not provide much in terms of the level of detail and the scope of the nuclear weapons programs as both sides were developing their nuclear arsenals and doctrines.

29. Interview with Jaswant Singh, *The Hindu Times* November 29, 1999.

30. Interview with Strobe Talbott, *The Hindu Times* January 15, 2000.

31. However, Pakistan offered basing rights in October 2001, so the United States did not require Indian bases.

32. Keith Payne and Mark Schneider, Office of Force Planning, Department of Defense, interviewed by the author, Washington, D.C., May 15, 2003.

33. *A Brief History of the FMCT*, 15–16.

34. Subhash Kapila, *United States War-Gaming on South Asia Nuclear Conflict: An Analysis*, South Asia Analysis Group, Paper no. 476, June 14, 2002.

35. Lee Feinstein, "Avoiding Another Close Call in South Asia," *Arms Control Today* (July/August 2002) <http://www.armscontrol.org/act/2002_07–08/feinsteinjul_aug02.asp>.

36. Outgoing U.S. Ambassador to India Robert Blackwill, "The Future of U.S.-Indian Relations," speech to the Confederation of Indian Industry, New Delhi, July 17, 2003. Blackwill cautioned that India, for one, could no longer be

lectured to paternalistically about its nuclear weapons program and that working as partners was a better approach.

37. Teresita Schaeffer, interviewed by the author, Washington, D.C., April 29, 2002. Schaffer points out that Prime Minister Vajpayee did not initially endorse missile defense in May 2001, but soon came to support it within the framework of counterproliferation. Counterproliferation is consistent with India's views that all powers should scale down and eventually eliminate nuclear weapons. India also has endorsed the process of consultation, which helped lead Russia to live with missile defense.

38. Rajesh Basrur, "Missile Defense and South Asia: An Indian Perspective," in Michael Krepon and Chris Gagne, eds., *The Impact of US Ballistic Missile Defenses on Southern Asia* (Washington, D.C.: Henry L. Stimson Center, Report 46, July 2002). Basrur writes that Russian TMD systems cost between $55 million and $150 million depending on type.

39. Interview with Col. Jack Gill, National Defense University, Near East and South Asia Center, May 1, 2002.

40. *The Impact of US Ballistic Missile Defenses on Southern Asia*. Krepon and Gagne find that, in the short term, U.S. missile defense would probably spark an arms race with China that would trickle down to cause an arms race between India and Pakistan. See also Gregory Koblentz, "Viewpoint: Theater Missile Defense and South Asia: A Volatile Mix," *Non-proliferation Review* 4, no. 43 (Spring–Summer 1997): 54–62.

41. Interview with Rodney Jones, Defense Threat Reduction Agency, Fort Belvoir, Virginia, April 30, 2002. In an arms race with China, India's technological shortcomings and economic weakness would be apparent. The BJP government is not committed to economic reform, which leads to economic backsliding.

42. Interview with Rodney Jones, Defense Threat Reduction Agency (DTRA), Fort Belvoir, Virginia, April 30, 2002. P. R. Kumaraswamy, *India and Israel: Evolving Strategic Partnership*, Begin-Sadat Center for Strategic Studies Bar-Ilan University, Mideast Security and Policy Studies, no. 40, September 1998.

43. Kerry Kartchner, Peter Almquist, Charles D. Frizzelle, Jr., Tom McIlvain, Jerome Bracken, and Robert Batcher, U.S. State Department, interviewed by the author May 12, 2003.

44. Interview with Alexander Lennon, editor-in-chief, *The Washington Quarterly* Center for Strategic and International Studies (CSIS), Washington, D.C., April 30, 2002.

45. Interview with Ted Andrews, India Desk Officer, State Department, Washington, D.C., April 29, 2002.

46. "Joint Statement Following U.S.-India Defense Policy Group Meeting: Defense officials of two countries met in Washington August 6–7," United States Department of Defense News Release, August 8, 2003.

47. Ibid.

48. Selig Harrison, "Nuclear Proliferation: North Korea and Pakistan," *International Herald Tribune* April 21, 2003 <http://www.iht.com/articles/93839.html>. See also, Bill Keller, "The Thinkable," *The New York Times Magazine* May 4, 2003, 48–53.

49. Gottemoeller, *Enhancing Nuclear Security in the Counter-Terrorism Struggle*; Harrison, "Nuclear Proliferation: North Korea and Pakistan"; Keller, "The Thinkable."

50. William J. Broad, David E. Sanger, and Raymond Bonner, "How Pakistani Built His Network, A Tale Of Nuclear Proliferation," *New York Times*, February 12, 2004.
51. "Editorial," *Daily Times*, Lahore, Pakistan, Sunday, May 23, 2004.
52. Interview with Eric Arnett, State Department, Washington, D.C., April 29, 2002.
53. Hoodbhoy and Mian, "The India-Pakistan Conflict."
54. Interview with Sohail Mahmood and Masood Khan, Pakistan Embassy, Washington, D.C., May 2, 2002.
55. Mutahir Ahmed, "Missile Defense and South Asia: A Pakistani Perspective," in Krepon and Gagne, *The Impact of US Ballistic Missile Defenses on Southern Asia.*
56. Gottemoeller, *Enhancing Nuclear Security in the Counter-Terrorism Struggle.*

16

The Nuclear Posture Review and Northeast Asia: Theoretical and Practical Implications

William E. Berry, Jr.

Domestic political issues dominated the 2000 presidential campaign between Al Gore and George W. Bush. Nonetheless, both candidates understood that issues related to national security and the international economy were important to many Americans, and would be at least mentioned in some of the presidential debates. For most of the campaign leading up to the 2000 elections, Northeast Asia occupied candidate Bush's attention principally in connection with larger policy considerations. For instance, in his September 1999 speech to the Citadel, Bush spoke of the People's Republic of China (PRC) as a threat to Taiwan and expressed reservations about China's development of missile technologies. Similarly, he warned that the Democratic People's Republic of Korea (DPRK, North Korea) could "reach across the oceans" to threaten the United States. Both of these examples were given places of prominence in Bush's arguments to develop and deploy missile defenses and to withdraw from the 1972 Anti-Ballistic Missile Treaty.[1]

In November 1999, Governor Bush's speech at the Reagan Library had more to say about Northeast Asia. He acknowledged that the United States and China shared some common goals such as preventing the proliferation of weapons of mass destruction (WMD) and avoiding conflict on the Korean peninsula. He specifically challenged the William Clinton administration's description of China as a strategic partner, however, by identifying the PRC as an American competitor. Bush accepted the "one China" concept that had been American policy since the Richard Nixon administration, but he made clear that, if elected, his administration would "help Taiwan defend itself."[2]

These two speeches were important because they contained many of the themes that were translated into policy documents once Bush became president. This chapter examines how the Bush administration incorporated many of these core beliefs into the 2001 Nuclear Posture Review (NPR), particularly in terms of policy toward China, North Korea, the Republic of

Korea (ROK, or South Korea), and Japan. This assessment also will examine two other important policy documents that were published just before and after the NPR: the 2001 Quadrennial Defense Review (QDR) and the National Security Strategy (NSS), published in September 2002. Counter-terrorism, nonproliferation of weapons of mass destruction, and keeping North Korea in check developed as key components of the administration's policy. The coincidence of interests in these issues has led to some positive reactions to the U.S. policy documents, in addition to some (largely predictable) negative interpretations.

U.S. POLICY DOCUMENTS AND THEIR IMPLICATIONS FOR NORTHEAST ASIA

Quadrennial Defense Review

The Department of Defense (DoD) published the QDR on September 30, 2001. Asia figured in the new QDR, which noted in its section on the changed international security environment: "Asia is gradually emerging as a region susceptible to large-scale military competition." More specifically, the QDR posited that "a military competitor with a formidable resource base will emerge in this region," and it identified the East Asian littoral from the Bay of Bengal to the Sea of Japan as a "particularly challenging area."[3]

Although China was not mentioned specifically in the QDR, the reference to the East Asian littoral included Taiwan and indirectly the relationship between China and Taiwan. Similarly, the reference to a "large scale military competitor" in East Asia realistically only could include China or Japan. Because Japan was an American treaty ally, it seems clear that this term was a less than subtle reference to the PRC.[4]

NUCLEAR POSTURE REVIEW

The Pentagon presented the classified version of the NPR to Congress late in 2001 and released an unclassified edited version in January 2002. The NPR offered several observations that had particular salience for countries in Northeast Asia. In the section titled "sizing the nuclear force," the NPR listed a series of immediate, potential, and unexpected contingencies that the United States must take into account when setting requirements for nuclear strike capabilities, which was a good example of the new capabilities-based approach adopted by the Bush administration. In the immediate category of contingencies were listed an Iraqi attack on Israel or its neighbors, a North Korean attack on the ROK, and a military confrontation in or near the Taiwan Straits. The NPR then offered a more controversial series of statements about North Korea, Iraq, Iran, Syria, and Libya as countries that have "long-standing hostility toward the United States and its security partners; North Korea and Iraq in particular have been chronic military concerns. All sponsor or harbor terrorists, and all have active WMD and missile programs."[5]

As far as China is concerned, the report stated that "due to the combination of China's developing strategic objectives and its ongoing modernization of its nuclear and nonnuclear forces, China is a country that could be involved in an immediate or potential contingency." Since the NPR had already stipulated that "a military confrontation over the status of Taiwan" was one of the three potential contingencies requiring American attention, this reference to China as part of that problem was clear.

Ehsan Ahrari, writing in the *Asia Times*, criticized the inclusion of China in the NPR because it might encourage Chinese officials to modernize their nuclear weapons to overcome American defensive systems and lead to increased proliferation. Similarly, he argued that including North Korea as one of the countries against which the United States might use nuclear weapons could lower the nuclear threshold, making nuclear war more likely.[6]

National Security Strategy

The September 2002 National Security Strategy was different from the QDR and NPR in several important aspects. First, the NSS was a White House document released under President Bush's signature, while the other two originated in the Pentagon. Second, the NSS was clearly a post–September 11 document.[7] The NSS began with the speech the president gave at the West Point graduation in early June 2002 in which he indicated that the American national security strategy was based on a "distinctly American internationalism." It is important to remember that this was the title of Bush's speech on the campaign trail in late 1999. This theme of American exceptionalism was one that the administration has attempted to develop and was very much in evidence in the NSS.

Perhaps the most important theme developed in the NSS was the premise that the international security environment in 2002 was more dangerous than during the Cold War. The combination of rogue states, terrorism, and technology (including weapons of mass destruction, or WMD) had changed the nature of U.S. national security policy. The president frequently referred to this threatening combination as "tyrants, terrorists, and technology."[8] For the administration, the traditional use of deterrence and containment against rogue states and terrorists, most significantly if weapons of mass destruction were available, had become ineffective, and a new strategy was required. This new strategy involved preemptive attacks against these types of adversaries and unilateral action if necessary.[9] Preemption and unilateral action became cornerstones of the Bush strategy to defend the country following the September 11, 2001, terrorist attacks.

As had been the case in the NPR, North Korea and China once again took center stage in this document. The NSS designated the DPRK as "the world's principal purveyor of ballistic missiles, and has developed its own WMD arsenal."[10] President Bush thereby identified North Korea as a country likely to assist terrorists with weapons of mass destruction, but this allegation of possible assistance to terrorists was implied rather that explicitly stated in the NSS. China received more extensive coverage. Although the NSS acknowledged that China and the United States were cooperating in the war against terrorism and efforts to bring stability to the Korean peninsula, problems remained in the areas of China's military modernization, proliferation, human rights, and the Taiwan situation.[11]

THE RESPONSES FROM NORTHEAST ASIA

What is clear from this review of the Bush administration's national security policy as evident in the QDR, NPR, and NSS is that there were several themes repeated throughout all of these documents. One was the concept of American exceptionalism, or as the president has said, the "distinctly American interna-tionalism." From the administration's perspective, the United States must focus on the development of democracy, freedom, and free market economic principles to contribute to international peace. Another theme was the emphasis on the use of U.S. military power, not necessarily as a last resort, to resolve problems. Preemption and unilateral action also emerge as important themes in these documents. While many Americans viewed these security themes as benign based on national values, U.S. leaders did not seem to understand how the policies played in Northeast Asian countries.

The People's Republic of China

Bush administration officials always maintained that their policies toward China would be different from those of the Clinton administration. One of the early ramifications of this policy change was the reference to China as a strategic competitor rather than a strategic partner. Early events in the new administration involving the PRC tended to reinforce suspicions on both sides. In early April 2001 an American EP-3 surveillance aircraft and its twenty-four-person crew collided with a Chinese fighter over the South China Sea, in international waters. The U.S. plane suffered damage and landed on China's Hainan Island, while the Chinese fighter crashed, killing the pilot.[12] After eleven days of negotiations, the Chinese released the crew, but the American ambassador in Beijing first had to express "sincere regret" about the death of the Chinese pilot, adding that he was "very sorry" the American plane had violated Chinese airspace to land on Hainan Island.[13] It took almost two more months before the Chinese agreed to allow the aircraft to be disassembled and returned to the United States.

Also in April 2001, President Bush announced his decision to make a $5 billion arms sale to Taiwan that included four *Kidd*-class destroyers, twelve PC-3 antisubmarine aircraft, eight diesel submarines, antiship missiles, advanced torpedoes, and minesweeping helicopters. Bush also gave an interview on national television at the time of the arms sale announcement and stated that the United States would do "whatever it took" to assist Taiwan in its defense. Although the president and his staff later tried to minimize the damage, Chinese leaders were incensed by these events.

In June 2001, Secretary of Defense Donald Rumsfeld announced that he was going to restrict future American–Chinese military contacts to a case-by-case review because of the EP-3 incident, which further strained the relations between the United States and China.[14]

U.S. national missile defense also remained a point of contention between Beijing and Washington. From the Chinese perspective, this system would limit China's nuclear deterrent and potentially stimulate an arms race. Later in 2001, the administration tried to reassure the Chinese by indicating the United States did not object if China decided to modernize part of its missile force if this action would reduce Chinese concerns over missile defense.[15] There is no question that the bilateral relationship with China has dramatically improved following the attacks of September 11, because officials in both countries understand that they have a mutual interest in fighting international terrorism. China has long expressed concerns about suspected Islamic terrorist groups in Xinjiang Province. One American expert on the bilateral relationship described this improvement as "the most important success for Bush administration policy in Asia."[16]

In the first months after the attacks, China's assistance to the United States was primarily through diplomatic support, working to restrict international terrorist financial networks, and intelligence sharing.[17] As a reflection of the improved bilateral ties, President Bush visited China in February 2002 and characterized the relationship as "constructive, cooperative, and candid." He explained to President Jiang Zemin that the United States intended to go forward with its missile defense program, but that he considered the mix of offensive and defensive systems to be stabilizing rather than destabilizing.[18] Although President Bush may well have believed this to be true, he seemed to have little understanding that the Chinese and others might believe that this combination of offensive and defensive nuclear systems could provide the United States with a first-strike capability.

Two of the best examples of increasing U.S.-China cooperation against terrorism were China's acceptance of an American military presence in Central Asia even after the conclusion of the war in Afghanistan that replaced the Taliban government, and the U.S. designation of the East Turkestan Islamic Movement (ETIM) as a terrorist organization. As the United States established military bases in Uzbekistan, Kyrgzstan, and Tajikistan, Chinese officials could see the U.S. military presence as a potential counter to ETIM and other alleged Islamic terrorist groups operating in Xinjiang Province. American forces provided some stability in this region. When Deputy Secretary of State Richard Armitage visited Beijing in August 2002, he announced the Bush administration's decision to place the ETIM on its terrorist list and freeze its assets in the United States. China viewed this policy change as important because the administration had been reluctant to recognize China's argument that there was a connection between terrorism and China's efforts to suppress such specific groups as the ETIM in northwest China.[19]

When the Chinese became aware of the NPR in March 2002, their reaction was predictable, yet muted. Vice Foreign Minister Li Zhaoxing called in U.S. Ambassador Clark Randt to protest China's inclusion on the list of countries against which the United States might use nuclear weapons. Li told Randt that his country would not submit to "outside intimidation including nuclear blackmail," and he charged the United States with "nuclear saber-rattling at the Chinese people." He insisted that the United States provide a more comprehensive explanation about possible uses of nuclear weapons against China and the other countries that were identified as targets by the NPR. In addition to this diplomatic protest, Chinese officials canceled a ship visit scheduled for New York later that year and denied permission for an American Navy vessel to visit Hong Kong.[20]

Despite the Chinese protest to Randt, it is evident the Chinese were more concerned that the Bush administration had approved the visit of Taiwan's defense minister to the United States to attend a nongovernmental business meeting in Florida in March 2002. While in the United States, this Taiwanese official met informally with Deputy Secretary of Defense Paul Wolfowitz and Assistant Secretary of State James Kelly. Li strongly protested to Randt about this contact and expressed the Chinese position that this visit and meeting were examples of American interference in China's internal affairs.[21]

Later in 2002, when the White House published the NSS, China expressed concern over the possibility of American preemptive attacks and unilateral action but indicated, "the consequences of such a strategy have yet to unfold." As 2002 approached its end, China was in the midst of a major political transition as President Jiang Zemin transferred power to Hu Jintao. This distraction may explain why China's reactions to Bush administration policy statements were not especially vigorous.[22] Chinese leaders also well understood that if China's remarkable economic growth and development were to continue, relations with the United States had to remain stable. This reality also helped to explain China's muted reactions to both the NPR and the NSS.

The NPR probably had its greatest impact on China's strategic nuclear modernization program. This is not to suggest that the Bush administration's policies were responsible for these modernization programs, because improvement efforts began well before the 2000 election. But U.S. policy justified China's modernization process. Since China developed nuclear weapons in 1965, it had followed basically a limited deterrence policy in that it maintained a relatively modest nuclear capability—though it was large enough to punish any aggressor.[23] The reference to the new triad in the NPR, particularly the emphasis on defensive systems, became a factor in the Chinese calculus as to how to structure its nuclear forces. The modernization program in ballistic missiles has progressed from the DF-3 and DF-5 models to the DF-31 that was first tested in 1995 and the DF-41 now under development. The most important technical developments have been the progression from liquid-fueled to solid-fueled missiles with much-improved accuracy, which has given the Chinese a counterforce capability. Improvements also have occurred in Chinese submarine-launched missiles through the expansion of ranges to reach the continental United States.[24]

Taiwan

It is more difficult to evaluate the effects of the NPR on Taiwan than on China. Although the Bush administration authorized a major arms sale to Taiwan early in 2001, Taiwan has been slow to purchase these weapons for organizational and fiscal reasons.[25] Chinese planners are concerned that Taiwan will be invited to participate in the American missile defense system that, from the Chinese perspective, could encourage an eventual Taiwanese declaration of independence. To preclude this eventuality, China has taken several steps to influence Taiwan's behavior. In a Department of Defense annual report on the Chinese military in July 2003, the Pentagon estimated that China had deployed approximately 450 short-range ballistic missiles (SRBMs) in provinces near Taiwan and was adding about seventy-five of these missiles per year. This report suggested that China's intent was to coerce Taiwan and to complicate any American responses to a replay of the 1995–1996 Taiwan Strait crisis.[26]

The situation in Taiwan has been further complicated for the United States since the election of Chen Shui-bian as Taiwan's president in 2000. During his reelection campaign in late 2003 and early 2004, President Chen proposed holding a referendum in conjunction with the presidential election scheduled for March 2004. This proposed referendum included the following question to the Taiwanese electorate: "Should mainland China refuse to withdraw the missiles it has targeted at Taiwan and to openly renounce the use of force against us, would you agree that the government should acquire more advanced antimissile weapons to strengthen Taiwan's defense capabilities?" China vehemently opposed this referendum because of its perception that any referendum was a step toward Taiwan's independence.[27] In December 2003, China's Prime Minister Wen Jiabao visited Washington and met with President Bush. At the conclusion of their meeting, they held a press conference during which Bush was asked to comment on the proposed Taiwan referendum. In a stinging rebuke to Chen Shui-bian, Bush responded that he opposed this referendum. The president went on to state, "the comments by the leader of Taiwan indicate that he may be willing to make decisions unilaterally to change the status quo, which we oppose."[28]

Chen won the Taiwanese presidential election, but by a very narrow margin—perhaps 30,000 votes out of 13 million ballots cast. The referendum on the question of increased defense spending to offset the Chinese missile threat was defeated because fewer than 50 percent of those participating in the election for president voted on the referendum.[29] The whole question of Taiwan's possible participation in the missile defense system was raised again in early April 2004 when the Pentagon announced that the United States was willing to sell Taiwan $1.78 billion in radar equipment to improve Taiwan's capabilities to detect the launch of ballistic missiles. China immediately responded that this proposed sale sent "the wrong message" to Taiwan and strenuously opposed the consummation of any such sale. At the same time, the U.S. Navy announced its intention to send an Aegis-class destroyer to the Sea of Japan to assist Japan with missile defense. China added its objections to this deployment along with its objection to the radar upgrade for Taiwan. For China, these two initiatives were related because they could contribute to Taiwan's participation in a regional missile defense.[30] It is not clear how this situation will be resolved, but it is evident that American missile defense as outlined in the NPR will continue to be an important issue in the bilateral relationship with China, particularly if there is the possibility of Taiwan's involvement in a regional missile defense scheme.

North Korea

Soon after assuming office in January 2001, President Bush announced that his administration would conduct a policy review regarding North Korea. During the course of this review, it became apparent that a significant debate was underway within the administration. On one side were those who wanted to pursue a policy of regime change in the DPRK and argued that negotiations should be avoided. The other side countered that it was necessary to negotiate with North Korea in a multilateral framework, while using traditional tools of containment to keep Kim Jong Il under control. Vice President Dick Cheney, Secretary Rumsfeld, and Deputy Secretary Wolfowitz were in the former group while Secretary Powell, Deputy Secretary Armitage, and Assistant Secretary Kelly were in the latter. The president announced the results of this policy review in June 2001 and directed his staff to begin "serious discussions" with North Korea. He also added human rights and conventional military forces to the list of topics to be addressed along with the North's nuclear weapons program and missile exports.[31] Despite this seeming victory for Powell and those supporting negotiations, no formal discussions occurred until October 2002.

The NPR probably had more of an effect on North Korea that any other country in Northeast Asia. The classified version of this review apparently listed the DPRK as one of the seven countries against which the United States might consider using nuclear weapons and it contained references to developing conventional and nuclear weapons that could attack deep underground bunkers. Because there have been estimates that North Korea may have as many as 15,000 underground sites, the DPRK is a likely target for the earth penetrating weapons outlined in the NPR. The North Koreans also viewed American missile defense systems, particularly those that may be deployed in Northeast Asia, as being directed against them.

The North Korean response to the NPR was quick in coming. A commentary published by the Korean Central News Agency described the NPR as "an inhuman plan to spark a global nuclear arms race" and predicted "strong countermeasures" against it.[32] This commentary continued by stating that North Korea would "not remain a passive onlooker" after being included on the list of countries the United States might attack with nuclear weapons; it even threatened attacks on the Pentagon. The News Agency concluded by warning that "a nuclear war to be imposed by nuclear fanatics would mean their ruin in nuclear disaster." The DPRK's apparent paranoia over the NPR was not an isolated event. President Bush included North Korea as a member of his "axis of evil" in his 2002 State of the Union address that also occurred in January; moreover, the NSS released in September identified North Korea as a rogue state, missile exporter, and supporter of terrorist organizations. The uses of preemptive attacks, threatened in the NSS, were employed against both Afghanistan and Iraq, and these attacks—along with the regime changes associated with them—no doubt further gripped the attention of the leadership in Pyongyang.

The administration sent Assistant Secretary of State Kelly to hold discussions with the North Koreans in October 2002. At these discussions in Pyongyang, Kelly presented evidence to his hosts that North Korea had embarked on a highly enriched uranium (HEU) program to develop nuclear weapons. After first denying this accusation, the North Koreans admitted they did have such a program and told Kelly they had pursued this option because of Bush administration hostility. Kelly retorted that American intelligence indicated the North Koreans had begun work on this program no later than 1999, which of course was during the Clinton administration.[33]

Whatever the North Korean motivations for its HEU program, the admission that it had such a program set in motion a series of events that have resulted in a very dangerous situation on the Korean peninsula. North Korea expelled International Atomic Energy (IAEA) inspectors, restarted its plutonium nuclear weapons program, and withdrew from the Nuclear Non-Proliferation Treaty. The United States, along with its South Korean and Japanese allies, cut off fuel oil shipments included in the 1994 Agreed Framework and threatened other punitive actions.[34]

There have been three multilateral negotiating sessions on North Korea held in Beijing (in April 2003, August 2003, and February 2004), but little substantive progress has been made to reduce the threat of the DPRK's nuclear weapon programs. The NPR certainly was not solely responsible for this impasse, but it must be viewed as part of the mix of factors that produced a deteriorating situation involving North Korea's nuclear weapon programs.

South Korea

The relationship between South Korea and the United States has also been troubled during the Bush administration. Differences between the two governments over policies toward North Korea contributed to this policy dispute, and the NPR reflects some of these differences. In March 2001, South Korean President Kim Dae Jung came to Washington to visit President Bush. By most accounts, this meeting did not go well. Kim's signature policy involving North Korea—referred to as the Sunshine Policy—represented an effort to separate political and economic relations between the two Koreas.[35] Kim wanted to encourage other countries such as the United States and Japan to engage the DPRK, especially with trade and aid initiatives. Although the Bush administration's North Korean policy review was still underway, the U.S. president expressed his reservations about negotiations with North Korea. From Kim's point of view, the emerging U.S. position would undercut his initiatives with Pyongyang.[36]

South Korea held its presidential election in December 2002, and Roh Moo Hyun won. There was a fair amount of anti-American sentiment expressed during this campaign, which is partly explained by unfortunate events involving American military personnel in South Korea. More important was the South Korean perception that the United States was impeding Seoul's efforts to improve relations with North Korea.[37] President Roh visited President Bush in May 2003 in an effort to establish a personal relationship between the two leaders. To a certain extent, this meeting achieved that goal. In a joint statement after the meeting, the two presidents stated that North Korea must agree to the complete, verifiable, irreversible dismantlement of all its nuclear weapons programs through peaceful means based on negotiations.[38] In March 2004, Foreign Minister Ban Ki Moon came to Washington for further discussions with his American counterparts. Ban reiterated his government's position that North Korea must disband its nuclear weapons programs. He also repeated the ROK's pledge to send 3,000 additional military forces to Iraq (South Korea already had about 600 noncombatant forces there) and to provide $260 million for Iraqi reconstruction.[39]

As the visits of Roh and Ban demonstrated, bilateral relations between the United States and South Korea have improved since 2002. The NPR has been a relatively unimportant impact on this improving relationship. At the time the NPR was released, a South Korean Ministry of Defense official was quoted as saying that his country probably would not object to the document "under the current security situation." He stated that the ROK desired for the United States to continue to consult with its allies in Seoul as to how the NPR would actually be implemented.[40] A member of the National Academy of Science in Seoul, however, was not so sanguine regarding the NPR. He opined that the review was causing "great confusion" in the ROK because it seemed to provide for additional nuclear weapons that could reduce the nuclear threshold rather than make a nuclear exchange less likely. He, too, called on the United States to consult with its South Korean counterparts so as not to damage security on the Korean peninsula.[41]

South Korea has not expressed interest in joining in the American-sponsored regional missile defense system primarily because it does not view DPRK nuclear weapons as the major threat to its security. Because Seoul is only thirty miles from the thirty-eighth parallel that divides the two Koreas, North Korean artillery is viewed as a more serious threat, and missile defense would not be effective against this threat. Also, South Korea is wary about missile defenses because of the potentially negative effects its participation would have on its relations with both North Korea and China. Therefore, although relations with the United States have improved, the possibility exists that differences over the implementation of the NPR could emerge in the future.

Japan

During his speech at the Reagan Library in November 1999, George Bush noted that he wanted to focus on such alliance partners as Japan, and he followed through after his election. Japanese–American relations are exceptionally strong, and the personal ties between Bush and Prime Minister Junichiro Koizumi are warm. The two governments cooperate on issues highlighted by the NPR and the NSS: counterterrorism and the North Korea threat. The international reaction to Japan's "checkbook diplomacy" after the first Gulf War in the early 1990s stung Japanese leaders, and Prime Minister Koizumi did not intend to make a similar mistake. Japan's support for the war against the Taliban in Afghanistan and against Saddam in Iraq has been much more robust and includes Japanese military personnel (approximately 600 soldiers) on the ground in Iraq. Deploying forces to Iraq was particularly controversial and required legislation in the Diet and specific cabinet authorization.[42]

Regarding North Korea, Koizumi visited Pyongyang in September 2002 and met with Kim Jong Il. This meeting came as somewhat of a surprise, but the Japanese Prime Minister had a definite agenda that was important in his country. Kim apologized for North Korean kidnappings of Japanese nationals during the Cold War and agreed to allow the survivors to return to Japan. Kim also agreed to continue the missile-testing moratorium on medium-range missiles that had been in place in the DPRK since 1998.[43]

In May 2003, President Bush invited Prime Minister Koizumi to visit his ranch in Crawford, Texas. At the conclusion of their two-day summit, they released a press statement that addressed North Korea. This press statement indicated the two leaders saw the DPRK problem the same way. It concluded: "We will not tolerate nuclear weapons in North Korea. We will not give into blackmail and will not settle for anything less than the complete, verifiable, and irreversible elimination of North Korea's nuclear weapons program."[44] Bush also indicated that he believed Japan should be added to the list of those countries participating in any future discussions with North Korea. As a result, the three-party talks were expanded, and Japan joined the August 2003 and February 2004 talks in Beijing with the South Korean, U.S., and Russian delegations. Japan also has joined the Proliferation Security Initiative (PSI) designed to impede North Korean exports of nuclear weapons, missiles, and other contraband. Japan is the only country in Northeast Asia to participate in the PSI as of April 2004.[45]

Another area of cooperation related to the NPR was Japan's decision to become more involved with missile defense. In 1998, Japan was shocked when North Korea tested a Taepo Dong missile that flew over parts of Japan. Its response to the North Korean missile, however, was been tempered by Japan's aggressive legacy in East Asia and constitutional questions over collective security measures. Nonetheless, Prime Minister Koizumi and other Japanese leaders have decided to move forward with missile defense by upgrading Japan's Patriot missile system and allocating longer-term resources totaling perhaps $10 billion over the remainder of this decade to develop a two-layered system including Aegis destroyers and the Patriot missiles.[46]

North Korean officials were not pleased with these cooperative American–Japanese efforts on missile defense. A Foreign Ministry official reacting to the planned destroyer deployment stated that this act represented a "grave obstacle to the process of resolving the nuclear issue through dialogue" and a "hostile act" against North Korea.[47] While it is unlikely that many in Japan or the United States will lose sleep over this North Korean response, this example of cooperation between the two countries on the North Korean threat and the possible proliferation of WMD was at the heart of positive U.S.-Japanese relations.

CONCLUSION

This chapter has placed the NPR in the larger context of the Bush national security policy involving Northeast Asia. Counterterrorism, nonproliferation of WMD, and keeping North Korea in check developed as key components of the administration's policy. The reactions from some of the most important regional powers were related to how these countries view these general themes in their own national security policies. Under normal circumstances, the NPR would have been viewed with alarm and disdain by officials in Beijing because of its references to China, its emphasis on missile defense, and its reflection of the U.S. proclivity to undertake unilateral actions. Chinese concerns about terrorism and proliferation on the Korean peninsula, however, have mitigated these potential concerns about the NPR. The Bush administration's policies toward China also have changed because of shared interests. There has been a shift away from strategic competitor to something closer to strategic partner. The issue of Taiwan and the possible extension of missile defenses to this island, however, would probably be a red line for China, and the Bush administration must be careful not to inflame this issue.

North Korean officials definitely viewed the NPR as a hostile document for good reasons: it was literally the "poster country" for the NPR. Whether Kim Jong Il will decide to give up his nuclear weapons program for improved political and economic relations with the region and the United States remains to be seen.

South Korea was somewhat ambivalent about the NPR because of different threat perceptions between Washington and Seoul regarding North Korea. The two governments also have different views about the possible peaceful reunification of the two Koreas. While relations have improved in the past few months, strong feelings of anti-Americanism or at least "anti-Bushism" exist in the Republic of Korea. No such ambivalence exists in Japan, and the bilateral relationship has increased in importance for both Tokyo and Washington. The NPR remains an important policy document, but how it is perceived in Northeast Asia depends on the individual national security policies of the countries in the region and particularly the relationships of these countries with the United States.

NOTES

1. George W. Bush, "A Period of Consequences," speech delivered at the Citadel, September 23, 1999 available at <www.citadel.edu/pao/addresses/pres_bush. html>.

2. George W. Bush, "A Distinctly American Internationalism," speech delivered at the Reagan Library, November 19, 1999 available at <www. mtholyoke.edu/ acad/inrel/bush/wspeech.html>. The observations that follow are taken from these two speeches.

3. Quadrennial Defense Review Report, September 30, 2001. A copy of this report is available at <www.defenselink.mil/pubs/qdr2001.pdf>. The reference to Asia is found on 4, to defense policy goals on 11–12, and to the capabilities based orientation on 13–14.

4. Michael McDevitt, "The Quadrennial Defense Review and East Asia," *PacNet Newsletter* no. 43 (October 26, 2001) <www.csis.org/pacfor/pac 0143.htm>.

5. The edited version of the Nuclear Posture Review, dated January 8, 2002, can be found at <www.globalsecurity.org/wmd/library/policy/dod/npr.htm>. This specific quote is found on 5.

6. Ehsan Ahrari, "U.S. Lowers Nuclear Barriers," *Asia Times* March 15, 2002 <www.atimes.com/front/DC15Aa02.html>.

7. The National Security Strategy of the United States of America, September 2002 <http://usinfo.state.gov/topical/terror/secstrat.htm>.

8. Ivo H. Daalder and James M. Lindsay, *America Unbound: The Bush Revolution in Foreign Policy* (Washington, D.C.: Brookings Institution, 2003), 120. For a specific reference in the National Security Strategy, see pp. 13–14.

9. See the National Security Strategy for a detailed discussion of preemption and unilateral action 15–16 and 31.

10. National Security Strategy, 14.

11. Specific references to China in the NSS, 27–28.

12. Elisabeth Rosenthal and David E. Sanger, "U.S. Plane in China After It Collides With Chinese Jet," *New York Times* April 2, 2001.

13. Bonnie S. Glaser, "Mid-Air Collision Cripples Sino-American Relations," *Comparative Connections* 2nd Quarter 2001, U.S.-China Relations, <www.csis. org/pacfor/ccejournal.html>. The references to the ambassador's remarks are on 2.

14. Ibid. 3–4. See also Michael R. Gordon, "Rumsfeld Limiting Military Contacts with the Chinese," *New York Times* June 4, 2001.

15. David E. Sanger, "U.S. Will Drop Objections to China's Missile Buildup," *New York Times* September 2, 2001; Dali l. Yang, "China in 2001: Economic Liberalization and Its Political Discontents," in *Asian Survey*, XLII, no. 1, (January/February 2002): 15–16.

16. Robert D. Sutter, "U.S. Leadership: Prevailing Strengths Amid Challenges," in Richard J. Ellings and Aaron L. Friedberg, eds., *Strategic Asia 2003–04: Fragility and Crisis* (Seattle, Wash.: National Bureau of Asian Research, 2002), 40.

17. Thomas J. Christensen, "China," in Ellings and Friedberg, eds. *Strategic Asia 2002–03: Asian Aftershocks* 55.

18. Bonnie S. Glaser, "Two Steps Forward, One Step Back," *Comparative Connections*, 1st Quarter 2002, U.S.-China Relations, 1–2.

19. For the U.S. military presence in Central Asia, see Kathleen A. Collins and William C. Wohlforth, "Defying 'Great Game' Expectations," in Ellings and Friedberg, eds., *Strategic Asia 2003–04: Fragility and Crisis*, 296–298. For the U.S. designation of the ETIM as a terrorist group, see Bonnie S. Glaser, "Playing Up the Positive on the Eve of the Crawford Summit," *Comparative Connections*, 3rd Quarter 2002, U.S.-China Relations, 2–3.

20. Glaser, "Playing Up the Positive," 6.

21. Ministry of Foreign Affairs of the People's Republic of China, "Vice Foreign Minister Li Zhaoxing Summons U.S. Ambassador Randt to Make Representations on Tang Yiau-min's Visit to the United States," March 18, 2002 <www. fmprc. gov.cn>.

22. Glaser, "Playing Up the Positive," 8–9.

23. Alastair Iain Johnston, "China's New 'Old Thinking,'" *International Security* 20, no. 3 (Winter 1995–1996): 17–23.

24. David Shambaugh, *Modernizing China's Military* (Berkeley, Calif.: University of California Press, 2002), 274–282.

25. Michael R. Gordon, "A Guppy-Size Force," *New York Times* April 18, 2001.

26. Bonnie S. Glaser, "The Best Since 1972 or the Best Ever," *Comparative Connections* 3rd Quarter 2003, U.S.-China Relations, 8.

27. Keith Bradsher, "Taiwan's Leader Tones Down Referendum Opposed By Beijing," *New York Times* January 17, 2004; Joseph Kahn, "Taiwan Voters Weighing How Far to Push China," *New York Times* March 8, 2004.

28. David E. Sanger, "Bush Lauds China Leader As 'Partner' in Diplomacy," *New York Times* December 10, 2003.

29. Keith Bradsher and Joseph Kahn, "Taiwan's Leader Wins Re-Election; Tally Is Disputed," *New York Times* March 21, 2004.

30. Norimitsu Onishi, "Japan Joining U.S. Missile Shield," *New York Times* April 3, 2004.

31. Statement of the President, June 11, 2001 <www.whitehouse.gov/news/releases/2001/06/20010611-4.html>.

32. All of these quotes are found in Don Kirk, "North Korea Denounces U.S. Nuclear Plan, Promises Response," *New York Times* March 13, 2002.

33. For a series of articles on the Kelly visit in October 2002, see *New York Times* October 17, 2002; October 18, 2002; and October 21, 2002.

34. For details on the 1994 Agreed Framework, see William E. Berry, Jr., "North Korea's Nuclear Program: The Clinton Administration's Response," *INSS Occasional Paper* 3 (Colorado Springs, Colo.: USAF Institute for National Security Studies, March 1995).

35. For more details on the Sunshine Policy, see Norman D. Levin and Yong-Sup Han, *Sunshine in Korea: The South Korean Debate over Policies Toward North Korea* (Santa Monica, Calif.: The RAND Corporation, 2002), especially 23–32.

36. For a good review of the Bush–Kim meeting in March 2001, see Morton I. Abramowitz and James T. Laney, "Meeting the North Korean Nuclear Challenge," Report of an Independent Task Force, sponsored by the Council on Foreign Relations, June 2003, 12.

37. Ralph A. Cossa, "Trials, Tribulations, Threats, and Tirades," *Comparative Connections* 4th Quarter 2002, U.S.-Korea Relations, 6–7.

38. Joint Statement Between the United States of America and the Republic of Korea, May 14, 2003 <http://www.whitehouse.gov/news/releases/20030514-17.html>.

39. "Remarks With South Korean Minister of Foreign Affairs and Trade Ban Ki-Moon After Their Meeting" <http://www.state/secretary/rm/30162.htm>. Ban also gave a speech at the Center for Strategic and International Studies while in Washington on March 5, 2004, in which he made several of these same points. For a good review of current U.S.-ROK relations, see Victor Cha, "South Korea: Adrift or Anchored," in Ellings and Friedberg, eds., *Strategic Asia 2003–04: Fragility and Crisis*, 117–120.

40. "ROKG Still Wants US Nuclear Umbrella, Reportedly Willing to Accommodate Nuclear Posture Review," *Korea Herald* March 12, 2002.

41. Ah Pyong Chun, "Is There a Diplomatic Strategy for Denuclearization?" Seoul *Tong-a Ilbo*, March 2, 2002 <http://www.donga.com>.

42. On Afghanistan, see Eric Heginbotham and Richard J. Samuels, "Japan" in Ellings and Friedberg, eds., *Strategic Asia 2002–03: Asian Aftershocks*, 103–104. For Iraq, see Michael H. Armasost, "Japan: Tilting Closer to Washington," in Ellings and Freidberg, *Strategic Survey 2003–04: Fragility and Crisis*, 86 and 93. The cabinet decision was announced in Norimitsu Onishi, "Japan Commits Itself to Sending Up to 600 Ground Troops to Iraq," *New York Times* December 10, 2003.

43. Donald G. Gross, "After the Koizumi-Kim Summit, Nothing is the Same," *Comparative Connections*, 3rd Quarter 2002, U.S.-Korea Relations, 3–4.

44. "President Bush meets with Prime Minister Koizumi, May 23, 2003," at <www.whitehouse.gov/news/releases/2003/05/20030523-4.html>.

45. For some background on the Proliferation Security Initiative, see the Chairman's Statement at the Brisbane Australia meeting, July 9–10, 2003 <http://www.dfat.gov.au/globalissues/psi/index.html>.

46. Armacost, 88–89; Norimitsu Onishi, "Japan Joining U.S. in Missile Shield," *New York Times* April 3, 2004.

47. "DPRK Radio Carries FM Spokesman's 31 March Criticism of US Aegis Deployment," Foreign Broadcast Information Service (FBIS), March 31, 2004 at <http://portal.rccb.osis.gov.servlet/Headlines>.

17

The Nuclear Posture Review: The Middle East Redux?

James A. Russell

The Nuclear Posture Review (NPR) promises to affect the shape and content of the nation's national security strategy writ large, and, U.S. security strategies tailored to geographic theaters around the world. Each of the National Command Authority's regional military commanders will inevitably adjust their plans, policies and resources to meet the requirements of operationalizing the NPR.

The muted foreign reactions to the NPR are surprising because the NPR identifies new roles and missions for nuclear weapons, especially in the Middle East and the Persian Gulf. The NPR makes the region a central focus of the redesigned strategic deterrent, now comprising nuclear and conventional components, with conventional long-range precision strike weapons functioning in a "strategic" context. While it might be too dramatic to suggest that the Middle East effectively replaces the Soviet Union as the central targeting requirement for sizing and configuring U.S. nuclear forces, regional contingencies will undoubtedly assume a more prominent role in the nation's nuclear strategy.[1] The NPR implies that the defense of Israel, for example, represents a core mission for the strategic deterrent by identifying several "near-term" contingencies involving an attack on Israel that could lead to the use of nuclear weapons by the United States.[2] Moreover, with two countries in the region—Syria and Iran—fostering programs to develop weapons of mass destruction (WMD) that support terrorism, the strategic force has two potential targets in the area. The region seems to be the archetypal situation that informs the NPR's treatment of the targeting problem posed by hardened and deeply buried targets that cannot be held at risk by conventional weapons.[3] As the NPR notes, these targets necessitate a new family of munitions that will be incorporated into the strategic deterrent.[4]

This chapter examines the implications of implementing the NPR for U.S. security strategy in the Middle East, framing NPR implementation in the context of the theoretical literature on the role of nuclear weapons in deterrence and coercive strategies. This theoretical framework will be applied to compellent Iraq from 1991 to 2003, as well as to current policy toward

Syria. The chapter concludes with an assessment of the ability of the strategic deterrent to assure allies, deter adversaries, dissuade adversaries from competing against the United States, and defeat adversaries if necessary.

THE NPR AND THE MIDDLE EAST

According to leaked sources, the NPR supposedly identified Iraq, Iran, Syria, and Libya (in addition to North Korea) as countries that " . . . could be involved in immediate, potential, or unexpected [nuclear] contingencies. All have longstanding hostility toward the United States and its security partners. . . . All sponsor or harbor terrorists, and all have active WMD and missile programs."[5] Saddam's forcible removal from power and Libya's apparent abandonment of its WMD programs presumably removed these countries from the potential list of contingencies, leaving Iran and Syria as countries in the region that might be involved in situations requiring the United States to use nuclear weapons. The NPR strongly implies a U.S. commitment to use nuclear weapons in the defense of Israel, identifying one "immediate contingency" that might lead to the use of nuclear weapons: an Iraqi attack on Israel. While such an attack clearly has been obviated with Saddam's ouster, it stands to reason that the same logic applies to a Syrian or Iranian attack on Israel. Both Syria and Iran maintain well-established WMD capabilities and both foster longstanding and overt hostility toward Israel.

While the NPR specifically refers to particular regional contingencies, the strategic deterrent is assigned a broad array of functions that are particularly relevant to U.S. policy in the Middle East. The NPR suggests that nuclear weapons and the strategic deterrent can be applied in many wartime scenarios short of massive retaliation and all-out war. The NPR envisions a variety of peacetime missions for the nuclear force; for example, as a deterrent to preserve the status quo and prevent the outbreak of interstate conflict. The strategic deterrent also can help change the behavior of states and other threatening actors in the international system. The strategic deterrent is one capability designed to support the concept of dissuasion—highlighted in the Bush administration's strategy documents—that looks to convince states of the futility of entering into a direct competition with the United States. These documents also emphasize the salience of threats coming from the spread of WMD and terrorism. The strategic deterrent is presented as a tool to keep states from providing WMD to terrorist clients and from attacking the United States and its friends and allies. While many of the Bush administration's strategy documents show a lack of confidence in applying deterrence to non-state actors, the documents expand the role of deterrence in other areas.[6]

For wartime missions, the Bush administration repeats formulations from previous administrations that allow for the use of nuclear weapons in certain contingencies. As the National Strategy to Combat Weapons of Mass Destruction states: "The United States will continue to make clear it reserves the right to respond with overwhelming force—including through resort to all our options—to the use of WMD against our forces abroad and friends and allies."[7] The deterrent also will be used to address the targeting problem posed by the proliferation of hardened underground targets that cannot be held at risk by conventional munitions. Additionally, the NPR calls for the replacement of the cumbersome Single Integrated Operational Plan with something called "adaptive planning," in which components of the strategic deterrent can be integrated into responses to ongoing contingencies on reasonably short notice. These broadly defined political and military missions suggest certain identifiable objectives within the Middle East:

- Deter and defend attacks against forward-deployed forces.
- Defend Israel from attack by adversaries using conventional or non-conventional weapons.
- Convince states with WMD or contemplating the pursuit of WMD to abandon these programs.
- Convince states that engage in or support terrorism to cease these activities.
- Deter states that possess WMD from passing these weapons to terrorist organizations targeting either the United States or Israel.
- Present the National Command Authority (NCA) with a flexible and diverse array of attack options (both conventional and nuclear) to defeat adversaries in regional contingencies, such as:
  ○ Counterforce operations against WMD and regime targets.
  ○ Tactical support to theater commanders.
  ○ Strategic use in situations requiring massive retaliation.
- Assure Israel of the U.S. defense commitment, which can act as a deterrent to aggressive Israeli actions against its neighbors.
- Assure coalition partners throughout the region that the United States can and will use force to deter attacks on these partners and to defend them using the strategic deterrent if necessary.

Although these functions are not articulated in any strategy document, they reflect how the NPR objectives can serve U.S. national security objectives in the Middle East.

THEORY, COMMUNICATIONS, AND DECISION MAKERS

The Middle East boasts not only all the salient threatening features of the international environment frequently identified by commentators (terrorism, WMD, and instability), but it also is a region where systemic interstate communications problems pose enormous obstacles for the United States in operationalizing complicated political and military strategies. These communications issues constitute a critical issue as policy makers determine the role for the strategic deterrent in regional security strategy.

Implementing the NPR in the region suggests an interesting confluence of theoretical approaches to the role of nuclear weapons in strategy and the role that perceptions, signals, and communications play in interstate relations. The NPR implies that the strategic deterrent has a prominent role to play in a family of coercive political and military strategies, in which states either threaten—or in some cases actually use—force to achieve political objectives. Associating the strategic deterrent with coercive and deterrent strategies suggests the applicability of a theoretical framework articulated during the late 1950s and early 1960s by Thomas Schelling in his works, *The Strategy of Conflict* and *Arms and Influence.*[8] Schelling argued that nuclear weapons could serve as a useful tool to policy makers engaged in what he called the "diplomacy of violence."[9] Schelling believed that nuclear weapons represented an instrument that could be wielded through strategies of deterrence, compellence, and coercion. The NPR's broadly defined missions for the strategic deterrent suggest that the Bush administration also believes this to be the case.

Schelling's distinctions between the concepts of deterrence and compellence remain as valid today as when he articulated them. Deterrence is the function of threatening the use of force to keep an opponent from taking certain actions. [10] Compellence is the initiation of actions (including the use of force) that will be administered until an adversary changes objectionable behavior or initiates certain desired behaviors.[11] The deterrent threat is more or less open-ended, whereas the compellent threat requires the initiation of action with a specific articulation of some sort of deadline or set of actions that must be taken before the compellent actions can cease. Schelling's view was that "coercion" was a concept encompassing both deterrence and compellence[12] and that both concepts functioned in the context of coercive strategies available for use as bargaining tools in interstate conflict.

Schelling believed that nuclear weapons could have a role in these strategies in both political and military contexts, meaning they could discourage an adversary from taking actions, force an adversary to change behavior, and, if necessary, serve as tools to achieve tactical and strategic objectives once hostilities had been initiated. In his view, nuclear weapons could play a role in limiting the scope of armed conflict once begun, since the escalation dominance it afforded could convince an adversary of the futility of continuing the conflict and hence bring the action to a close on favorable terms. He took this point to an extreme in *Arms and Influence*, arguing that destruction of enemy cities could form part of a coercive strategy to inflict successive and unacceptable levels of pain on an adversary in order to terminate a conflict on favorable terms.[13]

The Strategy of Conflict provides another vital supporting element in the theoretical framework linking nuclear weapons and their potential roles in coercive strategies. Schelling believed that interstate conflict could be analyzed as part of a bargaining process. Strategies of deterrence, compellence, and coercion, Schelling argued, could be placed into a framework of game theory called "a theory of interdependent decision." His theory posited that deterrence, compellence, and coercion could be applied to achieve objectives as part of the interstate bargaining process.[14] Under Schelling's theory, operationalizing the concepts of deterrence and compellence occurred when states threatened the use of force or used force to inflict successive levels of pain on an adversary to achieve a desired outcome.[15] Schelling acknowledged that the bargaining process had one important limitation; asymmetries in communications might prevent actors from receiving signals of intent.[16] The issues of actor rationality and the function of interstate communications have always troubled analysts as they thought about assigning roles to nuclear weapons in deterrent and coercive strategies. Former Defense Secretary Robert McNamara cogently expressed these doubts during his University of Michigan commencement address in June 1962, when he stated: "[T]he mere fact that no nation could rationally take steps leading to a nuclear war does not guarantee that a nuclear war cannot take place. Not only do nations sometimes act in ways that are hard to explain on a rational basis, but even when acting in a 'rational' way they sometimes, indeed disturbingly often, will act on the basis of misunderstandings of the true facts of a situation. They misjudge the way others will react, and the way others will interpret what they are doing."[17] McNamara's misgivings about the supposed rationality of actors involved in deterrent relationships are reflected in much of the literature on deterrence theory.[18]

The problem of interstate communications—central to the application of Schelling's coercive bargaining framework—is systematically addressed by Robert Jervis in his seminal work, *The Logic of Images in International Relations*.[19] Jervis analyzed how policy makers drew inferences from the actions of other states and, in addition, how decision makers could influence the inferences being drawn by their counterparts.[20] Jervis suggested that policy makers communicate with one another through a series of images; an internal image developed for internal audiences and an external image presented to the world at large. These images constitute powerful tools: "The image of a state can be a major factor in determining whether and how easily the state can reach its goals. A desired image (the substance of which will depend on the actor's goals and his estimate of the international environment) can often be of greater use than a significant increment of military or economic power." [21] A central feature of this convention of communication described by Jervis is that images constructed by states constitute a powerful tool for deception; they can be used to confuse actors. One of the main points in *The Logic of Images* is the role that deliberate deception plays in international relations.[22]

Jervis suggests that interstate communication takes place through a series of "signals," which are "statements or actions, the meanings of which are established by tacit or explicit understandings among the actors."[23] "Indices" represent another feature of the communication system, which are "statements or actions that carry some inherent evidence that the image projected is correct because they are believed to be inextricably linked to the actor's capabilities or intentions."[24] Both signals and indices can be manipulated by the actors both to deceive another actor and to convince the actor of intent. Jervis believed that actors engaged in the delivering and receiving process had a tendency to "decouple" these signals and "couple" those signals to new meanings that inevitably diverged from the initiating party's intended meanings.[25]

In addition to these systemic communications problems, Jervis also believed that misperception substantially clouded the ability of decision makers to convey and receive intentions accurately.[26] Misperceptions stem from the tendency of decision makers to fit incoming information into their existing theories and images, from the tendency for actors to establish their theories and expectations prematurely, or from historical traumas that influence future perceptions. When messages are sent from a different background of concerns and information than is possessed by the receiver, misunderstanding is likely to occur. Information and actions also can convey unwanted messages. Decision makers often see other states as more hostile than they are, and actors tend to believe that the behavior of others is more centralized than it really is.[27]

Jervis' discussion of perception and signaling suggests that effective interstate communications are at best problematic and at worst haphazard. Sources of misperception combined with the complicated system of communicating intent and developing indices produce what can only be described as a communication process prone to uncertainty and unpredictability. These inherent frailties of the system can be exacerbated in cross-cultural communications, but they can occur almost as easily between states with well-developed political and cultural relationships.[28]

Cognitive psychology and game theory suggest that several propositions must be taken into consideration by those who seek to achieve the objectives specified in the NPR. First, coercive strategies are more likely to succeed in the presence of common assumptions, mutual dependence, rational actors, and effective communications. Second, coercive strategies are more likely to succeed if the communications system allows actors to convey and receive information about intentions accurately, to promote the interstate bargaining process.

IMPLICATIONS IN THE MIDDLE EAST

During the Cold War, arms control played an important role in establishing a relatively structured communications system between the United States and the Soviet Union. Summit talks and the accompanying informal interactions on the margins of these meetings helped establish a communications framework that enabled the deterrent relationship at the strategic level. The arms control process fostered strategic stability by helping both Soviets and Americans sort through the complicated process of drawing correct inferences from signals and indices. It also allowed the actors to take unambiguous concrete actions (e.g., limiting strategic nuclear delivery vehicles) pursuant to an agreed-upon framework that sought to introduce predictability into force structures. Consistent with Schelling's formulations, this framework meant that the actors in the bargaining process shared a basic set of assumptions and could agree to pursue compromise in certain aspects of their relationships, even while allowing and even encouraging conflict to continue in other areas at the same time. And, consistent with Jervis's ideas, the actors had a structured forum to convey intention and develop indices to gauge the impact that their signals were having.

In the Middle East, however, there exists no institutionalized process for adversaries to ensure structured communications on a routine basis outside of formal political channels—and even these rarified channels do not exist, in many cases, for communications between Iran and the United States or between Iran and Israel. Instead, interstate communications with and within the Middle East tend to occur through the media and more traditional forms of political or diplomatic communications. These forms of communication leave much to be desired. The language of diplomacy, Jervis notes, effectively constitutes its own "code" with ambiguous and open-ended meanings.[29] He summarized the characteristics of diplomatic language as a "complex signaling system [that] is not noiseless and unambiguous, and thus signals are often intentionally unclear even at the first, or semantic, level. This allows actors to issue signals they can disown and give[s]them more flexibility to explore possible politics without changing others' images of themselves to their detriment."[30] Communications through the media are even more problematic, particularly in the Middle East. Government-controlled media throughout much of the Arab world routinely push pronounced anti-American and anti-Semitic messages, which make state-run news outlets poor channels through which to communicate signals.

Further confusing the interstate communications process are differences flowing from history, religion, ethnicity—particularly distinct "national" identities—as well as the personalities of the leaders themselves. Defining differences between the United States and the countries in the Middle East as "cultural" seems somehow inadequate, because a more complicated analytical category really is required. The interaction of all these variables provides an important founding basis for the images that Jervis suggested are integral parts of the interstate communications system. If these images are opaque, obscured, or just plain misperceived by U.S. officials, they do not convey intent completely or accurately.

Coercive and Compellent Failure: The United States and Iraq, 1991–2003

It is difficult to underestimate the impact of misperception and miscommunications on the coercive strategy employed from 1991 through 2003 by the United States against Iraq.[31] The stated objectives of U.S. policies were threefold—though not necessarily mutually supportive. U.S. policy objectives were: to deter Iraqi attacks against its neighbors and to mitigate Iraq's military threat to the region; to seek Iraq's compliance with a variety of UN Security Council resolutions, the most important of which was verifiable disarmament; and, from 1997 onward, to topple Saddam by encouraging internal and external opponents of his regime. Throughout the decade, the United States used a variety of diplomatic, economic, and military tools in the context of a broadly based strategy of compellence and deterrence to achieve these objectives. The United States deployed forces engaged in ongoing military operations to enforce a United Nations trade embargo and to deny Iraq control over much of its airspace. The United States used its influence in the United Nations Security Council to isolate Iraq politically and tried to ensure the efficacy of the United Nations' arms inspection process pursuant to UN Security Council Resolution 687. The United States used force repeatedly throughout the period in response to various objectionable behaviors by the Iraqi regime.

The U.S. approach to Iraq represented a classic mix of deterrent and compellent strategies. The threat of force was always present, varying in intensity throughout the period, depending on the crisis at hand, and sustained attacks were launched in 1993, 1996, and 1998. A pattern emerged during the decade. Defiance by Saddam resulted in U.S. military deployments into the region, accompanied by repeated statements of intent to use force. These crises were resolved with either a political compromise at the United Nations or, alternately, U.S. attacks. This pattern continued until December 1998, when the UN withdrew its inspectors and the United States mounted Operation Desert Fox. Following these strikes, the rules of engagement for U.S. forces patrolling the no-fly zones were expanded, allowing a more systematic and sustained military campaign against the Iraqi air defense system and command and control network throughout southern Iraq.

The approach taken by the United States reflected important elements of Schelling's bargaining process. Both the threat and the actual use of force took place in tandem with public statements that conveyed intent in pursuit of an objective. Escalation followed rhetoric if Saddam did not comply. Saddam's defiance during the period also supported a prevailing view that the United States was dealing with a dangerous and recalcitrant "realist," whose main motivation was to remain in power and continue defying the international community by preserving his WMD programs. Saddam's refusal to provide information to correct discrepancies in declarations to the UN weapons inspectors and the discovery of the so-called concealment mechanism during the tenure of UN Special Commission Chairman Richard Butler only confirmed a prevailing view that Saddam had stocks of WMD stored just out of the inspectors' reach. After all, so the reasoning went, why else would he go to such lengths and endure the wrath of the international community?

But in retrospect, it appears that Saddam, the other actor in the coercive bargaining framework, was working with an asymmetrical series of motivations and had developed images that were for the most part opaque to the United States (if not the entire international community). The asymmetrical interests and opaque images meant the signals and indices used by both sides were more like ships passing in the night rather than signals conveyed by rational actors communicating in a calculated interstate bargaining process. Evidence to support this assertion has emerged in interviews with former high-ranking Iraq officials, and seemingly incredible incongruencies have emerged. For example, there are questions about whether Saddam ever knew the specific requirements of UN Security Council Resolution 687 that banned all WMD programs (including research) and missiles exceeding 150 kilometers in range. According to former Iraqi foreign minister Tariq Aziz, Saddam insisted as late as 1999 that UNSCR 687 only prohibited long-range missiles that carried WMD.[32] A variety of Iraqi interlocutors also have stated that the 150-kilometer missile range limit represented the most important restriction in the entire series of disarmament obligations imposed on Iraq.[33] Despite U.S. beliefs to the contrary (reflected in intelligence estimates), Iraq apparently abandoned programs to develop biological and chemical agents shortly after the first Gulf War.[34] The programs were not regime priorities. But Saddam deemed a long-range missile capability essential to preserve political and military credibility with his hostile neighbors, Iran and Syria, which maintained similar capabilities.

Preserving credibility and not losing face with his neighbors, in hindsight, seemed more important to Saddam than meeting his mandated obligations to the international community. The importance of preserving credibility may have been fed by what some Iraqis have described as Saddam's "inferiority complex," in which he saw himself as weak.[35] The United States never caught on to this nuance of Saddam's belief structure and assumed that the long-range missile programs constituted only one in a variety of programs (chemical, biological, and nuclear weapons) that were of strategic importance to the regime. Additionally, it now appears that Iraq's WMD concealment program was created to prevent the international community from knowing that Iraq, for the most part, had already disarmed. Saddam apparently believed that Iraq would no longer be seen as a powerful regional state if his neighbors realized he had abandoned his most dangerous weapons. Others suggest that the concealment program was primarily intended to prevent internal actors from realizing that Iraq had already disarmed.[36] U.S. officials believed that the concealment mechanism was meant to prevent inspectors from finding hidden weapons, and the existence of the program only confirmed suspicions that Saddam had something to hide. The fiction that Iraq retained WMD stocks was maintained up until the U.S. invasion of Iraq in March 2003. Debriefs with Iraqi military commanders, for instance, indicate a nearly universal belief among them that "other" units had WMD to counter the invasion.[37]

Saddam had grown increasingly isolated in the last years of his regime, receiving only filtered information from a limited number of sources. There was a breakdown in the regime's command structure from 1998 onward.[38] By contrast, the United States continued to see Saddam as an unyielding, all-powerful dictator with an iron grip on power. This view missed the gradual disintegration of the regime's command structure after Operation Desert Fox in December 1998.

Saddam consciously manipulated both signals and indices to deceive a variety of different internal and external actors. It seems he was successful in his deception. The United States and the international community swallowed his deception hook, line, and sinker. Saddam's motivations and images also were strongly rooted in the region's cultural and behavioral norms—a critical one of which is not losing face. Saddam's need to preserve credibility with his neighbors and internal opponents formed an important element in Iraq's external image. Saddam clung to these core beliefs and the supporting image long after rational analysis would have advocated change. Although U.S. officials understood the importance Saddam attached to his WMD programs for regional and international credibility, they never caught on to the deception in part because it seemed illogical and counterintuitive. U.S. diplomatic and military actions had some coercive and deterrent value, but these actions also had the unintended effect of reinforcing what Saddam wanted the rest of the world to believe: that he retained significant WMD stocks. Iraqi officials failed to perceive accurately U.S. coercive messages.

Asymmetrical interests, misperception (fed by intelligence failures) and communications problems affected the coercive bargaining framework. Indeed, in retrospect it is unclear whether the framework was operating at all in accordance with Schelling's paradigm. The implications of this analysis for the months preceding Operation Iraqi Freedom are significant. As was the case in the 1991 Gulf War, a variety of senior U.S. officials, including President George W. Bush, stated that Iraqi use of chemical or biological weapons against U.S. forces or coalition partners would be met with an overwhelming response. U.S. troops expected that Iraq would, in fact, use its chemical and biological weapons in response to the invasion, suggesting that the National Command Authority would have to decide whether to use nuclear weapons against Iraqi targets. From the U.S. perspective, public declarations and the history of Iraqi chemical and biological weapons nonuse in the first Gulf War suggested that deterrence could play a role in the coercive framework and discourage Saddam from using weapons of mass destruction.

The preceding analysis of the weaknesses in the coercive framework suggests that both parties had entered a blind alley in the months before the war. U.S. officials believed that the coercive framework was fully operational and that deterrence could play a useful role. But it seems that Saddam was incapable of "rational" actions or failed to receive intended signals from the United States. In short, the United States and Iraq were in a strategically unstable environment, in which uncontrolled escalation could have occurred relatively easily due to actions by either party.

Deterrence, Extended Deterrence, and Compellence: Syria, the United States, and Israel

Preliminary analysis of the historic record in Iraq provides some useful insights into applying coercive and compellent strategy against Syria. The NPR suggests that Syria is a specific target of the strategic deterrent.

Damascus continues to receive particular attention from U.S. policy makers because of its active support of terrorist groups, its overt hostility to Israel, and its well-developed WMD infrastructure, particularly its missile and chemical warfare programs. The strategic deterrent is expected to support a variety of deterrent and compellent objectives that involve the threat and, if necessary, the actual use of force against Syria. In the aftermath of Operation Iraqi Freedom, Bush administration officials made a variety of statements implying that the same calculations that informed the decision to use force against Iraq also apply to Syria.[39] The strategic deterrent is expected either to directly support or to help accomplish the following objectives: (1) deter an attack on Israel; (2) defeat Syria (using nuclear weapons if necessary) should it attack Israel with WMD; (3) convince Syrian leader Bashar Assad to stop supporting terrorist groups targeting the United States and its allies; (4) convince Assad to forego Syria's WMD programs and disarm; and (5) provide the National Command Authority with an array of nuclear and conventional counterforce attack options related to Syria's WMD infrastructure, some of which is buried underground.

Policy toward Syria also is interesting since the United States is developing an extended deterrent to bolster an existing deterrence relationship between Israel and Syria. This relationship is based on Israeli nuclear weapons and overwhelming conventional superiority on the one hand, and Syria's well-developed WMD capabilities (mainly long-range missiles and chemical weapons) and inferior conventional capabilities on the other. Deterrence in this situation is a multifaceted phenomenon.

While the U.S. strategic deterrent is directed primarily at Syria, a secondary objective is to assure Israel of the strength of the U.S. commitment to Israel's security in the region. This commitment is intended to influence Israeli behavior, most obviously to constrain Israel's use of force against its neighbors. In the best of all worlds, the strategic deterrent can thus act both as a tool to restrain overly aggressive Israeli actions and to control the potential escalation of a conflict. But these are perhaps best-case assumptions. In fact, the strategic deterrent could encourage Israel to act more aggressively than it would otherwise because Israeli officials might assume that their actions would be backed by the thousands of warheads in the U.S. arsenal and the array of U.S. standoff conventional munitions used to great effect in Afghanistan and Iraq.

To assess the impact that the U.S. strategic deterrent might have on Israeli behavior, an analysis of Israeli views of compellence and deterrence is essential. A review of literature on Israeli deterrence suggests a striking and potentially dangerous variance between U.S. and Israeli views of compellence and deterrence. The U.S. view of compellence generally involves the avoidance of escalation, while the Israelis actively seek to escalate conflicts.[40]

The Israelis have developed a compellent/deterrence model that is founded on several assumptions. Israeli leaders have sought to provoke hostile Arab reactions to establish escalation dominance. Israeli policy makers often seek excuses to escalate the use of force against their adversaries. Bureaucratic inertia and the role of military officials in the decision-making process have contributed to a de facto default position of conventional escalation. This approach has failed to achieve Israel's objectives of security and in fact has played a role in compromising the ability of all concerned states and actors to create a political framework for negotiations.[41]

Israeli views also raise the possibility of unwanted and potentially unlimited escalation in a crisis situation that would invariably involve the United States and its strategic deterrent. Particularly for U.S. policy makers attempting to articulate how and when the strategic deterrent will come to bear in and on the Israeli compellent/deterrent model, it is important to arrive at a common set of assumptions recognized by all parties to this communication to avoid the potential for misunderstanding and misperception resulting from Israeli actions that are intended to provoke a response.

These issues assume particular significance in assessing the impact of NPR implementation on the Israeli–Syrian deterrent relationship. That relationship is highly unstable. Each side is hostile toward the other. Syria uses terrorist surrogates to attack Israel, while Israel responds with conventional attacks on those surrogates. In October 2003, for example, in the first such attack deep into Syria since the 1973 war, Israel bombed a target near Damascus that allegedly was associated with terrorist activities. In response to the attack, Syrian Foreign Ministry official Boushra Kanafani reserved for his state "the right to retaliate by all means at its disposal."[42] Hezbollah officials made similar statements of intent to respond in the event of further Israeli attacks.[43] Israeli Prime Minister Ariel Sharon responded in an equally defiant tone, stating: "Israel will not be deterred from protecting its citizens and will strike its enemies in every place and in every way."[44] The Bush administration's response was to caution both parties while emphasizing Israel's right to defend itself.

The Israeli attack on Syria must be seen in the context of Israel's desire to provoke a response from Syria, which Israel would then meet with overwhelming escalation. Thus, judging the stability of the Syria–Israel deterrent relationship is problematic. Both actors may well have intuitively agreed upon a series of "red lines" that form the basis of a coercive bargaining framework. Israel mounted the raid into Syria as a signal of sorts, which, if nothing else, demonstrated its overwhelming military superiority and Israel's willingness to use force whenever it felt warranted. Syria's response recognized its inherent weakness but also conveyed that there are limits beyond which Syria cannot be pushed. It is equally plausible that Israel would have welcomed escalation by the Syrians as a pretext for a wider war.

Layering the U.S. strategic deterrent over this situation creates additional uncertainties. For example, it is unclear to what extent either Israel or Syria are aware that they both are being subjected to deterrent and compellent strategies in this incident as suggested in the NPR. So, it is unclear exactly how the strategic deterrent is functioning in its task of assuring Israeli decision makers of U.S. commitment to Israel's security.

If it is difficult for the United States to convey its intentions to its close ally Israel, Syria is another matter altogether, especially in connection with integrating Syria into a coercive framework backed by the strategic deterrent. It is unclear whether Bashar Assad realizes that he is being subjected to coercive and compellent strategies that are potentially backed up by nuclear weapons. It also is unclear whether the U.S. strategic deterrent plays any role in the Syrian decision-making calculus on conflict escalation or even surprise attack. If one takes seriously the NPR's assertions about the central importance of the United States deterring attacks against Israel and actively defending it, one would expect that Bashar Assad should be made aware that escalation in situations such as the October 2003 attacks could lead to a U.S. response in defense of Israel.

In Syria and its leader Bashar Assad, the United States faces a similar situation to the one it confronted in Iraq with Saddam Hussein during the 1990s: an authoritarian leader operating with limited information within a decision-making environment characterized by relatively few actors. Assad's priority is to maintain his hold on power. The internal political environment in Syria is opaque to U.S. decision makers—as it was in Iraq—and yet understanding this environment is crucial to devising a communications strategy that can convey both sides' intent accurately. In seeking to operationalize coercive and compellent strategies against Syria, the United States confronts communications shortfalls. Accurately conveying intent is critical. To overcome these communications weaknesses requires U.S. analysts to discern Bashar Assad's structure of internal and external images through which he views the world.

CONCLUSION

The NPR suggests that the strategic deterrent and its nuclear component is expected to have a variety of political and military roles in the Middle East. A critical issue facing policy makers over the coming decade is determining how these roles will be operationalized. Over the next ten years, a new arsenal must be designed, tested, and fielded with a parallel effort to develop doctrine, tactics, techniques, and procedures. While a host of domestic, political, and legal hurdles to fielding new weapons remain, the technical and operational issues associated with the new families of weapons seem relatively straightforward.

It will be manifestly more difficult to determine how the new weapons will function in support of broadly defined political objectives—such as assurance and dissuasion, for example, at the strategic level. To be sure, leaving these issues somewhat ambiguous and open-ended has its uses and may even serve to strengthen deterrence. After all, as Schelling noted, the value of nuclear weapons in a coercive framework partly stems from the unstated threat to use force. But while the United States can leave these issues ambiguous for external actors (such as Syria and Iran), these issues certainly should be subjected to rigorous and ongoing internal review so policy makers have an idea of how the strategic deterrent is expected to function and in what situations it will be employed in direct support of compellent and coercive strategies.

In the Middle East, the United States must address communications issues surrounding the conveyance of intent. Lessons from the thirteen-year experience trying to shape Iraqi behavior are not encouraging. A review of the U.S. interaction with Iraq suggests serious breakdowns in communications. While the United States "got lucky" because Saddam did not use WMD against U.S. forces, it would be a mistake to conclude that Iraq's nonuse of WMD augurs well for the future. An unfortunate conclusion from the Iraq case is that systemic communications difficulties make preemptive action more attractive in situations where there can be no confidence that the coercive framework is functioning with any degree of predictability.

These lessons seem particularly germane to the ongoing Israeli–Syrian relationship—with the potential for escalation on both sides—which involves the United States and its commitment to Israel. Variances between U.S. and Israeli views of deterrence and compellence should be resolved if the United States wants its strategic deterrent to function in a constructive way to achieve its policy objectives with both Israel and Syria. Moreover, correctly deciphering the images motivating Syrian leader Bashar Assad seems equally important if the United States is to construct a communications system that can accurately convey intent.

NOTES

The views in this article are the author's own and do not reflect the views or positions of the Naval Postgraduate School or the Department of Defense.

1. Concern over the potential use of nuclear weapons in the region predates the NPR. See John Donnelly, "DIA: Mideast Most Likely Place Nukes Could Be Used," *Defense Week* 21, no. 19, May 8, 2000. Donnelly quotes testimony from then-director of the Defense Intelligence Agency Lt. Gen. Patrick Hughes to the Senate Armed Services Committee in 1999: "The Middle East will become the region of greatest concern in terms of using nuclear weapons within the next 10 to 20 years."
2. Nuclear Posture Review, January 8, 2002, 6 (all page references according to original indicated in excerpts posted at <www.globalsecurity.org/wmd/library/policy/dod/npr.htm>).
3. A good description of the generic problem of targets impervious to conventional strikes can be found in the Office of the Secretary of Defense, *Proliferation: Threat and Response*, January 2001, 90–91 <www.defenselink.mil/pubs/ptr20010110.pdf>.
4. The Iranian nuclear site at Natanz, about 200 miles from Tehran, is said to have centrifuges and other equipment housed in bunkers seventy-five feet deep with walls eight feet thick. See Doug Frantz, "Iran Closes in on Ability to Build a Nuclear Bomb," *Los Angeles Times* August 4, 2003. Syria also is believed to have developed an extensive hardened underground infrastructure for WMD storage and production activities. See Dany Shoham, "Poisoned Missiles: Syria's Doomsday Deterrent,"

Middle East Quarterly IX, no. 4 (Fall 2002) <http://www.meforum.org/article/510>. Also see Anthony Cordesman, "Weapons of Mass Destruction in the Middle East: Regional Trends, National Forces, Warfighting Capabilities, Delivery Options, and Weapons Effects," Center for Strategic and International Studies strategic assessment (April 15, 2003), 51–59.

5. *Nuclear Posture Review*, 6.
6. For an expanded discussion of this issue, see James J. Wirtz and James A. Russell, "U.S. Policy on Preventive War and Preemption," *The Nonproliferation Review* 10, no. 1 (Spring 2003): 113–123.
7. The White House, "National Strategy to Combat Weapons of Mass Destruction," press release, December 2002, 3 <http://www.whitehouse.gov/news/releases/2002/12/WMDStrategy.pdf>.
8. Thomas Schelling, *The Strategy of Conflict* (Cambridge, Mass: Harvard University Press, 1960); Schelling, *Arms and Influence* (New Haven, Conn.: Yale University Press, 1966).
9. Schelling, *Arms and Influence*, 34.
10. Ibid., 72.
11. Ibid., 70–71.
12. Ibid., 71.
13. Ibid., 190–220.
14. Schelling, *The Strategy of Conflict*, chap. 2; chap. 4.
15. Schelling, *Arms and Influence*, 16; 31.
16. Schelling, *The Strategy of Conflict*, 146–150.
17. Defense Secretary Robert McNamara, "The No Cities Doctrine," University of Michigan Commencement, June 1962. In this speech, McNamara also argued that "basic military strategy in a general nuclear war should be approached in much the same way that more conventional military operations have been regarded in the past. That is to say, principal military objectives, in the event of a nuclear war stemming from a major attack on the alliance, should be the destruction of the enemy's forces, not his civilian population."
18. For example, in his book *Deterrence: A Conceptual Analysis* (Beverly Hills: Sage Publications, 1977), Patrick Morgan notes that the circumstance of threat and reaction can create psychological reactions in the minds of the actors that can introduce "some influence from irrational objectives and perceptions . . ." into an otherwise rational decision-making process (78).
19. Robert Jervis, *The Logic of Images in International Relations* (Princeton, N.J.: Princeton University Press, 1970).
20. Ibid., 3.
21. Ibid., 6.
22. Ibid., 11.
23. Ibid., 18.
24. Ibid.
25. Ibid., 139–173.
26. Jervis lays out a series of ideas on the sources of misperception in "Hypotheses on Misperception," *World Politics* 20 (April 1968): 454–479. Jervis expands on these ideas in *Perception and Misperception in International Politics* (Princeton, N.J.: Princeton University Press, 1976).
27. Ibid., 454–479.
28. Richard Neustadt, *Report to JFK: Skybolt in Perspective* (Ithaca, N.Y.: Cornell University Press, 1999).

29. Jervis, *Logic of Images*, 115.

30. Ibid., 138.

31. An excellent treatment of the record of U.S. coercive strategy with Iraq is contained in Dan Byman and Mathew Waxman, *Confronting Iraq: U.S. Policy and the Use of Force Since the Gulf War* MR-1146-OSD (Santa Monica, Calif.: RAND Corp., 2000).

32. Steve Coll, "Hussein Was Sure of His Own Survival," *Washington Post*, November 3, 2003. The information given by Aziz in these debriefs is somewhat suspect in light of his checkered history, but his suggestion that Saddam fundamentally misunderstood one of the essential requirements of UNSCR 687 seems particularly fascinating.

33. Ibid.

34. James Risen, "Ex-Inspector Says CIA Missed Disarray in Iraqi Arms Program," *New York Times* January 26, 2004.

35. Coll, "Hussein was Sure of His Own Survival." Coll quotes Iraq Army Logistics Chief Maj. Gen. Walid Mohammed Taiee as saying that Saddam "had an inferiority complex."

36. Kenneth M. Pollack, "Spies, Lies, and Weapons: What Went Wrong," *The Atlantic Monthly* (January/February 2004) <www.theatlantic.com/issues/2004/01/pollack.htm>.

37. Coll, "Hussein Was Sure of His Own Survival."

38. As recounted in Risen's "Ex-Inspector Says CIA Missed Disarray in Iraqi Arms Program," David Kay, who headed the U.S. efforts to find WMD in Iraq after the invasion, described the disintegration as a "vortex of corruption," in which government activities spun out of control in 1997 and 1998, with scientists going directly to Saddam to get money for various fake WMD-related activities.

39. In an interview on April 5, 2003, Undersecretary of of State John Bolton said that the invasion of Iraq would send a message to Syria that "the cost of their pursuit of weapons of mass destruction is potentially quite high . . . [and] the determination of the United States . . . to keep these incredibly dangerous weapons out of the hands of very dangerous people should not be underestimated." Bolton's was one of a series of statements expressing concern about Syria's WMD following the U.S. invasion of Iraq. On April 16, 2003, Bolton further stated that the United States intends to exert "a maximum diplomatic effort" to persuade "states like Syria, Libya and Iran, among others, to give up their pursuit of nuclear, chemical, and biological weapons and long range ballistic missile delivery systems. . . . We want a peaceful resolution to all of these issues, but the determination of the United States, especially after September 11, to keep these incredibly dangerous weapons out of the hands of very dangerous people should not be underestimated." For the Bolton quote and for a good summary of statement of various U.S. officials following the invasion of Iraq, see Paul Kerr, "Top U.S. Officials Voice Concern About Syria's WMD Capabilities," *Arms Control Today*, Arms Control Association, Washington, D.C., May 2003. <www.globalsecurity.org/military/ops/syria-intro.htm>.

40. Zeev Maoz, "The Unlimited Use of the Limited Use of Force: Israel and Low Intensity Warfare, 1949–2004," unpublished paper presented at the annual meeting of the International Studies Association, Montreal, March 17–20, 2004. Cited with the author's permission.

41. Ibid., 29–30.

42. As quoted in Kim Ghattas, "Syria Warns Israel of Retaliation," *BBC News* October 11, 2003 <http://news.bbc.co.uk/1/hi/world/middle_east/3183788.stm>.

43. Ibid.

44. As quoted in "Syrian Ambassador Promises Military Responses to Further Attacks," *Guardian Unlimited* October 8, 2003 <www.guardian.co.uk/israel/Story/0%2C2763%2C1058599%2C00.html>.

CONCLUSION

18

CONCLUSION

Jeffrey A. Larsen

What was the ultimate goal and purpose of the 2001 Nuclear Posture Review (NPR)? Has it changed the way the U.S. military plans future operations and investment strategies? What is the likely impact of the NPR on the global norms of nonproliferation and nuclear nonuse? In the volume at hand, our purpose was to address such questions by tracing the logic of the NPR and to identify what remains to be done to make it a reality. Our underlying assumption was that the NPR offered a reasonable response to the political, technical, and strategic challenges and opportunities faced by U.S. policy makers and planners and that this threat environment will likely dominate planning for at least the next decade. We asked each of our contributors to discuss the policy implications of the NPR in terms of a variety of issue areas and regional settings. We hoped thereby to provide an objective view of evolving U.S. deterrence strategy, allowing us to assess the strengths and weaknesses of the NPR and to identify the roadblocks in the path of any effort to transform the U.S. nuclear arsenal into a new type of strategic deterrent that embodies nuclear and conventional weapons and missile defenses. We wanted to avoid both extremes in our assessment of the new policy; blanket denunciation or automatic acclamation. Somewhere in the middle was fertile ground for rigorous and unbiased analysis.

A close reading of the chapters in this book illuminates several findings and themes as our contributors raise questions about the NPR's impact on U.S. national security strategy.

THE NPR: A CONSTRUCTIVE DEPARTURE IN U.S. DEFENSE POLICY?

Mark Trachtenberg began our study by pointing out that the United States has been more attracted to preemptive strategies, such as the one we find in the NPR, than is generally realized. He reviewed American national security strategies back to the Harry Truman administration to demonstrate that the first use of military force has been a central tenet of American foreign policy for decades. Moreover, in promulgating the NPR, according to Trachtenberg, the George W. Bush administration was merely carrying forward ideas and concepts that were begun in the William Clinton administration. Furthermore, he argues, the reason preemptive strategies have been so commonly used throughout history is that they are rooted in the structure of international politics.

Trachtenberg notes that three arguments are usually presented by detractors of the NPR and its new policy provisions. First, they say the NPR will make nuclear weapons more useable. Without arguing whether or not this statement is true, Trachtenberg points out that during the Cold War, the United States continually designed and improved its warfighting options, theater nuclear forces, and plans for first use of such weapons. Second, opponents of the NPR argue that preemption is a rare and illegitimate policy in international relations. In contrast, Trachtenberg believes that preemption has always been an option within international relations; it was almost used during the Cuban Missile Crisis some forty years ago and against China in the 1950s. Third, critics of the NPR charge that terrorism is a totally new phenomenon that requires a new rule book. Trachtenberg acknowledges that today's terrorist does pose a significant challenge to U.S. national security, but the same was true of the challenges created by nuclear weapons at the outset of the Cold War.

In their evaluation of the Bush administration's effort to create a strategic deterrent, Steve Fetter and Charles Glaser foresee a very limited role for nuclear weapons in the missions identified by the NPR. They addressed three questions: Are there certain targets that can only be destroyed with nuclear weapons? If so, what would be the costs and benefits of actually using a nuclear weapon? And if the benefits make use worthwhile, does the United States need new tailored weapons? They believe that adversaries are unlikely to attack the United States or its vital interests with weapons of mass destruction (WMD), because the United States already possesses highly capable deterrent forces and the will to use them in response to a WMD attack. Moreover, if deterrence fails, U.S. conventional forces can destroy or disable the types of targets the NPR identifies for nuclear weapons, with much smaller collateral effects. Consequently, there is at best a limited role for nuclear weapons in many of the missions identified by the NPR.

As Fetter and Glaser further point out, no matter how well the United States designs its deterrent policy, there will always be some possibility that deterrence could fail and conventional weapons would be ineffective against strategically critical targets. Were the United States actually to use nuclear weapons, it would obviously generate a variety of costs, particularly to the United States' international reputation and to the goals of WMD nonproliferation and nonuse.

For Fetter and Glaser, the NPR raises more questions than it answers. It also overstates the extent to which nuclear weapons can be used to undertake new mission contemplated by U.S. military planners. They believe that a more thorough study of possible targets—and the risks and costs of nuclear attacks on these targets—will lead to a more measured nuclear doctrine in which there are, at most, a few scenarios in which the United States might use nuclear weapons preemptively.

Dennis Gormley agrees with Fetter and Glaser. According to Gormley, it should not have come as any surprise that the NPR was greeted by its detractors as evidence that U.S. policy makers intended to rely increasingly on nuclear weapons. Until very recently, after all, nuclear deterrence formed the foundation of U.S. national security strategy. Nuclear weapons were expected to deter strikes not only on the American homeland but also on allies in Europe and Asia. Many hoped that the end of the Cold War represented a rare turning point in the long-standing quest to eliminate nuclear weapons globally. Some observers expected nuclear arsenals to dwindle in size and importance in the new strategic circumstances, and they remain sensitive to changes in U.S. nuclear weapons policy that portend the persistence of these weapons. Thus, the fact that the NPR mentions the potential need for new types of nuclear weapons to deal, for example, with targets that may not be susceptible to increasingly effective nonnuclear strike forces provoked a firestorm of criticism.

Amid the uproar, according to Gormley, few scholars or commentators have paid attention to the truly revolutionary features of the NPR. In particular, they have failed to highlight the continuing marginalization of nuclear weapons and the corresponding dependence on nonnuclear solutions to form the basis of a new national security strategy. A truly revolutionary effect of the NPR is the quiet transformation now taking place to achieve nonnuclear solutions to what have previously been nuclear missions in support of U.S. national security strategy. Gormley also notes that despite the overall reduction in the role of nuclear weapons in the emerging U.S. strategic deterrent, nuclear weapons still are needed to hold certain types of targets at risk. In this sense, having a few earth penetrating nuclear weapons in the strategic mix could make declaratory policy more credible by reducing the prospect of collateral damage.

THE NPR'S "NEW TRIAD"

The new triad includes strategic strike forces (both nuclear and conventional), strategic defenses, and an enhanced infrastructure. Joe Pilat considers the new triad to be an evolutionary rather than a revolutionary development in U.S. defense policy. In the new strategic framework, deterrence no longer holds its central Cold War position, and it is no longer expected to be based exclusively (or even primarily) on nuclear weapons. The new triad is designed to meet the full range of possible requirements created by emerging threats. In the past, just as the United States had distinct military forces for nuclear and conventional missions, there also were distinct command and control systems for nuclear, conventional, missile defense, and theater forces. Now planners face the challenge of integrating those different command and conrol networks into one seamless system. To give U.S. policy makers confidence in their ability to respond to a changing world, the United States must develop and prototype a range of adaptable conventional and nuclear weapons, including missile defenses. The United States also requires a modernized, reinvigorated, and revitalized conventional and nuclear defense infrastructure.

The three legs of the new triad are inextricably linked. Global strike aims to deny an adversary the capacity to use WMD against the United States or its allies and forces stationed overseas. The defense leg is an insurance policy in the event that the first leg fails. And the infrastructure and command, control, and intelligence leg enhances the effectiveness of the offensive and defensive legs of the new triad. The NPR thus reflects a logical and integrated strategy that was meant to provide decision makers with a range of options.

At the same time, the NPR shows some dramatic rethinking of some familiar issues and concepts. One new aspect of the NPR's triad is the formal removal of nuclear forces as the central focal point of U.S. strategic capabilities. A second radical departure from past defense policy is the importance placed on damage limitation and strategic defenses. In light of these new and developing policy and strategic considerations, Pilat notes that key challenges faced by emerging U.S. strategic defenses include technical issues, cost, international support, operational integration, and political sustainability.

Kerry Kartchner highlights two factors that will prove decisive when it comes to the future of missile defense. If the United States and its allies realize verifiable and enduring success in peacefully disarming states such as Libya, such continued diplomatic progress will diminish the priority assigned to missile defense. But if missile defense proves itself in actual combat, beyond the handful of lower-range missiles intercepted in Operation Iraqi Freedom—say by intercepting a long-range missile destined for the United States or one of its allies—missile defense will be transformed into a key component of the U.S. global military posture. The NPR envisions such a future role for strategic defenses.

A responsive defense research, development, and production infrastructure for U.S. strategic forces is, in principle, equal in status with strategic strike and defense capabilities. Steve Maaranen notes that the responsive infrastructure is the least well defined, most poorly understood, and arguably the least effectively implemented component of the new triad. The function of the responsive infrastructure is to provide the flexibility needed to address threats successfully, especially unexpected strategic challenges to U.S. interests. It is meant to add a powerful element of dissuasion to U.S. strategy by demonstrating America's technological superiority.

The challenges involved in creating an effective, coordinated new triad research and development program and responsive infrastructure are myriad. According to Maaranen, a viable research and development program will require the U.S. government to make a compelling case for the NPR strategy and to create a comprehensive planning process for strategic forces. Development of this infrastructure also will require officials to overcome deeply embedded roles and responsibilities within DoD, which will require a significant investment of political influence and scarce dollars for at least a decade. This is true for both the DoD's industrial base and the

Department of Energy's nuclear weapons complex. Improving the condition of the nuclear weapons research and development and production infrastructure is mandatory if the United States intends to rely on nuclear deterrence for the foreseeable future. Historically, however, the United States has found it difficult to sustain investment in capabilities that do not meet clear, near-term requirements.

COMMAND, CONTROL, AND INTELLIGENCE

Nathan Busch describes the command and control (C^2) requirements that will empower the NPR's new triad. According to Busch, DoD is making progress in addressing several of the difficult objectives outlined by the Quadrennial Defense Review and the NPR. These include the creation of U.S. Northern Command, the elimination of U.S. Space Command, and the establishment of a new U.S. Strategic Command (USSTRATCOM) that will provide C^2 support to the other unified commands.

Other issues remain to be solved, however. According to Busch, military planners have yet to define the roles of the combatant commands and their relationship to USSTRATCOM in the overall command and control network. The United States needs an information and command system that allows the combatant commanders and U.S. allies to access information and command channels. It also needs a plan to integrate U.S. strategic nuclear forces with conventional forces. Policy makers will have to determine if the new strategic deterrent will require the same system of authorization and use-control devices that were utilized by the old nuclear triad. The global missile defense system has to be integrated so that it will work in conjunction with regional combatant commands. Busch states that while it appears that a central role for USSTRATCOM will be to provide early-warning information about incoming missile attack, it remains unclear exactly how U.S. conventional forces worldwide will be integrated into the missile defense command and control network.

Charles Ball amplifies these themes in his chapter on intelligence requirements. The NPR explicitly states that in order to reduce reliance on nuclear weapons and to address concerns prompted by WMD proliferation, the United States will require significantly better intelligence capabilities than it currently possesses. Secretary of Defense Donald Rumsfeld stated in his introduction to the NPR that its success will require "exquisite intelligence." According to Ball, the perceived requirement for intelligence of such an extraordinarily high caliber is a reflection of the extent to which the Bush administration believes that the geopolitical environment confronting the United States has been transformed in an extraordinary way. The current administration believes that the threat of terrorists and rogue states armed with weapons of mass destruction make today's security environment more complex and dangerous than it was during the Cold War.

Ball avers that obtaining intelligence of this fidelity will prove to be so difficult that policy makers will conclude that it cannot be done. This situation, in turn, will reinforce the belief that the mere existence of regimes with potential WMD capabilities and ties to terrorists pose a threat so inherently dangerous that it constitutes an immediate challenge to U.S. security.

James Smith expands on Busch's description of some changes the military has made to ensure better command and control of its strategic forces. Smith reminds us that all organizations adapt to changes in their particular operating environment. Often the environmental changes are evolutionary, and the resulting process of organizational change can be limited to adaptation and accommodation. Fundamental or revolutionary changes in the environment, however, demand similar changes in the organizations that carry out operations in that new environment. According to Smith, this is the situation facing the U.S. military services today. They are tasked with preparing and presenting strategic capabilities to achieve the objectives outlined in the NPR under significantly changed—and changing—strategic circumstances. Reorganization may be necessary to ensure the military can achieve effects-based planning, full integration, and the culture change necessary to achieve its primary missions. During the Cold War, there were separate and distinct militaries not necessarily linked to a specific service: nuclear deterrence forces, conventional forces, and special operations forces. In today's more complicated world, those distinctions are disappearing as missions increasingly call for mixed and varied capabilities.

Smith argues that today's strategic services must develop institutions to achieve the new strategic mission, organizations that understand what strategic threats and effects mean today. They must develop effective organizational structures and advocacy channels to organize, train, and equip forces for these mission sets. They also must develop the systems and personnel with the required technical and policy expertise to accomplish those missions.

While we can expect resistance from the services to these needed changes, the fact is that the strategic mission outlined in the NPR is a national tasking to the military services. The strategic landscape has changed, and the clear imperative is for the military services to transform to embrace this revised mission set. The process of transformation outlined by the NPR has defined the new strategic framework and outlined new strategic objectives. But, as Smith notes, those points are not endpoints, they are merely guideposts on a continuing journey of change and transformation.

ARMS CONTROL, DISARMAMENT, AND NONPROLIFERATION

Jeffrey Knopf argues that the NPR and the direction taken by the Bush administration in terms of U.S. national security are fundamentally incompatible with the goals of nonproliferation and, by implication, arms control in general. But Jeff Larsen argues that the Bush approach to world affairs *is*, in fact, arms control, albeit an approach that many in the traditional arms control and disarmament community—as well as members of the Bush administration—find difficult to accept.

According to Larsen, the current emphasis on self-reliance, preemption, and preventive war against terrorism reflects a different, activist approach to arms control that seeks many of the same objectives that were sought by the traditionalists in the heyday of arms control during the late Cold War. More than forty years ago, Thomas Schelling and Morton Halperin put forward three criteria for determining whether a policy fell under the rubric of arms control. According to this taxonomy, an arms control agreement or approach must lessen the chances of war, reduce the consequences should war occur, and lower the cost of preparing for war. In Larsen's perspective, the Bush administration's preemptive policy and the NPR's recommendations all meet these criteria. They represent a new, radically different means of handling international challenges formerly dealt with through arms control. Still, he argues, the NPR is a new type of arms control.

Larsen admits that the NPR was not written with arms control in mind. Yet, it and related national security documents put forth by the George W. Bush administration, can achieve many of the same effects as formal arms control treaties. The nuclear reductions that the Moscow Treaty calls for further the goal of eventual disarmament that the Nuclear Non-Proliferation Treaty seeks. The ability to conduct conventional and information operations as strategic strikes, something that could previously only be done using nuclear weapons, may actually raise the nuclear threshold, making the use of nuclear weapons less likely than in the past.

The new strategies of the Bush administration, with their emphasis on preemption, preventive war, enhanced national military capabilities, and a willingness to undertake unilateral actions, are simply a different, more effective means of handling challenges formerly dealt with by arms control. The arms control community must accept, adapt, and embrace these new approaches if it wants to avoid becoming marginalized.

Knopf disagrees with Larsen's assessment. According to Knopf, American policy makers must remember that many people around the world think of themselves as members of an "international community." Knopf suggests that there are standards of right and wrong and customs and conventions that help each member of this global community form expectations about how other members will behave. The international community has developed norms of these types with respect to nuclear weapons—norms that have been largely formalized since the 1960s in the nonproliferation regime. The nonproliferation regime rests on widely shared beliefs that nuclear arms are unconventional weapons, the use of which should be taboo, the proliferation of which—both vertically and horizontally—should be stopped in the short term, and the abolition of which should be pursued in the long term.

A handful of states and non-state actors reject and defy the norms of the international community, including nonproliferation norms. The United States government calls these actors rogue states and terrorists, and has, for good reasons, grown increasingly concerned about what might happen if these actors acquire WMD. These concerns have been a driving force in the formulation of a new national security strategy, including the new nuclear posture.

Unfortunately, according to Knopf, the proposals for how the United States should respond to the increased urgency of threats from rogue states and terrorists include several elements that are themselves incompatible with the principles and rules of the nonproliferation regime. Proposals to consider developing new nuclear weapons, especially if they lead to resumption of testing, and suggestions the United States might use or threaten to use nuclear weapons preemptively against nonnuclear targets, pose the sharpest challenges to the nonproliferation regime.

Knopf suggests that greater sensitivity to existing international norms could help the United States reconcile these objectives. The NPR and national security strategy are based on the principles that the United States should be willing to act on its own if necessary, using military force preventively, including nuclear options for striking nonnuclear targets. The nonproliferation regime is based on the principle that every effort should be made to avoid the use of nuclear weapons, including serious efforts to eliminate the possession of such weapons. In short, the tendency to conventionalize nuclear weapons that underlies the new U.S. strategy diverges greatly from the basic understanding—that nuclear arms are different—that underlies the nonproliferation regime. This puts U.S. policy on a collision course with regime principles against the use and possession of nuclear weapons. Because the underlying principles of the NPR and the NPT are so divergent, Knopf argues, the United States cannot fully achieve both its new defense objectives and its objective of strengthening the existing nonproliferation regime. Before the United States implements a new posture, it must make a choice about where to set the balance between alternative policy approaches and priorities in this area.

THE REGIONAL RESPONSE TO THE NPR

Has U.S. reliance on nuclear weapons and nuclear posturing in the past accelerated the proliferation of weapons of mass destruction? Some would argue that it has. For example, India may have pursued an independent nuclear capability as a result of America's nuclear signaling during past crises on the South Asian littoral. If that is true—if there really is a causal linkage resulting in unintended consequences—what might result from renewed reliance on nuclear weapons in the 2001 NPR? These and other questions are posed and answered by our authors who address specific regions of particular concern to the United States: Europe, Russia, South Asia, Northeast Asia, and the Middle East.

NATO: Cooperation in Missile Defenses

David Yost reminds us that Europe is concerned about the NPR and the Moscow Treaty, not just because the Bush administration appears interested in developing new nuclear strike forces, but also because Europeans have an immediate interest in a benign future for Russia. Some concepts, such as deterrence by punishment, are noncontroversial because they represent continuity with Cold War strategies. Other concepts, such as dissuasion and deterrence by denial, are more speculative and are not embraced enthusiastically by North Atlantic Treaty Organization (NATO) allies. And at least one concept—preemption—is highly controversial among U.S. allies.

America's NATO allies will only have a secondary role in NPR implementation, especially if the process of nuclear transformation in practice is confined to U.S. strategic nuclear forces. The NPR, however, also calls for advanced nonnuclear capabilities and improved defenses, notably against missile attacks. The full scope of the NPR thus identifies a potentially significant role for U.S. allies, if they choose to participate in implementing key initiatives that fall within its broad strategic framework. Yost provides several examples of this potential cooperation. If the allies decided to construct a missile defense architecture capable of protecting the territories and populations of all nations in North America and Europe (the subject of a feasibility study called for at NATO's Prague Summit in November 2002), this plan would require far-reaching cooperation and participation in NPR programs. Similarly, the establishment of a more flexible and promptly responsive military posture, with enhanced nonnuclear capabilities, as foreseen in the Prague Capabilities Commitment and the NATO Response Force, can only be achieved through multinational allied efforts.

Russia: Ambivalent Response

Alexander Saveliev points out that Russian interest in the NPR is not just theoretical; it also is based on practical politics. Russian officials do not treat their nuclear arsenal as an instrument of a victory, and they are confident that other nuclear states do not plan to launch a massive strike against the Russian Federation. But Russian officials are ready to abandon the mission of deterrence by punishment in the event of new arms control negotiations that call for further deep reductions of nuclear forces as confidence building measures.

A multifaceted approach to deterrence that combines negotiations with deterrence measures tailored to the new environment offers a positive and constructive Russian response to the Bush administration's NPR. U.S.-Russian dialogue about contemporary security threats is a critical first step in addressing the role of nuclear weapons in world politics, a problem that exceeds the framework of U.S.-Russian relations. Saveliev recommends that the United States and Russia slowly include other nuclear states in this dialogue about today's security threats because nuclear issues can no longer be addressed only on a unilateral or bilateral basis.

South Asia: The NPR and Regional Stability

According to Stephen Burgess, the NPR has had a significant impact on both India and Pakistan. The changes in U.S. policy that the NPR expresses have brought about changes in U.S. relations with India and Pakistan and in the behavior of South Asia's major powers toward one another. On the one hand, says Burgess, the U.S. stance almost automatically ends discussions that urge India and Pakistan to give up their nuclear weapons programs. On the other hand, the new U.S. policy establishes a framework that can encourage greater responsibility and accountability with the recognition of India and Pakistan as nuclear weapon states.

In some respects, this changed global nuclear policy situation has already improved the prospects for a peaceable South Asia. U.S. arms control efforts in South Asia before 2001 helped India and Pakistan agree to confidence-building measures, which could have led to greater transparency and improved nuclear weapons command and control. Also, major changes in the U.S. approach toward South Asia have been associated with the Bush administration's National Security Strategy and the NPR. Before 2001, the approach was more detached, as diplomats attempted to induce India and Pakistan to join the Nuclear Nonproliferation Treaty and the Comprehensive Test Ban Treaty. The Bush administration moved the United States closer to India and Pakistan, especially after September 11, 2001, and eased sanctions for violating arms control measures, which sent a message to both countries that it was acceptable for them to remain as de facto nuclear weapons states. The Bush administration strategy was designed to improve relations with India as a rising power in Asia that could assist in balancing a rising China. The Indian government reciprocated by welcoming a U.S. defensive nuclear weapons strategy, missile defense, and deep reductions in warheads and missiles.

Northeast Asia: A Mixed Impact

According to Bill Berry, how the NPR is perceived in Northeast Asia depends on the relationship of specific countries with the United States. The reactions to the NPR from some of the most important regional powers also are related to how these countries treat weapons of mass destruction and deterrence issues in their own national security policies. Under normal circumstances, the NPR would have been viewed with alarm and disdain by officials in Beijing because of its references to China, its emphasis on missile defense, and its reflection of the U.S. proclivity to undertake unilateral actions. Chinese concerns about terrorism and proliferation on the Korean peninsula, however, mitigated these potential concerns about the NPR. The Bush administration's policies toward China also have softened after the September 11, 2001, terrorist attacks because of shared interests. There has been a shift away from China's Cold War role of strategic competitor to something more akin to a strategic partner. The issue of Taiwan and the possible extension of missile defenses to this island, however, would probably be a red line for China, according to Berry, and the Bush administration must be careful not to allow the NPR to inflame the "offshore island" issue for Beijing.

Berry points out that North Korean officials viewed the NPR as a hostile document, and for good reason—it was literally the "poster country" for the notional threat articulated in the NPR. Whether Kim Jong Il will decide to give up his nuclear weapons program for improved political and economic relations with other states in the region and with the United States remains to be seen. South Korea, on the other hand, was ambivalent about the NPR because of different threat perceptions between policy makers in Washington and Seoul regarding North Korea. The two governments also have different views about the possible peaceful reunification of the Korean peninsula. No such ambivalence exists in Japan, and the bilateral security relationship between the United States and Japan has increased in importance for both Tokyo and Washington.

Middle East: NPR Target Region

James Russell closes out our section on international reactions to the NPR by reviewing the situation in the Middle East. According to Russell, the muted foreign reactions to the NPR in this region were surprising because the NPR makes the region a central focus of the redesigned U.S. strategic deterrent. Russell suggests that the Middle East effectively replaces the Soviet Union as the central targeting requirement for sizing and configuring U.S. nuclear forces. The NPR implies that the defense of Israel, for example, represents a core mission for the strategic deterrent by identifying several near-term contingencies involving an attack on Israel that could lead to the use of nuclear weapons by the United States. Moreover, two countries in the region—Syria and Iran—maintain programs to develop weapons of mass destruction and support terrorism. The region seems to be the archetypal situation that drives the NPR's focus on the targeting problem posed by hardened and deeply buried facilities that cannot be held at risk by conventional weapons. As the NPR notes, these targets necessitate a new family of munitions that will be incorporated into the strategic deterrent.

In the Middle East, the United States must address communications issues surrounding the conveyance of intent. Lessons from the thirteen-year experience trying to shape Iraqi behavior are not encouraging. An unfortunate conclusion from the Iraq case is that systemic communications difficulties make preemptive action more attractive in situations where there can be no confidence that the coercive measures are functioning with any degree of predictability. This bodes ill for U.S. relations with Syria.

CONCLUSION

It will be extremely challenging to determine how new nuclear weapons might support the Bush administration's broadly defined political objectives, such as enhancing assurance and dissuasion at the strategic level. Leaving these issues somewhat ambiguous and open-ended has its uses and may even serve to strengthen deterrence. Either way, the analysis in these chapters has shown that ambiguity is still very much in vogue when it comes to the evolving U.S. strategic deterrent.

We have considered but not definitively answered several questions about the relationship between the NPR and U.S. national security. For example, is the NPR moving U.S. national security strategy in a direction that is incompatible with the goals of nonproliferation? Or is it simply a new way of achieving the same goals traditional arms control pursued? How strong is the nuclear taboo? Can the United States violate that taboo by crossing the nuclear use threshold one time without destroying the underlying international norm against the use of nuclear weapons in combat? And what is more important: the maintenance of a norm, or doing what is necessary to ensure a state's security? If nuclear use leads to proliferation, of course, integrating nuclear and conventional forces into a single strategic strike force may be self-defeating.

We do not anticipate that either supporters or critics of the proposed changes in U.S. strategic policy would be completely satisfied with our description and analysis of the Bush administration's NPR. Nevertheless, we believe that a debate on the current and potential U.S. response to the emerging strategic environment is crucial to global security. We hope that this volume provides some insights into the prospects and pitfalls facing policy makers as they face today's evolving and uncertain security environment while highlighting the panoply of concerns and considerations that inform the decisions that have been and will be made about U.S. nuclear policy.

Appendix 1

The Nuclear Posture Review
in the Annual DoD Report
to Congress[1]

Chapter 7: Adapting U.S. Strategic Forces

The Department of Defense has completed a comprehensive review of the U.S. nuclear posture. This chapter summarizes the conclusions of that review.

Nuclear forces continue to play a critical role in the defense of the United States, its allies and friends. They provide credible capabilities to deter a wide range of threats, including weapons of mass destruction and large-scale conventional military force. Nuclear capabilities possess unique properties that give the United States options to hold at risk classes of targets important to achieve strategic and political objectives.

The transformation of the nation's nuclear posture complements the transformation of America's conventional forces and capabilities. President Bush directed the Department of Defense to transform America's military forces to meet the challenges of the new century. In response to his direction, the Department of Defense used the Congressionally-mandated Quadrennial Defense Review to develop a new defense strategy and program for transforming U.S. conventional forces. Building on the strategic premises of the QDR report, the Nuclear Posture Review (NPR) offers a blueprint for transforming our strategic posture and signifies a major departure in our approach for managing strategic issues. Indeed, the findings of the NPR form the foundation for the Moscow Treaty signed by President Bush and Russian President Putin and awaiting ratification by the Senate.

The Nuclear Posture Review began with the recognition that the security situation at the start of the 21st century differs substantially from that of the early 1990s when the last Nuclear Posture Review was conducted. The end of the Cold War can no longer be considered a recent phenomenon. Russia is no longer an enemy and the collapse of the Soviet Union is now more than a decade past. At the same time, new dangers have emerged that are both less familiar and less predictable, including terrorists and rogue states intent on acquiring and using weapons of mass destruction. Unlike the former Soviet Union, their leaders are subject to few institutional restraints on using such weapons. Their decision-making processes are obscure and behavior at times unpredictable. Their actions increase the complexity of managing international security. In this environment, the probability of surprise and ubiquity of uncertainty are dominant strategic considerations for the U.S.

Meeting the challenges of surprise and uncertainty requires a new approach to deterrence. While nuclear forces made an indispensable contribution to deterring Warsaw Pact aggression during the Cold War, a strategic posture that relies solely on offensive nuclear weapons is insufficient to support the nation's defense policy goals. The Nuclear Posture Review concluded that deterrence should not be limited to the threat of retaliation, nor rely exclusively on nuclear forces. The U.S. will need a broader range of capabilities to assure friends and foe alike of its resolve. Nuclear forces, moreover, are unsuited to many of the contingencies for which the U.S. prepares. A mix of capabilities, offensive and defensive, nuclear, and conventional is required. Such a mix will provide additional military options that are credible to enemies, reassuring to allies, and appropriate to Americans.

Following the direction laid down for U.S. defense planning in the QDR, the Nuclear Posture Review shifts the basis for strategic forces planning from specific threats to emerging capabilities that could exploit U.S. vulnerabilities or confer advantages on adversaries.

This capabilities-based approach is the foundation for transforming the U.S. nuclear posture: replace the Strategic Triad of the Cold War with a New Triad that integrates conventional and nuclear offensive strategic strike capabilities, active and passive defenses, and a responsive infrastructure to provide a more diverse portfolio of capabilities against immediate, potential and unforeseen contingencies; and Adopt a new approach to strategic nuclear force reductions that provides the flexibility to respond to changes in the security environment and to technological surprise.

THE NEW TRIAD

The application of a capabilities-based approach to U. S. nuclear forces has resulted in a decision to transform the existing triad of U.S strategic nuclear forces 3/4; intercontinental ballistic missiles (ICBMs), heavy bombers, and submarine-launched ballistic missiles (SLBMs) 3/4; into a New Triad composed of a diverse portfolio of offensive and defensive, nuclear, and conventional systems. The New Triad is designed to give the President and the Secretary of Defense a broad array of options to address a wide range of possible contingencies.

The elements of the New Triad are depicted in figure A1.1 and summarized below: strike capabilities, both nonnuclear and nuclear, and their associated

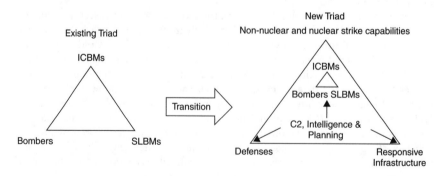

Figure A1.1 The New Triad.

command and control; active and passive defenses, including the command and control for air and missile defenses; and research and development (R&D) and industrial infrastructure for developing, building, and maintaining offensive forces and defensive systems.

The efficiency and military potential of the individual elements of the New Triad are maximized by timely and accurate intelligence, adaptive planning, and enhanced command and control. Enhancing these capabilities is critical to realizing the potential inherent in the New Triad concept.

With respect to nuclear forces, once the planned warhead reductions are completed, the New Triad will include about one-third of the operationally deployed warheads of the current strategic nuclear force. It will retain a vital role in deterring Weapons of Mass Destruction (WMD) threats, assuring allies of U.S. security commitments, holding at risk an adversary's assets and capabilities that cannot be countered through nonnuclear means, and dissuading potential adversaries from developing large-scale nuclear, biological, chemical, or conventional threats.

As other elements of the New Triad are developed and integrated, they could assume tasks now assigned exclusively to nuclear forces. Under such circumstances the required number of operationally deployed nuclear weapons might be further reduced.

ELEMENTS OF THE NEW TRIAD

There are six underlying elements that support the legs of the New Triad:

Strike Capabilities. Non-nuclear strike capabilities include advanced conventional weapons systems, offensive information operations, and Special Operations Forces. Deployed nuclear strike capabilities include the three legs of the existing strategic triad and theater-based, nuclear-capable dual-role aircraft. Nuclear-armed sea-launched cruise missiles, removed from ships and submarines under the 1991 Presidential Nuclear Initiative, are maintained in a reserve status.

Defenses. Active defenses include ballistic missile defense and air defense. Passive defenses include measures that reduce vulnerability through mobility, dispersal, redundancy, deception, concealment, and hardening; warn of imminent attack and support consequence management activities. This element of the New Triad comprises defenses for the U.S. homeland, forces abroad, allies, and friends.

Infrastructure. The R&D and industrial infrastructure includes the research facilities, manufacturing capacity, and skilled personnel needed to produce, sustain, and modernize the elements of the New Triad. A responsive infrastructure that can augment U.S. military capabilities in a timely manner provides strategic depth to the New Triad.

Planning. Careful planning will be critical to integrate and balance the three elements of the New Triad. Planning for the New Triad must consider multiple goals, a spectrum of adversaries and contingencies, and the many uncertainties of the security environment.

Command and Control. A reliable, survivable, and robust command control system will serve as a critical portion of the New Triad.

Intelligence. "Exquisite" intelligence access to an adversary's secrets without his knowledge is essential to provide insight into the intentions as well as the capabilities of opponents. Such intelligence should enable the United States to tailor its deterrent strategies to the greatest effect.

CREATING THE NEW TRIAD

Development and deployment of elements of the New Triad will require several initiatives.

Major Initiatives. Developing and sustaining the New Triad will require investment in the areas of: (1) advanced nonnuclear strike, (2) missile defenses, (3) command and control, and (4) intelligence. These investments will reinforce the nation's strategic deterrent capabilities and contribute significantly to the improvement of the military's operational capabilities.

Overhaul of Existing Capabilities. To meet the demands of the New Triad, an overhaul of existing capabilities is needed. This includes improving the tools used to build and execute strike plans so that the national leadership can adapt pre-planned options, or construct new options, during highly dynamic crisis situations. In addition, the technology base and production readiness infrastructures of both DoD and the National Nuclear Security Administration must be modernized so that the United States will be able to adjust appropriately to changing situations.

Nuclear Force Reductions and System Modifications. As elements of the New Triad are deployed and the number of operationally deployed nuclear warheads is reduced, adjustments may be needed to match the capabilities of the remaining nuclear forces to new missions. The large size of the Cold War nuclear arsenal allowed planners to develop weapons optimized for specific tasks. The large number of warhead types in the arsenal served to reduce the risk that technical problems with one type of warhead would substantially reduce the capability of the force overall. For the New Triad, the reduced size of the force will require more reliable systems. In addition to the efforts needed to refurbish aging weapons in the stockpile, a need may arise to modify, upgrade or replace portions of the extant nuclear force or develop concepts for follow-on nuclear weapons systems better suited to the nation's needs. It is unlikely that a reduced version of the Cold War nuclear arsenal will be precisely the nuclear force the United States will require in 2012 and beyond.

The New Triad will take time to develop as its elements are adjusted and adapted to each other. Nuclear forces assigned to the New Triad and their command and control systems are mature, but are in need of refurbishment. Advanced nonnuclear strike capabilities are comparatively new, their operational effectiveness is still developing, and planning for their employment is still evolving. Missile defenses are beginning to emerge as systems that can have an effect on the strategic and operational calculations of potential adversaries. They are now capable of providing active defense against short- to medium-range threats. The defense and nuclear infrastructure is well established, but in many respects neither is sufficiently flexible to respond quickly to new requirements.

Sizing the Nuclear Force for Immediate, Potential and Unexpected Contingencies. In setting requirements for nuclear strike capabilities, distinctions can be made among the contingencies for which the United States must be prepared. Contingencies can be categorized as immediate, potential, or unexpected.

Immediate Contingencies involve well-recognized, current dangers. During the Cold War, Soviet threats to the United States and Western Europe represented the immediate contingency for which U.S. nuclear forces were primarily prepared. Current examples of immediate contingencies include an attack using WMD on U.S. forces or a key friend or ally in the Middle East or Asia.

Potential Contingencies are plausible, but not immediate, dangers. They are contingencies which the U.S. leadership can anticipate and about which it has received timely warning. For example, the emergence of a new, hostile military coalition against the United States or its allies in which one or more members possess WMD and the means of delivery is a potential contingency that could have major consequences for U.S. defense planning. The re-emergence of a hostile peer competitor is another example of a potential contingency.

Unexpected Contingencies are sudden and unpredicted security challenges. They could occur in the near term or well into the future. Contemporary illustrations might include a sudden regime change by which an existing nuclear arsenal comes into the hands of a new, hostile leadership group or an adversary's surprise acquisition of WMD capabilities.

The operationally deployed forces are sized to provide the capabilities required to meet U.S. defense goals in the context of immediate and unexpected contingencies. That is, a sufficient number of forces must be available on short notice to counter known threats while preserving a small, additional margin in the event of a surprise development. The United States plans to reduce its operationally deployed nuclear forces over the next decade to 1,700 to 2,200 warheads, while maintaining the flexibility necessary to accommodate changes in the security environment that could affect U.S. nuclear requirements. This reduction will provide a credible deterrent at the lowest possible number of nuclear weapons consistent with national security requirements and alliance obligations.

The United States will also maintain an ability to augment the operationally deployed force to meet unanticipated or surprising potential contingencies. This augmentation would be accomplished by moving the required number of individual warheads from storage to an operational unit. This capability is also an important tool to assure allies and friends and dissuade potential competitors. It will allow the United States to augment its operational forces over weeks, months and years to meet any potential contingencies. Depending on the time available, the United States could also pursue diplomatic, political, and economic measures to improve conditions. Additionally, it could choose to improve other elements of the New Triad.

ADOPTING A NEW APPROACH TO STRATEGIC FORCE REDUCTIONS

Figure A1.2 depicts the department's approach toward reductions in strategic nuclear arms. The objective is an operationally deployed strategic nuclear force with 1700 to 2200 operationally deployed strategic nuclear warheads by 2012. Reductions are planned through a phased program beginning in FY 2002 that eliminates Peacekeeper ICBMs, removes 4 Trident SSBNs from strategic service, and downloads weapons from Trident SLBMs, Minuteman III ICBMs, and B-52H and B-2 bombers.

The precise method of achieving the reductions will be determined in the course of the periodic reviews the department will conduct. The periodic reviews will: review the progress to date in the reduction schedule; evaluate existing assumptions regarding the risks facing U.S. national interests for the next one to three years and the role of nuclear forces in meeting those risks; and Review the progress made

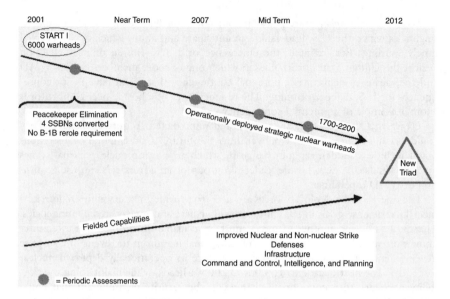

Figure A1.2   Path for nuclear reductions.

Note: The downward arrow illustrates a trend. U.S. reductions are unlikely to occur in a linear fashion.

in the development of the New Triad and the capability of nonnuclear forces, defenses, intelligence, command and control, and the defense infrastructure to meet emerging risks.

As the President's announced reductions are implemented, the existing verification regime established by the first Strategic Arms Reduction Treaty (START I) that entered into force December 5, 1994 will remain in effect. The START I Treaty includes provisions that provide a useful baseline of transparency for offensive strategic forces. The U.S. will assess options for additional transparency and confidence-building options in the context of the new strategic relationship with Russia. In this regard, President Putin has announced that the Russian Federation also will reduce nuclear forces in line with its requirements. The United States will continue consultations with the Russian Federation on how to achieve increased transparency and predictability regarding reductions in offensive nuclear forces.

The U.S. Senate did not provide its advice and consent to the Comprehensive Test Ban Treaty (CTBT). The Administration does not support ratification of the CTBT but continues to support observance of the U.S. testing moratorium. The U.S. test readiness posture under a moratorium is an important aspect of the U.S. infrastructure. The Department of Defense is working with the Department of Energy to determine the appropriate test readiness standard that exercises the range of skills necessary to sustain this readiness posture and to be able to respond appropriately to unforeseen problems with the nuclear stockpile.

In sum, the U.S. strategy for its strategic forces will be transformed and adapted to meet the challenges of the decades to come. The risks associated with reductions in deployed nuclear warheads will be offset by the development and fielding of nonnuclear offensive and defensive capabilities and a revitalization of the infrastructure.

The new strategy puts aside Cold War practices and planning and represents an important step in defense transformation.

NOTE

1. Donald H. Rumsfeld, Secretary of Defense, *Annual Report to the President and the Congress* (Washington, D.C.: Department of Defense, 2002), available at <www.defenselink.mil/execsec/adr2002/toc2002.htm>.

APPENDIX 2

NUCLEAR POSTURE REVIEW LETTER OF TRANSMITTAL FROM SECRETARY OF DEFENSE RUMSFELD[1]

Nuclear Posture Review Report

Foreword

The Congress directed the Defense Department to conduct a comprehensive Nuclear Posture Review to lay out the direction for American nuclear forces over the next five to ten years. The Department has completed that review and prepared the attached report.

Early on, we recognized that the new security environment demanded that the Department go beyond the Congressional mandate in developing a strategic posture for the 21st century. President Bush had already directed the Defense Department to transform America's military and prepare it for the new, unpredictable world in which we will be living. The result of his direction is the Quadrennial Defense Review (QDR). Building on the QDR, this Nuclear Posture Review puts in motion a major change in our approach to the role of nuclear offensive forces in our deterrent strategy and presents the blueprint for transforming our strategic posture.

This report establishes a New Triad, composed of:
- Offensive strike systems (both nuclear and non-nuclear);
- Defenses (both active and passive); and
- A revitalized defense infrastructure that will provide new capabilities in a timely fashion to meet emerging threats.

This New Triad is bound together by enhanced command and control (C2) and intelligence systems.

The establishment of this New Triad can both reduce our dependence on nuclear weapons and improve our ability to deter attack in the face of proliferating WMD capabilities in two ways:
- The addition of defenses (along with the prospects for timely adjustments to force capabilities and enhanced C2 and intelligence systems) means that the U.S. will no longer be as heavily dependent on offensive strike forces to enforce deterrence as it was during the Cold War.
- The addition of non-nuclear strike forces–including conventional strike and information operations–means that the U.S. will be less dependent than it

has been in the past on nuclear forces to provide its offensive deterrent capability.

The combination of new capabilities that make up the New Triad reduce the risk to the nation as it draws its nuclear forces toward the goal of 1,700–2,200 operationally deployed strategic nuclear warheads announced by President Bush on November 13, 2001.

The following is a summary of the highlights in this report.

First and foremost, the Nuclear Posture Review puts the Cold War practices related to planning for strategic forces behind us. In the decade since the collapse of the Soviet Union, planning for the employment of U.S. nuclear forces has undergone only modest revision, despite the new relationship between the U.S. and Russia. Few changes had been made to the size or composition of the strategic nuclear force beyond those required by the START Treaty. At the same time, plans and funding for sustaining some critical elements of that force have been inadequate.

As a result of this review, the U.S. will no longer plan, size or sustain its forces as though Russia presented merely a smaller version of the threat posed by the former Soviet Union. Following the direction laid down for U.S. defense planning in the Quadrennial Defense Review, the Nuclear Posture Review shifts planning for America's strategic forces from the threat-based approach of the Cold War to a capabilities-based approach. This new approach should provide, over the coming decades, a credible deterrent at the lowest level of nuclear weapons consistent with U.S. and allied security.

Second, we have concluded that a strategic posture that relies solely on offensive nuclear forces is inappropriate for deterring the potential adversaries we will face in the 21st century. Terrorists or rogue states armed with weapons of mass destruction will likely test America's security commitments to its allies and friends. In response, we will need a range of capabilities to assure friend and foe alike of U.S. resolve. A broader array of capability is needed to dissuade states from undertaking political, military, or technical courses of action that would threaten U.S. and allied security. U.S. forces must pose a credible deterrent to potential adversaries who have access to modern military technology, including NBC weapons and the means to deliver them over long distances. Finally, U.S. strategic forces need to provide the President with a range of options to defeat any aggressor.

To meet the nation's defense goals in the 21st century, the first leg of the New Triad, the offensive strike leg, will go beyond the Cold War triad of intercontinental ballistic missiles (ICBMs), submarine-launched ballistic missiles (SLBMs), and long-range nuclear-armed bombers. ICBMs, SLBMs, bombers and nuclear weapons will, of course, continue to play a vital role. However, they will be just part of the first leg of the New Triad, integrated with new non-nuclear strategic capabilities that strengthen the credibility of our offensive deterrence.

The second leg of the New Triad requires development and deployment of both active and passive defenses–a recognition that offensive capabilities alone may not deter aggression in the new security environment of the 21st century. The events of

September 11, 2001 underscore this reality. Active and passive defenses will not be perfect. However, by denying or reducing the effectiveness of limited attacks, defenses can discourage attacks, provide new capabilities for managing crises, and provide insurance against the failure of traditional deterrence.

The third leg of the New Triad is a responsive defense infrastructure. Since the end of the Cold War, the U.S. defense infrastructure has contracted and our nuclear infrastructure has atrophied. New approaches to development and procurement of new capabilities are being designed so that it will not take 20 years or more to field new generations of weapon systems. With respect to the nuclear infrastructure, it needs to be repaired to increase confidence in the deployed forces, eliminate unneeded weapons, and mitigate the risks of technological surprise. Maintaining our ability to respond to large strategic changes can permit us to reduce our nuclear arsenal and, at the same time, dissuade adversaries from starting a competition in nuclear armaments.

The effectiveness of this New Triad depends upon command and control, intelligence, and adaptive planning. "Exquisite" intelligence on the intentions and capabilities of adversaries can permit timely adjustments to the force and improve the precision with which it can strike and defend. The ability to plan the employment of the strike and defense forces flexibly and rapidly will provide the U.S. with a significant advantage in managing crises, deterring attack and conducting military operations.

Constructing the New Triad, reducing our deployed nuclear weapons, and increasing flexibility in our strategic posture has resource implications. It costs money to retire old weapons systems and create new capabilities. Restoring the defense infrastructure, developing and deploying strategic defenses, improving our command and control, intelligence, planning, and non-nuclear strike capabilities require new defense initiatives and investments. However, these investments can make the U.S. more secure while reducing our dependence on nuclear weapons.

The Quadrennial Defense Review established the foundation for America's post-Cold War defense strategy. Building on the Quadrennial Defense Review, the Nuclear Posture Review will transform the Cold War era offensive nuclear triad into a New Triad designed for the decades to come.

Donald H. Rumsfeld
Secretary of Defense

NOTE

1. Donald H. Rumsfeld, "Nuclear Posture Review Report," letter of transmittal to the U.S. Congress, January 2002, available at <www.defenselink.mil/news/Jan2002/d20020109npr.pdf>.

INDEX